MODELS AND EXPERIMENTS IN RISK AND RATIONALITY

THEORY AND DECISION LIBRARY

General Editors: W. Leinfellner (*Vienna*) and G. Eberlein (*Munich*)

Series A: Philosophy and Methodology of the Social Sciences

Series B: Mathematical and Statistical Methods

Series C: Game Theory, Mathematical Programming and Operations Research

Series D: System Theory, Knowledge Engineering and Problem Solving

SERIES B: MATHEMATICAL AND STATISTICAL METHODS

VOLUME 29

Editor: H. J. Skala (Paderborn); *Assistant Editor:* M. Kraft (Paderborn); *Editorial Board:* J. Aczél (Waterloo, Ont.), G. Bamberg (Augsburg), H. Drygas (Kassel), W. Eichhorn (Karlsruhe), P. Fishburn (Murray Hill, N.J.), D. Fraser (Toronto), W. Janko (Vienna), P. de Jong (Vancouver), T. Kariya (Tokyo), M. Machina (La Jolla, Calif.), A. Rapoport (Toronto), M. Richter (Kaiserslautern), B. K. Sinha (Cattonsville, Md.), D. A. Sprott (Waterloo, Ont.), P. Suppes (Stanford, Calif.), H. Theil (St. Augustine, Fla.), E. Trillas (Madrid), L. A. Zadeh (Berkeley, Calif.).

Scope: The series focuses on the application of methods and ideas of logic, mathematics and statistics to the social sciences. In particular, formal treatment of social phenomena, the analysis of decision making, information theory and problems of inference will be central themes of this part of the library. Besides theoretical results, empirical investigations and the testing of theoretical models of real world problems will be subjects of interest. In addition to emphasizing interdisciplinary communication, the series will seek to support the rapid dissemination of recent results.

The titles published in this series are listed at the end of this volume.

MODELS AND EXPERIMENTS IN RISK AND RATIONALITY

edited by

BERTRAND MUNIER

Ecole Normale Supérieure, Cachan, France

and

MARK J. MACHINA

University of California, San Diego, U.S.A.

KLUWER ACADEMIC PUBLISHERS
DORDRECHT / BOSTON / LONDON

Library of Congress Cataloging-in-Publication Data

```
Models and experiments in risk and rationality / edited by Bertrand
  Munier and Mark J. Machina.
       p.    cm. -- (Theory and decision library. Series B,
  Mathematical and statistical methods ; v. 29)
    Includes bibliographical references.
    ISBN 0-7923-3031-5 (acid-free)
    1. Risk--Mathematical models. 2. Decision-making--Mathematical
  models.    I. Munier, Bertrand. II. Machina, Mark J. III. Series.
  HB615.M63 1994
  368--dc20                                                  94-22976
```

ISBN 0-7923-3031-5

Published by Kluwer Academic Publishers,
P.O. Box 17, 3300 AA Dordrecht, The Netherlands.

Kluwer Academic Publishers incorporates
the publishing programmes of
D. Reidel, Martinus Nijhoff, Dr W. Junk and MTP Press.

Sold and distributed in the U.S.A. and Canada
by Kluwer Academic Publishers,
101 Philip Drive, Norwell, MA 02061, U.S.A.

In all other countries, sold and distributed
by Kluwer Academic Publishers Group,
P.O. Box 322, 3300 AH Dordrecht, The Netherlands.

Printed on acid-free paper

All Rights Reserved
© 1994 Kluwer Academic Publishers
No part of the material protected by this copyright notice may be reproduced or
utilized in any form or by any means, electronic or mechanical,
including photocopying, recording or by any information storage and
retrieval system, without written permission from the copyright owner.

Printed in the Netherlands

TABLE OF CONTENTS

INTRODUCTION TO THE VOLUME   vii

1. PSYCHOLOGICAL ASPECTS OF RISK BEARING   1

The Psychogenetic Approach to Risk
    Jean-Pascal Assailly   3

Contextual Effects and the Influence of the Frame on Decision Making
    Bernard Cadet   17

CE-PE Bias and Probability Level: An Anchoring Model of their Interaction
    Paul J.H. Schoemaker and John C. Hershey   35

2. NEW DEVELOPMENTS IN THE THEORY OF RISK AVERSION   57

Non-Additive Probabilities and the Measure of Uncertainty and Risk Aversion: A Proposal
    Aldo Montesano   59

A Precautionary Tale of Risk Aversion and Prudence
    Louis Eeckhoudt and Harris Schlesinger   75

Embodied Risk: 'Framing', Consumption Style and the Deterrence of Crimes of Passion
    Jerome Rothenberg   91

3. NON-EXPECTED UTILITY MODELS AND TESTS   117

Estimation of Expected Utility and Non-Expected Utility Preference Functionals Using Complete Ranking Data
    Enrica Carbone and John D. Hey   119

The 'Closing In' Method: An Experimental Tool to Investigate Individual Choice Patterns Under Risk
    Mohammed Abdellaoui and Bertrand Munier   141

Gains and Losses in Nonadditive Expected Utility
    Rakesh Sarin and Peter Wakker   157

An Outline of My Main Contributions to Risk and Utility Theory: Theory, Experience, and Applications
    Maurice Allais   173

4. MULTIPLE CRITERIA DECISION-MAKING UNDER UNCERTAINTY   223

Multiattribute Analysis Based on Stochastic Dominance
    Kazimierz Zaras and Jean-Marc Martel   225

Aggregation and Uncertainties in Deliberated Evaluation
    Quingsan Cao and Jean-Pierre Protzen   249

Multicriteria Decision Model and Decision Making Process in an Organization: An Application in Industrial Management
    Claude Pellegrin   261

5. PRODUCTION, FIRMS AND MARKETS   273

Expected Profits and Information Under Uncertainty
    Eirik Romstad and Per Kristian Rørstad   275

Market Preferences Revealed by Prices: Non-Linear Pricing in Slack Markets
    Alain Chateauneuf, Robert Kast and Alain Lapied   289

Risk, Time and Financial Decision
    François Quittard-Pinon and Jacques Sikorav   307

6. GAMES AND SOCIAL CHOICE   323

Ambiguity-Aversion and Non-Additive Beliefs in Non-Cooperative Games: Experimental Evidence
    Colin F. Camerer and Risto Karjalainen   325

On Regular Composed Tournaments
    Gilbert Laffond, Jean Laine and Jean-Francois Laslier   359

Market Games with Asymmetric Information: The Core with Finitely Many States of the World
    Beth Allen   377

Information Transmission in Signalling Games: Confrontation of Different Forward Induction Criteria
    Gisèle Umbhauer   413

INTRODUCTION TO THE VOLUME

Decision making under conditions of risk or uncertainty was a popular subject among scientists in the 17th and 18th centuries. At that time, it was primarily developed in connection with parlor games, such as Daniel Bernoulli's famous analysis of the Saint Petersburg Paradox or Waldegrave's solution to de Monmort's game, although it was also applied to such far ranging issues as the sentencing or freeing of court defendants[1] and even to the very issue of religious faith, as with Pascal's famous wager[2]. Epistemic uncertainty, indeed, was studied earlier than economic risk, and it took a long time before the latter was recognized as being of a formally distinct nature from the former.

When interest in the topic of risk resurfaced among scientists in the 20th century, due to the seminal work of von Neumann and Morgenstern, it initially took a rather different aspect, with an emphasis on economic and strategic behavior. Since then, it has taken on additional and more varied psychological, social and logical aspects, along with its original epistemic one.

As a result of this enlarged scope, the field of decision making under risk and uncertainty has become much more complex : not only are the "rules" of social and economic situations more complicated (and ambiguous) than those of simple parlor games, but the underlying criterion of "rationality" comes off as more difficult to model in all but the simplest of situations, and even the notion of "risk" itself emerges as being more subtle than had been thought in the 1950' s.

The papers in this volume focus on a selection of these modern-day issues.

---

[1] George M. von Fürstenberg, Ed., 1990, *Acting Under Uncertainty: Multidisciplinary Conceptions*, Dordrecht/Boston, Kluwer Academic Publishers. See chs.1-3 in particular.

[2] Blaise Pascal, *Oeuvres complètes*, Paris, Lafuma, 1963.

General Background

Some of the topics scrutinized in this book originate in the challenge to the expected utility paradigm exemplified by Maurice Allais' famous Paradox, first presented in 1952 and pursued in numerous subsequent contributions, notably Allais' and Ole Hagen's 1979 volume *Expected Utility Hypotheses and the Allais' Paradox* [3]. Hagen and Allais (who was awarded the 1988 Nobel Memorial Prize in Economic Science) were among the first to question the theoretical and empirical hegemony of the expected utility model and, as is often the case with intellectual pioneers, met with stiff opposition. However, as a result of their continued efforts and those of subsequent researchers, the field of "non-expected utility theory" has emerged as an important part of the literature on choice under uncertainty. Experimental, empirical, and theoretical research in this area now appears beside more traditional articles in all of the leading journals.

An important part of this questioning of the expected utility paradigm has been an increased amount of experimental work in a discipline which had heretofore given the experimental method much less than its proper recognition, and an increased amount of scientific exchanges with psychologists. The experimental approach has become a major tool in economics as well as in management science, and indeed, has opened new insights into the connection between these two disciplines. It is thus important to give a picture of what these recent results have taught us. The first questions that come to mind concern the level of performance of the above-mentioned non-expected utility models: how well do they describe observable behavior, and how well do they allow us to deliver prescriptions to decision-makers ?

The questioning of the classical expected utility paradigm has also raised a set of related questions : namely, how do individuals perceive information in situations of risk and uncertainty ? Experimental research has shown, for example, that the method of "framing" the description of a risky situation has a significant impact on choice behavior, although we do not yet have precise knowledge of the processes by which such "framing effects" operate. In a related context, experimenters have found that the "response mode" presented to the subject also has an impact on the elicitation of the subject's risk preferences. These findings are of decisive importance when it comes to the prescriptive modeling of decision-making under risk : how could one use *any* of the models put forward by researchers - expected utility or otherwise - if subjects' underlying preferences cannot be elicited independently of the "frame of reference"

---

[3] Maurice Allais and Ole Hagen, eds., *Expected Utility Hypotheses and the Allais' Paradox: Contemporary Discussions of Decisions under Uncertainty with Allais' Rejoinder*, Dordrecht/Boston, D. Reidel Publishing Co., 1979.

(either the question description or the response mode) of the observer ? After all, the very definition of a prescriptive decision model requires the analyst to be able to advise the decision-maker as to the best decision to make according to *the latter's own preferences.*

Given these difficulties in eliciting preferences, and also given the fact that analysts, when advising the executives of an organization, thereby influence the standards of behavior of the organization, many management scientists hold the view that preferences are in fact not *elicited*, but rather, *constructed* in cooperation between the decision-maker and the analyst. Multi- criteria decision models play an important role in such construction procedures. They are, in some sense, the bounded rationality equivalent of a well-defined utility function, which would be too hard to uniquely observe *or* construct. But how should one accomodate the phenomenon of *risk* in multi-criteria decision modeling ? And how should these models be applied within an organization, in order to best meet the properties required of decision-making schemes under uncertainty ?

The answer to this last question becomes even more complex when we recognize that the agents in any organization have at least partially conflicting interests, and are at least partially aware of that fact. This interaction between agents in a social system leads us back to where we started when describing these new developments in modern decision-making, namely to the theory of games of strategy. In fact, researchers who have questioned the expected utility version of classical "instrumental rationality" have often found themselves questioning the very concept of instrumental rationality altogether. The use of non-expected utility in a backward induction setting leads to quite a few problems, be it in a situation of individual sequential decision-making or in a multi-stage, multi-player game. In any event, the arguments against the validity of backward induction in game theory are probably stronger than anywhere else, and this has led many scientists to question backward induction schemes of instrumental rationality. *Forward* induction schemes have been proposed, which are one form of what has been called "cognitive" or "interactive" rationality. Here, "rational behavior" does not require an agent to make the absolute best use of limited means towards a set of given ends using objective information (information on the "fundamentals" of a stock, for example), but it does require agents to make the best use of what they can know (or guess) about each others' beliefs and ends, and of what they can know (or guess) about their own constraints, beliefs and ends.

Although game-theoretic situations constitute the height of these difficulties, much of the problem already emerges in the one player sequential decision-making scheme represented by decision trees. Indeed, the connection between questioning expected utility theory and questioning the concept of instrumental rationality very likely lies within the domain of "dynamic consistency" in sequential individual decision-making, as studied a couple of years ago in McClennen's *Rationality and Dynamic Choice* [4] ... Here, in fact, the questions of memory, belief formation and belief revision cannot be avoided: instrumental rationality appears as an incomplete model of human rationality.

This is not to say that classical game theory cannot remain a useful tool for modeling questions of social choice, equity and justice. It only means that game theory, if it is to be considered as a prescriptive tool for decision-makers, must admit some fundamental changes in its traditional design. Making these adaptations will undoubtedly require further experimental studies of behavior in games, in order to gauge concepts similar to the ones that have been studied in individual choice: namely risk-attitudes, ambiguity attitudes, etc... Much remains to be done along these lines.

Detemining the final implication of these emerging designs and concepts for economics and management science is of great importance. One difficulty in achieving this is that we know too little concerning the impact of risk and uncertainty on production, consumption and financial economics or management, *even* within the classical framework, or perhaps, *because* we have historically imposed the classical framework, which, by oversimplifying risk attitudes, might hide many significant phenomena. How then, for example, is production economics affected by uncertainty ? Does arbitrage pricing in financial markets relate in any substantial way to the particular measure of risk used in modeling financial market behavior ? Would the management of risk in nuclear plants be substantially affected, if we were to recognize that concavity of the utility function alone is simply not enough to represent risk attitudes when it comes to the far tail of a probability distribution bearing on collectively catastrophic accidents ?

Contents of the Volume

Original contributions to the above-mentioned areas of individual choice, experimental economics, operations analysis, multiple-criteria decision making, market uncertainty, game theory, and social choice can be found in this volume. The papers are arranged so as to appear in order of increasing complexity of the decision environment or social context in which they situate themselves.

The first group of papers, titled "Psychological Aspects of Risk-Bearing", consider choice at the purely individual level, and for the most part, free of any specific economic or social context.

The second, third and fourth groups of papers study the behavior of the individual in standard economic settings, as for example when choosing over monetary lotteries. The second group, titled "New

---

[4] Edward F. McClennen, *Rationality and Dynamic Choice: Foundational Explorations*, London, Cambridge University Press, 1990.

Developments in the Theory of Risk Aversion", examines individual choice within the classical expected utility approach. The third section, titled "Non-Expected Utility Models and Tests" examines this same topic, but from a perspective that also includes non-expected utility preferences over lotteries. The fourth group of papers, titled "Multiple Criteria Decision-Making Under Uncertainty", considers the more specialized but crucial context of uncertain choice involving tradeoffs between competing criteria - a field which is becoming of increasing importance in applied decision analysis.

The final two sections examine uncertain choice in social or group contexts. The section "Production, Firms and Markets" does so by looking at applications in production economics and finance. The final section of the volume, "Games and Social Choice", presents new experimental and theoretical findings concerning agents' interaction in games of strategy and new theoretical findings regarding mechanisms for societal choice.

The original versions of these papers were presented at the 6th *Foundations and Applications of Utility, Risk and Decision Theory* (FUR VI) conference, held at the Ecole Normale Supérieure de Cachan, just outside of Paris. Additional papers from this conference appear in a special issue of *Theory and Decision* (Vol. 35, No. 3, November 1993), which forms a companion volume to the present one.

Bertrand Munier
Cachan, France

Mark J. Machina
La Jolla, California, USA

1. PSYCHOLOGICAL ASPECTS OF RISK-BEARING

The three papers in this section consider a range of psychological aspects of individuals' perception of, and behavior toward, risk. With the first paper, by Jean-Pascal Assailly, we truly "begin at the beginning". This paper discusses the development of the concept of risk and the evolution of risk-taking behavior in the child. Drawing on psychological studies of Piaget and Infelder and others, the author provides an overview of the various stages of the child's development and understanding of the contradictory concepts of "risk" and "causality" (in the sense that the latter is taken to denote "necessity"). During these early stages, the child often exhibits systematic misunderstandings of such concepts as equiprobability, statistical independence, etc. Formal probabilistic reasoning only begins to develop in adolescence.

Assailly also points out that a similar progression can occur in attitudes toward taking risks. At an earlier stage, risk taking can actually be more pronounced, as children are much better able to concretely visualize the potential prize in a gamble than the fact that it might only have a small probability of occurrence. Besides chronological age, the many studies reported by the author also examine the influence of gender, culture, and physical (i.e., bodily) versus material (i.e., commodity) risks, with a special reference to road and traffic safety.

The second paper in this section, by Bernard Cadet, seeks to empirically examine the relative influence of a number of different "framing" and "contextual" effects on choice in a well-known decision problem, namely the "unusual Asian disease" example of Kahneman and Tversky. This problem is itself an important example of the influence of the "reference point" in choice under uncertainty, as pointed out over four decades ago by Harry Markowitz. Specifically, it has been found that subjects' preferences for or against a more risky versus a less risky vaccination program are heavily influenced by whether the alternative possible outcomes are expressed in terms of "lives lost" from the status quo, or in terms of "lives saved" relative to the worst-case scenario.

In his paper, Cadet delves even more deeply into such contextual effects. He considers the effects of the number of attributes used in describing each outcome, the qualitative form of information presentation, and subjects' previous knowledge upon choice in the above example, as well as additional older and newer examples of framing effects. He interprets his findings as signaling the need for greater attention to the study of decision-making as a unified cognitive process.

By way of contrast with the above study on the effect of question framing, the final paper in this section, by John Hershey and Paul Schoemaker, examines the effect of "response mode," that is to say, the form in which the subject is asked to respond to questions aimed at uncovering his or her underlying level of risk aversion. In this study, the two alternative modes are the standard "sure monetary equivalent" measure and the "probability equivalent" measure, where the latter is defined as that chance of winning a prespecified prize that would leave the individual indifferent to a given sure amount of money.

Earlier studies of the effects of response mode, including some by Hershey and Schoemaker themselves, have found that the two different modes can elicit quite different degrees of risk aversion from the same subject. In the present paper, the two authors extend these findings by examining the degree of interaction of various attributes with this disparity. In particular, they find that the disparity increases with the probability of winning, and they develop a psychologically-based "anchoring" model to account for this effect.

THE PSYCHOGENETIC APPROACH TO RISK

Jean-Pascal Assailly*

INTRODUCTION

Risk accompanies existence from its very beginning; indeed we know from studies of newborn animals and humans that every individual is confronted from birth with the necessity of satisfying two contradictory needs ; the search for security, expressed particularly by all forms of attachment behavior aiming to maintain a certain proximity with the maternal organism or its substitute, and the search for stimulation, expressed particularly by the exploration of environment, exploration which constitutes a source of risk. Risk is therefore inscribed, like security, in the very dynamic of development. This initial and fundamental ambivalence (the search for and avoidance of risk), continues and manifests itself at different ages and in diverse spheres of existence.

Moreover, the concept of risk, as approached by the experts in social sciences, implies the understanding and manipulation of other concepts such as probability, utility and chance, since risk is defined as the product of probability by utility. In the perspective of genetic psychology, this would suggest a first question : what degree of understanding do children and adolescents have of these concepts ? Then we can ask ourselves if the level of understanding reached is related on the one hand with risk-taking and on the other hand with risk perception. Finally, we will consider the specific nature of the risk of accident which is the major cause of mortality during childhood and adolescence. These four issues form the subject of this article.

---

* Chargé de recherche à l'**INRETS**, Institut National de Recherche sur les Transports et leur Sécurité, 2, Avenue du Général Malleret-Joinville, 94114, Arcueil Cédex, France.

CONSTRUCTION OF THE CONCEPT OF RISK

Risk is undoubtedly one of the most complex concepts which the child has to understand and handle during the course of his development. The main reason for this phenomenon is that this cognitive construction is indissociable from that of two other concepts, probability and chance, because the intrinsic nature of the concept of risk is probabilistic. From the very beginning of his existence, the child learns to select in reality what comes from regularity, from law and what originates in chance ; probability being an intermediary phenomenon, it is not immediately understood but is the subject of a long and arduous construction. The genetic model for the concept of risk could thus be outlined by the following diagram :

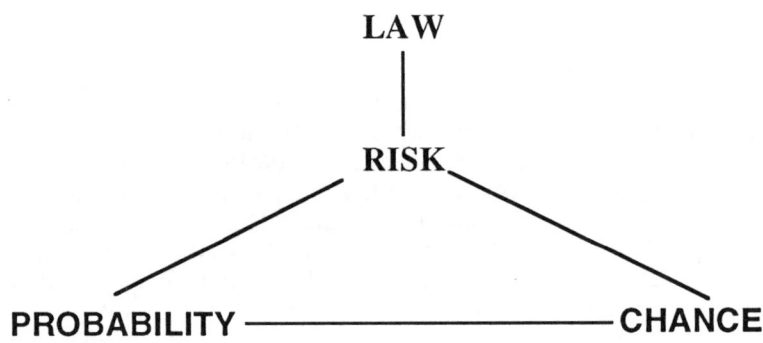

The cognitive roots of the concept of risk are thus to be sought in the initial elaboration of the child with regard to chance and probability.

The difficulty for the child in understanding chance will be better understood when the numerous cases where chance is not integrated by the adult are considered[1] : the most frequent is the urge to believe, which is as ancient as humanity itself and manifested in very

---

[1] At the extreme it can be thought that the negation rather than the acceptance of chance is the more natural disposition of man.

different forms (religions, mysticism, astrology, superstition, etc..) but whose common denominator is precisely to deny chance by substituting different determinisms ; certain types of personality or more seriously of nosographic entities of psycho-pathology (e.g. obsessional neurosis or paranoia) lead to a negation of chance by systematically attributing a meaning to any event whatsoever; the gambling situation brings about a regression in the player's intuition of probability because of the illusory will for control.

More generally, the tendency of the human being to establish cause and effect relationships between independent events has been conceptualised in four main ideas :

— the illusion of contingency ; most individuals, when they produce causal attributions in connection with negative events (such as accidents, cancer, rape, bereavement, for example), resist the idea that the event may be uncertain and search for a cause, particularly in themselves. The central principle of causal attribution is that of co-variance, i.e. effects are generally attributed to causes which appear to vary with the effects : this seems logical but numerous distortions can alter attribution judgements.

— the illusion of justice ; the feeling of justice also allows the elimination of chance if we consider that "everyone gets what he deserves and only deserves what he gets". Thus, the illusion of justice is expressed for example with regard to road accidents in the idea that they result from the "fault" of a guilty driver : it is therefore more reassuring to think that you are different from bad drivers or that you would have behaved differently in the same situation. In the same way, this "theory of fairness" can produce a certain number of cognitive and moral dissonances when the subject is confronted with injustices of flagrant social absurdity (e.g. dying young, famine amongst African children, etc.); the resolution of the dissonance will therefore imply a restructuring of the opinion (e.g. : "I deserve what others who are like me or in a comparable situation get"....)

— the illusion of control : the expectation of a probability of success much greater than the objective probability in the situations of the type - financial bet is a well known result of studies on the subjective utility of risk.

— the fundamental error : in explaining a certain type of behavior, the individual generally has a tendency to overestimate the individual, dispositional variables ("such a person behaves thus because he or she is like that"); thus fundamental error also expresses in a certain way the illusion of control since it attributes the responsibility to the individual and his characteristics.

In other respects, the questioning of chance does not spare the much more "rational" world of scientists and scientific research since Einstein's famous "God does not play dice"...If chance has taken center stage since quantum mechanics and the concept of the "threshold of uncertainty", its role is contested in practically all fields of research. Let us simply mention the controversies between physicists and mathematicians on the morphogenesis of the universe, between neo-Darwinian and stochastic biologists or anthropologists with regard to the "uncertain" character of phylogenesis and of genotype transformations, etc...

It is therefore not surprising that the notion of chance does not initially have any sense for the child. As in other domains (e.g. speed, time), the psychological functioning of the child has been compared to that of "primitive" mentalities. It is particularly well known that the absence of the notion of chance is one of the essential characteristics of the latter : "primitive", "magic" or "animist" thinking always attributes a cause, known or unknown, to every event. In the same way, the child remains reluctant to accept the idea of chance for a long time : every parent can notice that shortly after the acquisition of language and for a long period, the most frequent and most insistent question of a child is the "why" which often provokes the embarrassment of said parent. If the child spontaneously and incessantly asks himself this question, it is because, for him, every event has a cause and he wants to discover it, especially if it is not apparent. In many cases, the adult's predicament is due to the fact that he considers the event in question as being totally accidental. It is therefore the finalism of the child which initially obstructs the construction of the concept of chance and which is at the root of the parallel between "childlike" and "primitive" mentalities, between ontogenesis and the history of the sciences, as it constitutes the essential characteristic of causal imputations and of the child's representations of the World.

Indeed, physical chance can be defined as the interference of independent causal series (Cournot's principle) : the typical example is that the causality particular to the series "a man is walking in the street" does not necessarily take in the intersection with the causality particular to the series "a tile falls from the roof"...However, this does not take risk exposure in account, since if a man never walked in the street, there would be no "chance" of a tile falling upon his head... It is precisely the concurrence of interference and independence which is precluded by finalism because, for the child, the interference of causes necessarily supposes the interdependence of phenomena.

Thus, chance is a derived notion, secondary, because what is primary is the search for order and law ; it is only when the latter are sufficiently constructed that the child will be able to integrate what resists them, that is to say, chance.

A model of this construction has been proposed by Piaget and Inhelder (1974): it involves three phases, corresponding as for the other physical phenomena such as space, time, speed, etc. to the more general stages in the development of the child's thought and logic.

— in a first phase covering the period from birth to 7 years and which corresponds to the first two general stages of sensorimotor intelligence and pre-operatory intuition, chance cannot be understood because the child cannot differentiate between the possible and the necessary ; thus when an infant hears noise behind a door, we can think he "expects" to see his mother without being sure, that her appearance is considered as possible or probable but not certain, and this phenomenon can be attributed to the precocious intuition of the unexpected, an intuition providing the genetic foundation for the concepts of chance and probability. However, the unexpected is not to be confused with the unforeseeable : the child notices the unexpected by contrast with expected regularities [2], he is even capable of anticipating as he already knows that this can be disappointed by reality, but he cannot conceive of the unforeseeable as his thinking only oscillates between the foreseeable and the unexpected. For him, nothing is definitely foreseeable as this deduction of a necessity involves mental operations which he does not yet control and nothing is definitely unforeseeable i.e. risky, for the same reason (understanding what is irreducible to deduction). The unexpected will thus be interpreted in a motivational and finalistic manner in terms of caprice or arbitrariness.

This functioning of causality during this first stage will lead the child to logical "aberrations", e.g. in a group B formed by one A and two C, the child often judges it more "sure" to fall on the A during a test with one draw precisely because the A is unique!... In fact, the child's predictions do not have a probabilistic structure of the relation between the part (the favourable cases) and the whole (all the possible cases). Likewise, the child can set processes in motion which are only apparently of a probabilistic nature, such as compensation : thus, confronted with two contingencies, A and B, A being the most often presented, the child will bet on B. However, if he acts in this way, it is not because he thinks that B now has a better chance of winning, but rather as the result of a moral judgement of the type "each one in his turn", of a "natural" order of things which would apply as much to gambling as to the alternation between good and bad weather...We see how the motivational component (here the eminently respectable sentiment of justice..) wins over reason. Finally, the analogy between "childlike" and "primitive" mentalities is clearly shown by the experiments where, unknown to the child, a dice is "fixed" so that it always falls on the same side. The child is not astonished at the "miracle" thus produced. Indeed, to be astonished at a "miracle", it must be understood that it is contrary to both necessity and chance. For the child, as for the "primitive" [3], everything can be a miracle as chance does not exist.

— in a second phase covering the period from 7 to 11 years and which corresponds to the general stage of concrete operations, the child progressively discovers chance as a reality incompatible with said operations, but he cannot yet integrate the notion of probability. It is

---

[2] Which moreover constitutes the fundamental psycho-biological process of emotions such as fear or laughter.

[3] Indeed more recently, since the miracle in antiquity (etymology : miraculum) was considered to be a natural thing.

from the foreseeable that the child is thus going to understand the unforeseeable : therefore, mastering the reversibility of concrete operations, he will be able, for example, to predict the trajectory of a moving object and he will immediately understand that this determination will escape deduction if other bodies intervene to modify the trajectories, speeds and durations as in the Brownian movement. This indetermination did not pose a problem in the preceding stage as all the movements, regular or not, were indeterminable before 7 years. From the moment that the foreseeable is constructed, the unforeseeable can acquire meaning : the child will classify in a separate, complementary area, accidental events, i.e. insufficiently determinate or indeterminable, and it is this area which will constitute the concept of chance. The discovery of indetermination(be it spatiotemporal or logicoarithmetic) involves the dissociation of the two forms of reality, the necessary (operatively determined) and the possible (the undetermined), whereas they were undifferentiated in the preceding stage. If the child understands the notion of chance between 7 and 11 years, he cannot yet integrate that of probability precisely because of the construction of chance. Indeed, the latter is discovered by opposing the operatory and the fortuitous, whereas probabilistic reasoning supposes a new synthesis between operations and chance, a re-introduction of the operation on the level of the uncertain. To estimate a probability is to assess the importance of the favourable cases in relation to all possible cases and it is precisely their exhaustive analysis of which the child is incapable before 11 years as it supposes another operatory level.

— in a third phase, covering the period from 11 to 15 years and which corresponds to the general stage of formal operations, probabilistic reasoning becomes possible. The principal characteristic of this stage is in effect a reversal of the relation between the possible and the real : before 11 years, the possible is part of the real, after, the real is part of the possible, it is only one of the forms. In the preceding stage, the child discovered chance and possibility but he intuitively applies the same operatory level to them, that of concrete operations bearing on the real, whereas, they are not adapted to the analysis of the possible which supposes formal thinking, i.e. a hypothetico-deductive thought which operates on abstractions : it is a matter of making an inventory of the possibilities in such a way that the distribution of the whole becomes foreseeable, then, of attributing a probability to each isolated case as a part of this whole. This supposes a combinatory analysis and the acquisition of the proportionality (the relation of two systems of simultaneous relations) which are only possible with the help of formal thinking. The concept of probability thus issues from a need, that of resolving the cognitive conflict between chance and deduction : when the child understands that the former creates an obstacle to the latter, his mind reacts in trying to interpret chance as if it were determinable "despite all", treating uncertain mechanisms as if they were not so : thus, even if an isolated case is unforeseeable, all cases together are, on the other hand, foreseeable, and the probabilistic composition will consist in linking the part and the whole.

The classic experiment which well illustrates this mechanism is that where the child must take two balls out of a bag containing thirty in different colors, each color being unequally represented, and predict the most probable couples. The solution thus supposes that the child predicts all the possibilities (the combinations two by two) and understands that chance will select certain cases amongst those possible, the latter becoming realities but that the realities cannot in any way exceed the possibilities. If chance realizes certain possibilities, it does not create any further ones : confronted with the unforeseeable and incomprehensible character of chance, the child's mind will translate it in terms of operations : the latter will have the particularity of being disorganized (absence of systematic order of events) and incomplete (chance does not exhaust the possible), but they will render chance "thinkable". This displacement of chance on the operatory ground will allow the judgement of probability. Thus, the child understands from this stage the relation between the rarity of a phenomenon and the number of attempts before it happens. Likewise, when the child takes as his own Bertrand's principle ("chance has neither conscience nor memory"), the law of big numbers becomes accessible to him. This constitutes the foundation of probabilistic reasoning as it supposes that the limit frequency is equal to the probability, i.e. the relative differences between events diminish with the number of attempts, because of the growing importance of compensations between fortuitous invervals. It is therefore the "equalising" role of chance which is going to be integrated by the child. The dispersion of the distribution being structured, an isolated case can be considered as a fraction of all the possibilities being gradually realized according to the law of big numbers, which constitutes precisely the definition of probability : a fraction of determination.

THE EVOLUTION OF RISK-TAKING

Studies based on gambling generally conclude that there is a reduction in risk-taking with age during childhood. Thus, Walesa (1975) observes in different experimental situations that the subjects (Polish) aged 8-10 years tend to take more risks and are more motivated by gain than the 14-18 year-olds who take less and are more motivated by the avoidance of loss. This result could be analysed in the light of the Piagetian theory previously presented : the ages 8-10 corresponding to the stage of concrete operations, the child does not master the concept of probability and thus centers himself on the utility of risk (loss or gain), the perceived value will be the expected value; the ages 14-18

corresponding to formal operations, the adolescent can coordinate utility and probability, and his expected value will be in keeping with the mathematical definition of the product of utility by probability. In other respects, this evolution equally demonstrates the more general capacities of self-decentration ; the adolescent has a better differentiated perception of uncertain factors and factors dependent on his own ability to control an event. However, the author points out that the inter-individual variability is clearly more important than the variability between age groups.
Similar observations have been made by Mc Ginnis and Berg (1973) on 60 American boys aged from 8 to 10 years ; all the subjects try to maximise potential gains without concerning themselves with the assessment of potential losses.

In a completely different cultural context (in Japan) but also drawing from Piaget, Nakajima and Ohta (1989) observe a similar phenomenon in 75 adolescents aged between 12 and 23 years : the subjective probability progressively comes closer to the age of objective probability in different types of lotteries. However, we should be cautious in using generalisations as Krishna (1981) does not observe any correlation between age and risk-taking in his study of 200 Indian adolescents aged from 13 to 18 years ; the sociocultural factors can thus interfere with ontogenesis.

More generally, it is the capacity to envisage the consequences of decision-making which develop from childhood to adolescence; so, in reply to the question "What must a good decision-maker do when he takes an important decision ?", Mann et al. (1984) note that 30% of the 13 year-old subjects and 51% of the 15 year-old subjects sponteaneously evoke consideration of the consequences.

The study of risk-taking in childhood also raises the problem of motivations for risk-taking. The role of motivation is particularly relevant concerning the values of a reinforcement at different ages : when children are confronted with dilemmas of the type : choose between 1) obtaining a candy bar, 2) having one chance in five of obtaining five bars, 3) having one chance in twenty-five of obtaining twenty-five bars, etc., a significant reduction in the tendency to take risks with age is indeed noticed. But can it really be concluded that the youngest are more inclined to take risks? It seems obvious moreover that candy has a much more important motivational value at nine years than at fifteen. Therefore the result obtained could rather reflect the evolution of attitudes towards candy than that of risk-taking...

THE EVOLUTION OF RISK PERCEPTION

As we have previously seen, studies on the evolution of risk-taking are based on well defined situations which generally specify the type, probability and stake of the potential loss. If we now leave the stuffy precision of the laboratories, it would appear that the situations presenting a risk for the child in daily life are clearly less well-defined and that he (like the adult moreover) does not clearly know the type (i.e. the consequences), the probability or the loss at stake. We can therefore ask ourselves if the child perceives certain risks and at what age he perceives such and such a risk.

Few studies exist in this field as its methodological approach is difficult. Indeed, verbal techniques, pertinent for situations of the type - gambling, show themselves to be less adapted to the study of other types of risk, particularly because of the child's problem in understanding the situation. It has turned out that graphic and audio-visual techniques improve this understanding. In employing them, Walesa (1977) has produced an interesting study on the perception of certain categories of risk (material loss, physical danger, loss of life, moral loss, other losses, no loss) according to age amongst 600 Polish subjects aged from 4 to 18 years. He notes :

— a U curve in the perception of a nil risk (no loss); it is frequent at 4-6 years and 16-18 years, infrequent at 8-11 years.

— a development of moral stakes after 9 years, which corresponds to the development of moral judgement as described by Piaget for example.

— a weak genetic evolution in the perception of physical dangers and loss of life, i.e. it depends more on the type of situation than on age. Likewise, Meyer and Vinje (1978) have shown that 92% of children aged from 4 to 6 years considered it dangerous to run on a highway, 89% on a road and 61% on a playground, which indicates quite a precocious differentiation of situations according to their potential danger. This differentiation has been studied more recently about the health risk behaviors (Jurs and al., 1990) of 113 American children aged 3 to 5 : comparing the danger of four situations, the children have assessed as the more dangerous the nonuse of restraints in cars, then smoking, then eating "junk food" and then not to wash their hands ...

Finally, another study (Dickson and Hutchinson 1988) carried out on 585 Scottish children aged from 9 to 12 years concludes with similar results and adds interesting complementary information, especially from a preventive angle; in effect, the subjects of this age, particularly the girls, perceive physical risks (injuries) better than material risks (loss of or damage to a possession), but, on the other hand, they produce responses less adapted to situations of physical danger than material danger. The authors conclude that security campaigns should not be uniquely centered on the child's awareness of danger but also on the relevant behavior for coping with risk.

ROAD RISK IN CHILDHOOD

Risk-taking or non perception of risk?

Since work by Sandels (1968,1979) which has now become a "reference study" on the behaviour of children in road traffic, a consensus has been established in this field with regard to the concept that the determinism of the accident is more likely to result from the non perception of danger by the child (together with the difficulty of his/her being detected by the driver) than risk-taking per se. The different factors which, for children, have an influence on the non perception of danger include characteristics related to morphology (size), perception (difficulties in locating sounds and peripheral vision), cognition (perception of a series of discrete, independent events, rather than the dynamic nature of traffic, difficulties understanding intentions and putting oneself in the place of the driver[4], difficulties in grasping time, space and speed, understanding road signs, etc.). Furthermore, if the child shows specific characteristics related to information acquisition, his/her involvement in accidents could also be linked to the way in which he/she processes the information, i.e. he/she would not compensate information acqusition shortfalls when making a decision, as would an adult.
Although this conclusion is similar to that drawn up with regard to understanding risk and probability concepts, namely that the characteristics of childhood lead us to see the nature of risk at this period in life in a different light, it would nevertheless be dangerous to conclude that children do not take risks on the road. Surveys carried out on children as pedestrians show clearly that young boys, for example, adopt more risky behaviour than do girls: less frequent use of pedestrian crossings, etc., these factors could undoubtedly be associated with their overinvolvement. In the same way, surveys carried out in Holland on the behaviour of child cyclists (e.g. Van Schagen et al., 1986) show that 11-14 year old children are particularly noted for less careful behaviour than for other age groups : they approach junctions at a high speed, reduce

---

[4] Which more generally relates to the concept of "egocentrism" proposed by Piaget.

speed less frequently when crossing junctions, are less likely to look sideways.
Furthermore, a factor which is frequently put foward with regard to risk-taking by child pedestrians is that of play. Reference studies carried out in Sweden by Sandels (op.cit.) on the etiology of accidents involving child pedestrians have shown that the great majority of accidents of this type result from the child "dashing-out" onto the roadway. In 31% of these cases, Sandels notes a social factor which "hastened" the accident : the child was running to someone or away from someone. Similar findings have been observed in Japan (Hoshi, 1976) and in Britain (Grayson, 1975). A street can therefore be a playground, an "open air theatre" for a child. Attention distracted in this way is a accident risk factor which must be taken into account for children of this age.
Similarly, road safety work concerning accident risks to children have clearly shown the multidimensional nature of this problem : although cognitive development influences risk perception, particularly when acquiring and processing information, other spheres of development such as socialisation or emotions also determine the way in which children behave in traffic.

CONCLUSIONS

The concepts of risk, probability and chance are therefore not immediate facts for the child but are the subject of a long and difficult construction ; the Piagetian contribution lies essentially in the analysis of each age's cognitive constraints, constraints which determine and structure the apprehension of these three concepts.
This construction allows us to partially understand the evolution of risk-taking between childhood and adolescence : before mastering formal operations, the child cannot estimate probability and thus centers himself on utility ; when these are acquired, coordination of both risk assessment components becomes possible.
On the other hand, work on differential perception of risks and road safety studies suggest that other phenomena interfere with this cognitive evolution ; the danger stakes and their meaning are not the least of these. We must therefore question what constitutes the experiential "texture" of risk : the emotions. Like cognitive structures, emotional structures have a history, a construction and their evolution[5] is a factor structuring the genesis of attitudes related to risk from childhood to the adult age.

---

[5] Here, we are only suggesting a point, which, in itself, would necessitate another publication.

REFERENCES

Dickson G.C.A. and **Hutchison** G.E., 1988, "Children's perception of and anticipated responses to risk", *Br. J. educ. Psychol.*, 58, pp. 147-151.

Grayson G.B., 1975, *The Hampshire child pedestrian accident study*, TRRL Report 668.

Jurs J. and **Mangili** L.and **Jurs** S., 1990, Preschool children's attitudes toward health risk behaviors, *Psychological Reports,* 66, pp. 754.

Hoshi T., 1976, Educating young children for traffic safety : activities of the children's traffic safety clubs, *The Wheel Extended*, 6, pp. 14-18.

Krishna K.P., 1981, Risk taking among Indian adolescents, *J. Soc. Psychol.*, 114, pp. 293-294.

Mann L. and **Harmoni** R.V. and **Power**, C.N., 1984, *Adolescents' knowledge and beliefs about decision making*, Unpublished manuscript, Flinders University of South Australia.

Meyer C.J.W. and **Vinje**, M.P., 1978, *Een onderzoek naar der kennis van verkeersbegrippen bij kinder van 4-6 jaar,* Groningen, Traffic Research Center.

Mc Ginnis J.H. and **Berg**, N.L., 1973, Effects of prior gains on risk-taking behavior by children, *Psychological Reports*, 32, pp. 543-549.

Nakajima Y. and **Ohta**, 1989, N. Developmental change in subjective probability during adolescence, *Psychological Reports*, 64, pp. 243-249.

Piaget J. and **Inhelder** B., 1974, *La genèse de l'idée de hasard chez l'enfant,* Paris, PUF.

Sandels S., 1968, *Children in traffic*, London, Elek.

Sandels S., 1979, *Unprotected road users : a behavioural study*, Skandia Report III, Stockholm.

Van Schagen I.N.L.G. and **Brookhuis**, K.A. ,1986, Following observations of young cyclists, in Lourens, P.F.(ed.), *Annual Report 1986,* Traffic Research Centre, University of Groningen, pp. 40-45.

Walesa, C., 1975, Children's approaches to chance- and skill-dependent risk, *Polish Psychological Bulletin*, 6, 3, pp. 131-138.

Walesa, C., 1977, Development of risk perception in children and adolescents, *Polish Psychological Bulletin*, 8, 3, pp. 171-176.

CONTEXTUAL EFFECTS

AND

THE INFLUENCE OF THE FRAME ON

DECISION MAKING

Bernard Cadet[*]

For the purposes of the present paper it would be helpful - though with the risk of some degree of over-simplification - to group the various theoretical studies which underlie research on decision-making under two broad and relatively distinct headings, as reflected in the title of the conference which brings us together today.
The first of these trends could be called formal: the aim is to indicate from a normative point of view and given the personal (or "subjective") values of the decider what constitutes a "good" decision. This assumes that people are "consistent" (Lindley, 1971 ; De Finetti, 1974), i.e. that they are able to rank their preferences in transitive order. Given the difficulties in assessing subjective values, it became immediately obvious that this condition is naturally encountered only in a very limited number of cases, so that almost all authors who belong to this school of thought recommend the use of axiomatic systems (Savage, 1954 ; De Finetti, 1974 ; Luce, 1959), thereby guaranteeing the formal validity of assessments of subjective values. These are then combined according to simple arithmetical rules (especially multiplication) in order to provide criteria for a decision-making model. The prototype of this procedure is illustrated by the theories of expected utility (EU) and subjective expected utility (SEU).

---

[*] Professor of Psychology Groupe TC2IP (Cognitive Processing of Uncertain or Probabilistic Information), Département de Psychologie, Université de Caen, 14032 Caen cedex, France.

This approach is perfectly valid from the formal point of view, but the complexity of the axiomatic propositions it entails and of the introspection it demands is such that its repercussions, though clearly logical, involve consequences which are difficult to appreciate for the great majority of deciders placed in situ. The conclusion must be that these formal theories do not describe real behavior, but rather that of an "idealised decider" (Savage, 1967), a mythical individual unaffected by error, lapses of memory or inconsistency.

The second school of thought derives from surveys conducted by Edwards (1954, 1961) and adopts an unequivocally behavioral approach developped in a serie of posterior works on multiattribute utility (Edwards, 1977 ; Edwards and Newman, 1982). The pursuit of formal optimality is replaced by the study of the cognitive functions used in processing data when individuals find themselves in a decision-making situation. The pre-eminence of realism over norms and of cognitive over formal aspects, together with repeated observations of bias led scientists working within this perspective to study decision-making by means of remarkably well-conceived experimental designs and thereby to assess the effect of certain variables on choice.

Three broad sets of conclusions can be drawn :

a) In "real-life situations", the preconditions required by utility theories are hardly ever satisfied. Generally speaking, preferences can be intransitive (Tversky, 1969); sequential ordering is so unreliable (Slovic, 1971) that there are cases when it can be reversed (Lichtenstein and Slovic, 1973).

b) The EU and SEU criteria appear to produce entities which are either too general or too abstract to be of any real use as references in decision-making. Some factors which deciders consider important are ignored - for example, the dispersion of different values : the importance of this factor was stressed some time ago by Allais (1953) and experimentally studied by Slovic and Lichtenstein (1968b) via comparison of standard versus duplex games of identical expected value.

c) Since formal theories aim to ascertain individual assessments they tend to ignore the contextual and presentational features of a decision-making situation, yet these factors would appear to play a decisive role in reaching a conclusion. The present study, in keeping with the cognitive approach, explores the influence of certain presentational characteristics on the decision-making process.

1. THE INFLUENCE OF FRAME AND CONTEXT ON DECISION MAKING

The generic term 'presentation', designating the general conditions under which a decision-making problem arises, can be subdivided into two component parts.

1.1. The role of the frame

The more general of the component parts is the frame, i.e. the environmental (or "ecological") features of the problem situation. Every decision problem is dealt within a given environment which comprises specific features or 'frame', presented in positive or negative terms.

The nature of the environment, the references adopted and the general conditions of presentation all have an impact on how a decision is reached. These connections have been clearly evidenced in studies by Kahneman and Tversky (1984) and by Tversky and Kahneman (1981), using a paradigm illustrated by the well-known example of the "Asian disease" in which two situations of equal expected utility (therefore of identical formal value) lead to a reversal in order of preferences.

THE EXEMPLARY PROTOTYPE DESCRIBED BY TVERSKY AND KAHNEMAN (1981)

"Imagine that the US is preparing for the outbreak of an unusual Asian disease, which is expected to kill 600 people. Two alternative programs to combat the disease have been proposed. Assume that the exact scientific estimates of the consequences of the programs are as follows :

1(A) If Program A is adopted, 200 people will be saved.

1(B) If Program B is adopted, there is one-third probability that 600 people will be saved and two-thirds probability that no people will be saved.

Which of the two programs do you favour ?"

Another group of subjects was given the same problem phrased in exactly the same way, but the two solutions were presented differently :

2(A) If Program C is adopted, 400 will die.

2(B) If Program D is adopted, there is a one-third probability that nobody will die and a two-thirds probability that 600 people will die."

It will be recalled that in the first problem 72% of subjects studied (N=152) chose option 1A, the no-risk option, whereas in the second problem, which has the same expected utility value, 78% of subjects in a different group (N=155) chose the risky option 2B. This reversal, in contradiction with the formal principles of expected utility, is caused by the fact that each version prompts subjects to use a distinct set of references, one of which emphasises the certainty of lives saved (Problem #1) whereas the other highlights the possibility of avoiding deaths (Problem #2).

Given that both versions of the problem are formally identical, this represents inconsistent behavior, running counter to what rational choice would expect.

This example is a neat illustration of the role of the decision frame, i.e. "the decision maker's conception of the acts, outcomes and contingencies associated with a particular choice" (Tversky and Kahneman, 1981), and underscores the fact that individual references are not limited to assessments of probability and utility; they influence also the overall apprehension of the set of available elements and the particular environmental tone or hue associated with them.

Thus we may say that the usefulness of any given sequence of data depends on contextual characteristics. This in turn recalls the phenomena described by the Gestalt school in their study of perceptual illusion. In the Gestalt view (Koffka, 1935 ; Kohler, 1940), perception is not conceived of as something which imposes itself on the individual; it is a constructive and dynamic0 activity, a form of data-processing strongly influenced by field factors expressed as centration effects.

The close relationship between perceptual and decisional behavior led Tversky and Kahneman (1983) to put forward the idea of "cognitive illusions" and Hammond (1990) to suggest that of "illusionism", referring to field effects on decision-making. According to this approach, adopted also in the present study, decision-making is the consequential result of cognitive activity comprising both the decider's personal characteristics (as evidenced by the utility theories) and field effects related to presentation (the contribution of the cognitive school).

1.2 The role of the informational context

In addition to frame conditions, every decision situation contains a specific network of information available to the decider. The generic term for this network is the 'informational context', and consists of elements which vary as to number, quality and organisational modality (structure). Together they define for any given situation a specific and highly individualised network configuration. Experimental studies of the informational context have led to conclusions which run counter to those forecast intuitively.

1.2.1. Quantitative increase in available data does not result ipso facto in a corresponding rise in quality of decisions. The relationship between these two elements is by no means linear. If data is initially restricted, additional information does result in better decisions, but beyond a threshold of around five or six items requiring simultaneous processing, additional data tends to cause inconsistency and mistakes. This phenomenon has been demonstrated in the field of diagnosis in psychopathology, and has the paradoxical corollary that the decider claims heightened confidence in the value of his chosen conclusion (Hogarth, 1975 ; Cadet, 1991).

1.2.2. Quality of data is assessed via "diagnosticity". A given data indicator is termed "diagnostic" if it produces a high probability of reducing uncertainty, thereby promoting the choice of a particular outcome (were such an item to eliminate uncertainty altogether, it would be pathognomonic). Every context contains items of different informative value: some are highly diagnostic, others are weak or even misleading. Beyth-Marom and Fischhof (1983) have demonstrated that subjects placed in situ use both diagnostic and "pseudo-diagnostic" indicators without seeking to verify the quality of the available data items.

1.2.3. Organisational modality or contextual structure refers to the way in which information is acquired or provided. Whether data is dispersed, serially arranged or loosely connected to the various available outcomes influences the decision-making process.

Several studies have demonstrated the importance of structure :

- Montgomery (1983, 1989) showed that deciders look first for an attractive choice i.e. treatment of those issues which strongly correspond to the personal values of the decision-maker to the exclusion of all others and then test for its general superiority over alternative choices before reaching a final decision. In cases like this, decisions depend on "predecisional information" rather than on overall estimates of utility : subjects seeking information with a view to decision-making "usually do not gather the same amount of information on different alternatives. Some alternatives are examined very thoroughly, others to a lesser extent while still others are entirely ignored" Tyszka (1985).

- It is, however, by no means certain that this procedure is typical ; in other contexts the strategies employed are more analytical. Some decisions are processed via the empirical application of multidimensional analysis, in which the values of the attributes specific to each outcome are estimated over different scales and if necessary weighted before global scores are determined. This procedure has been studied in different ways by Aschenbrenner et al (1986) and by Svenson (1979) ; they demonstrated that only a small amount of available information is actually used. Sundstroem (1989) related these variations to different decisional rules - additive, conjunctive or eliminatory (type EBA, in terms of Tversky's (1972) theory).

2. RESEARCH HYPOTHESES AND EXPERIMENTAL PROCEDURE

The above mentioned studies lead quite clearly to the conclusion that both frame and context influence decision-making. This, however, tells us nothing about how they operate and under what conditions their influence on behavior may be reinforced or attenuated. Also, observation per se cannot enhance our understanding of the impact of presentation, since it is too circumstantial as to conditions and insufficiently specific about effects. The cognitive modalities which we presume to be operating must be experimentally activated so as to bring about change in decisions.
The optimal research strategy implies setting up an experimental protocol in which frame and context variations represent the independent variables (IV) and the decisions reached the dependent variable influenced by them.

2.1 Hypotheses

The present study follows Gestalt principles, and targets a more explicit definition of the convergent or antagonistic effects of frame and context on decision-making.

Possible factors which might cause these effects to vary are :

a) The number of attributes available to the decider. One hypothesis would be that an increase in information leads to a reduced influence of frame, insofar as the impact of a more prolific and more elaborate context will accrue either positively or negatively to frame effects.

b) The presentation of information. Does the way in which information is presented - scattered or structured - modify frame influence ?

c) The effect of prior knowledge available to subjects when they make their decision. Decision reversal can be induced in "simple game" situations in which available information is scanty (for example in the "Asian disease" situation). Is this still the case where subjects can call upon information in decision contexts with which they are more familiar and which concern them directly ?

2.2 Modifications to the original paradigm

The prototype is Kahneman and Tversky's (1981) paradigm in which subjects have to decide between alternative actions presented in frames which, though contrasted ("positive" - "negative"), possess equivalent expected utility.

In order to test the above hypotheses, the prototype was subjected to two series of modifications, one relative to structure, the other to response assessment modality.

2.2.1. There are three structural modifications :

- The number of attributes ("Q" - quantity) which describe each available option: 2, 4 or 6 items of information (utility and probability) instead of a single item.

- Presentation ("P") of these attributes can take on one of two modalities : either scaled along dimensions ("D"), so that for each option the value of a given attribute can be compared to each of the others, or in a structured whole ("S") in which the set of attributes pertaining to each option is sufficient to define it. Procedure D corresponds to what is commonly called the analytical method, in which comparative evaluation is paramount, whilst procedure S is akin to the global approach in its attempt to formulate an overall assessment.

- Prior knowledge ("K") of the problem situation is a variable which may influence frame effects. The cognitive effort required in choosing between options probably depends on the decider's degree of familiarity with the problem situation. When decisions involve situations previously encountered (modality K1), prior knowledge "referentials" (Cadet, 1991) are made use of, whereas choosing between unfamiliar options (modality K2) in games or social decisions (Eiser, 1988) excludes recourse to such a strategy. The expectation is that the latter situation will be more sensitive to presentational effects than the former.

2.2.2. Modifications to response modality and quantification of decisions

Each problem is presented separately using Tversky and Kahneman's (1981) code - numbers designate frame (1 = "positive", 2 = "negative"), and letters classify options (A : sure option, B : probabilistic option).

Statement of the problem is accompanied by a response sheet on which the two competing options are set out in tree diagram form, an arrangement recommended by Raiffa (1968). Subjects give to each branch a personal appeal value ("PAV") scored from 1 (very low appeal level) to 5 (very high appeal). Each proposed outcome is thereby quantified, a procedure which appears more instructive than the mere indication of dominant preference. For each option (2 outcomes) and for each subject the algebraic difference is calculated : $1A - 1B = x$ or $2A - 2B = y$.

The modified protocol continues to produce $x>0$ in all Type 1 situations and $y < 0$ in all Type 2 situations. Scores close to +/-5 can be interpreted as highly indicative of the existence of frame effect, whereas those approximating to 0 imply zero frame effect.

3. THE EXPERIMENT : MATERIAL AND PROCEDURE

3.1. The decision situations

Three experimental decision situations were designed in accordance with the fundamental rules of the paradigm (equal expected value presented in contrasting frames) but incorporating the modifications described supra.

- The first problem is similar to that of Kahneman and Tversky (1981), modified as to number of available attributes and as to presentation.
- The second situation is a simple probability game with financial gains and losses, and follows Slovic and Lichtenstein's (1968a) procedure for the experimental study of decisions.
- The third situation incorporates the idea of familiarity : at the beginning of the academic year, subjects have to rent a small apartment. This has proved to be a highly suitable decision problem (Sundstroem, 1989).

3.2. The experimental design

For each problem the protocol follows a randomised factorial pattern containing 2 (frame) * 3 (Q) * 2 (P) = 12 modalities. The effect of familiarity will be dealt with separately through comparison of responses to situations #2 and #3.

3.3. Population

Subjects are psychology students in the first two years of the curriculum (DEUG), (mean age : 21.4 ; sd : 1.6). Participation in the project is voluntary and unpaid, but credits valid for the final examination are granted to the students, who have had neither instruction nor training in decision problem-solving. Five subjects are randomly assigned to each modality (N = 60 for each problem). The problems are presented to each group following the factorial design.

4. RESULTS AND ANALYSIS

In keeping with the experimental layout, the investigation of possible factors influencing the decisions was carried out by means of statistical analysis of variance.
Two procedures were chosen :
- on a more general level, multiple analysis of variance (MANOVA) to determine whether the experimentally-introduced factors have an overall effect on decision-making.
- simple analysis of variance (ANOVA) to determine the importance of these factors on the decisions reached in each of the problem situations.

4.1. Multiple analysis of variance

TABLE 1 : Results of the multivariate analysis (WILKS' test)

SOURCES	FACT.1 F2.3	FACT.2 F1.2.3	FACT.3	F1.2	F1.3
ddl	(3.46) (6.92)	(6.92) (6.92)	(3.46)	(6.92)	(6.92)
F	39.63 0.690	1.23 1.06	0.728	5.08	0.690
Proba.	$p < .001$ $p = .660$	$p = .299$ $p = .389$	$p = .544$	$p < .0001$	$p = .660$
	n.s	n.s. n.s.	n.s.		n.s.

It is clear that significant effects are found, viz :

- factor #1: frame has a significant influence on all three decisions- interaction between factors #1 and #2 (frame * quantity of information). This result tends to confirm the fact that interactions between certain factors play a significant role in decision-making, and that these interactions are highly specific. No other interaction between factors reaches significance.These overall findings will now be adjusted by examining their impact on each problem situation.

4.2. Decisions in problem #1 (ANOVA)

TABLE 2 : Incidences of independant variables on decisions computed from "PAV" (Problem # 1)

	S.SQ.	df	M.S.	F
Proba.				
TOTAL VAR.	306.16	59	5.19	
FAC1 VAR.			126.12	1	126.12
63.04 .0000				
FAC2 VAR.			7.22	2	3.61
1.80 .1738				
FAC3 VAR.			3.76	1	3.76
1.88 .1737				
FAC1.2 INTERVAR.	65.69	2	32.85	16.42
.0000				
FAC1.3 INTERVAR.	0.82	1	0.82	0.41
.5326				
FAC2.3 INTERVAR.	2.09	2	1.05	0.52
.6017				
FAC1.2.3 INTERVA	4.42	2	2.21	1.11
.3403				
RESIDUAL VAR.	96.04	48	2.00	

This first problem entirely confirms MANOVA conclusions: factor #1 and interaction #1 * #2 both have a significant impact on the decisions reached.

4.3. Decisions in problem #2 (ANOVA)

TABLE 3 : Incidences of independant variables on decisions computed from "PAV" (Problem # 2)

	S.SQ.	df	M.S.	F	Proba.
TOTAL VAR.	224.92	59	3.81		
FAC1 VAR.	96.22	1	96.22	53.20	.0000
FAC2 VAR.	3.88	2	1.94	1.07	.3516
FAC3 VAR.	0.26	1	0.26	0.14	.7081
FAC1.2 INTERVAR.	2.03	2	1.02	0.56	.5791
FAC1.3 INTERVAR.	29.40	1	29.40	16.26	.0003
FAC2.3 INTERVAR.	0.64	2	0.32	0.18	.8405
FAC1.2.3 INTERVA	5.69	2	2.85	1.57	.2163
RESIDUAL VAR.	86.81	48	1.81		

Once again frame is the only factor which has a dominant influence when taken singly, and in this case interaction with factor #3 (presentation) produces a significant result.

4.4. Decisions in problem #3 (ANOVA)

TABLE 4 : Incidences of independant variables on decisions computed from "PAV" (Problem # 3)

Proba.	S.SQ.	df	M.S.	F
TOTAL VAR.	202.57	59	3.43	
FAC1 VAR. 12.44	.0011	36.80	1	36.80
FAC2 VAR. 1.46	.2416	8.63	2	4.31
FAC3 VAR. 0.68	.4194	2.01	1	2.01
FAC1.2 INTERVAR. .9287	0.43	2	0.22	0.07
FAC1.3 INTERVAR. .6075	0.82	1	0.82	0.28
FAC2.3 INTERVAR. .3814	5.85	2	2.92	0.99
FAC1.2.3 INTERVA .3703	6.03	2	3.01	1.02
RESIDUAL VAR.	142.00	48	2.96	

When content is familiar, only factor #1 has a significant influence.

5. DISCUSSION

These results clearly demonstrate the important role played by frame, which in the present experiment is the only factor which consistently influences outcome. Tversky and Kahneman's (1981) findings on the importance of frame effect on decision-making are thus broadly confirmed, and may even be further adjusted.

The present study, because of the methodological changes mentioned above, actually quantifies differences in appeal (DA) as between options proposed, and does not simply express crude choice reversal in terms of percentages. This means that two complementary features can be underlined :

(1) the magnitude of frame effect, present in all three situations and producing highly significant primary impact. The nature of the information involved, and in particular reference to prior knowledge is not a discriminatory variable, but the structure of the decision situation, identical in all three cases, appears to be the crucial factor in producing similarity of effect.

(2) significant interactive effects, in which frame (factor #1) consistently participates. Frame is associated to quantity of information (F #1 * #2) in the first problem, and to presentation (F #1 * #3) in the second. Though limited in number - these are the only significant interactions - these two results are epistemologically important in that they imply the possibility of associations and the existence of what MEEHL (1954) called "configural effects" in which different items of information influence one another.

On a more detailed level, the F#1 * F#2 interaction in the first decision appears to be based on information intake procedures. This has two aspects. Firstly, mean differences A-B decrease regularly for both types of frame when the number of attributes pertaining to each option increases from 2 to 6 (note, however, that dispersion is always higher when frame is negative). Secondly, dispersion is always less for 2 or 6 attributes than for 4. In other words, both sparse (2 elements) and high-density (6 elements) contexts interfere with assimilation of information ; ordinary limitations on human capability, particularly "flux" capacity, make the simultaneous processing of several indicators increasingly difficult (Hogarth, 1975). The present writer has previously shown (Cadet, 1991) that beyond a threshold of about 5 items per option, any additional information tends to generate more inaccurate empirical judgments because of data overload. It is quite possible that a similar kind of cognitive overload forms the basis for F#1-F#2 interaction.

The F#1-F#3 interaction, significant in problem #2, indicates that frame and presentation taken together have a crucial impact on decision-making. A detailed scrutiny of A-B mean scores and dispersion reveals for both types of frame a decrease in mean scores from dimensional to global presentation, whilst standard deviations remain fairly homogeneous (lying between 1.34 and 1.63).

This suggests that, dispersion being equal, information intake procedures generate the interactive effect. When "pre-packed" information is provided (i.e. in global modality), frame effects are quite significantly weakened; in dimensional procedures, where subjects themselves decide on the value of a given option after processing data pertaining to it, frame influence is maintained.

From this we may conclude that the structured quality of global modalities produces contextual effects which run counter to frame effects and thereby tend partly to diminish their impact. This confirms one of our initial hypothesis - though we must stress that the phenomenon concerns interactive operations and not one of the primary effects.

6. CONCLUSION

The present study brings us more in tune with how certain frame characteristics influence decision-making. The importance of frame effect is a salient feature in various decision settings : social, game and familiar situations. Even prior knowledge of theme leaves frame impact undiminished : the effect is just as significant in situation #3 as in the other two.

It would nevertheless be advantageous to analyse frame effect in terms of the overall cognitive field created by the situation, since the present investigation reveals significant interactions with quantity of information and with modes of presentation. These hybrid results point to different modalities of information intake and processing, and would appear to indicate that decisions are the consequence of a "modus vivendi" between field influences.

These results complement other analyses based on the same paradigm and dealing with verbal protocols (Maule, 1989). Although the latter start from a different perspective, they too lay emphasis on the effect of presentation on the conclusions reached. The present study, albeit limited as to choice of situations and subjects (including size of sample), shows that future research must conceptualise decision-making as an overall process consequential upon the interplay of reciprocal cognitive influences.

REFERENCES

Allais (M.), Le comportement de l'homme rationnel devant le risque Critique des postulats et axiomes de l'Ecole Américaine, Econometrica, 1953, 21, 503-546.

Aschenbrenner (K.M.), Bockenholt (V.), Albert (D.), Schmalhofer (F.), The selection of dimensions when choosing between multiattribute alternatives, in (R.W.) Scholtz (Ed), Current issues in West German Decision Research, Frankfurt, Lang, 1986.

Beyth-Marom (R.), Fischhof (B.), Diagnosticity and pseudo-diagnosticity, Journal of Personality and Social Psychology, 1983, 45, 1185-1195.

Cadet (B.), Le diagnostic comme activité cognitive d'expertise, Psychologie Médicale, 1991, 23, 141-146.

De Finetti (B.), Theory of probability : a critical introductory treatment, Vol. 1, New York, Wiley, 1974.

Edwards (W.), The theory of decision making, Psychological Bulletin, 1954, 51, 380-417.

Edwards (W.), Behavioral decision theory, Annual Review of Psychology, 1961, 12, 473-498.

Edwards (W.), How to use multiattribute utility measurement for social decision making ?, IEEE Transactions on Systems, Man and Cybernetics, 1977, SMC-7, 326-340.

Edwards (W.) ; Newman (J.R.), Multiattribute Evaluation, Beverly Hills, Sage, 1982.

Eiser (J.R.), Prise de risque social, conservatisme et piège social, Bulletin de Psychologie, 1988, 41, 186-192.

Hammond (K.R.), Functionalism and illusionism : Can integration be usefully achieved ? in (R.M.) HOGARTH (Ed), Insights in decision making. A tribute to Hillel J. EINHORN, Chicago, University of Chicago Press, 1990.

Hogarth (R.M.), Cognitive processes and the assessment of subjective probability distributions, <u>Journal of the American Statistical Association</u>, 1975, <u>350</u>, 271-289.

Kahneman (D.), Tversky (A.), Choice, values and frames, <u>American psychologist</u>, 1984, <u>39</u>, 341-350.

Koffka (K.), <u>Principles of Gestalt Psychology</u>, New York, Harcourt Brace, 1935.

Kohler (W.), <u>Dynamics in Psychology</u>, New York, Liveright, 1940.

Lichtenstein (S.), Slovic (P.), Response-induced reversal of preference in gambling decision : An extended replication in Las Vegas, <u>Journal of Experimental Psychology</u>, 1973, <u>101</u>, 16-20.

Lindley (D.V.), <u>Making decisions</u>, New York, Wiley, 1971, Second Edition 1985.

Luce (R.D.), <u>Individual choice behavior : a theoretical analysis</u>, New York, Wiley, 1959.

Maule (J.A.), Positive and negative decision frame : a verbal protocol analysis of the Asian disease problem of TVERSKY and KAHNEMAN, in (H.) MONTGOMERY and (O.) SVENSON (Eds), <u>Process and structure in human decision making</u>, New York, Wiley, 1989.

Meehl (P.E.), <u>Clinical vs Statistical Prediction : A theoretical Analysis and a Review of the Evidence</u>, Minneapolis, University of Minnesota Press, 1954.

Montgomery (H.), Decision rules and the search for a dominance structure : towards a process model of decision-making, in (P.C.) Humphreys, (O.) Svenson and (A.) Vari (Eds), <u>Analysing and aiding decision processes</u>, Amsterdam, North Holland, 1983.

Montgomery (H.), From cognition to action : the search for dominance in decision making, in (H.) MONTGOMERY and (O.) SVENSON (Eds), <u>Process and structure in human decision making</u>, New York, Wiley, 1989.

Raiffa (H.), <u>Decision Analysis : Introductory Lectures on Choice under Uncertainty</u>, Reading Massachusetts, Addison Wesley, 1968.

Savage (L.J.), <u>The foundations of statistics</u>, New York, Wiley, 1954.

Savage (L.J.), Difficulties in the theory of personal probabilities, Philosophy of Science, 1967, 34, 305-310.

Slovic (P.), Information processing, situation specificity and the generality of risk taking behavior, Report of the Oregon Research Institute, Eugene, Oregon, 1971.

Slovic (P.), Lichtenstein (S.), Relative importance of probabilities and payoffs in risk-taking, Journal of Experimental Psychology, 1968a, 78, 1-18.

Slovic (P.), Lichtenstein (S.), Importance of variance preferences in gambling decisions, Journal of Experimental Psychology, 1968b, 78, 646-654.

Svenson (O.), Process description of decision making, Organizational Behavior and Human Performance, 1979, 23, 86-112.

Sundstroem (G.), Information search and decision making : The effets of information displays, in (H.) MONTGOMERY and (O.) SVENSON, Process and structure in human decision making, New York, Wiley, 1989.

Tversky (A.), Intransitivity of preferences, Psychological Review, 1969, 76, 31-48.

Tversky (A.), Elimination by aspects : a theory of choice, Psychological Review, 1972, 79, 281-299.

Tversky (A.), Kahneman (D.), The framing of decisions and the psychology of choice, Science, 1981, 211, 453-458.

Tversky (A.), Kahneman (D.), Extensional versus intuitive reasoning : the conjunction fallacy in probability judgment, Psychological Review, 1983, 80, 293-315.

Tyszka (T), Variability of predecisional information seeking behavior, Polish Psychological Bulletin, 1985, 16, 275-282.

CE-PE BIAS AND PROBABILITY LEVEL: AN ANCHORING MODEL OF THEIR INTERACTION[1]

Paul J. H. Schoemaker and John C. Hershey
The Wharton School
University of Pennsylvania

1. Introduction

It was established over a decade ago that the certainty equivalence (CE) and probability equivalence (PE) methods for measuring basic risk attitudes yield different results (Hershey, Kunreuther, and Schoemaker, 1982). The typical design used presents subjects with a choice between a sure amount S and a gamble G offering a probability p of a larger payoff and a complementary probability of a smaller payoff. The amount S typically equals the expected value of the gamble. In the CE mode, S is adjusted to some point of indifference. In the PE mode, the probability p used for the gamble is adjusted. The probability equivalence method typically yields greater risk aversion than the certainty equivalence method for both gain and loss gambles. Several explanations have been offered.

The first one is the PE-reframing hypothesis (Hershey and Schoemaker, 1985; Schoemaker and Hershey, 1992). According to this explanation, some subjects reframe a given gain or loss gamble as a mixed one when in the PE mode, by subtracting the sure amount S from each of the gamble's outcomes. The sure amount S and the expected value of the reframed gamble thus become 0, and the gamble's two outcomes are viewed as a gain and a loss relative to this new reference point of 0. Since mixed gambles tend to evoke more risk aversion than pure loss or gain gambles, the net effect of PE reframing is an increase in risk aversion. Such reframing is less plausible in the CE mode since the sure amount itself is the figure to be adjusted and thus cannot serve as a fixed anchor.

Johnson and Schkade (1989) have accounted for CE-PE discrepancies using an anchoring and adjustment model. This

---

[1]We thank Jon Baron, Mark Machina, J. Edward Russo, and Elke Weber for helpful comments.

explanation was initially rejected by Hershey and Schoemaker (1985) for situations in which subjects anchor on S (in the CE method) or on the probability p (in the PE method). Johnson and Schkade, however, introduced <u>variable</u> anchoring and adjustment which can explain the results. Also, they found in their experiments that the differences in risk attitude elicited by the two methods depend on the reference probability used in the questions posed to subjects. The CE-PE discrepancy is greatest for low probabilities, getting smaller as the probability increases. They show that this pattern can arise from an anchoring and adjustment model where the response is a weighted average of <u>varying</u> starting points and a target utility function.

In this paper, we seek to verify the interaction between response mode effects and reference probability since Johnson and Schkade used procedures that differed from our initial designs. For example, they used standard gambles in which both gamble outcomes were nonzero; we use simple gambles in which one outcome is zero. For some of the questions, Johnson and Schkade did not prompt subjects with the risk neutral value of the parameter to be elicited, nor did they ask subjects if the risk neutral response made them indifferent. We always prompt subjects with the starting point and permit indifference.

Johnson and Schkade used linked two-stage questions to assess response mode effects (as we did initially). However, as shown in Schoemaker and Hershey (1992), this design introduces complex interactions with response mode and reference probability due to nonlinear propagation of noise. In the present study, we therefore analyze single, non-linked responses. Finally, we manipulate other factors known to influence responses in standard gamble questions -- stimulus levels, domain of the questions, direction of risk transfer, and context -- and, in the present study, examine possible interactions between these factors and response mode.[2]

In addition to replicating the interaction between response mode bias and reference probability, we offer a simpler anchoring and adjustment model to explain it. This model assumes that subjects adjust a <u>fixed</u> percentage of the maximum allowable adjustment from the risk neutral starting point in the direction of their ordinal risk attitude. We present a formal proof that this model predicts the observed interaction. Thus, the explanation for the interaction does not depend on variable anchors and adjustments. We also show that the interaction is not found in simulated responses based on prospect theory.

---

[2]In Hershey and Schoemaker (1994), we report the full results for all factors and their interactions.

2. Experiment

A two-stage questionnaire was administered to 140 MBA students. The stages were separated one week in time. In each stage, subjects answered either certainty-equivalence (CE) questions or probability-equivalence (PE) questions for both the gain and loss domains. The stimulus levels were the same for each of the two stages, for all subjects.

2.1 Experimental Design

Subjects. The respondents were MBA students taking an introductory course in Behavioral Decision Making at the Graduate School of Business at the University of Chicago. The questionnaire was administered near the beginning of the course, prior to any discussion of probability and risk. The median age of subjects was 27; 23% of subjects were female.

Stimuli. Within each questionnaire, all gambles had one possible nonzero outcome and one possible zero outcome. The stimulus levels for the 12 questions differed only in terms of the probability levels used, the absolute value of the nonzero outcome, and the sign (i.e., domain) of the nonzero outcome. As an illustration, consider the following prototype question:

> Imagine you are in a situation where you have a 20% chance of winning $200. Would you be willing to take a sure gain of $40 in exchange for this gamble?
>
> CIRCLE YOUR ANSWER: YES NO INDIFFERENT
>
> If **yes**, how small would the sure gain have to be for you to be just indifferent between the sure gain and the gamble? $_____ (Write an amount less than $40.)
>
> If **no**, how large would the sure gain have to be for you to be just indifferent between the sure gain and the gamble? $_____ (Write an amount greater than $40.)

The twelve questions in each questionnaire were constructed by using all combinations of three probability levels — 20%, 50% and 80%, two absolute values for the gambles' outcomes — $200 and $5000, and two domains — gains and losses. These same stimuli were used in the second-stage questionnaire, but there were differences in the wording as described in the next two subsections. The twelve questions posed in each of the two stages are summarized in Figure 1.

Eight different orderings of the questions were generated and balanced across subjects. For each stage, half of the subjects received the six gain questions first and half had the six loss questions first. Within each set of six questions, half received the three "$200 questions" first and half the three "$5000 questions" first. The question order was held constant within subjects for the gain and loss domains. Within each group of three questions, half saw probability levels in ascending order and half in descending order. (Again, the order was the same within subjects for all four sets of three questions.) The ordering of the twelve questions was unchanged within subject across the two stages.

2.2 Two Preference Elicitation Methods

The critical variation between questionnaires that we examine in this paper is **response mode**. The prototype question presented above asks for a certainty equivalent (**CE**), i.e., a sure dollar amount that is just as attractive as the gamble. The alternative response mode asks for a probability equivalent (**PE**), i.e., a probability level for the gamble's nonzero outcome that makes the gamble just as attractive as the sure outcome. This PE variation uses the same top part as the prototype question, but differs in the followup questions as follows:

> If **yes**, how large would the probability of winning the gamble have to be for you to be just indifferent between the sure gain and the gamble? _____%
> (Write a probability greater than 20%)
>
> If **no**, how small would the probability of winning the gamble have to be for you to be just indifferent between the sure gain and the gamble? _____%
> (Write a probability less than 20%)

2.3 Procedure

In the first stage, half of the subjects answered CE questions and half PE questions. In the second stage, about half within each group had a change to the opposite response mode and half had no change in response mode. Thus the between-subjects factors in our design are the ORDER controls. MODE is partly a between-subjects variable and partly a within-subjects variable. The exclusively within-subjects factors are DOMAIN, AMOUNT, AND PROBABILITY.

	Gamble's Nonzero Outcome	
Domain	$200	$5000
Gains	$p = 0.20$ $p = 0.50$ $p = 0.80$	$p = 0.20$ $p = 0.50$ $p = 0.80$
Losses	$p = 0.20$ $p = 0.50$ $p = 0.80$	$p = 0.20$ $p = 0.50$ $p = 0.80$

Figure 1. Stimulus levels for the twelve questions each subject answered in each stage.

Two other factors were also manipulated in these questionnaires, as reported in Hershey and Schoemaker (1994). One concerns the direction of risk transfer; in half of the questionnaires the potential risk was to be assumed by the subject, rather than divested as in our prototype question. The other factor involved context; in one-quarter of the questionnaires, a more specific contingent claim scenario was specified, in contrast to an abstract description. The data revealed no interaction between either of these two factors and MODE, so they are not discussed further in the present paper.

3. Analysis

The General Linear Model (GLM) procedure of SAS (1985) was used to analyze the data. Two pairs of runs were performed, one pair for each of two dependent variables (as described below). Each pair consisted of one run to examine main effects for all of the independent variables, and a second run involving only the most significant (p<.001) main effects plus their possible interactions.

Dependent Variables

To compare subjects' responses across questions (which differ in dollar size, response mode, and domain), the following rescaling was used. For CE responses, the dollar amounts were linearly transformed to a scale from zero to one. Zero corresponds to the smaller of the gamble outcomes (i.e., zero for gain gambles and the negative outcome for loss gambles) whereas one represents the larger outcome. For example, a CE response of $90 for a $200 gain gamble would have a rescaled CE value of 0.45; a CE response of -$1500 for a $5000 loss gamble would have a rescaled CE value of 0.70. In the PE mode, no rescaling is necessary for gains, since the responses all refer to the probability of the larger outcome -- $200 or $5000. For loss gambles, we rescaled to (1-PE) so that p refers to the chance of losing $0.

To transform these rescaled response variables into risk-attitude measures, two dependent variables were calculated. The first is the parameter of an exponential function estimate; the second is the negative log of the parameter of a power function estimate. We explain each below.

(1) **Exponential Function.** Each rescaled response corresponds uniquely to a c parameter in the exponential utility function $U(x) = (1-e^{-cx})/(1-e^{-c})$, assuming expected utility (EU) theory (Von Neumann and Morgenstern, 1947) applies. This c parameter, which is positive for risk-averse answers and negative for risk-seeking ones, was used as one dependent variable. We followed the usual custom of

projecting this function from the lower amount for gains and the higher amount for losses (which would be zero on the original response scale). Numerical methods were used to estimate the value of this parameter for each response.[3] This measure may especially appeal to economists who often favor exponential utility because of its wealth independence (Arrow, 1971, and Pratt, 1964).

(2) **Power Function.** Each response also corresponds uniquely to an alpha (α) parameter in the power utility function $U(x) = x^\alpha$. This parameter ranges between 0 and 1 for risk-averse answers and is greater than 1 for risk-seeking responses. To facilitate comparisons with the exponential measure, and to make the scales for risk-averse and risk-seeking responses symmetric, we used the negative logarithm of the power function parameter, $-\log \alpha$, as our second dependent variable. As with the exponential measure, the function was projected from the lower amount for gains and the higher amount for losses. Psychologists may be especially partial to power or logarithmic functions in view of their strong psychophysical support (Stevens, 1974).[4]

4. Results

Extreme outliers were first eliminated from the data set. Outliers were defined as responses that yielded an exponential function parameter greater than 10 in absolute value. These same outliers were removed for both dependent variables to maintain comparability across runs. After eliminating responses involving (i) missing data, (ii) ordinal inconsistencies between categorical preference and numerical response, and (iii) extreme outliers (as defined above), the number of observations was reduced from 3,360 to 3,055 (i.e., about 9% were eliminated).

No single run showed a significant main effect for question order; the results described in this section focus on the remaining

---

[3] A closed form answer is not attainable since the exponent c appears in both the numerator and denominator. Upon reduction of the EU equality, we are left with $e^{-c(CE)} = 1-p+pe^{-c}$ from which c cannot be isolated.

[4] The power function exhibits constant proportional risk aversion (or seeking) (Keeney and Raiffa, 1976). This means that scaling a gamble up or down by a fixed multiplicative factor would lead to identical values of alpha. For example, adding three zeros to all outcomes will not affect alpha (a kind of scale insensitivity).

factors. The results for the two pairs of GLM runs are shown in Table 1. The two dependent variables yield similar results.

The DOMAIN*AMOUNT variable is by far the most significant one. This is quite easily justified; differences in responses by domain and amount are not inconsistent with utility theory. PROBABILITY and MODE are also significant main effects for most runs. The most important interaction is PROBABILITY*MODE. Using the power function as an example, we show in Table 2 the mean values of - log α for the main factors, along with the standard deviations and sample sizes. The PROBABILITY*MODE interaction, which is the focus of this paper, is graphed separately for gains and losses in Figure 2.

As seen in Table 2, there is more risk aversion for gains than for losses, and more risk aversion for larger absolute amounts than for smaller. The former result is consistent with prospect theory (Kahneman and Tversky, 1979). The latter result, however, is inconsistent with the assumption of constant proportional risk aversion (or seeking) that is implied by the power utility function. Despite this, the power function offers the best overall fit of the data.

4.1 Main Effects

There is increasing risk aversion with increasing probability level. Recall that the values .2, .5, and .8 refer to the probability of the larger outcome, which for losses is $0. The results confirm our earlier finding for the loss domain that preference for actuarially fair insurance (and hence risk aversion) increases monotonically as the probability of a zero loss increases (Hershey and Schoemaker, 1980).

One explanation for this increase in risk aversion is a nonlinear probability weighting function, f(p), which induces increasingly risk-averse responses for increasing p. Within subjective expected utility theory (Schoemaker, 1982), this would happen if the ratio $f(p_2)/p_2$ is less than the ratio $f(p_1)/p_1$ for $p_2 > p_1$. The probability weighting function in prospect theory might also produce this result, depending on its exact shape. Karmarkar's (1978) subjectively weighted utility model could likewise account for these results for most of the probability range, assuming his alpha parameter is less than 1. Machina's (1982) fanning out model, as well as other generalized utility models (see Camerer, 1989), also predict increased risk aversion as the probability of gain increases.

Table 2 shows more risk aversion for probability equivalence questions than certainty equivalence ones, a finding that is consistent with the CE-PE literature. It is unlikely that this is due to variable anchors across the two conditions in our design. Every question prompted the subject with the gamble's expected value when asking

Main Effects	Deg. Free.	Exponential Function	Power Function
R-square		0.363	0.387
Domain*Amount	3	205.8 **	238.9 **
Probability	2	4.6	64.4 **
Mode	1	13.0 **	23.1 **

Main Effects + Inter.	Deg. Free.	Exponential Function	Power Function
R-square		0.413	0.436
Domain*Amount	3	219.1 **	248.5 **
Probability	2	6.4 **	74.6 **
Mode	1	14.7 **	26.5 **
Dom*Amt*Prob	6	2.3	1.6
Dom*Amt*Mode	3	1.0	12.8 **
Prob*Mode	2	48.1 **	29.5 **
Dom*Mod*Prob*Mode	6	1.9	0.5

* $p < .001$ (none)
** $p < .0001$

Table 1. Results of General Linear Model for two specifications of dependent variable, for main effects only and for main effects plus all interactions. Entries are F values. The actual model (and R-squares) include other factors not included in this table, as described in the text.

			- log α	
Factor(s)	Level	Mean	Standard Deviation	N
Domain* Amount	Dom=Gains, Amt= 200	.279	.718	783
	Dom=Gains, Amt=5000	.617	.840	733
	Dom=Losses, Amt= 200	-.197	.745	780
	Dom=Losses, Amt=5000	-.081	.758	759
Probability	Prob=0.2	-.023	.830	1015
	Prob=0.5	.154	.775	1038
	Prob=0.8	.318	.845	1002
Mode	CE	.071	.706	1467
	PE	.221	.921	1588

Table 2. Mean values, standard deviations, and sample sizes for main effects using the dependent variable based on the power utility function. The precise measure used is - log α, where α is the coefficient of the power function.

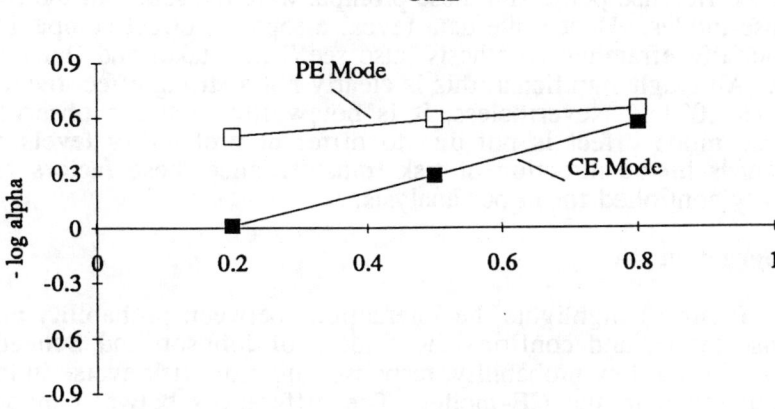

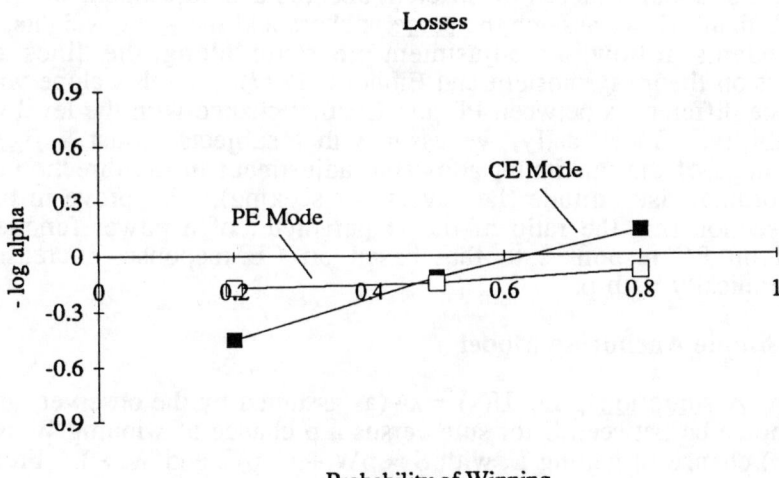

Figure 2. Mean values of - log α for each response mode, as a function of probability level. α is the parameter of a power function. Higher points denote greater risk aversion.

for an indifference point, and these prompts were the same for the two response modes. Hence, the data reveal a separate effect compatible with our PE-reframing hypothesis (also see Schoemaker and Hershey, 1992). Although significant, this is clearly not a strong effect overall (.221 vs. .071). Nevertheless, it is noteworthy that the observed response mode effect is not due to different probability levels or differences in the direction of risk transfer, since these factors are explicitly controlled for in our analysis.

4.2 Interaction With p

Figure 2 highlights the interactions between probability and response mode, and confirms the finding of Johnson and Schkade (1989). For the low probability, responses are more risk averse in the PE mode than in the CE mode. The differences between modes declines as the probability increases. In fact, in the loss domain, the two lines cross. We now turn to our explanation of the interaction between probability and response mode. (The interaction between domain and response mode is discussed in Hershey and Schoemaker, 1994.)

We propose a considerable simplification of Johnson and Schkade's model. Instead of different anchors and adjustment weights for CE than PE, we assume the <u>same</u> anchors and the <u>same</u> weights. If respondents follow an adjustment heuristic along the lines of expression theory (Goldstein and Einhorn, 1987), then this alone will produce differences between PE and CE that change with the level of probability. Specifically, we assume that subjects adjust a <u>fixed</u> percentage of the maximum allowable adjustment in the direction of their ordinal risk attitude (i.e., averse or seeking). We prove in the next section that the ratio of the α parameter of a power function based on PE responses to that based on CE responses increases monotonically with p.

5. A Simple Anchoring Model

<u>Assumptions.</u> Let $U(x) = x^\alpha$ (as assumed by the observer) and the choice be between S for sure versus a p chance of winning W and a (1-p) chance of getting L, with $S = pW + (1-p)L$ and $W > L$. From an EU perspective, CE and PE judgments would be encoded as:

$$U(CE) = (p)U(W) + (1-p)U(L), \text{ and}$$

$$U(S) = (PE)U(W) + (1-PE)U(L)$$

Without loss of generality, we may set W=1 and L=0 such that if $U(x) = x^\alpha$ we get:

$CE^\alpha = p$ or $\alpha_{CE} = \log(p)/\log(CE)$, and

$p^\alpha = PE$ or $\alpha_{PE} = \log(PE)/\log(p)$.

Note that $\alpha_{CE} = \alpha_{PE} = \alpha$ since $CE = p^{1/\alpha}$ and $PE = p^\alpha$.

The Model. We now assume that the CE and PE judgments are in fact generated by a fixed percentage adjustment w, with the S and p values serving as the CE and PE anchors, respectively. The adjustment is in the direction of the subject's ordinal risk preference (e.g., downward for CE under risk aversion), with w applied to the maximum allowable distance. For risk averters, the adjustments are:

$CE = w(0) + (1-w)p = p(1-w)$, and

$PE = w(1) + (1-w)p = p+w(1-p)$.

For risk seekers, the adjustments are:

$CE = w(1) + (1-w)p = p+w(1-p)$, and

$PE = w(0) + (1-w)p = p(1-w)$.

Note the symmetry in adjustments between risk attitudes.

If the above CE and PE responses are encoded with EU theory, the α_{CE} and α_{PE} coefficients will no longer be equal in general. For example, if we assume $U(x) = x^\alpha$, we get, for risk averters:

$$\alpha_{CE} = \frac{\log(p)}{\log(p(1-w))}, \text{ and } \alpha_{PE} = \frac{\log(p+w(1-p))}{\log(p)}.$$

For risk seekers:

$$\alpha_{CE} = \frac{\log(p)}{\log(p+w(1-p))}, \text{ and } \alpha_{PE} = \frac{\log(p(1-w))}{\log(p)}.$$

Note that the ratio α_{PE}/α_{CE} is the same for risk seekers and risk averters, namely:

$$R = \frac{\alpha_{PE}}{\alpha_{CE}} = \frac{\log(p(1-w))\log(p+w(1-p))}{(\log(p))^2}.$$

To simplify notation, let:

$x = \log(p)$
$y = \log(p(1-w))$
$z = \log(w+p(1-w)) = \log(p+w(1-p))$

with x, y and z < 0.

Proof. We now prove that $R = y \cdot x/x^2$ increases with p, or that $\partial R/\partial p > 0$. Let $R = f/g$ where $f = y \cdot z$ and $g = x^2$. We want to prove that

$$\frac{\partial R}{\partial p} = \frac{f'g - g'f}{g^2} > 0, \text{ or } f'g > g'f, \text{ where}$$

$$f' = z'y + y'z = \frac{(1-w)\log(p(1-w))}{w+p(1-w)} + \frac{(1-w)\log(w+p(1-w))}{p(1-w)},$$

$$g' = \frac{2\log(p)}{p}.$$

That is, we want to prove that

$$\left[\frac{(1-w)y}{w+p(1-w)} + \frac{(1-w)z}{p(1-w)}\right](\log(p))^2 > \frac{2\log(p)}{p} \cdot y \cdot z.$$

To simplify further, let $k = p(1-w)$ with $0 \leq p, w, k \leq 1$. Multiplying both sides by $((w+k)k/\log(p))^2$ yields:

$$k(1-w)\log(k) + (w+k)(1-w)\log(k+w) > \frac{2k(w+k) \cdot y \cdot z}{(p)\log(p)}.$$

Substituting k for (w+k) and log(k) for log(k+w) on the left-hand side lowers its value. If we can prove the inequality below, which is more tight, we shall also have proved the above inequality. In other words, is

$$k(1-w)\log(k) + (k)(1-w)\log(k) > \frac{2k(w+k)(z)\log(k)}{(p)\log(p)} \quad ?$$

Dividing both sides by the negative term $(2k)\log(k)$ leaves

$$1-w < \frac{(w+k)z}{(p)\log(p)}, \text{ or } \frac{p(1-w)}{w+k} < \frac{\log(p+w(1-p))}{\log(p)}, \text{ or}$$

$$\frac{k}{w+k} < \frac{\log(p+k)}{\log(p)}.$$

Since the left-side ratio is less than one, and the right-side greater than one, we have proved the inequality (for any positive k, w and p).

In sum, an anchoring and adjustment model based on expression theory can account for the observed interaction with the probability level p.

6. Prospect Theory Predictions

Finally we examine the predictions of prospect theory (PT) regarding the interaction with p. The calculations in this section assume one prototypical PT subject. It would require a much more complex analysis to derive predictions for a heterogeneous population of PT and non-PT subjects. We first examine PT without assuming PE-reframing and then with.

<u>Without PE-Reframing</u>. Table 3 shows the gambles we used to derive predictions from PT. We examine two domains -- gain and loss -- corresponding to the first two sections of the table. The probability in each domain goes from .9 to .1 in increments of .2. The basic gamble examined offers $200 or $0 in the gain domain (denoted win and lose respectively in the table) and is translated downward by $200 to obtain the loss gambles. The column PT-value shows each gamble's value as predicted by PT, assuming

$$V(x) = \begin{cases} x^{.88} \text{ if } x \geq 0 \\ -2.25(-x)^{.88} \text{ if } x < 0, \end{cases}$$

$$\pi(p) = p^{.65} / (p^{.65} + (1-p)^{.65})^{1/.65}.$$

These parameter estimates were obtained from Tversky and Kahneman (1992), assuming the same π functions for gains as losses.

The next columns in the table list each gamble's EV and the PT-value of that EV (denoted V(EV)). These output values were then used to calculate CE values for this hypothetical PT subject, as follows:

$$CE = V^{-1}[\pi(p)V(W) + \pi(1-p)V(L)].$$

The PE values were iteratively estimated in order to make the following equation hold:

$$V(EV) = \pi(PE)V(W) + \pi(1-PE)V(L).$$

For example, for gamble C, which offers even chances of receiving $200 or $0, the prototypical PT-subject would specify a CE of $78.43 (well below the gamble's EV of $100) or would require a probability of 67% to find the gamble as attractive as receiving $100 for sure.

Gamble	Prob.	Win	Lose	PT-Value	EV	V(EV)	CE	PE	Alpha CE	Alpha PE
Gain-side Gambles										
A	0.9	200	0	79.0	180	96.5	143.2	0.98	0.32	0.14
B	0.7	200	0	59.6	140	77.4	104.0	0.89	0.55	0.33
C	0.5	200	0	46.5	100	57.5	78.4	0.67	0.74	0.57
D	0.3	200	0	34.3	60	36.7	55.6	0.34	0.94	0.90
E	0.1	200	0	18.9	20	14.0	28.3	0.06	1.18	1.24
Loss-side Gambles										
F	0.9	0	-200	-42.6	-20	-31.4	-28.3	0.94	0.85	0.81
G	0.7	0	-200	-77.3	-60	-82.6	-55.6	0.66	1.06	1.11
H	0.5	0	-200	-104.6	-100	-129.5	-78.4	0.33	1.35	1.74
I	0.3	0	-200	-134.0	-140	-174.1	-104.0	0.11	1.83	3.00
J	0.1	0	-200	-177.6	-180	-217.2	-143.2	0.02	3.17	6.97
Translated Gambles										
K	0.9	20	-180		0	0		0.99		0.14
L	0.7	60	-140		0	0		0.92		0.24
M	0.5	100	-100		0	0		0.78		0.36
N	0.3	140	-60		0	0		0.53		0.54
O	0.1	180	-20		0	0		0.15		0.82

Table 3. Gambles used to provide predictions from prospect theory.

The last step in this PT simulation was to infer an α parameter for each CE and PE response, assuming an EU framework. Assuming $U(x) = x^\alpha$ for gains, we get for CE:

$$U(CE) = pU(200) + (1-p)U(0), \text{ or}$$

$$CE^\alpha = p \cdot 200^\alpha + (1-p) \cdot 0^\alpha, \text{ or}$$

$$\alpha_{CE} = \frac{\log(p)}{\log(CE) - \log(200)}.$$

Similarly, PE values were mapped into alphas as follows:

$$U(200p) = PE \cdot U(200) + (1-PE)U(0), \text{ or}$$

$$(200p)^\alpha = PE \cdot 200^\alpha + (1-PE) \cdot 0^\alpha, \text{ or}$$

$$\alpha_{PE} = \frac{\log(PE)}{\log(200p) - \log(200)}.$$

Similar calculations were conducted for the loss domain, projecting the power function from the higher amount (corresponding to $0).

Figure 3 plots ($-\log \alpha_{CE}$) and ($-\log \alpha_{PE}$) for gain and loss gambles and reveals a strong interaction with p for both. The interactions, however, are in the opposite direction from what was found empirically. Whereas PT predicts a greater slope for PE than CE in both domains, Figure 2 shows exactly the opposite. PT does predict that both CE and PE judgments become more risk averse as p rises.

<u>With PE-Reframing</u>. Finally, we test whether PE-reframing can explain the observed interaction with p. The bottom panel of Table 3 shows the translated gambles. Note that the gain and loss gambles yield identically reframed gambles once the EV is subtracted from each. Hence, we only need to analyze the five gambles labeled K through O. The same calculations were performed as before, yielding the CE and PE values shown in the far right columns. Figure 4 plots for each domain ($-\log \alpha_{CE}$) and ($-\log \alpha_{PE_t}$), where PE_t refers to the PE value implied by PT under PE-reframing. For both gains and losses, PE reframing predicts that both curves slope upward, and again the empirically observed interaction is not predicted.

7. Conclusions

This paper offers several contributions to the complex and diverse literature on individual risk taking. We replicate the finding of Johnson and Schkade (1989) that the extent of CE-PE bias depends on the probabilities used. Specifically, the effect of response mode is

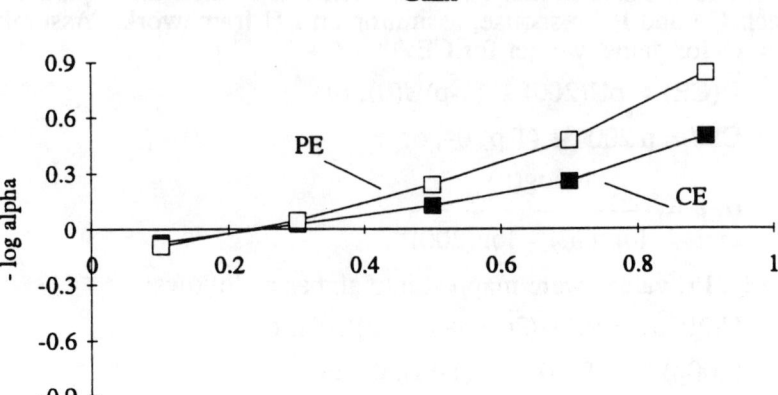

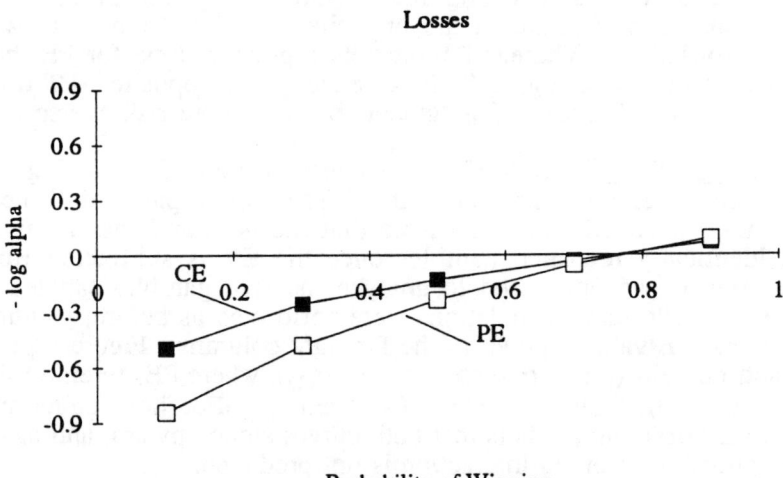

Figure 3. Predicted values of - log α for each response mode for prospect theory responses, with no PE-reframing. Higher points denote more risk aversion.

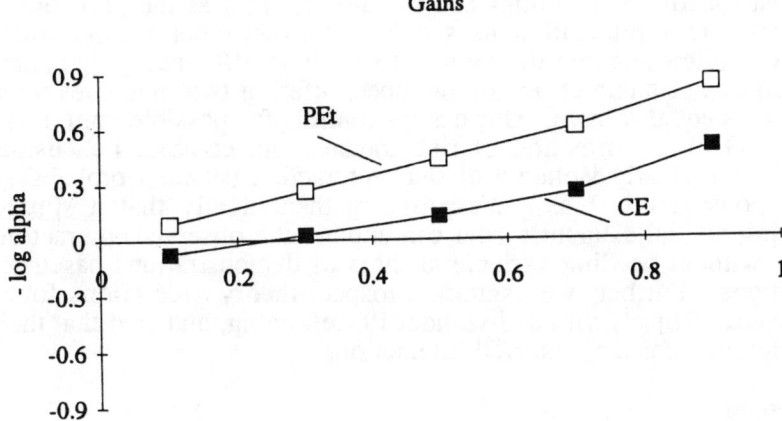

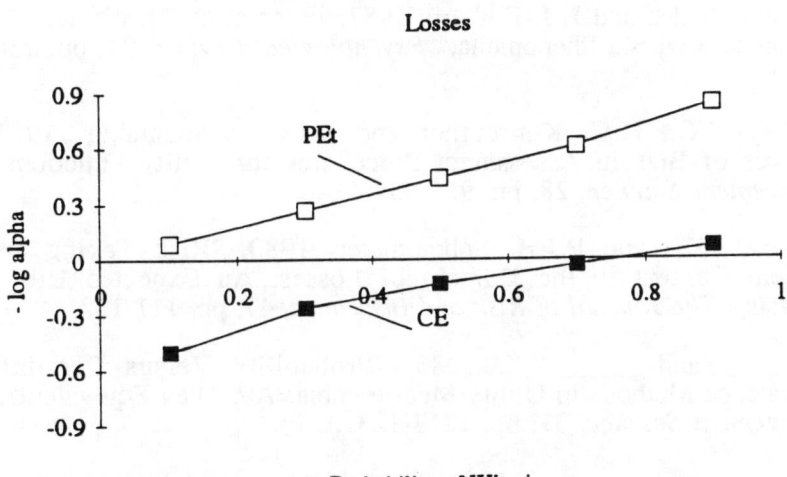

Figure 4. Predicted values of - log α for each response mode for prospect theory responses, <u>with</u> PE-reframing. Higher points denote more risk aversion.

strongest for low probabilities and steadily declines as the probability increases. Our replication uses different experimental conditions, notably explicit anchors throughout to elicit indifference judgments. Also, all of our gambles are simple ones, offering two outcomes with one always equal to zero. Our design controls for possible confounding effects of the direction of risk transfer and context; i.e., using ANOVA we clearly isolate a distinct interaction between probability and response mode bias. We prove mathematically that a simple anchoring and adjustment model can explain the observed interaction with p, without needing variable anchors or demonstrations based on simulations. Further, we examine prospect theory predictions for a prototypical subject, with and without PE reframing, and find that they are different from the observed interaction.

References

Arrow, K.J., 1971, *Essays in the Theory of Risk-bearing*, Markham Publishing Co., Chicago.

Camerer, C.F., 1989, "An Experimental Test of Several Generalized Utility Theories," *Journal of Risk and Uncertainty*, 2, pp. 61-104.

Goldstein, W.M. and H.J. Einhorn, 1987, "Expression Theory and the Preference Reversal Phenomena," *Psychological Review*, 94, pp. 236-254.

Hershey, J.C., H.C. Kunreuther and P.J.H. Schoemaker, 1982, "Sources of Bias in Assessment Procedures for Utility Functions," *Management Science*, 28, pp. 936-954.

Hershey, J.C., and P.J.H. Schoemaker, 1980, "Risk Taking and Problem Context in the Domain of Losses: An Expected Utility Analysis," *The Journal of Risk and Insurance*, 47, pp. 111-132.

_____ and _____, 1985, "Probability Versus Certainty Equivalence Methods in Utility Measurement: Are They Equivalent?," *Management Science*, 31, pp. 1213-1231.

_____ and _____, 1994, "Main Effects and Interactions in Risky Choice," Department of Operations and Information Management, The Wharton School, University of Pennyvania.

Johnson, E.J. and D. Schkade, 1989, "Bias in Utility Assessments: Further Evidence and Explanations," *Management Science*, 35, pp. 406-424.

Kahneman, D. and A. Tversky, 1979, "Prospect Theory: An Analysis of Decision Under Risk," *Econometrica*, 47, pp. 263-291.

Karmarkar, U.S., 1978, "Subjectively Weighted Utility: A Descriptive Extension of the Expected Utility Model," *Organizational Behavior and Human Performance*, 21, pp. 61-72.

Keeney, R.L. and H. Raiffa, 1976, *Decisions With Multiple Objectives: Preferences and Value Tradeoffs*, John Wiley, New York.

Machina, M., 1982, " 'Expected Utility Analysis' Without the Independence Axiom," *Econometrica*, 50, pp. 277-323.

Pratt, J.W., 1964, "Risk Aversion in the Small and in the Large," *Econometrica*, 32, pp. 122-136.

SAS Institute, 1985, *SAS User's Guide: Statistics*, Version 5 Edition, SAS Institute, Cary, ND.

Schoemaker, P.J.H, 1982, "The Expected Utility Model: Its Variants, Purposes, Evidence and Limitations," *Journal of Economic Literature*, 20, pp. 529-563.

_____ and J.C. Hershey, 1992, "Utility Measurement: Signal, Noise, and Bias," *Organizational Behavior and Human Decision Processes*, 52, pp. 397-424.

Stevens, S.S., 1974, "Perceptual Magnitude and its Measurement," in E.C. Carterette and M.P. Friedman (eds.), *Handbook of Perception* (Volume 2), Academic Press, New York.

Tversky, A. and D. Kahneman, 1992, "Advances in Prospect Theory: Cumulative Representation of Uncertainty," *Journal of Risk and Uncertainty*, 5, pp. 297-324.

Von Neumann, J. and O. Morgenstern, 1947, *Theory of Games and Economic Behavior* (2nd ed.), Princeton University Press, Princeton.

2. NEW DEVELOPMENTS IN THE THEORY

OF RISK AVERSION

The three papers in this section represent qualitatively new extensions of the standard theory of risk aversion. The first paper, by Aldo Montesano, proposes a new and rigorous measure of the heretofore elusive concept of "uncertainty aversion". Whereas standard risk aversion seeks to measure an individual's attitudes toward outcome variability in a setting of well-defined "objective" probabilities, this new notion seeks to adopt a "subjective" setting, where uncertainty is represented by "events" or "states of nature," and pre-specified numerical probabilities do not exist.

Specifically, the author seeks to decompose an individual's aversion to a subjectively uncertain prospect (as compared to a sure prospect) into that portion due to outcome variability ("risk aversion") and that portion due to the non-existence of objective probabilities ("uncertainty aversion"). This is accomplished by adopting the Schmeidler/Chateauneuf/Gilboa nonadditive probability model of preferences over subjective prospects, and from this, deriving an associated additive probability measure for each specific prospect. The difference between the certainty equivalent of the prospect and its expected value using the additive probabilities gives a natural generalization of the standard risk premium, and the difference between the latter expected value and the expectation using the individual's non-additive probability measure gives the new measure of uncertainty aversion.

The paper by Louis Eeckhoudt and Harris Schlesinger extends recent work on the new notion of "prudence", which, if $U(\cdot)$ is a von Neumann-Morgenstern utility function, is given by the measure $-U'''(\cdot)/U''(\cdot)$. This measure has been shown to be linked to the comparative statics of individual behavior under risk in much the same way that the standard measure $-U''(\cdot)/U'(\cdot)$ is linked to the individual's level of risk aversion. As such, it provides an extremely useful analytical device for the prediction of economic behavior.

In their paper, the authors examine conditions for one individual's utility function to be globally more prudent than another's. They also examine the various logically possible manners in which a pair of individuals can be compared in terms of both their risk aversion and prudence levels. These results can be expected to significantly extend the scope of comparative statics analysis under uncertainty.

The third paper in this section, by Jerome Rothenberg, relates the style of consumption of economic actors to risk, using a new approach. Rothenberg calls this approach the "embodied risk" approach, and applies it to many practical problems.

NON-ADDITIVE PROBABILITIES AND THE MEASURE OF UNCERTAINTY AND RISK AVERSION: A PROPOSAL

Aldo MONTESANO[1]*

1. Introduction

Risk aversion is intuitively connected to the risk premium, which is the difference between the expected value and the certainty equivalent. The certainty equivalent is described by the preference function, which associates to every act a certain consequence indifferent to it according to the agent's preferences. The expected value is determined once the probabilities of the events and the correspondent consequences are known.

For a lottery with consequences $c_1, \ldots, c_k$ (where $c_i \in R$) and probabilities $p_1, \ldots, p_k$, risk aversion is measured by $\mu = (c^* - x)/\sigma$, where $c^* = \Sigma_{i=1}^{k} p_i c_i$ is the expected value, x is the certainty equivalent and σ is the standard deviation, i.e. $\sigma = (\Sigma_{i=1}^{k} (c_i - c^*)^2 p_i)^{1/2}$

---

[1]* Bocconi University, Milan, Italy

(Montesano 1991).

Risk aversion is measured by the preceding relationship in any situation where it is defined, including for instance the two stage model proposed by Segal (1991) in order to describe the preferences considered by the Ellsberg paradox (which cannot be described by one stage models with additive probabilities). In this model the expected value is known since events with given probabilities are associated to the possible consequences.

An analogous measure for uncertainty and risk aversion can be introduced with reference to models which describe situations where the probabilities of the events are not known (or objective) and, consequently, the expected value of the act is unknown. For these situations we must introduce a valuation of the (additive) probabilities of the events associated to the possibile consequences. Such a situation occurs with the model of expected utility with non-additive probabilities (EUNAP) proposed by Schmeidler (1989), Chateauneuf (1988), Gilboa (1987) and other authors in order to describe also the preferences considered by the Ellsberg paradox. The determination of additive probabilities from non-additive probabilities and the corresponding measure of uncertainty and risk aversion are the subject of the present paper.

(We define as uncertain a situation where objective probabilities are unknown: there is no uncertainty aversion or propensity if the agent's subjective probabilities are additive. We define as risky a situation where the possibile consequences are not all equal to each other: there is no risk aversion or propensity if the expected value is equal to the certainty equivalent, where the expected value is obtained considering the agent's subjective probabilities, which are not necessarily additive).

2. The expected utility model with non-additive probabilities (EUNAP), uncertainty and risk aversion.

In the EUNAP model, if S is the set of states of the world and 2^S is the set of events (which are subsets of S), the non-additive probability is a function $v: 2^S \to R$ which satisfies the conditions $v(\emptyset)=0$, $v(S)=1$, and $E \subseteq F \Rightarrow v(E) \leq v(F)$. The additivity (or modularity) condition $v(E)+v(F)=v(E \cup F)+v(E \cap F)$ for all pair $E_1 F \in 2^S$ is not required. In the present paper only the finite case is considered, i.e. where the possibile consequences (payoffs) are associated to events which are a finite partition $(E_i)_{i=1}^k$ of S. Then there are k possible consequences $(c_i)_{i=1}^k$ and any act is a function $a: S \to R$ such that $a(E_i)=c_i$ with $i=1,\ldots,k$.[2]

The EUNAP model describes preferences between acts by means of the utility function

$$U(a)=U(c_k)+\sum_{q=1}^{k-1}(U(c_q)-U(c_{q+1}))v(\sum_{i=1}^{q}E_i)$$

once the consequences ore ordered so that $c_1 \geq c_2 \geq \ldots \geq c_k$ and $U: R \to R$ is an increasing function.

Following a current definition, which is equivalent to others under certain conditions (Karni-Schmeidler, 1991, pp. 1805-1806), there

---

[2] Alternatively we can consider a finite set of events. Their constituents allow us to individuate the k events $(E_i)_{i=1}^k$, to which the consequences $(c_i)_{i=1}^k$ are associated.

is uncertainty aversion if the non-additive probability is convex (or supermodular), i.e.
$$v(E)+v(F) \le v(E \cup F)+v(E \cap F)$$
for all pairs of events $E, F \in 2^s$. We can also say that there is uncertainty propensity if the non-additive probability is concave, while there is no indication if the non-additive probability is neither convex or concave.

When $k=2$ and probabilities are symmetrical, i.e. $v(E_1)=v(E_2)$, then we can immediately refer the measure of uncertainty aversion to the quantity $1-2v(E)$, where $v(E)=v(E_1)=v(E_2)$. No measure of uncertainty aversion has been proposed yet to my knowledge when $k>2$.

3. The measure of uncertainty aversion in the EUNAP model.

Let us define c^*-x as the uncertainty and risk premium, where $c^* = \sum_{i=1}^{K} p_i c_i$ is the expected value with additive probabilities (to be introduced) of an act and x is its certainty equivalent, i.e.
$$x = U^{-1}\left(U(c_k) + \sum_{q=1}^{k-1}(U(c_q)-U(c_{q+1}))v(\cup_{i=1}^{q}E_i)\right).$$

Let the uncertainty and risk premium be divided in two parts: the uncertainty premium $c^*-c^*_v$ and the risk premium c^*_v-x, where
$$c^*_v = c_k + \sum_{q=1}^{k-1}(c_q-c_{q+1})v(\cup_{i=1}^{q}E_i)$$
is the expected value with non-additive probabilities, while
$$c^* = c_k + \sum_{q=1}^{k-1}(c_q-c_{q+1})\sum_{i=1}^{q}p_i$$
is the expected value with additive probabilities, where p_i is the probability (to be determined) of event E_i.

The determination of the uncertainty

premium requires the introduction of additive probabilities. Since the agent's preferences allow us to observe only non-additive probabilities, the additive probabilities must be determined from the non-additive probabilities.

The determination of probability p_i proposed here takes into account all the non-additive probabilities which measure event E_i, i.e. $v(E_i+F)-v(F)$ for any $F \subseteq S\setminus E_i$. In the finite case under examination, $v(E_i+f_{ij})-v(f_{ij})$, where $f_{ij} \in F_{ij}$ and $F_{ij} = \{\sum_{h=1}^{j-1} E_{a_h} : a_h \in K\setminus\{i\}, a_h \neq a_{h'}\}$, with $F_{i1} = \emptyset$ and $K=\{1,\ldots,k\}$, for any $f_{ij} \in F_{ij}$ and $j \in K$. Consequently,

$$p_i = \sum_{j=1}^{k} \alpha_{jf} \sum_{f_{ij} \in F_{ij}} (v(E_i+f_{ij})-v(f_{ij}))$$

where $(\alpha_j)_{j=1}^{k}$ are parameters which are determined by the condition $\sum_{i=1}^{k} p_i = 1$. Their value is (see Appendix A) $\alpha_j = \dfrac{1}{j\binom{k}{j}}$ so that[3]

$$p_i = \sum_{j=1}^{k} \frac{1}{j\binom{k}{j}} \sum_{f_{ij} \in F_{ij}} (v(E_i+f_{ij})-v(f_{ij}))$$

Obviously, if subjective probabilities are additive, then $p_i = v(E_i)$.

If $k=2$ we find
$$p_1 = \frac{1}{2}(1+v(E_1)-v(E_2))$$
$$p_2 = \frac{1}{2}(1-v(E_1)+v(E_2))$$

if $k=3$

---

[3] This formula determines a value which is completely analogous to the Shapley value in the theory of cooperative games (e.g. Myerson 1991, pp.436-444).

$$p_1 = \frac{1}{6}(2+2v(E_1)-v(E_2)-v(E_3)+v(E_1+E_2)+$$
$$+v(E_1+E_3)-2v(E_2+E_3))$$
$$p_2 = \frac{1}{6}(2-v(E_1)+2v(E_2)-v(E_3)+v(E_1+E_2)+$$
$$-2v(E_1+E_3)+v(E_2+E_3))$$
$$p_3 = \frac{1}{6}(2-v(E_1)-v(E_2)+2v(E_3)-2v(E_1+E_2)+$$
$$+v(E_1+E_3)+v(E_2+E_3))$$
etc.

These additive probabilities can be interpreted as a mean of the probabilities the agent takes into consideration i.e., p_i is the expected value of $v(E_i+f_{ij})-v(f_{ij})$ for a random sequences of the elementary events), or as the mean composition of the urn from which events are drawn.

The proposed construction of the additive pobability measure is robust with respect to a suddivision of the events into subevents the measure of which is additive: for instance, if we create new events by flipping a coin, so that an event E_h is suddivided into the two events E'_h and E''_h, with E'_h+E_h and $v(E'_h+F)+v(E''_h+F)=(E_h+F)+v(F)$ for any $F\subseteq S\setminus E_h$, then this suddivision does not change p_i for $i\neq h$, while $p'_h+p''_h=p_n$.

The uncertainty premium is then
$$c^* - c^*_v = \sum_{q=1}^{k-1}(c_q - c_{q+1})(\sum_{i=1}^{q}(\sum_{j=1}^{k}\frac{1}{j\binom{k}{j}}\sum_{f_{ij}\in F_{ij}}(v(E_i+f_{ij})+$$
$$-v(f_{ij})))-v(\sum_{i=1}^{q}E_i))$$

If $k=2$, then
$$c^* - c^*_v = (c_1 - c_2)\frac{1}{2}(1-v(E_1)-v(E_2))$$
if $k=3$, then

$$c^*-c^*_v=(c_1-c_2)\frac{1}{6}(2-4v(E_1)-v(E_2)-v(E_3)+v(E_1+E_2)+$$
$$+v(E_1+E_3)-2v(E_2+E_3))+(c_2-c_3)\frac{1}{6}(4+v(E_1)+v(E_2)+$$
$$-2v(E_3)-4v(E_1+E_2)-v(E_1+E_3)-v(E_2+E_3))$$
etc.

If subjective probabilities are symmetrical, i.e. $v(E_i)=v(E_j)$, $v(E_i+E_j)=v(E_h+E_m)$, etc. for $i,j,h,m \in K$, $i \neq j$ and $h \neq m$, then we find:
if $k=2$
$$c^*-c^*_v=(c_1-c_2)(\frac{1}{2}-v(E_1))$$
if $k=3$
$$c^*-c^*_v=(c_1-c_2)(\frac{1}{3}-v(E_1))+(c_2-c_3)(\frac{2}{3}-v(E_1+E_2))$$
in general
$$c^*-c^*_v=\sum_{q=1}^{k-1}(c_q-c_{q+1})(\frac{q}{k}-v(\sum_{i=1}^{q}E_i)).$$

We can demonstrate (see Appendix B) that, if the non-additive probability is convex (concave), then the uncertainty premium is nonnegative (nonpositive) whatever the consequences,[4] i.e. $c^*-c^*_v \geq 0$ (≤ 0) for any $(c_q)_{q=1}^{k}$ with $c_q \in R$ and $c_1 \geq c_2 \geq ... \geq c_k$.

However, the opposite implication does not hold: there are non-convex probabilities which determine a positive uncertainty premium whatever the consequences (unless all are equal). As an example: $k=3$, $v(E_1)=v(E_2)=v(E_3)=0.3$, $v(E_1+E_2)=v(E_2+E_3)=0.65$, and $v(E_1+E_3)=0.55$. This probability is not convex since $v(E_1)+v(E_3)>v(E_1+E_3)$. We find $p_1=p_3=19/60$ and $p_2=22/60$, so that, for any

---

[4] Taking into account the analogy with the Shapley value, the Appendix B corresponds to the property that for every convex nonnegative game the Shapley value belongs to the core.

triplet $c_a \geq c_b \geq c_c$ with $c_a > c_c$, we obtain
$c^* - c^*_v = (c_a - c_b)(p_a - v(E_a)) + (c_b - c_c)(p_a + p_b - v(E_a + E_b)) > 0$ since $p_a > v(E_a)$ and $p_a + p_b > v(E_a + E_b)$ for any poir a,b=1,2,3 with a ≠ b.

The measure of uncertainty aversion is given by the index

$$\mu_u = \frac{c^* - c^*_v}{\sigma}, \text{ where } \sigma = \left(\sum_{i=1}^{k}(c_i - c^*)^2 p_i\right)^{1/2}.$$

If k=2 we find

$$\mu_u = \frac{1 - v(E_1) - v(E_2)}{(1 + v(E_1) - v(E_2))^{1/2}(1 - v(E_1) + v(E_2))^{1/2}}$$

which is, in the symmetrical case,
$$\mu_u = 1 - 2\,v(E)$$

If $k \geq 3$ the measure μ_u also depends on consequences $(c_i)_{i=1}^{k}$, not only on subjective probabilities. For instance, if k=3, we find

$$\mu_u = (c_1 - c_2)(p_1 - v(E_1)) + (c_2 - c_3)(p_1 + p_2 - v(E_1 + E_2)) \times$$
$$\times ((c_1 - c_2)^2 p_1(1-p_1) + (c_2 - c_3)^2 p_3(1-p_3) + 2(c_1 - c_2)(c_2 - c_3)p_1 p_3)^{-1/2}$$

where p_1, p_2, and p_3 have the already determined values. In the case of symmetrical probabilities

$$\mu_u = \frac{1}{\sqrt{2}} \frac{(c_1 - c_2)(1 - 3v(E_1)) + (c_2 - c_3)(2 - 3v(E_1 + E_2))}{((c_1 - c_2)^2 + (c_2 - c_3)^2 + (c_1 - c_2)(c_2 - c_3))^{1/2}}$$

The measure of uncertainty aversion does not vary if all consequences converge to a same value, i.e. if we put $c'_i = c + t(c_i - c)$ in place of c_i and we make t approach zero.

In fact uncertainty substantially concerns the valuation of the probabilities while risk also entails the valuation of the consequences.

4. The measure of risk aversion in the EUNAP model.

Let us now consider the measure of risk aversion

$$\mu_r = \frac{c^*_v - x}{\sigma}$$

which leads to the measure of the uncertainty and risk aversion when added to the measure of uncertainty aversion,

$$\mu = \mu_u + \mu_r = \frac{c^* - c^*_v}{\sigma} + \frac{c^*_v - x}{\sigma} = \frac{c^* - x}{\sigma}$$

We can determine the measure of local risk aversion by putting $c'_i = c + t(c_i - c)$ for c_i for any $i = 1, \ldots, k$ and by approaching t to zero, i.e.

$$m_r(c) = \lim_{t \to 0} \frac{c^{*\prime}_v - x'}{\sigma'}$$

Since $\lim_{t \to 0} c^{*\prime}_v = c$, $\lim_{t \to 0} x' = c$, and $\lim_{t \to 0} \sigma' = 0$, we have

$$m_r(c) = \lim_{t \to 0} \frac{\frac{d}{dt}(c^{*\prime}_v - x')}{\frac{d}{dt}\sigma'} = \frac{c^*_v - c - \lim_{t \to 0} \frac{dx'}{dt}}{\sigma}$$

where, in the EUNAP model,

$$\lim_{t \to 0} \frac{dx'}{dt} = c_k - c + \sum_{q=1}^{k-1}(c_q - c_{q+1}) v(\sum_{i=1}^{q} E_i) = c^*_v - c$$

Consequently, we find $m_r(c) = 0$.

Therefore, the measure of local risk aversion of the first order is equal to zero also in the case of non-additive probabilities, since utility is linear with respect to probabilities. (The same result for the standard model of expected utility is discussed in Montesano 1985). Locally, i.e. for acts whose consequences differ very little from one another, risk is negligible with respect to uncertainty.

If uncertainty is absent, i.e. probability is additive, then the EUNAP model becomes the standard model of expected utility and the measure of risk aversion of the second order, which is defined by

$$r(c) = \lim_{t \to 0} 2 \frac{c^{*\prime} - x'}{(\sigma')^2},$$

results equal to the Arrow-Pratt index.

5. Conclusion

The measure of uncertainty and risk aversion has been introduced for the EUNAP model by determining additive probabilities from non-additive ones which describe an agent's preferences under uncertainty together with his/her utility function. We have demonstrated that for small acts (i.e. whose consequences differ very little from one another) risk aversion is negligible if there is uncertainty aversion. However, risk aversion can be comparable to uncertainty aversion if we introduce models which are not linear in (non-additive) probabilities. For instance, a EURDNAP (expected utility with rank-dependent non-additive probabilities) model can be envisaged, which would describe not only preferences of the kind considered by the Ellsberg paradox but also preferences of the kind considered by the Allais paradox.

***

References

Chateauneuf Alain, 1988, Uncertainty Aversion and Risk Aversion in Models with Non-Additive Probabilities, in Bertrand R. Munier ed., *Risk, Decision, and Rationality*. Dordrecht: Reidel, pp. 615-627.

Gilboa Itzhak, 1987, Expected Utility with Purely Subjective Non-Additive Probabilities, *Journal of Mathematical Economics* 16, 65-88.

Karni Edi and David Schmeidler, 1991, Utility Theory with Uncertainty, in Werner Hildenbrand and Hugo F. Sonnenschein eds., *Handbook of Mathematical Economics*, Volume IV. Amsterdam: North Holland, pp. 1763-1831.

Montesano Aldo, 1988, The Risk Aversion Measure without the Independence Axiom, *Theory and Decision* 24, 269-288.

Montesano Aldo, 1991, Measures of Risk Aversion with Expected and Nonexpected Utility, *Journal of Risk and Uncertainty* 4, 271-283.

Myerson Roger B. 1991, *Game Theory (Analysis of Conflict)*, Cambridge (Mass.): Harvard University Press.

Schmeidler David, 1989, Subjective Probability and Expected Utility without Additivity, *Econometrica* 57, 571-587.

Segal Uzi, 1991, Two-Stage Lotteries without the Reduction Axiom, *Econometrica* 58, 349-377.

Appendix A

Determination of additive probabilities from non-additive probabilities.

Since $p_i = \sum_{j=1}^{k} \alpha_j \sum_{f_{i,j} \in F_{i,j}} (v(E_i + f_{i,j}) - v(f_{i,j}))$ for $i \in K$, where $K = \{1, \ldots, k\}$, $F_{i,j} = \{\sum_{h=1}^{j-1} E_{a_h} : a_h \in K \setminus \{i\}, a_{h-} \neq a_h\}$ with $F_{i,1} = \emptyset$, and $\sum_{i=1}^{k} p_i = 1$, then

$$\alpha_j = \frac{1}{j} \frac{1}{\binom{k}{j}} \text{ for } j \in K.$$

Proof. Let us introduce the sets
$F_j = \{\sum_{h=1}^{j} E_{a_h} : a_h \in K, a_{h\sim} \neq a_h\}$. Since these sets are composed of $\binom{k}{j}$ elements while the sets $F_{i,j}$ are composed of $\binom{k-1}{j-1}$ elements and since consequently

$$\sum_{i=1}^{k} \sum_{f_{i,j} \in F_{i,j}} v(E_i + f_{i,j}) = k \frac{\binom{k-1}{j-1}}{\binom{k}{j}} \sum_{f_j \in F_j} v(f_j)$$

$$\sum_{i=1}^{k} \sum_{f_{i,j+1} \in F_{i,j+1}} v(f_{i,j+1}) = k \frac{\binom{k-1}{j}}{\binom{k}{j}} \sum_{f_j \in F_j} v(f_j)$$

the condition

$$1 = \sum_{j=1}^{k} \alpha_j \sum_{i=1}^{k} \sum_{f_{i,j} \in F_{i,j}} v(E_i + f_{i,j}) +$$
$$- \sum_{j=0}^{k-1} \alpha_{j+1} \sum_{i=1}^{k} \sum_{f_{i,j+1} \in F_{i,j+1}} v(f_{i,j+1}) =$$

$$= \sum_{j=1}^{k-1} \left(k \frac{\binom{k-1}{j-1}}{\binom{k}{j}} \alpha_j - \frac{k \binom{k-1}{j}}{\binom{k}{j}} \alpha_{j+1} \right) \sum_{f_j \in F_j} v(f_j) + k\alpha_k$$

requires

$$\alpha_k = \frac{1}{k}, \qquad \alpha_j = \frac{k-j}{j} \alpha_{j+1}$$

i.e. $\alpha_j = \frac{1}{j} \frac{1}{\binom{k}{j}}$ for $j \in K$.

Appendix B

Theorem. If the non-additive probability is convex, then the uncertainty premium is nonnegative, i.e. $\sum_{i=1}^{q} p_i \geq v(\sum_{i=1}^{q} E_i)$.

Proof. Let us introduce the following sets
$B_{i,q,s-1} = \{\sum_{h=1}^{s-1} E_{a_h} : a_h \in \{1,\ldots,q\} \setminus \{i\}, a_h \neq a_{h\sim}\}$

MEASURE OF UNCERTAINTY AND RISK AVERSION   71

with $B_{i,q,0} = \emptyset$, which are defined for $0 \le s-1 \le q-1$, and

$$G_{q,q+j-s} = \{ \sum_{h=1}^{j-s} E_{a_h} : a_h \in \{q+1,\ldots,k\}, \ a_h \ne a_{h\sim} \}$$

with $G_{q,q} = \emptyset$, which are defined for $0 \le j-s \le k-q$. Both these sets are consequently defined for $\max(1, q+j-k) \le s \le \min(j,q)$.

Let us also introduce the sets

$$B_{q,s} = \{ \sum_{h=1}^{s} E_{a_h} : a_h \in \{1,\ldots,q\}, \ a_h \ne a_{h\sim} \}$$

with $B_{q,0} = \emptyset$, which are defined for $0 \le s \le q$.

Then, since the sets $B_{i,q,s-1}$ are composed of $\binom{q-1}{s-1}$ elements, which are all disjoint with respect to E_i, and the sets $B_{b,s-1}$ are composed of $\binom{q}{s-1}$ elements, we find

$$\sum_{i=1}^{q} \sum_{f_{i,j} \in F_{i,j}} v(f_{i,j}) =$$

$$= \sum_{s=\max(1,q+j-k)}^{\min(q,j)} \sum_{g_{q,q+j-s} \in G_{q,q+j-s}} \sum_{i=1}^{q}$$

$$\sum_{b_{i,q,s-1} \in B_{i,q,s-1}} v(b_{i,q,s-1} + g_{q,q+j-s}) =$$

$$= \sum_{s=\max(1,q+j-k)}^{\min(q,j)} (1+q-s) \times$$

$$\times \sum_{b_{q,s-1} \in B_{q,s-1}} \sum_{g_{q,q+j-s} \in G_{q,q+j-s}}$$

$$v(b_{q,s-1} + g_{q,q+j-s}).$$

Analogously, since the sets $\{E_i\} + B_{i,q,s-1}$ are composed of $\binom{q-1}{s-1}$ elements and the sets $B_{q,s}^q$ are composed of $\binom{q}{s}$ elements, we find

$$\sum_{i=1}^{q} \sum_{f_{i,j} \in F_{i,j}} v(E_i + f_{i,j}) =$$

$$= \sum_{s=\max(1,q+j-k)}^{\min(q,j)} \sum_{g_{q,q+j-s} \in G_{q,q+j-s}} \sum_{i=1}^{q}$$

$$\sum_{b_{i,q,s-1} \in B_{i,q,s-1}} v(E_i + b_{i,q,s-1} + g_{q,q+j-s}) =$$

$$= \sum_{s=\max(1,q+j-k)}^{\min(q,j)} s \sum_{b_{q,s} \in B_{q,s}} \sum_{g_{q,q+j-s} \in G_{q,q+j-s}}$$

$$v(b_{q,s} + g_{q,q+j-s}).$$

Consequently, since

$$\sum_{j=1}^{k} \sum_{s=\max(1,q+j-k)}^{\min(q,j)} = \sum_{s=1}^{q} \sum_{j=s}^{s+k-q}$$

we find

$$\sum_{i=1}^{q} p_i = \sum_{s=1}^{q} \sum_{j=s}^{s+k-q} \frac{1}{j} \frac{1}{\binom{k}{j}}$$

$$\sum_{g_{q,q+j-s} \in G_{q,q+j-s}} (s \sum_{b_{q,s} \in B_{q,s}} v(b_{q,s} + g_{q,q+j-s}) +$$

$$- (1+q-s) \sum_{b_{q,s-1} \in B_{q,s-1}} v(b_{q,s-1} + g_{q,q+j-s})).$$

The assumption that probability is convex implies that

$$(1+q-s) \sum_{b_{q,s-1} \in B_{q,s-1}} v(b_{q,s-1} + g_{q,q+j-s}) +$$

$$+ s \sum_{b_{q,s} \in B_{q,s}} v(b_{q,s}) \leq$$

$$\leq (1+q-s) \sum_{b_{q,s} \in B_{q,s}} v(b_{q,s} + g_{q,q+j-s}) +$$

$$+ s \sum_{b_{q,s-1} \in B_{q,s-1}} v(b_{q,s-1})$$

since for any set $b_{q,s-1} \in B_{q,s-1}$ there is in $B_{q,s}$ at least one set $b_{q,s} \supseteq b_{q,s-1}$ so that for these sets we have $b_{q,s} \cup (b_{q,s-1} + g_{q,q+j-s}) = b_{q,s} + g_{q,q+j-s}$ and $b_{q,s} \cap (b_{q,s-1} + g_{q,q+j-s}) = b_{q,s-1}$ and the convexity assumption requires

MEASURE OF UNCERTAINTY AND RISK AVERSION

$$v(b_{q,s-1}+g_{q,q+j-s}) + v(b_{q,s}) \leq$$
$$\leq v(b_{q,s}+g_{q,q+j-s}) + v(b_{q,s-1})$$

and since the $\binom{q}{s-1}$ sets of $B_{q,s-1}$ and the $\binom{q}{s}$ sets of $B_{q,s}$ can be arranged in order to satisfy the preceding inequality. We have consequently

$$\sum_{i=1}^{q} p_i \geq \sum_{s=1}^{q} \sum_{j=s}^{s+k-q} \frac{1}{j}$$

$$\frac{1}{\binom{k}{j}} \Sigma_{g_{q,q+j-s} \in G_{q,q+j-s}} (s \Sigma_{b_{q,s} \in B_{q,s}} v(b_{q,s}) +$$

$$- (1+q-s) \Sigma_{b_{q,s-1} \in B_{q,s-1}} v(b_{q,s-1}))$$

i.e., since the sets $G_{q,q+j-s}$ are composed of $\binom{k-q}{j-s}$ elements, we find

$$\sum_{i=1}^{q} p_i \geq \sum_{s=1}^{q} \sum_{j=s}^{s+k-q} \frac{1}{j} \frac{\binom{k-q}{j-s}}{\binom{k}{j}} (s \Sigma_{b_{q,s} \in B_{q,s}} v(b_{q,s}) +$$

$$- (1+q-s) \Sigma_{b_{q,s-1} \in B_{q,s-1}} v(b_{q,s-1})), \text{ i.e.}$$

$$\sum_{i=1}^{q} p_i \geq \sum_{j=q}^{k} \frac{q}{j} \frac{\binom{k-q}{j-q}}{\binom{k}{j}} v(\sum_{i=1}^{q} E_i) +$$

$$+ \sum_{s=1}^{q-1} \Sigma_{b_{q,s} \in B_{q,s}} v(b_{q,s}) (\sum_{j=s}^{s+k-q} \frac{s}{j} \frac{\binom{k-q}{j-s}}{\binom{k}{j}} +$$

$$- \sum_{j=s+1}^{s+1+k-q} \frac{q-s}{j} \frac{\binom{k-q}{j-s-1}}{\binom{k}{j}})$$

Now

$$\sum_{j=q}^{k} \frac{q}{j} \frac{\binom{k-q}{j-q}}{\binom{k}{j}} = \frac{1}{\binom{k}{q}} \sum_{r=0}^{k-q} \binom{r+q-1}{q-1} = 1$$

and

$$\sum_{j=s}^{s+k-q} \frac{s}{j} \frac{\binom{k-q}{j-s}}{\binom{k}{j}} - \sum_{j=s+1}^{s+1+k-q} \frac{q-s}{j} \frac{\binom{k-q}{j-s-1}}{\binom{k}{j}} =$$

$$= \sum_{r=0}^{k-q} \frac{s}{s+r} \frac{\binom{k-q}{r}}{\binom{k}{s+r}} - \frac{q-s}{s+r+1} \frac{\binom{k-q}{r}}{\binom{k}{s+r+1}} =$$

$$= \frac{1}{\binom{k}{q}\binom{q}{s}} \sum_{r=0}^{k-q} \binom{s+r-1}{r}\binom{k-s-r}{k-q-r} - \binom{s+r}{r}\binom{k-s-r-1}{k-q-r} =$$

$$= \frac{1}{\binom{k}{q}\binom{q}{s}} \sum_{r=0}^{k-q} \binom{k-q+s-r-1}{k-q-r}\binom{q-s+r}{r} - \binom{s+r}{r}\binom{k-s-r-1}{k-q-r} = 0$$

since

$$\sum_{r=a}^{k-q} \binom{q-s+r-a}{r-a}\binom{k-q+s-r-1}{k-q-r} - \binom{s+r-a}{r-a}\binom{k-s-r-1}{k-q-r} =$$

$$= \sum_{r=a}^{s-q} \binom{q-s+r-a-1}{r-a}\binom{k-q+s-r-1}{k-q-r} \frac{r-a}{q-s} +$$

$$- \binom{s+r-a-1}{r-a}\binom{k-s-r-1}{k-q-r}\frac{r-a}{s}$$

which is equal to zero if $a = k-q$ and if $a < k-q$ equal to

$$\sum_{r=a+1}^{k-q} \binom{q-s+r-a-1}{r-a-1}\binom{k-q+s-r-1}{k-q-r} - \binom{s+r-a-1}{r-a-1}\binom{k-s-r-1}{k-q-r}$$

which is in its turn equal to zero if $a = k-q-1$, and so on until $a = 0$.

Consequently, we find

$$\sum_{i=1}^{q} p_i \geq v\left(\sum_{i=1}^{q} E_i\right)$$

which implies $c^* - c^*_v \geq 0$ for all $(c_q)_{q=1}^{k}$.

A PRECAUTIONARY TALE OF RISK AVERSION AND PRUDENCE*

Louis Eeckhoudt
Catholic Faculties of Mons (Belgium) and Lille (France)

Harris Schlesinger
University of Alabama

1. INTRODUCTION

The expected-utility framework of von Neumann and Morgenstern (1944) and the theory of risk aversion, as developed by Pratt (1964) and Arrow (1965), remain cornerstones in the economics of choice under uncertainty. Although much recent work has focused on non-expected utility theory, the general preference functionals found in these models typically resemble those generated by expected-utility preferences locally. Moreover, the expected-utility model itself has been extended to account for more complex settings, and the Arrow-Pratt rankings have been shown to be robust in many of these extensions. For example, Kihlstrom, Romer and Williams (1981) and Nachman (1982) show that the Arrow-Pratt rankings extend to models with multiple sources of risk.[2] Pratt and Zeckhauser (1987) complement this work by imposing some additional structure on preferences in the presence of multiple risks.

---

*The research was undertaken while Schlesinger was a Visiting Professor at the Catholic Faculty of Mons and CORE, Catholic University of Louvain. Financial support for the former visit from the Intercollegiate Center for Management Science (CIM) in Brussels is gratefully acknowledged.

[2] For independent, additive risks, a restriction to nonincreasing absolute risk aversion is sufficient to extend the Arrow-Pratt rankings. Less restrictive sufficient conditions, as well as conditions for nonadditive risks are presented by Nachman (1982) and Pratt (1988).

Kimball (1990, 1993) recently extended the Arrow-Pratt and Pratt-Zeckhauser results to account for the precautionary-savings motive. By considering the concept of prudence, defined by a convex marginal utility of wealth, certain types of behavior under uncertainty become clearer, such as behavior in the intertemporal consumption/savings models of Sandmo (1970) and Drèze and Modigliani (1972). More recently, prudence has been shown to be useful in the signing of certain comparative statics.[3] Moreover, defining absolute prudence as $p(W) = -U'''(W)/U''(W)$ for the von Neumann-Morgenstern utility function U, the property of decreasing absolute prudence has been shown by Kimball (1993) to be a canonical extension of the property of decreasing absolute risk aversion and to have implications for models of choice under uncertainty.[4]

Although the formal concept of prudence is still in its infancy, it already seems to be having an impact on choice-theoretic models under uncertainty. Our purpose in this paper is to examine the link between changes in prudence and changes in risk aversion. In general, preferences that are locally more prudent can be either less risk averse or more risk averse. This is true even if preferences are uniformly more prudent. However, the structures of risk aversion and prudence are not independent and increases in prudence do have effects on risk aversion.

Given two utility functions U and V, with V uniformly more prudent than U, it is possible for either U or V to be uniformly more risk averse than the other. A key result of this paper is that if neither of the above rankings holds, then we obtain a type of single-crossing property, whereby V is more risk averse at lower wealth levels and U is more risk averse at higher wealth levels. Furthermore, we provide additional conditions needed on preferences to ensure that greater prudence implies greater risk aversion.

We also consider the reciprocal issue of whether greater risk aversion implies greater prudence. An important result of Pratt (1964) is that V is more risk averse than U if and only if there exists a monotone increasing and concave function $k:\mathbb{R}\to\mathbb{R}$, such that

---

[3] See Eeckhoudt, Gollier and Schlesinger (1991), for example.

[4] See also Eeckhoudt and Kimball (1992), who show that insurance demand increases in the presence of a random background wealth, if preferences display both decreasing prudence and decreasing risk aversion.

$V(W) = k[U(W)]$. We show in this paper that, if U locally exhibits nondecreasing absolute risk aversion, or at least risk aversion that is not decreasing too quickly (in a way made explicit in the text), then k' convex is sufficient to imply that V is also (locally) more prudent than U.

The paper is organized as follows. Section 2 sets out the basic definitions and their importance. In section 3, we extend Pratt's (1964) main theorem on equivalences for "uniformly more risk averse" to equivalences for "uniformly more prudent." We also examine the connection between "more risk averse" and "more prudent." Section 4 discusses some of the implications of decreasing prudence and decreasing risk aversion. Section 5 is a brief conclusion.

2. THE CONCEPT OF PRUDENCE

Consider a risk-averse expected-utility maximizer who owns nonstochastic wealth W along with random wealth $\tilde{y}$, where $E(\tilde{y}) = 0$ and the random variable $W + \tilde{y}$ is assumed to have a nonnegative support. Pratt (1964) defines the risk premium, $\pi(W,\tilde{y})$, implicitly via

(2.1) $\qquad U(W-\pi(W,\tilde{y})) = E[U(W+\tilde{y})]$

where U is a von Neumann-Morgenstern utility function of wealth (assumed throughout the paper to be strictly risk averse and thrice differentiable) $U : \mathbb{R}_+ \to \mathbb{R}$, and E is the expectation operator. Since we assume a zero mean for $\tilde{y}$, $-\pi$ represents the certainty equivalent for $\tilde{y}$.

Kimball (1990), extends Pratt's notion by defining the precautionary premium, $\psi(W,\tilde{y})$, by

(2.2) $\qquad U'(W-\psi(W,\tilde{y})) = E[U'(W+\tilde{y})]$.

The precautionary premium is positive if U' is convex; here, if U''' > 0. Since many economic problems entail a solution which equates marginal utilities, e.g. across time periods or across states of nature, this measure can prove useful, as shown by Kimball.

As a simple example, consider a two-period time horizon with zero interest and additively separable utility of consumption. Specifically, consider the following consumption/savings program

(2.3) $\quad \max_c U(c) + EV(W-c+\tilde{y})$,

where $c>0$ represents first-period consumption and V is a risk-averse utility function for second-period consumption. In the simplest case where U and V are identical, it follows that the optimal first-period consumption satisfies

(2.4) $\quad s = c + \psi(W-c,\tilde{y})$,

where $s = W-c$ denotes first-period savings, which equals average second-period consumption. Consequently, if $U''' > 0$, $s \geq c$ with equality holding only in the case where $\tilde{y}$ has a degenerate distribution. Indeed, optimal first-period consumption is given by $c = \frac{1}{2}(W-\psi)$, which is decreasing in the precautionary premium.

The condition $U''' > 0$ is referred to as "prudence" by Kimball (1990). Using Taylor series expansions it follows that for $\tilde{y}$ with a small variance, the precautionary premium ψ can be approximated by $\psi \approx \frac{1}{2}\sigma^2[-U'''/U'']$, exactly as Pratt (1964) approximates the risk premium $\pi \approx \frac{1}{2}\sigma^2[-U''/U']$. Indeed, Kimball (1990) uses the analogy between π and ψ to extend many of Pratt's results on risk aversion to results about precautionary savings. The degree of absolute prudence is defined as $p(W) = -U'''(W)/U''(W)$. In much the same way that the degree of absolute risk aversion, $r(W) = -U''(W)/U'(W)$, is a measure of the local concavity of utility, the degree of absolute prudence is a measure of the local convexity of marginal utility.

In addition to a precautionary savings demand, the concept of prudence has already found its way into other models of choice under uncertainty. For example, Eeckhoudt, Gollier and Schlesinger (1991) show how prudence is sufficient to sign comparative statics for certain localized increases in risk in a deductible insurance model; Eeckhoudt and Kimball (1992) show how decreasing absolute prudence (DAP) together with decreasing absolute risk aversion (DARA) is sufficient to guarantee that more insurance is purchased when background wealth is random; and McAfee (1991) shows how DAP is sufficient to ensure the existence of a solution within a particular class of bargaining games.[5] Since prudence and decreasing prudence are both fairly natural extensions of DARA, and since they seem to be making an impact on expected-utility-based models of choice, we turn our attention towards a more thorough examination of prudence and its relation to risk aversion.[6]

3. INCREASES IN RISK AVERSION AND INCREASES IN PRUDENCE

Pratt (1964) showed the following equivalences for "V is uniformly more risk averse than U."

THEOREM 3.1 (Pratt): *Let U and V represent two von Neumann-Morgenstern utility functions. The following are equivalent:*

i) $r^v(W) \geq r^u(W)$ $\forall W$ with strict inequality for at least one W in every interval.

ii) $\pi^v(W,\tilde{y}) > \pi^u(W,\tilde{y})$ $\forall W$ and $\forall$ nondegenerate $\tilde{y}$.

iii) $\exists\, k : \mathbb{R} \to \mathbb{R},\ k'>0,\ k''<0$ such that $k[U(W)] = V(W)$ $\forall W$.[7]

This result is easily extended to account for "V is uniformly more prudent than U" as follows.[8]

THEOREM 3.2: *The following are equivalent:*

i) $p^v(W) \geq p^u(W)$ $\forall W$ with strict inequality for at least one W in every interval.

ii) $\psi^v(W,\tilde{y}) > \psi^u(W,\tilde{y})$ $\forall W$ and $\forall$ nondegenerate $\tilde{y}$.

---

[5] McAfee defines $\delta(W) = -p(W)$ as the prudence measure. DAP above refers to the p(W) measure.
[6] See Kimball (1993), who shows the relationship between DAP, DARA and Proper Risk Aversion as defined by Pratt and Zeckhauser (1987).
[7] For simplicity in exposition, we omit the weak form of Pratt's Theorem. A weak form of Theorem 3.2 follows in a manner analogous to Pratt's Theorem 3.1.
[8] The proof follows by applying Theorem 3.1 to the functions -U' and -V' directly.

iii) $\exists\, g: \mathbb{R}_+ \to \mathbb{R}_+ ^*$, *where* $\mathbb{R}_+^*$ *denotes the extended real half line* $[0, \infty]$, $g \geq 0$, $g' \geq 0$, $g'' \geq 0$ *with these inequalities strict for g restricted to the image of U' and with* $g[U'(W)] = V'(W)$.

Note from Theorem 3.2 (iii) that if V is uniformly more prudent than U, then V' is a convex transformation of U'.[9]

A seemingly natural question to ask is: does an increase in prudence necessarily imply an increase in risk aversion? What of the converse? The answer to both questions is generally "no." However, there is a fair amount of structure to the relationships "more risk averse" and "more prudent." This is shown in the following two theorems along with the accompanying examples.

THEOREM 3.3: *Suppose that* $p^v(W) > p^u(W)$ $\forall W$. *Then* $\exists W^* \in \mathbb{R}_+^*$, *such that* $r^v(W) > [<] r^u(W)$ *if and only if* $W < [>] W^*$.

PROOF: It follows from Theorem 3.2 (iii) that $V'' = g'U''$. Thus, $-V''/V' = -g'U''/g > [<] -U''/U'$ as $g/U' < [>] g'$. Now g is increasing and convex, strictly so over the image of U', $\text{Im}[U']$. Define $x_1 \equiv \inf \text{Im}[U']$ and $x_2 \equiv \sup \text{Im}[U']$. Thus, $\text{Im}[U'] = (x_1, x_2]$. We consider four mutually exclusive and exhaustive cases.

  (a) If $g(x_2)/x_2 \geq g'(x_2)$, then $g(x)/x > g'(x)$ for $x \in \mathbb{R}_+$, $x < x_2$. It follows that $r^v(W) < r^u(W)$ $\forall W$. Hence, $W^* = 0$.

  (b) If $x_1 > 0$ and $g(x_1)/x_1 \leq g'(x_1)$, then $g(x)/x < g'(x)$ for $x > x_1$. Consequently, $r^v(W) > r^u(W)$ $\forall W$ and $W^* = \infty$.

  (c) If $x_1 = 0$ and $g(x_1) = 0$, then $g(x)/x < g'(x)$ for $x > 0$. Thus, $r^v(W) > r^u(W)$ $\forall W$ and $W^* = \infty$.

---

[9] We note, however, that while the underlying preferences are invariant to affine changes in k in Theorem 3.1, they are only invariant to scale changes in g in Theorem 3.2. Also note that Theorem 3.2(iii) implies that g will be integrable. The mapping in part (iii) above requires an image of the extended real half line in the case that $V'(0) = \infty$ but $U'(0) < \infty$. In this case, we define $g(x) = \infty$ for $x \leq U'(0)$.

(d) Finally, if none of the above cases hold, $\exists x^* \in (x_1, x_2)$ such that $g(x^*)/x^* = g'(x^*)$. Since $x^* \in \text{Im}[U']$, define W^* such that $U'(W^*) = x^*$. The conclusion follows.[10]

■

From Theorem 3.3, we see that it is possible for more prudent preferences to be everywhere more risk averse or everywhere less risk averse. However, it is also possible to have more prudent preferences that are more risk averse at "low" wealth levels ($W < W^*$) and less risk averse at "high" wealth levels ($W > W^*$), a type of single-crossing property. An example of case (d) in the proof of Theorem 3.3 is illustrated in Figure 1. In Figure 1, x^* is clearly seen as where $g(x)/x = g'(x)$. If $g[0] > 0$, as drawn, then $\exists x^* \in \mathbb{R}_+ ^*$ satisfying the above equality. However, x^* is not always contained in (x_1, x_2), as in cases (a) and (b) in the proof.

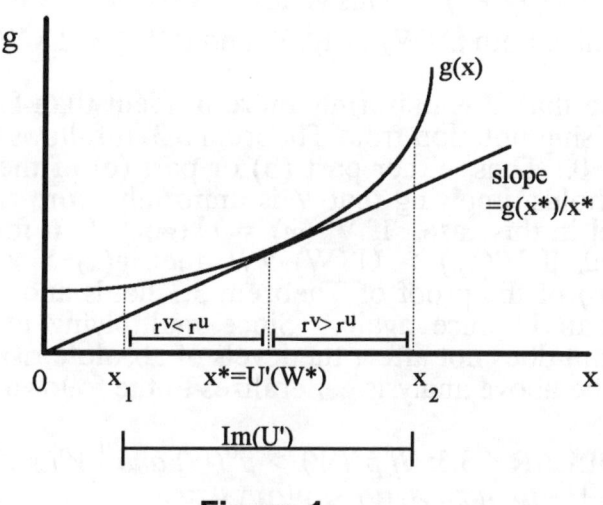

Figure 1

Suppose V is uniformly more prudent than U. We can use the proof of Theorem 3.3 to generate examples where r^v and r^u have alternative rankings.

---

[10] The behavior of g in our proof is useful in the examples that follow. A direct proof of Theorem 3.3 can also be given. Define $h(w) = r^u(w)/r^v(w)$. If $h = 1$, it can be shown, using equation (3.4) below, that $h'(w) = p^v(w) - p^u(w) > 0$. Therefore $h(w) = 1$ has at most one solution and the Theorem follows.

EXAMPLE 3.1: Let $U(W) = (1/\gamma)W^\gamma$ for $\gamma < 1$. Then $r^u(W) = (1-\gamma)/W$ and $p^u(W) = (2-\gamma)/W$. Letting $g(x) = x^2$, $p^v(W) = p^u(W) + r^u(W)$, verifying that V is more prudent.[11] Similarly, we find $r^v(W) = 2r^u(W) > r^u(W)$ $\forall W$. Integrating g over $U'(W)$ yields $V(W) = (2\gamma-1)^{-1}W^{2\gamma-1}$.

EXAMPLE 3.2: Use Example 3.1 but with $g(x) = x^2+1$. Then $p^v(W) = p^u(W) + r^u(W)$ once again, but $r^v(W)$ is a bit more complex. It is not difficult to show, however, that $W^* = 1$ in this case with $V(W) = W + (2\gamma-1)^{-1}W^{2\gamma-1}$. In other words, $r^v > [<]r^u$ as $W < [>]1$.

EXAMPLE 3.3: Let $U(W) = -e^{-W}$. Then $p^u(W) = r^u(W) = 1$ $\forall W$. Let $g(x) = x + (x+1)^{-1}$. This yields $V(W) = -e^{-W} + W + \ln(1+e^{-W})$, for which both $p^v(W) > 1$ $\forall W$ and $r^v(W) < 1$ $\forall W$.

Suppose that V is uniformly more prudent than U and that $V'(\infty) = 0$. Using notation from Theorem 3.3, it follows that $g(x_1) = 0$ with $x_1 \geq 0$. Thus, either part (b) or part (c) of the proof of Theorem 3.3 holds, implying that V is uniformly more risk averse than U as well in this case. If $V'(\infty) = U'(\infty) > 0$, it follows that $g(x_1) = x_1$ and, if $V'(W) > U'(W)$ $\forall W$, then $g(x) > x$ $\forall x > x_1$. Hence, part (b) of the proof of Theorem 3.3 holds and V is more risk averse than U once again. Since multiplying utility by a positive constant does not affect the levels of absolute risk aversion or prudence, the above analysis generalizes to the following.[12]

COROLLARY 3.3: *If $p^v(W) > p^u(W)$ and $[V'(\infty)/V'(W)] \leq [U'(\infty)/U'(W)]$ $\forall W$, then $r^v(W) > r^u(W)$ $\forall W$.*

The Corollary gives an additional condition needed to ensure that greater prudence implies greater risk aversion. We now turn our attention to when greater risk aversion implies greater prudence. Given Theorem 3.3, it is apparent that such an implication cannot generally hold. From Theorem 3.1, if V is more

---

[11] Note that, in general, $p^v = p^u - (g''/g')U''$.
[12] The authors thank Miles Kimball for suggesting this result.

risk averse than U, then $V(W) = k[U(W)]$ $\forall W$, where $k' > 0$, $k'' < 0$.

THEOREM 3.4: *Suppose $r^v(W) > r^u(W)$ $\forall W$. Then $p^v(W) > p^u(W)$ if and only if*

(3.1) $\qquad p^u(W) < 3r^u(W) - \{k'''[U(W)]/k''[U(W)]\}U'(W).$

PROOF: Induce g via k and U by $g[U'(W)] \equiv k'[U(W)] \cdot U'(W)$.

It follows that

(3.2) $\qquad g' = k' - k''U'/r^u > 0 \; \forall W$

and

(3.3) $\qquad g'' = (1/r^u)^2 \left[k''(p^u - 3r^u) + k'''U' \right].$

Now from Theorem 3.2 (iii), $p^v(W) > p^u(W)$ if and only if $g'' > 0$.

The conclusion follows ∎

Some practicality can be added to Theorem 3.4 by noting that [see Kimball (1990, p.65)]

(3.4) $\qquad dr^u(W)/dW = r^u(W)\left[r^u(W) - p^u(W)\right].$

Thus, $p^u(W) > [<;=] r^u(W)$ if $U(W)$ locally exhibits decreasing [increasing; constant] absolute risk aversion. With CARA or IARA, we obviously have $p^u < 3r^u$; but not necessarily with DARA. Consequently, we have the following extension of Theorem 3.4.

COROLLARY 3.4: *If $k : \mathbb{R} \to \mathbb{R}$ represents a concave transformation of U into the more risk averse utility function V, then $k''' > 0$ is sufficient for $p^v(W) > p^u(W)$ if U locally exhibits nondecreasing absolute risk aversion. More generally, $k''' > 0$ will be sufficient whenever $p^u(W) < 3r^u(W)$.*

The Corollary implies that a concave ($k'' < 0$) and prudent ($k''' > 0$) transformation of utility will not only increase the degree of absolute risk aversion but so long as risk aversion is not too decreasing in wealth, will increase the degree of absolute prudence as well. For instance, in Example 3.1, $p^u < 3r^u$ if $\gamma < \frac{1}{2}$, i.e. if the degree of (constant) relative risk aversion, $1-\gamma$, exceeds $\frac{1}{2}$.

Consider the two-period consumption/savings program (2.3). The optimal consumption plan will generally satisfy $U'(c^*) = E[V'(W - c^* + \tilde{y})]$. If both U and V are made more risk averse, even by the same concave transformation k, it does not generally follow that the optimal first-period consumption, c^*, will fall. On the other hand, using a common convex transformation g on both U' and V', it follows that c^* will fall.[13]

One needs to be careful, however, about misapplying Theorem 3.4 and its Corollary. For example, suppose the same concave transformation k is applied to U and V and that $p(W) < 3r(W)$ ∀W for both U and V. Then if $k''' > 0$, one might think that the increased risk aversion of U and V leads to increased savings by the argument given in the preceding paragraph. Indeed, from Corollary 3.4, it follows that both U and V will transform into more prudent utility functions. Note however that the induced convex transformation of U' in Theorem 3.4 depends upon the function U(W). Consequently, although the identical transformation k is applied to both U and V, the induced transformations on U' and V' need not be identical. Thus, optimal first-period consumption c^* need not fall.

Further consider the case where second-period utility is simply a discounted value of first-period utility, $V = \delta U$, where $\delta < 1$. Then one must include the discount factor in the second-period transformation, in order to ensure that c^* will fall. Applying a convex transformation g to U' in both the first and second periods will not generally ensure an increase in savings. In particular, this can be ensured only if the transformation g applied to U' in the first period is applied to $V' = \delta U'$ in the second period.[14]

---

[13] This follows trivially since $E\{g[V']\} > g\{E[V']\}$ by Jensen's inequality. Also note that although a concave transformation of U and V is insufficient to ensure increased savings, a concave transformation of two-period utility, $k[U(c) + V(W-c+y)]$, is sufficient.

[14] Thus, after the transformation, second-period utility is no longer merely a discounted first-period utility. Note also that even when g is properly applied to yield increased savings, the marginal rates of intertemporal substitution (under certainty) are altered by the transformation. Epstein and Zin

4. DECREASING RISK AVERSION AND DECREASING PRUDENCE[15]

The condition of DARA is typically viewed as having empirical support. At the least, risk aversion is typically viewed as nonincreasing. Similarly, arguments can be made for decreasing absolute prudence, or at the least, nonincreasing prudence. For instance, CARA utility also exhibits constant absolute prudence (CAP), and constant relative risk aversion (which implies DARA) also implies constant relative prudence (which in turn implies DAP). This is easily seen in Example 3.1. The rationale for DAP, together with DARA, is explored at length by Kimball (1993), who shows that these two conditions together are equivalent to standard risk aversion.[16]

One consequence of standard risk aversion is that it always reduces the level of investment in a risky security [or increases the investment in insurance] in the presence of an independent, zero-mean background risk. Consider wealth given by $W + \tilde{\varepsilon} + \tilde{y}(\alpha)$ where α is a control variable and $W + \tilde{\varepsilon}$ is considered a random background wealth, $\tilde{\varepsilon}$ and $\tilde{y}(\alpha)$ independent $\forall \alpha$, $E(\tilde{\varepsilon}) = 0$. Kihlstrom, Romer and Williams (1981) and Nachman (1982), assuming the integral on the right-hand side below exists and is finite, define the derived utility function by

(4.1) $$Z(W) \equiv \int_R U(W + \varepsilon) \, dG(\varepsilon),$$

where G is the cumulative distribution of ε.

THEOREM 4.1: *Consider the natural homeomorphism* $k: Im[U] \to Im[Z]$. *If U satisfies standard risk aversion, k is concave.*

(1989), Kocherlakota (1990) and Schlee (1992) discuss this problem with regards to risk aversion, but their comments are also relevant for prudence.

[15] In a recently completed unpublished paper, Kimball (1993) also examines these concepts. Rather than duplicating many of Kimball's results, we attempt in this section to present a set of results that complement those of Kimball.

[16] Preferences satisfy standard risk aversion if any risk that makes a small reduction in wealth more painful (as measured by the reduction in expected utility) also makes any undesirable, independent risk more painful [Kimball (1993)]. Standard risk aversion also implies proper risk aversion, as defined by Pratt and Zeckhauser (1987).

PROOF: $\forall W$, note that

(4.2) $\quad Z'(W) = \int_R U'(W+\varepsilon)dG(\varepsilon) = U'\bigl(W - \psi(W,\tilde{\varepsilon})\bigr)$

and

(4.3) $\quad Z''(W) = [1 - d\psi/dW]U''(W - \psi).$

Consequently,

(4.4) $\quad -\dfrac{Z''(W)}{Z'(W)} > -\dfrac{U''(W-\psi)}{U'(W-\psi)} > -\dfrac{U''(W)}{U'(W)},$

where the first inequality above follows from DAP and the second follows from DARA. The conclusion follows from Theorem 3.1. ∎

Theorem 4.1 says that the derived utility function Z is more risk averse than U. Since $E[U(W + \tilde{\varepsilon} + \tilde{y}(\alpha))] = E[Z(W + \tilde{y}(\alpha))]$, qualitative changes in the optimal choice of α due to adding $\tilde{\varepsilon}$ are identical to changes due to an increase in risk aversion. Eeckhoudt and Kimball (1992), for example, use this result to show that randomizing background wealth increases the quantity of insurance demanded when preferences exhibit standard risk aversion.

Although standard risk aversion is given a canonical justification by Kimball (1993), in general DARA preferences do not require prudence to be decreasing. Indeed, it is quite possible to have dp/dW and dr/dW differ in sign, as in the following examples.[17]

---

[17] The restricted domain in Example 4.1 is noteworthy. Indeed, Kimball (1993) shows that DAP over an interval (W_0, ∞) implies DARA over that interval as well. This result follows easily in our model. Define $V(W) = U(W-\delta) \; \forall W \geq \delta > 0$ and assume DAP of U. Thus V is more prudent than U over (δ, ∞). Kimball's result now follows as an application of Corollary 3.3.

EXAMPLE 4.1: Consider the following three utility functions restricted to the domain $W < \frac{1}{2}$.

$$U_1(W) \equiv -e^{-W}.$$
$$U_2(W) \equiv W - W^2.$$
$$U_3(W) \equiv U_1(W) + U_2(W)$$

It is then straightforward to show that

$$r_1 = p_1 = 1 \ \forall W.$$
$$r_2 = 2/(1-2W), \ p_2 = 0 \ \forall W.$$
$$r_3 = (e^{-W} + 2)/(e^{-2W} + 1), \ p_3 = e^{-W}/(e^{-W} + 2).$$

Both U_1 and U_2 exhibit constant absolute prudence while U_1 exhibits CARA and U_2 exhibits IARA. However, U_3 exhibits both IARA and DAP.[18]

∎

EXAMPLE 4.2: Let $U(W) \equiv W - W^2 + W^3$, restricted to the domain $W < \frac{1}{3}$. Then

$$r = (2 - 6W)/(1 - 2W + 3W^2) \text{ and } p = 6/(2 - 6W).$$

It is then straightforward to show that U exhibits DARA along with IAP.

∎

In each of the above cases, we can construct examples where the addition of an independent random background wealth does not lead to the purchase of more insurance, so that both DARA and DAP are critical for this conclusion.

5. CONCLUDING REMARKS

The concept of prudence seems to have many applications in choice - theoretic models under uncertainty. This paper has examined the relationship between risk aversion and prudence, paying particular attention to whether or not increases in risk

---

[18] Note that, although U_1 and U_2 exhibit CAP, the mixture of U_1 and U_2 yields DAP. In other words, mixtures of CAP utility functions do not necessarily remain CAP. A similar point was made about risk aversion by Brocket and Golden (1985).

aversion and increases in prudence necessarily imply each other. Although they generally do not, the two measures are inextricably entwined. For example, an increase in prudence is always accompanied by one of three types of changes in risk aversion: (1) everywhere higher, (2) everywhere lower, or (3) higher at lower wealth levels and lower at higher wealth levels. A sufficient condition on preferences for (1) to apply is that $[V'(\infty)/V'(W)] \leq [U'(\infty)/U'(W)]$.

We also showed that an increase in risk aversion leads to an increase in prudence, whenever the concave transformation into more risk-averse preferences is also a "prudent" transformation (k''' > 0) and preferences do not exhibit risk aversion that decreases too quickly in wealth.

The similarity of structure between risk aversion and prudence allowed Kimball (1990) to extend many of Pratt's results on risk aversion to account for a precautionary-savings motive. In this spirit, Pratt's main Theorem is extended in this paper to show that preferences are made more prudent only through a convex transformation of marginal utility. This transformation appears to be useful in obtaining general results stemming from increases in prudence, such as for the simple two-period consumption/savings model discussed in the text.

Finally, we considered decreasing absolute prudence and its relationship to decreasing absolute risk aversion. The value of these two conditions in tandem for settings including multiple sources of risk was examined. In particular, when both of these conditions on preferences hold, adding an independent background risk was shown to be tantamount to increasing the degree of risk aversion with no added background risk.

As the concept of prudence finds a wider range of applications over time a knowledge of its relationship to risk aversion should prove more and more useful. Hopefully, our paper makes a good preliminary contribution towards this end.

REFERENCES

Arrow, K. J. (1965): "Aspects of a Theory of Risk Bearing," Yrjo Jahnsson Lectures, Helsinki.

Brocket, P. L. and L. L. Golden (1985): "A Class of Utility Functions Containing All the Common Utility Functions," *Management Science*, 33, 955-964.

Drèze, J. H. and F. Modigliani (1972): "Consumption Decisions Under Uncertainty," *Journal of Economic Theory*, 5, 308-335.

Eeckhoudt, L., C. Gollier and H. Schlesinger (1991): "Increases in Risk and Deductible Insurance," *Journal of Economic Theory*, 55, 435-440.

Eeckhoudt, L. and M. Kimball (1992): "Background Risk, Prudence, and the Demand for Insurance," in *Contributions to Insurance Economics*, ed. by G. Dionne, Boston: Kluwer Academic Publishers.

Epstein, L. and S. Zin (1989): "Substitution, Risk Aversion and the Temporal Behavior of Consumption and Asset Returns: A Theoretical Framework," *Econometrica*, 57, 937-970.

Kihlstrom, R. E., D. Romer and S. Williams (1981): "Risk Aversion with Random Initial Wealth," *Econometrica*, 49, 911-920.

Kimball, M. S. (1990): "Precautionary Savings in the Small and in the Large," *Econometrica*, 58, 53-73.

Kimball, M. S. (1993): "Standard Risk Aversion," *Econometrica*, 61, 589-611.

Kocherlakota, N. (1990): "Disentangling the Coefficient of Relative Risk Aversion from the Elasticity of Intertemporal Substitution," *Journal of Finance*, 45, 175-190.

McAfee, R. P. (1991): "Efficient Allocation with Continuous Quantities," *Journal of Economic Theory*, 53, 51-74.

Nachman, D. C. (1982): "Preservation of 'More Risk Averse' Under Expectation," *Journal of Economic Theory*, 28, 361-368.

Neumann, J. von and O. Morgenstern (1944): *Theory of Games and Economic Behavior*, Princeton: Princeton University Press.

Pratt, J. W. (1964): "Risk Aversion in the Small and in the Large," *Econometrica*, 32, 122-136.

Pratt, J. W. (1988): "Aversion to One Risk in the Presence of Others," *Journal of Risk and Uncertainty*, 1, 105-113.

Pratt, J. W. and R. J. Zeckhauser (1987): "Proper Risk Aversion," *Econometrica*, 55, 143-154.

Sandmo, A. (1970): "The Effect of Uncertainty on Savings Decisions," *Review of Economic Studies*, 37, 353-360.

Schlee, E. E. (1992): "Multivariate Risk Aversion and Intertemporal Substitution," *GENEVA PAPERS on Risk and Insurance Theory*, 17, 159-169.

"Embodied Risk: 'Framing,' Consumption Style and
the Deterrence of Crimes of Passion"

Jerome Rothenberg
Massachusetts Institute of Technology
Cambridge, Massachusetts, U.S.A.

I. Embodied Risk: An Overview

In the author's, "Consumption Style as Choice Under Risk: Static Choice, Dynamic Irrationality and Crimes of Passion,"[1] a novel concept of "embodied risk" was developed, and it was argued there that in circumstances which favored the appearance of "embodied risk," consumer behavior could well systematically differ from what it would be if the same quantitative probability prospects were present in the conventional disembodied, or "abstract" risk context. These behavioral differences occurred in both a static and dynamic setting, and rather unusual dynamic anomalies could emerge in the "embodied" context. Finally, the paper demonstrated how the phenomenon of "crime of passion" could be straightforwardly rationalized in terms of "embodied risk" processes.

The present paper extends the analysis to examine explicitly the production and use of the central instrument for generating embodied risk situations, "consumption style," processes of some complexity. The extension permits a deeper insight into both the static and dynamic anomalies arising out of embodied risk behavior, and permits as well an illumination of further unconventional phenomena—not only crimes of passion but also

---

[1] In John Geweke ed., *Decision-Making under Risk and Uncertainty: New Models and Empirical Findings*, Kluwer Academic Publishers, Dordrecht, Netherlands, 1992.

spouse abuse.

Conventional theory for risky choices, what I call "abstract risk," deals with situations where individuals select among prospects whose risk characteristics are set exogenously outside the individual: participants passively await the outcomes generated by stochastic processes. "Embodied risk," on the other hand, deals with situations in which, after the choice of some such prospect, its stochastic outcome will be considerably, but not perhaps decisively, determined by the participant's own active efforts applied to the external stochastic process—efforts characterized by motivation, skill, resources, courage, and ingenuity. Indeed, the participant's testing of his/her efforts against the process becomes an important component of his/her overall payoff. As a meaningful test of the participant's capabilities, it becomes a meaningful test of his/her inherent personal worth. In this sense the risk situation is "embodied." Passive processes are "abstract."

Ordinary activities can be modified to create challenges for the individual to overcome. They may be made more difficult by the way the individual carries them out: with more flair, taking more chances, erecting unnecessary obstacles, setting performance goals considerably above the average—in eating, dressing, driving, engaging in sports, carrying out amours, etc. The degree and character of challenge for any activity, whether production or consumption, is called its "style." Style involves the inputs used (consumer commodities for consumption activities), the manner in which they are used—in terms of the demandingness of the situation—and the extent to which this combination of goals and manner can be "framed" as a relevantly perceived challenge to the participant. In the earlier paper we concentrated on inputs and manner; in this paper we introduce the crucial importance of "framing."

Activities do not naturally come with a given style; style is chosen by the participant: indeed, it must be produced by the participant. The three components are in fact inputs into a production process, with technology and cost functions.

In the stochastic process context in which an activity

appears, the probability distribution of outcomes varies with the style produced. In general low styles—with low degree of demandingness: conservative—generate outcome profiles relatively flat over various resulting states of nature, but slightly more favorable for favorable states of nature. High styles stretch the range of performance in both high and low directions, increase variance, and show much more steeply varied outcomes. For very high styles, performance is extremely high for a small subset of extremely favorable states of nature, but is apt to be very low—sometimes disastrously so—for wide stretches of states of nature.

Activities differ in their susceptibility to production of varied styles, especially very high styles. So individuals intent on engaging in high style activities will concentrate their efforts on those amenable to style variation. But participants also differ, probably even more widely, in the attractiveness of high style behavior. Our model characterizes this inclination in a novel form of utility function—in terms of fulfillment of different needs. The relevant need is "ego validation," and individuals are assumed to differ markedly in the contribution of this argument to their overall welfare. So it is preponderantly individuals with high ego validation needs that will resort to producing high styles. Since only a subset of activities will conveniently lend themselves to style augmentation, this subset of participants will choose high style behavior over a subset of activities but conservative low styles for other activities—those which are not "style-friendly."

Since high style increases the riskiness of any activity, will it be chosen only by individuals with risk preference? No. Our model contains an additional vital element in the static choice situation. A participant may well accept a fair risky gamble to a fair gamble less risky. This is because the underlying attraction to high style behavior lies in the individual's determination to prove his/her merit. The objective probability distribution characterizing the fair bet refers to expected outcomes for the general mass of participants—but the determination to test oneself lies in just the notion that one is better than that general mass. So the probability distribution perceived for oneself is <u>systematically more favorable</u> than the "objective" distribution. Thus the inclination to engage in high style behavior is generally accompanied by a "subjective" probability distribution corresponding to each "objective" distribution that is more favorable than the latter. So the choice of a high style over a low style gamble looks to the participant as rational—even where the participant believes him/herself to be risk averse!

II "Framing," Consumption Style and Risk Embodiment

Each individual's welfare is determined by a "primal welfare function."

(1) $W = W(U_1, U_2, \ldots U_n, U_{EV})$

W "primal welfare"; $U_1, U_2, \ldots$ bio/social needs 1, 2, ... n: i.e., need utility levels 1, 2, ..., m; U_{EV} level of satisfaction of ego validation needs: i.e., ego validation utility level.

Embodiment styles are direct attempts to gratify the ego validation needs, EV. We assume individuals differ greatly (the size of $\frac{\partial W}{\partial EV}$) and thus in their likelihood of resorting to risk embodiment for overall welfare maximization.

Satisfaction of the needs (U) occurs within consumption activities,[2] via the performance levels achieved in these activities.

(2a) $U_i = U_i [\alpha_1 (X_1, S_1, E), \alpha_2 (X_2, S_2, E), \ldots \alpha_m (X_m, S_m, E)]$
       $i = 1, 2, \ldots, m$

(2b) $U_{EV} = U_{EV} [[\alpha_1 (X_1, S_1, E), \alpha_2 (X_2, S_2, E), \ldots \alpha_m (X_m, S_m,$

---

[2]Generically "consumption." "Production" activities can easily be included.

E)]

(3) $N_i = N_i(U_i)$

U_i determinant of gratification of need i; α_j performance level of activity j   j = 1, ..., m; X_i commodity/labor use in activity j; S_j consumption style of activity j; E outcome of stochastic environmental process; N (.) need gratification function.

Performance level in an activity depends on the resources used, the style, and the result of the stochastic contextual process. Activity outcomes are stochastic, as is, therefore, welfare.

Consumption style is the process by which challenges are built into any activity. Low style involves little or no challenge beyond its inherent nature. Higher styles construct progressively greater challenges. So choice of S_j affects the range, variance, and other features of the probability distribution of outcomes. Higher S generates higher risk. Attraction to high S_j also tends to generate parallel "subjective" probability distributions more favorable to the relevant participant than the corresponding "objective" distribution. The basis for the optimism may or may not be in fact warranted.

This linkage of style, riskiness and optimism generates distinctive choosing behavior. Its divergence from conventional abstract risk situations stems from the fact that the individual literally sees "objectively" similar risk prospects differently in high and low style contexts.

Beyond the analysis of the first paper we now enrich the notion of embodiment. Individuals with a strong need for ego validation, who must deliberately build-in challenges for themselves to overcome to achieve validation, generally do not fully trust themselves to know their own worth. They often need the recognition or acknowledgement of others to confirm them. Arranging challenges thus becomes arranging a "performance" played for others. An "audience" is required. The test of self is done "in public."

Something more is implied. Others do not automatically

understand that our individual is embarking on an important self-challenge though the latter may know it well. The individual must create that understanding in the desired audience. The act of creating such a perceptual structure is called "framing." Style is chosen, not in a vacuum, but in a social perceptual structure: the frame. "Framing" has two aspects: obtaining an audience, and structuring the situation to create in them a social perception of the self-test. Both are necessary.

Framing is thus a form of production. What is produced we call a "contest." It varies from a trivial to an extremely demanding creation, requires the use of productive resources, and has various production technologies. Thus, it incurs real costs. Different types of contest, and the same type of contest in different circumstances, have different cost functions. Choice among style levels therefore requires balancing off a subjectively perceived set of stochastic gains against both a higher overall risk position and the resource cost of the necessary framing without which the high style alone would generate little utility gain.

III Contests: Necessary Conditions and Types

What is required for a consumption activity to be framed into a contest? First are requirements for an activity to be capable of high style context performance: (1) Existence of generally understood (consensual) norms, rules, and expectations concerning the nature of the contest and of contest performance—permitting a monotonic ordering of performance quality; (2) Performance level and its range consensually related to the demandingness of obstacles overcome in the performance; (3) Nature of the contest, strength of obstacles, and performance level visible to outsiders—the audience: what is at stake in the performance clearly perceivable by the audience; (4) A proximate (consensual) metric to describe both size of obstacles and level of performance.

Second is the requirement that high style performance be integrated into a contest structure by the presence of an audience knowledgeable about the structural features just itemized and important to the performer. The performance must be accessible and comprehensible to this audience. Importance refers to legitimacy for judgment concerning the performer's ego validation. This will be discussed further below.

Two features are stressed: structure that is publicly perceived as a contest with consensually quantifiable parameters about obstacles and performance; an appropriate and legitimizing audience. Both are important, and neither generally represents a trivial task.

Clearly, not all consumption activities meet these conditions. Probably most do not. So embodiment will tend to cluster in a special subset of activities.

We classify contests into four general types: demonstrations, competitions, rivalries, intimate interdependencies.

1. Demonstrations (K_d).

The subject performs "before" an audience who know the rules, difficulties, measures of performance level—usually because they participate in the activity also. There is not explicit competitive confrontation; the activity is generally ongoing, and the audience appreciate special achievements by comparison with their own separate performances, e.g., auto drivers as a group, well-dressed people, roulette players, etc. They are genuinely strangers to our player, and typically only casually present. Their legitimization potential is likely to be weak per capita but capable of being offset by large numbers. Some situational structuring is needed to alert the audience to the fact that a test is in the offing, and that the stakes are considerable. Different demonstration types will vary in potential ego validation but typically be weakest of the four types of contests.

2. Competitions (K_c).

The subject performs "before" an audience, who are themselves currently engaged in the same activity, and the joint activity is structured as a competitive process: there are explicit winners and losers, depending on differential performance; this active audience knows the rules, the metrics and what is at stake.

Since they explicitly compete against our subject, they are very sensitive to the latter's situation and achievement. Competitions may have many participants, and not all may be physically present to witness our subject's performance; but information is widely and rapidly disseminated.[3]

Competitors in this audience will be highly sensitive to our subject's performance, so their judgment matters. With direct inverse interpersonal welfare linkage, each audience member will tend to have a larger per capita ego validation effect. Legitimization here stems from the representativeness of the audience.

A competition context does not mean that the subject's every action is part of the competition. For example, competitive observance of fashion leadership does not make every clothing action by the subject an active head-to-head confrontation—yet the audience knows that the subject's performance bears on their recent past and near-future behavior—in another time and place.

3. <u>Rivalries, K_R.</u>

The subject performs interactively in rivalry relation with one or a small number of others. Regardless of the height of the literal winnings in the contest, this structure generates high affect levels in all participants, including our subject. Rivalries differ in the formal stakes at issue, but high affect makes the ego validation stakes high, higher than in competitions with even considerably higher formal stakes. Audience appropriateness depends on the readiness and intensity with which a necessary few others are prepared to enter into the rivalry contention.

4. <u>Intimate Interdependencies, K_I</u>

The subject performs before a most significant other (moral

---

[3]Where competition involves partners or teams, not all members of the audience need be the subject's competitors (R. Pope, personal communication, 1992).

leader, spouse, lover, close friend, etc.), seeking approval, or admiration, or love, or some general positive judgment. The expectation of such positive response stems from the close nature of the relationship and the multi-dimensionality of points of contact, such that a wide repertoire of behavior can be advanced for positive recognition. There is a contest in that the subject attempts to play his/her role in the relationship in so exemplary a manner as to elicit a stronger than normal positive response—often leading to the recursive interactive elevation of performance, each one's response being a further stimulus to increasingly exemplary, increasingly inspired performance.

This type of contest is unique, however, in that what is normally a most positive interaction may become equally a negative interaction. Because of the affectively unique status of each for the other, a disappointment of our subject at the hands of the other may lead to an aggressive contest in which she/he and then the other vie with one another to signal the intensity of dissatisfaction, or a punishment to fit the "crime," or a demonstration of the ability to control the hurt by displaying power or mastery or control over other aspects of the relationship, etc.

The relationship thus represents an interdependency which is inherently ambivalent. The importance of each to the other makes it possible for each to generate for the other either extremely positive or extremely negative stimuli, and the responses are typically mutually interactive with a powerful dynamism.

IV. Contests: Adequacy of Audience

Assembly and preparation of an audience is essential to framing a contest. The audience is the sounding board for the subject's performance to generate ego validation.[4] But the audience

---

[4]It should be pointed out that the importance of an audience to these contests does not mean that the activities on which they are built are themselves interpersonal. They may well consist entirely in using purely material market commodities. The essential

must be adequate to the task. One reason for classifying contests into types is that adequacy of audience means something different for each type.

a. <u>Demonstrations (K_D)</u>

This is the most impersonal type. Audience members must know the rules of the contest, understand its structure, recognize performance obstacles and know how to judge performance level. Given its more tenuous challenge character, high accessibility to outside observation is needed to facilitate recognition of its subtle test structure. For this, the larger the audience the better. The "reference group" that possesses necessary expertise from their own experience is likely to be substantial. Framing requires assembling enough of them, or joining opportune concentrations of them, to provide adequate representation. Thus, a possible adequacy index for the "reference group" is:

(4) $$m_D = n_D(N_D) \qquad n_D' > 0$$

m_D is the demonstration audience adequacy index; N_D is the absolute number of audience members taken from the appropriate "reference group."

b. <u>Competitions (K_c)</u>

These contests are more explicitly interpersonal, but, because of large numbers, individual members are not closely <u>personified</u>. Relevant groups may be: all auto drivers, all liquor drinkers of a given socio-economic or age group, or in the same bar, all "well-dressed" persons in a neighborhood or a given socio-economic or ethnic group, etc. Audience members must be

---

interpersonal aspect consists in the manner of their commission being subject to outsider judgment, and in conveyance of such judgment to the subject.

currently actively involved in the activity, and engaged in a competitive mode—i.e., all trying to perform in a superior way, and conscious of the relative performance of others. The competitions need not involve face-to-face competitive confrontation. Some competitor members of this audience need not even be physically present at the subject's performance. But those physically present must be aware that the subject's performance should be compared to their own; those not physically present must dependably and promptly receive news about the subject's performance, and refer it to their own performance—<u>and</u> the subject must expect that such information transmission will in fact occur. Audience adequacy here refers to the "competition group":

(5) $$m_{ci} = \frac{N_{ci}}{N_c} \leq 1$$

m_{ci} is the competitive group audience adequacy for action type i undertaken by the subject; N_c is the size of "reasonably representative" competition group; N_{ci} is the size of competition group audience for the subject's action type i.

c. <u>Rivalries (K_R)</u>

These contests are explicitly negative interpersonal processes, and, because of the significant fewness of participants (rivals or antagonists), are highly <u>personified</u>. There is generally, not always, a head-to-head confrontation. The exposed antagonistic, highly personified nature of the contest generally makes for strong affect. The stakes for ego validation are thus likely to consist of both the formal objective of the rivalry—the "prize"—and the resolution of the emotional arousal: the emotional vindication.

Rivalries differ in size of both aspects of the stakes, but the emotional often exceeds the formal prize. Rivals generally are inherently mutually aware of their rivalry, but not always, and not always to the same degree (as in the absence of head-to-head physical confrontation). Their rivalry status implicitly entails their being cognitively competent to serve as an audience; but their variable degree of perceivable consciousness of the rivalry contest qualifies their adequacy. As an index of rivalry group adequacy:

$$(6) \qquad m_{Ri} = \frac{b_{Ri} N_{Ri}}{N_R} \leq 1$$

m_{Ri} is the level of rivalry group adequacy for action type i; N_R is the reasonably complete set of rivals (in number); N_{Ri} is the number of rivals in the subject's audience for action type i; b_{Ri} is the average perceivable consciousness of rivalry contest.

d. <u>Intimate Interdependencies (K_I)</u>

These are explicitly and profoundly interpersonal—and certainly personified. Generally the only relevant audience is a single, specific person—and that person is "available." But this does not guarantee an entirely adequate audience. The audience may not be paying full attention, may not be fully aware of the challenge structure of the performance. This is possible because the relationship between subject and significant other is not inherently either a positive or negative confrontation or challenge. Lack of attention or awareness may be sincere, or it may be a deliberate strategy to avoid either hurt or the burden of a required positive response. Adequacy of intimacy group audience is:

$$(7) \qquad m_{Ii} = b_{Ii} \leq 1$$

m_{Ii} is the level of intimacy group adequacy; b_{Ii} is the degree of attention/awareness by significant other.

IV <u>The Decision Context and the Cost of Framing</u>

A. <u>Decision Context</u> We now express the decision context in terms of activities, framing, contests and styles, and their costs.

The individual must allocate his/her budget over a set of activities, $A_1, A_2, \ldots A_n$, and over the discretionary style in which each will be performed: its degree of contest intensity:

(8) $$K = K(S, m)$$

K is the degree of contest structuring; S is the consumption style; m is the degree of adequacy of contest audience. Its operations cost is:

(9) $$X = (P_y \cdot y + P_1 \cdot q)$$

X is the value of market commodities and labor used in the activity: i.e., $P \cdot Q$. Since P, price per unit, is assumed constant in the model, X is a quantity index (i.e., Q) of such commodities; y is the quantity of market commodities used (adjusted for quality); q is the quantity of labor used (adjusted for quality), and P_y, P_1 their respective prices. So:

(10) $$A_i = [K(S_i, m_i), X_i]$$

A_i is the intensity of activity i.

B. Cost of Framing

Framing represents a transformation of resources: it is a kind of production, with distinctive production functions, using resources, structuring a pattern of performance, collecting an appropriate audience—and as such it has a real cost associated with it. Audience assembly may incur travel costs, waiting, mobilizing the necessary performance inputs to a specific time and place opportunistically. High style structuring may incur considerable training costs, special types and variety and turnover of market goods, extra labor outlay in time and demandingness.

Our discussion of the different forms of contest makes clear that their costs, for given style levels, S_i, will generally be different. The cost function for each K must be differentiated for each K_z (z is contest type):

(11) $$C_{zi} = C_z [K_z (S_i, m_z)]$$

C_z is the cost of framing a contest of type z on activity i.

C. Performance Outcomes of Activities

1. Physical Outcomes

Let T_i be the performance level of activity i[5]. Outcomes are the result of a stochastic process (E) operating on the decision characteristics of the activity: S_i and X_i. They form a probability distribution:

(12) $$G [T_i \mid S_i, X_i]$$

In the prior paper we argued that this distribution has the following properties:

1. An increase in consumption style S_i raises both the range and variance of G:

(13) a. $\dfrac{\partial (\text{Range of G})}{\partial S_i} > 0$ b. $\dfrac{\partial (\sigma^2 \text{ of G})}{\partial S_i} > 0$

2. Higher intensity increases expected performance, but an increase in S_i has ambiguous effects on expected performance:

(14) $$\frac{\partial ET_i}{\partial X_i} > 0 \gtreqless \frac{\partial ET_i}{\partial S_i}.$$

S_i, by affecting the demandingness of obstacles involved in the activity, and opportunities for transcending them, affects the

---

[5]T corresponds here to the notation α (achievement level) in equations 2.

riskiness of the activity prospect without dependably changing its average performance level in either directions.

2. Need Satisfaction Impact of Activity Outcomes

A high S_i is adopted to demonstrate to oneself that one is capable of superior performance—better than the mean, indeed, better even in the face of <u>avoidable</u> unusual obstacles which are here voluntarily faced (in fact, overtly or covertly <u>deliberately</u> placed in the way). This trial therefore constitutes an asymmetric test: the extent to which performance <u>exceeds</u> normal expectation is more important than the extent to which it <u>falls below</u>.

The utility impact of activity outcomes is given as follows:

(15a) $\quad U_j = U_j [T_1, T_2, \ldots, T_n] \quad j = 1, 2, \ldots, n$

(15b) $\quad\quad\quad U_{EV} = e(m_i) \, V [T_i - \mu_1 (G (S_i))]$

$U_j [T_1, T_2, \ldots, T_m]$ is simply equation (2a) with T substituted for α: i.e., satisfaction of need j as an input into equation (1); U_{EV}^i is a <u>new</u> representation of the satisfaction of ego validation from activity i, based on performance divergence from the mean of the probability distribution generated by S_i; $V (T_i - \mu_i)$ is the ego validation impact of divergences from mean performance level in activity i. It is discontinuous at $T_i - \mu_i = 0$: for $T_i - \mu_i > 0$, it is a convex rising function, with rising V'; for $T_i - \mu_i < 0$, it is a concave falling function, with falling $|V'|$. Thus, for success the <u>degree</u> is very important; for failure, the <u>fact</u> is more important than its actual degree. The size of V depends on the extent to which unusual achievement via high style consumption enhances ego validation, and the importance of ego validation to the individual's primal welfare. We assume the former to be fairly uniform across individuals but the latter to differ markedly: i.e., $\partial W / \partial EV$ varies considerably among people. High style behavior is likely to be concentrated very unequally among the population. So the size of V depends on the size of $\partial W / \partial EV$

for the particular individual considered; $e(m_i)$ is the framing adequacy function. It measures the affective adequacy of framing in terms of audience adequacy (m). So the ego validation impact of performance depends partly on how adequate is the audience as a means of transforming sheer performance into ego validation via the sense of <u>success in a contest</u>. Since $0 \leq e(m) \leq 1$, e acts as a discount factor for potential validation.

V Static Choice

Consider an individual choosing between a lower and a higher style for some activity i, S_{0i} and S_{1i} respectively. In light of our discussion above, S_0 gives rise to the objective probability distribution G_0, with μ_0, σ_0; S_1 gives rise to the objective probability distribution G_1, with μ_1, σ_1. Assume $\mu_0 = \mu_1$, and $\sigma_0 < \sigma_1$. Due to the anxious self-confidence that would be required validation if S1 were considered, G_1 is superseded for the individual by a <u>personal achievement</u> distribution, G_1', more optimistic than the objective G_1 distribution. Thus, $\mu_1' > \mu_1$, $\sigma_1' = \sigma_1$.

Assume now that $ET = \mu$. To distinguish our model results from those stemming simply from risk preference attitudes, we further assume that the utility need gratification level is based on a mean-variance criterion. Then the utility differences involved in the comparison between S_0 and S_1 are as follows:

(16)   a. $U_{j0} = \mu_0 - g(\sigma_0)$

         b. $U_{j1} = \mu_1' - g(\sigma_1) > \mu_1 - g(\sigma_1)$,

for need gratification j.

To simplify without misrepresenting the central issue, assume that activity i only affects need gratification j. So only two terms of equation (1) are affected by the choice: U_j and U_{EV}. The differential for term U_j is:

(17) $\Delta U_j \equiv U_{j1} - U_{j0} = (\mu_1' - \mu_0) - (g(\sigma_1) - g(\sigma_0))$

For dramatic emphasis, let us assume that the individual is reasonably risk averse. Then it is quite possible that $\Delta U_j < 0$. Nonetheless, it is still possible for S_1 to be preferred to S_0: i.e., that $W(S_1) > W(S_0)$. The issue concerns the term U_{EV} in equation (15b). U_{EV} does not have to be risk-adjusted. Its value for S_1 stems from the anxious self-confidence implied by a high $\partial W/\partial EV$ (a high need for ego validation) that perceives greater reality for G_1' than for G_1 for that individual. The higher variance of G_1 and G_1' reflects higher risk, but $\mu_1' > \mu_1$ is perceived as personal worth, not risk. So the U_{EV} comparison is:

$$\Delta U_{EV} \equiv U_{EV,1}' - U_{EV,0} = e(m_i) V[\mu_1' - \mu_1] - e(m_0) V[\mu_0 - \mu_0]$$
(18)
$$= e(m_i) V[\mu_1' - \mu_1] > 0$$

where expected performance levels are μ_1' and μ_0 respectively. So the sharply non-linear rising V function can easily make $\Delta U_{EV} > 0$. With a strong ego validation need (large $\partial W/\partial U_{EV}$), positive $\partial W/\partial U_{EV} \Delta U_{EV}$ may well exceed a negative $\partial W/\partial U_j \Delta U_j$.

The final choice between S_0 and S_1 depends also on the cost of framing S_1 into a high K. This cost uses up resources that would otherwise permit higher level operation of all activities (the X and C(K)). The general decrease in all activity levels could well reduce W by more than it would be increased by comparing activity i impacts on U_j and U_{EV}.

The upshot of this analysis is that for some individual systematic choices between high and low S across activities favor higher S—and thus higher risk, contrary to predictions about such choice for abstract risk—where: 1) the individual has a high ego validation need ($\partial W/\partial U_{EV}$ is large); 2) the activity is one for which high S so stretches the positive range of potential performance that an optimistic interpretation of reality leads to an expected non-trivial performance level superiority over the population average; 3) the individual is not <u>heavily</u> risk-averse, although some risk aversion is possible; 4) the cost of framing a meaningful contest with that activity consistent with the higher S is low. Such systematic choices, moreover, counter-intuitive in conventional abstract risk theory, do not depend on the individual having risk preference. Thus, the circumstances favoring high S choices are different from those in "abstract" risk analysis. Risk embodiment does make a difference to behavior prediction.

VI Dynamic Implications of Framing

The major dynamic insight of the model in the earlier paper is that where high S is consistently chosen over a number of activities (or even one important one), optimistic modification of high S probability prospects will often prove empirically unwarranted, making the individual suffer big ego losses over time. These will result in a cumulative increase in frustration of ego validation, over time, which, via a systematic increase in implicit stakes by a temporal carryover of accumulated frustration, will induce further choice of progressively higher risk prospects, resulting in still further ego embarrassment, again which will, in turn, prove empirically more embarrassing still, but thereby promoting even more radical plunges into riskiness. This self-promoting runaway into rising risk commitment represents a dynamic inconsistency, because it is self-destructive, and simple insight is not enough to stop it.

The present elaboration of the approach does not run counter to the spirit of this finding. But it gives greater detail to dynamic changes and makes more plausible how the runaway inflation of riskiness may be deterred. Two finer-grained aspects of the dynamic process will be briefly noted: (1) opportunistic, impulsive behavior and (2) changes in high S, low S mix across activities.

A. Opportunistic, Impulsive Behavior

The attraction of, and opportunity for, high S framing of

contests depends importantly on the cost of framing. This cost varies for different types of contest, but also for different instances of the same kind of contest. Much of this variation involves obtaining an adequate audience. For example, a certain level of adequacy may require substantial travel. If one should stumble on a large, appropriate aggregation of people accidentally, engaging in the activity in this time and place could save considerable cost—could even decide the choice between high and low S. So there is a big temptation to act opportunistically, even impulsively, in such instances, to take advantage of the unplanned low cost framing opportunity.

This systematic tendency to opportunistic action is damaging to predictability. It also may weaken the possibility of <u>controlling</u> the impetus to the dynamic runaway pattern both internally and externally. Yet the reverse could also be argued. High costs of framing could systematically discourage high S behavior. The few chance encounters with notably low cost opportunities may so slow down the cumulative increase in ego frustration over time that its emotive effect may simply dissipate—the emotive motor of the increasing desperation may sputter. Thus, the resulting slowing down and unevenness of the process weakens the possibility of dynamic inconsistency.

Furthermore, a form of deliberate deterrence can thereby be envisaged via either internal or external control. Behavioral rules might be established by or for a vulnerable individual to decrease the probability of encountering such unplanned low cost framing opportunities. External attempts to deter this addictive type behavior might even take the form of making it more difficult for such assemblages to form or be recruited as audiences. Penalties, regulations, diversionary activities might be deliberately developed.

In sum, the cost of framing has distinct implications for the temporal unfolding of behavior, both for analysis and intervention designed to modify.

B. <u>Dynamic Changes of Mix</u>

The accumulation of ego frustration over time—what we

call a "cumulative stake"—does often induce progressively riskier choices. But the need to find attractive higher risk opportunities exposes the individual to progressively higher framing costs and less inherently ego-validating impacts. The afflicted individual is likely to seek out progressively more effective, less costly contest opportunities.

Both impact and costs are involved. The impact of higher S operates by stretching out both the positive and negative ranges of the performance level distribution—which permits the typical anxious self-confidence of the subject to anticipate highly unusual performance attainments. It is the upper range that is chiefly at issue. So, writing $\overline{R}$ for that range, $\partial \overline{R}/\partial S$ is the measure of the potential source of extraordinary performance—call it a "desperation productivity." Different activities will tend to offer different desperation productivities. An addicted individual will progressively seek out such activities, and shift the locus of high S behavior toward a narrower, more specialized set of embodying activities.

The dominant aspect of the cost of framing is the difficulty of assembling an appropriate size and character of audience. But this difficulty refers mostly to demonstration and competition contests. These may offer low cost instances where previous audiences can be re-recruited to repeat, continue, or finish contest processes begun earlier. Conventionally ongoing contests can have this property, but they are rare.

Greater opportunities for low cost framing naturally occur in rivalries and intimate interdependencies, especially the latter. The high personification means that two or a few people have a continuing relationship, with lively memories of previous contest instances contesting, thus nurturing expectations that make re-recruitment and structuring relatively easy. The situation can often be successfully manipulated by the subject into seeming simply <u>continuations</u> of previously <u>unfinished</u> contests.

Over and above these advantages, intimate interdependencies have three additional attractions in this context:

the significant other is the same person, with a continuing relationship fed by strong memories of past interchanges; the other's spatial availability is likely to be easily arranged; there are generally very high inherent ego stakes for the subject in the relationship as a whole, so contest structuring is likely to tap into highly ego-important elements. In the desperation status that often characterizes late stages of accumulated stakes, what interdependencies have to offer—admiration, approval, love—are sorely needed.

The foregoing suggests that as cumulative ego frustration proceeds, the cumulative stake growing, the subject will systematically shift the locus of high S behavior away from demonstrations and competitions toward rivalries and intimate interdependencies, subsequently concentrating further toward intimate interdependencies. The inherent capability of intimate interdependencies to develop both positive and negative climates leads toward greater emphasis on contesting to elicit the negative effects. In very late stages this can lead to actual physical abuse patterns. We shall attempt to elaborate an application to spouse abuse in the last section of this paper.

VII Deterrence of Crimes of Passion

Space does not permit more than a sketch of the rationale of crimes of passion under this approach. A crime of passion is an act of violence which was not intended beforehand, but was generated out of a heightening of emotions in the course of an interpersonal interactive process, and whose consequences are typically (but not always) sorely regretted by the perpetrator. It is an irrational act because of the combination of absence of intent and ex post regret.

Our approach interprets such acts as arising out of the dynamic process of building a cumulative stake by adopting unsuccessful and thereby progressively higher S strategies. Here the failures come not from "games of nature" which had been misperceived, but from poorly predicted interactive responses by one or a few other persons. The others' responses are defensive/hostile, high S responses to our subject's high S behavior toward them. Each such round frustrates ego validation further for all concerned, and the cumulative stake rises, an induced round of higher S and further reciprocal frustration, so the present stakes rise again interactively. This is a vicious cycle of defensive aggressiveness. When the interactive interplay moves rapidly toward very high mutual S strategies, perspective is lost, either symmetrically or asymmetrically, and there often follows a sudden eruption of violence as the final, highest S strategy of all. We have termed this rapid loss of perspectival control "funnel fugue." Its frequent outcome is the kind of violence that we described as a crime of passion.

Since this represents an irrational act, the notion of deterring it is not intuitively plausible. But our present model offers insight into how some form or degree of deterrence might be brought into the situation, although not guaranteed to be successful.

The key lies in preventing the framing of activities into contests, thereby weakening the process by which cumulative stakes are generated over time. The availability of this tack differs for the four kinds of contests. It appears hardest for K_D and K_C, somewhat less difficult for K_R and K_I. The goal is to decrease the subject's ability to structure situations as contests.

1. If <u>generic</u> imitation/competition by many actors exists all the time for a certain activity the subject can simply join in at will to form a demonstration contest. But the stakes here are usually <u>less</u> than for K_R and K_I contests, so a funnel fugue is less likely anyway.

2. If recognized multi-party competition exists independently of the subject, again the subject can simply join in at will: a competition contest. But here too the stakes are usually low.

3. Where the situation in the real world is currently unstructured for contest framing, the subject has to create it: this can be costly, difficult, sometimes even infeasible. So the subject seeks

adventitiously favorable circumstances where structure and audience are easily available. This leads to impulsive opportunism. This is rare, but when relevant it is very hard to deter (little predictability).

4. Where rivals already exist, and aspects of rivalrous situations <u>remain</u> indigenous over time, structure and audience recruitment are easier to organize simultaneously. Deterrence here requires <u>recognition by others</u> of the incipience of contesting. Potential/sometime rivals cannot easily neutralize their rival status—but they <u>can</u> avoid being a participant/audience.

This is crucial. Audience adequacy requires not simply physical presence, but attention to the structuring and understanding it as a contest. Potential "opponents" can help to self-neutralize themselves by degrees of either physical or participatory absence. They must intellectually/emotionally "walk away" from the confrontation. They may evince little interest, understanding, perception of what challenge the subject is mounting. Deterrence here may moderately succeed, but the stakes are high.

5. Highest of all are the stakes in the intimate interdependency situations. The significant other is not necessarily a rival, but the elaborate mutual needs and expectations can make him/her one. Such relationships are inherently ambivalent—both very high positive <u>and</u> negative rewards exist, almost side by side. Indeed, these relationships are the site of the largest percentage of crimes of passion.

The key to deterrence here is very much like that of rivalry relationships, but here the significant other is both more unambiguously the unique target and, because of spatial intimacy, more constantly physically available. Again the crux of deterrence is the other's ability to sense the incipient onset of the subject's framing a new challenge—or repeating an old one. Sensing it, the appropriate deterrence strategy is "participatory absence": low key, low S inattention: "tuning out"—deliberately failing to perceive the subject's attempt to put him/her to a test. While the incidence of crimes of passion in this kind of contest is too dishearteningly high for much optimism about successful deterrence, it may be that a considerably higher incidence would occur if such kinds of deterrence were not sometimes successful.

VIII Application to "Spouse" Abuse
The previous model could not illuminate spouse abuse. This version can.

1. High cumulative stake leads to a higher S orientation. This leads to a shift in the focus of S away from K_D and K_C—safer contests—toward K_R and K_I—more dangerous contests.

2. K_I The subject needs greater gains from the intimate relationship than heretofore. How? By demonstrating how strong the relationship is, how important the subject is to the relationship, how admirable the subject is—if the spouse still grants all the rewards of the relationship while the subject deliberately makes it harder and harder for the spouse normally to do so. So the subject tests, strains, abuses the spouse to elicit these bigger gains—in the form of respect, admiration for being masterly, fear, obedience, even love for being the creator of the spouse's abject obedience. Often those elements appear as a sequence of progressive degradation. But the growing abuse makes these gains less and less probable (under normal expectations of what people like and dislike and will tolerate.) So $\Delta S > 0$ here is a growing abuse, a stretching out of $\overline{\partial R}/\partial S$ but with lower and lower probabilities in that progressively more extreme range of negative treatment.

3. Cumulative Process: Since each new contest is with the same actor(s), both (or all) have the same memories of previous "plays." If a previous play of some high S in fact succeeded, that level of S is perceived as in fact being a new mean (expected) level of success; therefore, even the same S in a new repeat of the contest may have to involve a higher level of abuse in order to

achieve the same sense of exceptional gain (i.e., the previous success showed that the win wasn't really that exceptional). So with repeated expectation contests, the T schedule (the measure of performance level) may be repeatedly redefined conservatively.

Thus, even choosing what is perceived as the same S may in fact lead to progressively more serious abuse. But especially if non-K_I contests are increasing the cumulative stake (accumulated ego validation losses) during the same period faster than these domestic gains can offset them, the subject will raise S domestically, and the resulting rising violence can lead to fatality.

This is a slow-moving cumulation, not like the accelerating "funnel-fugue" interactive process that characterizes the dynamic of crimes of passion. The latter is more rapid and generates genuine regret at the end. Here regret is probably absent; the subject does not "lose control" of himself/herself, but is deliberate.

Deterrence here is like that for crimes of passion: the spouse should move off, disappear. But here this strategy is less safe or successful than with crimes of passion, since here the tormentor is not simply momentarily misguided, but rather has come to depend on habitual abuse of the spouse—is addicted—and will fight to continue the abuse pattern: attempted spouse withdrawal will lead to active hot pursuit.

References

Rothenberg, J. 1992. "Consumption Style as Choice Under Risk: Static Choice, Dynamic Irrationality and Crimes of Passion." In *Decision-Making under Risk and Uncertainty: New Models and Empirical Findings*, edited by John Geweke. Kluwer Academic Publishers, Dordrecht, Netherlands.

3. NON-EXPECTED UTILITY MODELS AND TESTS

Although they consist of both theoretical and empirical contributions, the five papers in this section share a common feature, namely that they all view the theory of individual behavior toward risk from a perspective much broader than the classical expected utility model, which dominated the field for so long. It is fitting that this is the largest section in this volume, for the six Foundations of Utility, Risk and Decision Theory (FUR) conferences have been instrumental in inspiring and disseminating new research in this area, an area that was once considered to be outside the mainstream.

The first paper, by Enrica Carbone and John Hey, addresses the issue of estimating preferences over lotteries. The authors provide an alternative to the standard pairwise ranking approach that has been the main vehicle for much of the original work in testing expected utility theory, such as the classic "Allais Paradox", the "common ratio effect", etc... They do this by eliciting individuals' complete rankings of large numbers of lotteries - in their actual experiments, 44 lotteries per subject! The authors find that approximately half of their subjects seem to conform to the expected utility model, and half depart from it in manner which can be better modeled by one or more of the non-expected utility models they consider. On the other hand, they also find that "error terms" are large, and suggest that such errors be explicitly considered in future estimation and testing.

The second paper, by Mohammed Abdellaoui and Bertrand Munier, provides still another alternative to the standard pairwise ranking approach for estimating and testing expected utility and non-expected utility preferences over lotteries. This paper develops a rigorous experimental method for estimating an individual's indifference curves over alternative lotteries. The method developed, termed the "Closing In Method", is a sequential process which determines several preference-equivalents of each arbitrarily chosen lottery. By obtaining actual equivalent lotteries rather than merely ordinal rankings, the authors are able to trace out the individual's indifference curves over lotteries, thereby allowing experimenters to conduct much more efficient estimation of preferences, and more powerful tests of expected utility versus non-expected utility models of preferences. One particularly interesting feature of the method is that it offers the possibility of an a posteriori check whether the main working hypothesis on which it rests is actually accepted or not by the sample of subjects: Few methodologies, indeed, make such an a posteriori check possible.

The paper by Rakesh Sarin and Peter Wakker offers a simple characterization of "non-additive expected utility," which is an extension of the well-known Quiggin model to situations of subjective uncertainty, in which the individual's beliefs regarding event likelihoods can be represented by a non-additive probability measure. Given that it ties together such seemingly disparate behavior as the Allais Paradox and the Ellsberg Paradox, the simplicity of this characterization is significant indeed.

The final paper in this section, by Maurice Allais, consists of an overview of his contributions to the theory of choice under risk over the last four and a half decades. As such, it provides a wide- ranging overview of his seminal work in this domain, as well as discussions of some recent work by others in the same area. It is especially appropriate that this personal description of his many contributions appear in this volume, as Allais was an instrumental force in the establishment of the FUR Conference series, and continues to make significant contributions to the field.

ESTIMATION OF EXPECTED UTILITY AND NON-EXPECTED UTILITY PREFERENCE FUNCTIONALS USING COMPLETE RANKING DATA[1]

Enrica Carbone and John D. Hey[2]

University of York

1 - INTRODUCTION

In recent years, there have been many empirical investigations into various alternative models of decision making under risk. Most of them have been experimental *tests* of the predictions (or the axioms) of the various theories - experiments testing the empirical validity of the various new theories against each other and against Expected Utility Theory (EU). In contrast, a number of recent experiments have followed the alternative route of *estimating* preference functionals, to discover whether the more general preference functionals explain observed behaviour significantly better than the less general functionals. The experiment discussed in this paper belongs to the second group of experiments and follows two previous experiments (Hey and Di Cagno (1990), Hey and Orme (1992)), which estimated the preference functionals implied by

---

[1]The authors are grateful to Colin Camerer, Mark Machina, Paul Shoemaker, Barry Sopher and other participants at the FUR VI Conference for helpful comments. Our thanks also to the Leverhulme Trust for generously providing the finance to pay the subjects who took part in this experiment.

Department of Economics, University of York, York YO1 5DD, UK.

several competing models. The first of these, Hey and Di Cagno (1990), reported on an experiment in which 68 subjects were asked 60 pairwise preference questions involving random prospects from four Marschak-Machina Triangles (see Machina 1987). The data obtained were used to estimate 3 preference functionals: Expected Utility, Difference Regret and Generalized Regret. The Difference Regret formulation fitted significantly worse than the other two but Generalized Regret did not appear to fit the data significantly better than Expected Utility, at least for the majority of the subjects. Hey and Orme (1992) followed the same line, using experimentally generated data from pairwise preference questions to estimate a number of preference functionals, but using more data and estimating more functionals. That experiment involved 80 subjects, each asked 100 pairwise preference questions, on two separate occasions. The resulting data was used to estimate the functionals implied by Expected Utility (EU), Regret, Weighted Utility, Disappointment Aversion, Prospective Reference Theories as well as two special cases of EU (namely Risk Neutrality and Constant Absolute Risk Aversion) and one special case of Regret (Difference Regret). For one half of the subjects (the apparently non-EU subjects), Regret and Prospective Reference seemed to fit somewhat better than the other theories, though it was clear that there was no overall "winner".

The present paper follows the above line of research but our experiment differs crucially from the earlier ones in that subjects were presented with 44 gambles and were asked to put the 44 gambles in order of preference. So our data is *complete ranking* data rather than *pairwise preference* data. Initially, because we wanted preference functionals with a reasonably small number of parameters, we restricted attention to preference functionals which satisfy betweenness. Such preference functionals have indifference curves in the Marschak-Machina triangle which are straight lines. If they are parallel straight lines, we have the Expected Utility representation. If the straight lines fan-out from a point to the south-west of the origin of the triangle we have Weighted Utility Theory (Chew 1983) with Chew and Wallers (1986)'s "light hypothesis"[3]. If the

---

[3]Weighted Utility theory is also consistent with straight line indifference curves fanning out from a point to the

straight lines fan out from a point to the South-West of the origin in the bottom right of the triangle and fan in from a point to the north-east of the hypoteneuse in the top left of the Triangle, we have Disappointment Aversion Theory (Gul 1991). With Prospective Reference Theory (Viscusi 1989) the straight lines are parallel within the Triangle but are discontinuous at the boundaries[4]. Note that, although Regret Theory (with statistically independent prospects) satisfies betweenness, and hence has linear indifference curves, it is not estimatible with the complete ranking data obtained from this experiment - since it is not a holistic theory, rather a theory of pairwise choice.

We added to this list of estimated preference functionals after discussions with Colin Camerer at the FUR VI conference. Camerer pointed out to us that we might estimate also the Rank Dependent Expected Utility functional if we used a particular weighting function, with just one parameter. So we added that to our list.

In the remainder of this paper we will use the following abbreviations: EU for Expected Utility Theory, WU for Weighted Utility Theory, DA for Disappointment Aversion Theory, PR for Prospective Reference Theory, RD for Rank Dependent Expected Utility (with the specific functional form mentioned later), RN for Risk Neutrality, and CA for (Expected Utility with) Constant Absolute Risk Aversion.

2 - THE EXPERIMENTAL DESIGN

The results reported in this paper are the findings of an experiment conducted with 24 individual subjects. The experiment involved each participant in placing 44 risky prospects in order of preference, from the most preferred through to the least preferred. We ran two separate such experiments: CIRCLE 1 and CIRCLE 2. In CIRCLE 1 all outcomes were one of four amounts: £0, £10, £20 and £30; while in CIRCLE 2 the outcomes were one of four

---

north-east of the the hypoteneuse of the triangle if this "light hypothesis" is not imposed. This "light hypothesis" is equivalent to Machina's Hypothesis II for the Weighted Utility model.

[4]Which strictly means that betweenness is *not* satisfied everywhere. But this theory is parsimonious in parameters - having just one more parameter than EU theory.

amounts: -£25, £5, £35 and £65 (note the minus sign in front of the first of these - this is a *loss* of £25). In both experiments the 44 gambles were placed in four separate piles of 11, each pile of 11 involving at most three outcomes. So the outcomes in the 4 piles were: in CIRCLE 1, £0, £10, £20; £0, £10, £30; £0, £20, £30; and £10, £20, £30; and in CIRCLE 2, -£25, £5, £35; -£25, £5, £65; -£25, £35, £65; and £5, £35, £65.

In order to simplify the participants' task of placing the 44 prospects in order of preference, the participants were advised to work pile by pile and first order the 11 prospects in each pile, from the most preferred through to the least preferred; then the subjects were asked to merge the four piles and rank the prospects all together so as to obtain a complete ordering of all 44 risky prospects.

Each of the 44 risky prospects were represented in the form of circles, with differentiated segments, where the size of each segment represented the probability of having a certain outcome while the colour represented the outcome[5]. Thus, for example, a risky prospect represented by a circle half of which was coloured medium blue, one-quarter of which was coloured white and one-quarter of which was coloured dark blue, represented a risky prospect with a one-half chance of winning £20, a one-quarter chance of winning £0 and a one-quarter chance of winning £30. In CIRCLE 1 we used the colour white to indicate the outcome £0, light blue to indicate £10, medium blue to indicate £20, dark blue to indicate £30; and in CIRCLE 2 we used the colour red to indicate a loss of £25, light blue to indicate £5, medium blue to indicate £35, dark blue to indicate £65. The gambles could be pictured as points in a Marshack-Machina triangle. The points were selected using a random number table in order to avoid systematic bias. We used the same points in CIRCLE 1 and CIRCLE 2. So in the two experiments, we have the same gambles, though denominated in different outcomes.

Perhaps we ought to comment as to why we carried out two separate experiments. Essentially we had a lingering suspicion, from earlier experiments testing EU and its alternatives, that many subjects behaved in non-EU ways

---

[5]The circles were printed on paper, attached on cardboard and cut, so people could easily handle them.

simply because the outcomes were not sufficiently large and there were very rarely real losses. We felt that if we made the outcomes sufficiently large and introduced serious real losses, subjects would have more reason to take the experiment seriously, and hence (we thought) behave in the 'more rational' EU way. Hence the numbers in CIRCLE 2, and indeed the reason for having *both* CIRCLE 1 *and* CIRCLE 2 - to see if our suspicions we correct. (It appears that they were not.) Of course, in order to induce (presumably risk-averse) subjects to participate in the experiment, we had to make CIRCLE 2, on average, more attractive that CIRCLE 1. For this reason, the expected payment from a randomly-chosen one of the 44 gambles was £14.57 on CIRCLE 1 and £18.68 on CIRCLE 2.

The subjects who participated in the experiments were all students at the University of York on **EXEC**'s computerised register[6]; they were recruited by mail-shot. We ran the experiment over a period of two days; the time we allowed for each participants was one hour[7], there were 15 slots available for each of CIRCLE 1 and CIRCLE 2 but only 9 volunteers were forthcoming for CIRCLE 2, despite the higher expected return. Details of the invitation and instruction posted to those who volunteered are given in an Appendix. To provide participants with an incentive to report their true ranking correctly, we employed the following payment mechanism: after the participant had completed the ranking, two of the risky prospects were chosen at random. (The subject drew two cloakroom tickets from a box containing tickets numbered from 1 to 44; behind each circle there was number to identify the circle.) After drawing the two numbers we played out the one of the two that was highest in the participant's ranking. The participant was paid according to the outcome. So the actual outcome depended on the ordering, on which two of the 44 prospects were randomly chosen, and upon the outcome of playing out the preferred prospect of the chosen two. The gamble was played out by

---

[6]**EXEC** is the Centre for Experimental Economics at the University of York. **EXEC** is mainly funded by the Economic and Social Research Council of the UK, though these particular experiments were funded by the Leverhulme Trust.

[7]The participants took on average about half an hour to rank the gambles in CIRCLE 1 and about an hour to rank the gambles in CIRCLE 2.

placing the copy of the chosen circle on top of a spinning device (a continuous roulette wheel) with a freely-spinning pointer, and letting the subject set the pointer spinning.

We should perhaps comment on a criticism voiced by some people to the effect that this mechanism does not provide a very strong incentive for the subject to report his or her true ranking, since the probability of any one gamble being drawn is so small (at 2/44) that the subject might just as well place the gambles in a random order. (Indeed, in pre-tests, one subject did just this: place the disks on the desk in front of her, and shuffle them around before picking them up in a random order.) To investigate the validity of this criticism we compared the expected payment that would have been obtained by a Risk Neutral Expected Utility maximiser using such a random ranking method with that which would have been obtained using the correct ranking. Using the random "ranking" the expected payment is £14.57 in CIRCLE 1 and £18.68 in CIRCLE 2; in contrast, using the Risk Neutral ordering the expected payment is £17.95 for CIRCLE 1 and £28.95 for CIRCLE 2. So the incentive is rather small for CIRCLE 1 (£3.38) but rather large for CIRCLE 2 (£10.27) - but each larger than the subjects' shadow wage rate over half-an-hour and one hour respectively.

Alternative payment mechanisms are, of course, possible. For example, we could put 44 copies of the highest-ranked disk into an urn, 43 copies of the second-highest-ranked disk into the urn, . . . , and just 1 copy of the lowest-ranked disk into the urn, letting the subject draw just one disk at random and playing it out. This has practical difficulties however[8]. Nevertheless, we agree that our mechanism may not be the best, and invite suggestions for (practical) alternatives[9].

3 - THE PREFERENCE FUNCTIONALS ESTIMATED

---

[8]Which could be overcome by using a computer to make the draw - but this might be mistrusted by subjects.

[9]In addition, of course, we are implicitly invoking the independence axiom at the randomisation stage (see, amongst others, Holt (1986) and Karni and Safra (1987)). That this may not be unreasonable in practice is suggested by Starmer and Sugden (1991).

First, some notation. Let $\mathbf{x} = (x_1, x_2, x_3, x_4)$ denote the four outcomes used in the experiment; let $\mathbf{r} = (r_1, r_2, r_3, r_4)$ denote the respective probabilities in a gamble. Let $V(\mathbf{r})$ denote the preference functional.

Subjective Expected Utility Theory
$$V(\mathbf{r}) = r_2 u(x_2) + r_3 u(x_3) + r_4 u(x_4)$$
Note that we have normalised[10] so that $u(x_1) = 0$; some such normalisation is needed for all preference functionals. For Expected Utility theory, as is well known, the utility function is unique only up to a linear transformation, which usually means that one can set *two* utility values arbitrarily. However the second normalisation is taken care of by our assumption concerning the nature of the error term (see later).

Prospective Reference Theory
$$V(\mathbf{r}) = \lambda[r_2 u(x_2) + r_3 u(x_3) + r_4 u(x_4)] + (1-\lambda)[c_2 u(x_2) + c_3 u(x_3) + c_4 u(x_4)]$$
where $c_i = 1/n(\mathbf{r})$ if $r_i > 0$ and 0 otherwise, and where $n(\mathbf{r})$ is the number of non-zero elements in the vector $\mathbf{r}$. (Prospective Reference's preference functional could be thought as a weighted average of the Expected Utility functional using the correct probability weights and the Expected Utility functional using equal probability weights for the non-null outcomes.) Here the normalisation is the same as the Expected Utility normalisation: $u(x_1) = 0$.

Viscusi (1989) refers to λ as the weight of the "relative information content ... associated with the stated lottery" and $(1-\lambda)$ as the weight of the "relative information content ... associated with the reference probability". Note that if $\lambda = 1$ then Prospective Reference Theory reduces to Expected Utility Theory.

Disappointment Aversion Theory

---

[10] An alternative interpretation, of course, is that $u(x_i)$ measures the difference between the utility of x_i and the utility of x_1. The difference is inessential.

Here our characterization appears different from that in Gul (1991), but it can be shown that they are identical; ours is more useful for our purposes.

$V(\mathbf{r}) = \min\{V_1, V_2, V_3\}$ where

$V_1 = [(1+\beta)r_2 u(x_2) + (1+\beta)r_3 u(x_3) + r_4 u(x_4)]/(1+\beta r_1 + \beta r_2 + \beta r_3)$
$V_2 = [(1+\beta)r_2 u(x_2) + r_3 u(x_3) + r_4 u(x_4)]/(1+\beta r_1 + \beta r_2)$
$V_3 = [r_2 u(x_2) + r_3 u(x_3) + r_4 u(x_4)]/(1+\beta r_1)$.

Again, we have normalised so that $u(x_1) = 0$. The parameter β is Gul's additional parameter; if $\beta = 0$, Disappointment Aversion Theory reduces to Expected Utility Theory.

Constant Absolute Risk Aversion
This is a special case of Expected Utility Theory with:
$u(x) = \gamma[1-\exp(-xR)]/[1-\exp(-x_4 R)]$, for all x

Note that $u(x_1)$ again is normalised to zero, and that γ is to be interpreted as the value of $u(x_4)$. We should emphasize that this particular parameterisation was chosen for computational reasons. The parameter R is the Arrow-Pratt index of absolute risk aversion. Note that Constant Absolute Risk Aversion reduces to Risk Neutrality if this parameter takes the value zero.

Risk Neutrality
This also is a special case of Expected Utility Theory, here with the restriction that:
$u(x) = x$, for all x.

Weighted Utility Theory
$V(\mathbf{r}) = [w_2 r_2 u(x_2) + w_3 r_3 u(x_3) + r_4 u(x_4)]/[r_1 + r_2 w_2 + r_3 w_3 + r_4]$.

Here w_2 and w_3 are the *weights* attached to x_2 and x_3. Once again, the normalisation is that $u(x_1)$ is put equal to zero; in addition, we set the weights attached to x_1 and x_4 equal to unity. Note that Weighted Utility Theory reduces to Expected Utility Theory if w_2 and w_3 are additionally both equal to unity.

Rank Dependent Expected Utility Theory (with specific weighting function)
$V(r) = u(x_2)[\pi(r_2+r_3+r_4)-\pi(r_3+r_4)] + u(x_3)[\pi(r_3+r_4)-\pi(r_4)]$

$$+ u(x_4)\pi(r_4)$$

where the weighting function π takes the specific form as follows:

$$\pi(r) = r^\gamma/[r^\gamma + (1-r)^\gamma]^{(1/\gamma)}$$

In RDEU the decision weight $\pi(r)$ is a non-linear function of probability, the weighting function[11] in the special case we consider has the particular shape illustrated in Figure 3. If $\gamma=1$ $\pi(r_i)=r$ then this preference functional reduces to EU. The normalisation again is that $u(x_1)$ is put equal to zero.

4 - THE ESTIMATION PROCEDURE

We used an Ordered Logit specification on the ranked data obtained from the experiment. This model was used by Beggs, Cardell and Hausman (1981) for analyzing survey data on potential consumer demand for electric cars. The probability model specification on ranked data yields the probability of the complete ordering rather than only the most preferred element among two or more elements. The basic specification we are using is the random utility model:

$$Y_i = V(\mathbf{r}_i, \mathbf{u}) + \varepsilon_i = V_i + \varepsilon_i \quad (i = 1, 2, \ldots, n)$$

where the $\mathbf{r}_i$ (the vector of probabilities for gamble i) are known and $\mathbf{u}$ (the vector of parameters for the functional in question) have to be estimated. V is the deterministic component of the model, while the stochastic component ε_i is assumed to follow an Extreme Value Distribution with unit variance[12] in which case :

$$\Pr(\varepsilon \leq t) = \exp\{-[\exp(-t)]\}$$

---

[11]This special case of RDEU was suggested to us by Colin Camerer at FUR VI; as Colin Camerer notes this is the weighting function used by Daniel Kahneman and Amos Tversky in "Advances in Prospect Theory: Cumulative Representation of Uncertainty".

[12]This is the second normalisation.

(which is the basis of the logit specification). The ε are assumed to be independently and identically distributed extreme value random variates. This assumption implies that the *relative* position of two lotteries in the ranking is independent of which other lotteries are to be ranked. Note further that one very attractive property of the extreme value distribution is that the expression $P(Y_1 > Y_2 > ..... > Y_n)$ can be explicitly stated whereas with the normal distribution (which was assumed by Hey and Di Cagno (1990) and Hey and Orme (1992)) the evaluation of this expression requires numerical approximation of an (n-1)-fold integral.

Then, for an observed ordinal ranking of the choices put in descending order, the probability of the subject's observed ranking is:

$$P(Y_1 > Y_2 > ..... > Y_n) = \prod_{i=1}^{n-1} \left[\frac{\exp[V(\mathbf{r}_i, \mathbf{u})]}{\sum_{j=i}^{n} \exp[V(\mathbf{r}_j, \mathbf{u})]} \right]$$

$$= \prod_{i=1}^{n} \left[\frac{\exp[V(\mathbf{r}_i, \mathbf{u})]}{\sum_{j=i}^{n} \exp[V(\mathbf{r}_j, \mathbf{u})]} \right]$$

Hence the log-likelihood function L(**u**) is given by

$$L(\mathbf{u}) = \sum_{i=1}^{n} V_i - \sum_{i=1}^{n} \log \left[\sum_{j=i}^{n} \exp(V_j) \right]$$

where $V_i = V(\mathbf{r}_i, \mathbf{u})$.

5 - ESTIMATION RESULTS

We estimated the 7 preference functionals described in section 3 for each of the 15 subjects in CIRCLE 1 and each of the 9 subjects in CIRCLE 2. Table 1 lists the maximised log-likelihoods for the fitted preference functionals for each model and each subject. The maximum likelihood routine[13] failed to converge in just 3 cases: WU for subject 9 on CIRCLE 1; WU for subject 6 on CIRCLE 2; and RD for subject 6 on CIRCLE 2. There are a number of reasons

---

[13] The programs were written and executed in GAUSS.

why that might be so, as the likelihoods are not always well-behaved. The DA model is of particular interest in this respect since the likelihood function is not necessarily always globally concave nor continuously differentiable; in some cases the likelihood function has a cusp at a β value of zero (the EU special case), in which case either the Maximum Likelihood occurs at β=0 or there are two local maxima either side of β which have to be checked numerically. The latter happens, for example, for subject 6 in CIRCLE 1. Additionally, and specifically in the three cases noted above, there are occasionally identification problems - perhaps not surprising in view of the nature of the data.

In order to make sense of Table 1 and subsequent analyses, we must make clear the nested structure of the various models; this is illustrated graphically in Figure 1. So, for example, 2 parameter restrictions take us from WU down to EU, a further restriction gives us CA and one more restriction take us down to RN. Of course this is all specific to our particular experimental setup, and in particular, to the fact that our experiment involved just 4 final outcomes. More generally, PR, DA and RD each have always just one parameter more then EU, while CA always has just one more parameter than RN; WU, in contrast, has (n-2) more parameters than EU (where n is the number of final outcomes), while EU has (n-3) more parameters than CA.

We can make use of this nested structure to test whether the more general models fit better than the less general models. So for example, since going from WU to EU requires two parameter restrictions, we can test the null hypothesis that the restricted model (less general) is accepted, and hence that the added parameters are not significant, using the usual likelihood ratio test. More specifically, if LL_a and LL_b are the estimated log-likelihoods for models a and b respectively, and if model a is obtained from model b by imposing k parameter restrictions, then under the null hypothesis that these restrictions are satisfied, the test statistic $2(LL_b - LL_a)$ has a chi-squared distribution with k degrees of freedom. As is conventional we have applied this test looking for significance at both 5% and 1%. Table 2 gives the results obtained.

Perhaps it would be helpful to comment on some of these. For example, for subject 1 in CIRCLE 1 the Expected Utility model (restricted model) is accepted against all the 'top-level' models. For the same subject, when we test EU against the special case of Constant Absolute Risk Aversion the latter (that is now is the restricted model) is accepted; while when we test CA against Risk Neutrality, this latter (which is now the restricted model) is rejected. So one might conclude for this subject that CA is, in some sense, the best. For subject 2 in CIRCLE 1 the restricted model is always rejected at 1%, so EU fits the data worse than all the 4 top level preference functionals (even though it fits better than CA and RN) but we have no information at this stage which one of the top-level functionals fits the data the best.

This problem arises since the four top level functionals are not nested within each other, and so it is not obvious how one should determine which is the best of any of the four which are significantly better than EU. There are non-nested tests available, but most are difficult to apply in this context, so we adopted a relatively crude approach, the starting point of which was the observation that if Model a was nested inside Model b by imposing k parameter restrictions, then the statistic $2(LL_b - LL_a)$ would (asymptotically) have a chi-square distribution with k degrees of freedom. Now suppose Models a and b are not nested within each other, but that Model b has k more parameters in its specification than Model a. One could argue that $2(LL_b - LL_a)$ would be *approximately* chi-squared with k degrees of freedom, and hence that the expected value of $2(LL_b - LL_a)$ would be approximately k. This line of argument suggests that one could correct the log-likelihood of Model b by subtracting $k/2$ from it to make it comparable with Model a. Or, more generally, one could construct a "corrected" log-likelihood of a model with m parameters by subtracting $m/2$ from the maximised log-likelihood. Applying this procedure across the board to all our seven models provides a way of correcting the log-likelihood to make them comparable. This give us a way of ranking the 7 functionals for each subject. Table 4 gives the details of the rankings which emerge from this exercise.

As we noted above, for subject 2 EU is rejected against all the more general models. If we look at the Corrected log-likelihood index, we see that the RD preference function ranks higher than the other models. For subjects 3 and 4 as well, EU is rejected and RD ranks highest on the corrected log-likelihood index. For subject

5 (like subject 1) EU is accepted against all the top level functionals at the 5% level. When we test EU against CA the latter is accepted while RN is rejected; so one could conclude that in this case CA fits the data no worse than the other preference functionals. For subject 6 again, the model that fits the data no worse than the others is EU. Subjects 7 and 8 are again two cases in which RD fits the data better than the other models. The case of subject 9 is a very peculiar case; first of all because the GAUSS routine does not converge for WU; second because EU is accepted only against PR, while being rejected against DA and RD; and third, because DA comes first in the corrected log-likelihood ranking; this is the only case in CIRCLE 1 where DA emerges as the 'best' model. Subject 10 is also a rather peculiar case because EU is always rejected against the more general models while PR is the best in the ranking of the corrected log-likelihoods; this is the only case where PR emerges as the 'best' model. For subject 11 the results are the same as for subjects 2 and 4. Subject 12 is the only case in CIRCLE 1 where RN fits the data no worse than the other models. Subjects 13, 14 and 15 are three cases in which EU fits the data no worse than the other models.

Now we turn to the results of CIRCLE 2. For subject 1, EU is rejected against all the more general models while RD emerges as the 'best' from the corrected log-likelihood ranking. For subject 2, PR is the best in the corrected log-likelihood ranking. Subjects 3 and 4 are similar to subject 1. For subjects 5 and 6, EU fits the data no worse than the other models (but note that in the case of subject 6 the Gauss routine does not converge for WU and RD). Subject 7 is similar to subjects 1 and 5 in CIRCLE 1. For Subject 8 EU is accepted against PR and WU at 5% and is accepted only at 1% against DA and RD. Subject 9 is very similar to subject 12 in CIRCLE 1: in this case RN is accepted against all other models. Finally, we note that our supposition that there would be more EU (and hence CA and RN) behaviour in CIRCLE 2 than in CIRCLE 1 does *not* appear to be borne out by our results.

In Table 5 we report for each subject the 'best' model and the coefficients for that 'best' model. For the purposes of this Table we define the 'best' model as the restricted one when it is accepted, or the first in the corrected log-likelihood ranking if EU is rejected in favour of at least one of the top level functionals. This Table provides a summary of the results discussed above.

TABLE 1: Log-likelihoods

Su	EU	CA	RN	DA	PR	WU	RD
CIRCLE 1							
1	-41.93	-42.57	-96.73	-41.93	-42.83	-40.61	-40.38
2	-34.68	-40.40	-102.8	-30.91	-30.76	-28.53	-23.82
3	-45.48	-53.45	-101.9	-44.28	-44.82	-43.22	-39.87
4	-59.30	-62.55	-97.57	-50.91	-53.82	-46.38	-42.45
5	-24.24	-24.25	-28.72	-24.24	-23.96	-22.22	-23.57
6	-6.34	-24.57	-103.9	-98.08	-6.32	-5.18	-6.06
7	-50.80	-52.06	-94.63	-50.80	-46.86	-46.62	-45.46
8	-52.22	-58.92	-93.33	-52.2	-51.86	-48.43	-47.80
9	-9.70	-18.51	-104.1	-1.47	-9.44		-4.80
10	-59.38	-60.88	-102.9	-56.00	-48.23	-53.49	-48.48
11	-59.01	-62.18	-97.99	-50.15	-50.00	-43.78	-38.23
12	-52.80	-52.86	-54.16	-52.80	-52.40	-51.19	-51.70
13	-52.06	-65.16	-95.74	-52.01	-50.59	-50.91	-49.08
14	-41.33	-43.39	-103.3	-41.31	-39.08	-41.03	-39.80
15	-59.27	-73.50	-86.37	-59.27	-59.08	-57.24	-59.00
CIRCLE 2							
1	-68.07	-69.72	-100.0	-61.63	-59.99	-58.00	-50.49
2	-41.57	-47.10	-100.8	-41.57	-32.01	-38.30	-32.89
3	-50.95	-56.29	-101.7	-50.92	-47.43	-49.50	-45.00
4	-39.00	-44.33	-101.9	-38.95	-33.82	-34.66	-30.54
5	-65.45	-72.92	-79.32	-65.45	-64.97	-64.70	-65.30
6	-12.01	-41.15	-104.1	-12.01	-10.52		
7	-33.71	-33.80	-45.08	-32.98	-32.59	-31.85	-32.61
8	-49.94	-52.05	-104.7	-47.50	-49.91	-49.38	-47.32
9	-44.52	-44.71	-45.32	-44.52	-44.04	-43.12	-44.23

TABLE 2: Result of Likelihood ratio test

Subject	PRv EU	DAv EU	WUv EU	RDv EU	EUv CA	CAv RN
CIRCLE 1						
1	a	a	a	a	a	r
2	r	r	r	r	r	r
3	a	a	a	r	r	r
4	r	r	r	r	*	r
5	a	a	a	a	a	r
6	a	a	a	a	r	r
7	r	a	*	r	a	r
8	a	a	*	r	r	r
9	a	r		r	r	r
10	r	r	r	r	a	r
11	r	r	r	r	*	r
12	a	a	a	a	a	a
13	a	a	a	*	r	r
14	*	a	a	a	*	r
15	a	a	a	a	r	r
CIRCLE 2						
1	r	r	r	r	a	r
2	r	a	*	r	r	r
3	r	a	a	r	r	r
4	r	a	*	r	r	r
5	a	a	a	a	r	r
6	a	a			r	r
7	a	a	a	a	a	r
8	a	*	a	*	*	r
9	a	a	a	a	a	a

KEY: a - accepted at the 5% level
 r - rejected at the 1% level
 * - rejected at the 5% but accepted at the 1% level

TABLE 3: Summary of likelihood ratio tests

PRv EU	DAv EU	WUv EU	RDv EU	EU CA	CAv RN
CIRCLE 1					
9a	10a	8a	6a	5a	1a
5r	5r	4r	8r	7r	14r
1*		2*	1*	3*	
CIRCLE 2					
5a	7a	5a	3a	3a	1a
4r	1r	1r	4r	5r	8r
	1*	2*	1*	1*	

KEY: a - accepted at the 5% level
 r - rejected at the 1% level
 * - rejected at the 5% but accepted at the 1% level

TABLE 4: Ranks based on corrected log-likelihood

Subjects	EU	CA	RN	DA	PR	WU	CC
			CIRCLE 1				
1	4	2	7	5	6	3	1
2	5	6	7	4	3	2	1
3	5	6	7	3	4	2	1
4	5	5	6	3	4	2	1
5	3	2	7	6	4	1	5
6	2	5	7	6	3	1	4
7	4	5	7	6	2	3	1
8	3	6	7	5	4	2	1
9	3	5	6	1	4		2
10	5	6	7	4	1	3	2
11	5	6	7	4	3	2	1
12	4	1	7	6	5	2	3
13	4	6	7	5	2	3	1
14	3	6	7	4	1	5	2
15	2	6	7	4	3	1	5
			CIRCLE 2				
1	5	6	7	4	3	2	1
2	4	6	7	5	1	3	2
3	4	6	7	5	2	3	1
4	4	6	7	5	2	3	1
5	1	6	7	4	2	3	5
6	2	4	5	3	1		
7	6	1	7	4	3	2	5
8	3	6	7	1	5	4	2
9	3	1	5	6	4	2	7

TABLE 5: summary of the "winning" models and coefficients

Su	Model	Estimated utility coeffs			Other coeffs
		CIRCLE 1			
1	CA		54.95	0.3186	
2	RD	87.34	104.57	113.72	0.7554
3	RD	47.23	54.22	60.6	0.7713
4	RD	36.41	47.0	54.98	0.6538
5	CA		117.83	0.9363	
6	EU	411.02	443.01	463.03	
7	RD	33.45	46.35	49.78	
8	RD	30.70	36.70	44.21	1.6882
9	DA	474.05	599.22	685.82	3.1936
10	PR	36.9	44.02	47.8	0.7407
11	RD	41.56	53.81	63.1	0.6481
12	RN			0.1672	
13	EU	29.	33.62	41.0	
14	EU	57.25	65.30	68.93	
15	EU	19.84	24.62	32.70	
		CIRCLE 2			
1	RD	27.80	37.43	43.65	0.5643
2	PR	69.55	77.2	84.51	1.1846
3	RD	37.07	43.79	49.97	0.7419
4	RD	64.19	78.6	86.88	0.7952
5	EU	13.57	19.19	27.21	
6	EU	315.36	324.39	351.49	
7	CA		40.71	0.4054	
8	EU	42.62	46.41	48.82	
9	RN			0.4394	

Figure 1: The Nested structure of the various functionals

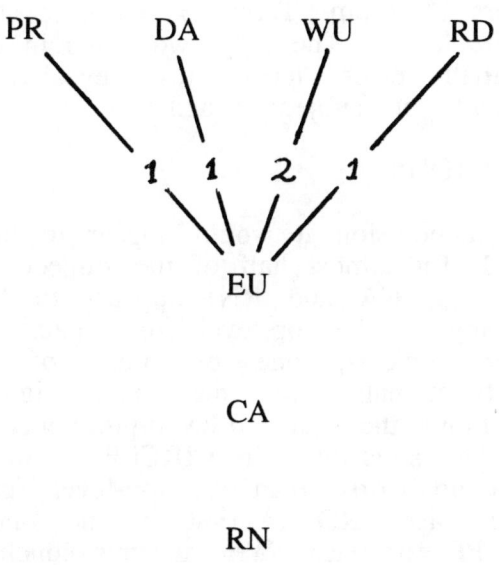

Key: XX ─────────── k ─────────→ YY

k indicates the number of parameter restrictions that reduce Model XX to model YY.

EU: Expected Utility
PR: Prospective reference
DA: Disappointment Aversion
WU: Weighted Utility
RD: Rank Dependent Expected Utility
CA: Constant Absolute Risk Aversion
RN: Risk Neutrality

Given that one of the two normalisations was achieved by setting the variance of the error term equal to unity, it follows that larger coefficients imply relatively smaller errors. From Table 5 we see that errors are generally quite large. The only two cases in CIRCLE 1 with relatively small error terms (as revealed by relatively large coefficients) are subjects 6 and 9.

7 - CONCLUSIONS

In conclusion it would appear to be the case that in CIRCLE 1, for almost half of the subjects EU (or one of its special cases, CA and RN) appears to fit the data no worse than any of the top-level functionals. For the other half of the subjects, one or more of the top level preference functionals fits the data significantly better than EU. Among the four top-level preference functionals RD emerges as the favourite. In CIRCLE 2, in five cases EU fits the data no worse than the top-level functionals, while in the other cases RD is first in the ranking for three subjects and PR for one. We can thus conclude, in spite of what we thought, that there appears to be no difference between the results of CIRCLE 1 and those of CIRCLE 2; in fact, both in CIRCLE 1 and 2, for about one half of the subjects EU appears to fit the data no worse than the other models while for the other half RD seems to fit better; just twice is PR and once DA the "winning" model.

It is important to notice that, for the more general models (with more parameters) on one hand there is an advantage in term of goodness of fit while on the other hand there is a disadvantage in term of loss of degrees of freedom. In other words the more we can explain by using a more general model the less we can predict.

Finally, we should emphasize the importance of the error term: as is clear from our results there is almost always a big error term. So: *either* none of the models considered in this paper are correct; *or* the subjects in this experiment reported their rankings with some (sizeable) error. This latter interpretation is consistent with previous experimental evidence and indeed is implicit in much modern theorising. It remains to explore the implications of this for the statistical properties of the test procedures reported elsewhere in the literature and for the estimation procedures used here and in previous literature. Given the findings of this experiment it is difficult to resist the conclusion that much of apparently non-EU behaviour is simply the result of decision making with error.

REFERENCES

Beggs S., Cardell S. and Hausman J. (1981), "Assessing the Potential Demand for Electric Cars", *Journal of Econometrics*, 16, 1-19.

Chew S.H. (1983), "A Generalization of the Quasilinear Mean with Applications to the Measurement of Income Inequality and Decision Theory Resolving the Allais Paradox", *Econometrica*, 51, 1065-1092.

Chew S.H. and Waller W.S. (1986), "Empirical Tests of Weighted Utility Theory", *Journal of Mathematical Psychology*, 30, 55-72.

Gul F. (1991), "A Theory of Disappointment Aversion", *Econometrica*, 59, 667-686.

Hey J.D. and Di Cagno D. (1990), "Circles and Triangles: An Experimental Estimation of Indifference Lines in the Marschak-Machina Triangle", *Journal of Behavioral Decision Making*, 3, 279-306.

Hey J.D. and Orme C.D. (1992), "Circles, Triangles and Straight Lines: Estimation of Betweenness-Satisfying Non-Expected-Utility Preference Functionals Using Experimental Data", **EXEC** Discussion Paper.

Holt C. A. (1986), "Preference Reversals and the Independence Axiom", *American Economic Review*, 76, 508-515.

Karni E. and Safra Z. (1987), "Preference Reversal and the Observability of Preferences by Experimental Methodes", *Econometrica*, 47, 263-291.

Machina M.J. (1987), "Choice Under Uncertainty: Problems Solved and Unsolved", *Journal of Economic Perspectives*, 1, 121-154.

Starmer C. and Sugden R. (1991), "Does the Random-Lottery Incentive System Elicit True Preferences? An Experimental Investigation", *American Economic Review*, 81, 971-978.

Viscusi W.K. (1989), "Prospective Reference Theory: Towards an Explanation of the Paradoxes", *Journal of Risk and Uncertainty*, 2, 235-264.

THE "CLOSING IN" METHOD :
AN EXPERIMENTAL TOOL TO INVESTIGATE
INDIVIDUAL CHOICE PATTERNS UNDER RISK

Mohammed Abdellaoui[*]
Bertrand Munier[**]

1. Introductory background

In view of the considerable evidence of systematic violations of expected utility by individual subjects, a number of alternative models generalizing expected utility have been developed. As P.Fishburn put it once [1988], we have entered "a new era" in the domain of decision under risk, but "we shall have to wait and see" during the "time of shakedown and sifting" ahead of us, i.e. until one or possibly several of the models put forward until now can attract a clear consensus. Most of these models weaken the independence axiom. But some of them retain some linearity properties, like Chew's *weighted utility theory* [1983] or Fishburn's *skew-symmetric bilinear utility theory* [1988]. Machina provided a quite general frame of reference, by dispensing altogether with the independence axiom and allowing one to envision different alternative hypotheses - among which his Hypothesis II [1982] is only one possibility. Other models emphasize the idea that decumulative probability distributions straightforwardly undergo a (necessarily non-linear) cognitive transformation, like Quiggin [1982], Yaari [1987], Allais [1988], Segal [1989], Wakker [1993].

[1*] CNRS Researcher at GRID, Ecole Normale Supérieure de Cachan
[**]Director of GRID, Professor at the Ecole Normale Supérieure de Cachan
The authors want to express their gratitude to D. Bouyssou, Ph. Delquié, J-Y. Jaffray, M. Machina, whose comments were very stimulating, as well as to several colleagues who attended the FUR VI conference. The usual caveat holds.

One question to ask, indeed, relates to which of these suggested models will emerge as most saliently describing individual behavior under risk. This question certainly does not encompass all remaining problems on the subject, but it is a most important one, pertaining to the validation of descriptive models of decision-making [Bell, Raiffa and Tversky, 1988] and, to the extent that prescriptive models need to be non-contradictory with descriptive ones, pertaining also to the validation of such prescriptive models.

In order to answer such a question, one can remark that all of these models do not select the same lotteries from adequately chosen pairs of lotteries : experimental tests as to how individuals choose among some of these given pairs of lotteries represent then one way [Munier, 1992] to deal with the question. Authors like Camerer [1989] or Harless [1992] as well as Hey and Orme [1992] have gone this way by using discrete lotteries entailing three possible payoffs. Such lotteries, as is well known, can be suitably represented in the Marschak-Machina triangle. Therefore, using the Marschak-Machina triangle as a frame of representation has recently been adopted by experimental investigations of individual preferences under risk. Several authors have tried to *rank* by a *single* index so-called "generalized expected utility models" by experimentally collecting and interpreting individual choices among *fixed* lotteries with particular locations within the triangle.

Another possible solution, which we would like to argue for in this paper, would consist in examining the shape of the indifference fields exhibited by subjects in experimental investigations. These fields should statistically exhibit properties which could make them consistent or not with such or such model. Indeed, every model suggested generates a specifically shaped indifference curve map, as will be recalled below.

In this perspective, we have designed a method of *direct and systematic* estimation of the indifference curves of subjects by experimental investigation, a method which we call the "Closing In" method. The idea is to systematically explore, starting out from several well-chosen points within the triangle, the shape of indifference curves in different "zones" of the triangle and to thus imply possibly complex indifference fields. This idea can be exploited in an experimental framework by using as well our interactive software "Maclabex", developed on microcomputers.

Section 2 contrasts in more details the two types of methods which can be used in this area of research : the fixed lotteries-single indexing method and the "Closing In" method. Section 3 is devoted to a detailed exposition of the procedure at the heart of the "Closing In" method as well as to the precautions to be taken in experimenting with this method, while Section 4 contains concluding remarks.

2. On two contrasted uses of the M-M Triangle

A field of possible choices under risk entailing fixed consequences x_1, x_2, x_3, with $x_1 < x_2 < x_3$, can be represented with the help of a Marschak-Machina triangle. All probability distributions on this support can be plotted like L (fig. 1) within the triangle, where p_3 is on the vertical axis, p_1 on the horizontal axis, p_2 being then measured as the horizontal segment between L and the hypotenuse.

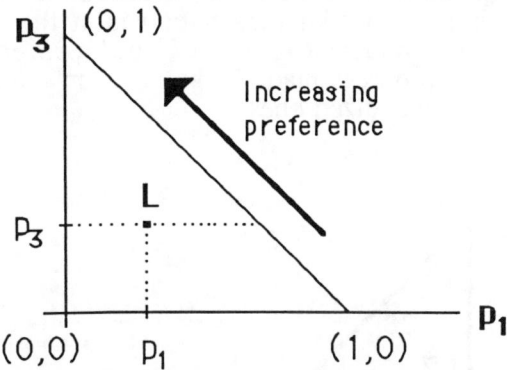

fig. 1. Marschak-Machina triangle. L figures the lottery L with probabilities p_1 on x_1, p_2 on x_2 and p_3 on x_3, with $x_1 < x_2 < x_3$, all fixed.

In the perspective of the first method mentioned above, it is interesting to visualize (fig. 2) the type of lotteries used by Harless [1992] in his experiments. Quite clearly, for example, the expected utility model allows for only two choice patterns to be consistent:

$C_1 \lesssim C_3 \lesssim C_5 \lesssim C_7$
or
$C_2 \lesssim C_4 \lesssim C_6 \lesssim C_8$

as the segments C_1C_2, C_3C_4, C_5C_6 and C_7C_8 are parallel. Other models would allow for less restrictive choice patterns. The idea of this first experimental perspective boils down to counting the percentage of choice patterns experimentally observed which can be regarded as consistent under the hypothesis that one given decision model underlies the expressed choices. Quite clearly, nothing can be said on the "true" shape of the individual indifference curves of the subjects investigated.

Harless and Camerer [1992] suggest several ways of designing an index of descriptive performance of the different models, based on matching the choice patterns allowed by each model and the experimentally observed patterns. An index of performance of the respective models is something which can indeed be devised and the new "generalized expected utility" models can thus be evaluated by a *single* index with respect to the expected utility model as well as with respect to each other. Consequently, some "hierarchy" between these models can be suggested. But this advantage of the method is at the same time what might make researchers reluctant to use it : does a *single* index fill our needs to evaluate the progress made in going from the expected utility models to any of the generalized ones ?

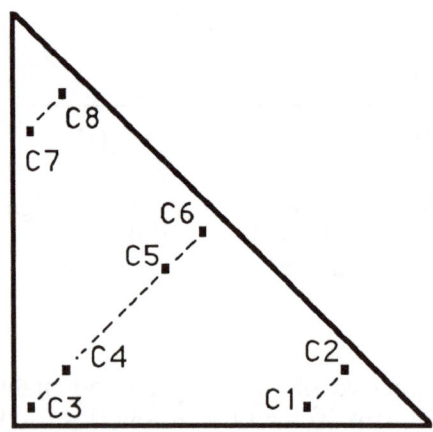

fig. 2. Fixed lotteries used by Harless[1992] to investigate patterns of preferences across subjects.

In risk theory, we all have learned that a single dimensional measure of risk is questionable [Rothschild and Stiglitz, 1971]. Could a single dimensional measure of the performance of these models be satisfactory ?

Hey and Orme [1992] used the choices made by their subjects among *given* lotteries to *econometrically estimate* the preference functionals associated with several models (assuming straight lines indifference loci) and then compare the respective degrees of statistical adjustment obtained. The econometric technique used generates the *single* index of performance thus implicitly advocated (whereas Harless and Camerer suggested to construct it in several heuristic ways). One can hope that the relative "poverty" of information collected on individual indifference loci can be partly compensated by some statistical sophisticated treatment. But it will only be partly compensated, for the basic hypothesis is the "betweenness" one (which implies straight lines indifference loci) and, unless this hypothesis is very cautiously tested (which would require our methodology or some equivalent one), one cannot be sure that the straight lines adjusted across points figuring fixed lotteries in the Marschak-Machina triangle are in effect indifference loci. The price paid to reach the convenience of a *single* index of descriptive performance of the different models seems to us to be again too high.

In contrast to these "fixed lotteries-single indexing uses" of the experimental method, the basic idea which we want to emphasize here emerges from another possibility opened to us by the Marschak-Machina triangle. This representation frame brings it indeed within our reach to visualize the "theoretical" indifference field associated with a given preference functional. In turn, this specific preference functional results from a given model of decision under risk, the expected utility model or one among the "generalized expected utility" models. The former, for example, implies that indifference curves are parallel straight lines, as is well-known, whereas weakening the independence axiom like in most of the last ones, leads to at least non parallel straight lines and possibly to more general indifference loci. Typical examples are given on figure 3.

Figure 3(a) illustrates an indifference field presenting a "fanning out" configuration compatible with Chew's "weighted utility theory" [1983]. Figure 2(b) shows an indifference field compatible with Gul's "theory of disappointment aversion" [1991]. In the latter case, the indifference lines are said to be "fanning in" in the above area within the triangle and "fanning out" in the bottom area of the triangle.

Other non-EU models discard any "straight lines shapes" of the indifference curves. Figure 2(c) shows, for example, an indifference field compatible with Kahneman and Tversky's "Prospect Theory" [1979]. Finally, figure 2(d) illustrates an indifference map which would be consistent with a preference functional of the Quiggin-Allais type, assuming monotonic convexity of the probability transformation function.

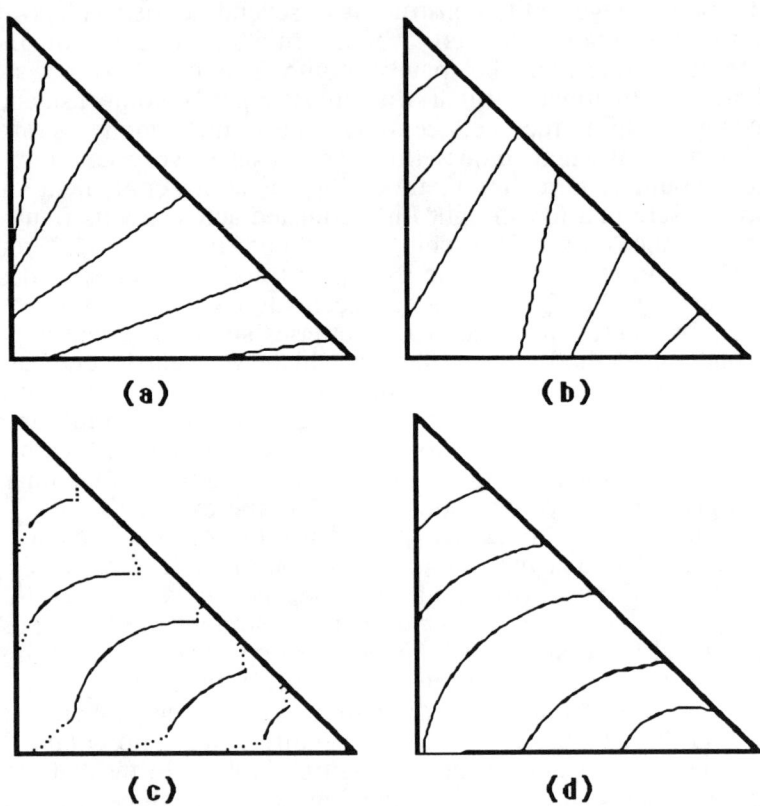

fig. 3. Some typical indifference fields :
  (a) "Weighted expected utility theory"
  (b) "Disappointment aversion theory"
  (c) "Prospect theory"
  (d) "Anticipated utility" under monotonically convex probability transformation functions

3. The "Closing In" method : Foundations and Operation

3.1. Basic Principle

Let us start from a discretionarily chosen lottery L within the Marschak-Machina triangle (fig.4). To a decision maker with preferences following the principle of first order stochastic dominance, it is always possible to find a lottery equivalent to L on the segment L'L" and another one on the segment MM' (fig. 4). It follows from the construction of the triangle that any point to the Northwest of any given point within the triangle represents a first order stochastically dominating distribution. Thus, L' (F.S.D.) L in the same way as L (F.S.D.) L" and, similarly, M (F.S.D.) L as well as L (F.S.D.) M', where (F.S.D.) denotes the corresponding binary relation, entailing strict preference. This is tantamount to say that the indifference curve at L necessarily cuts these two segments at some point in each case.

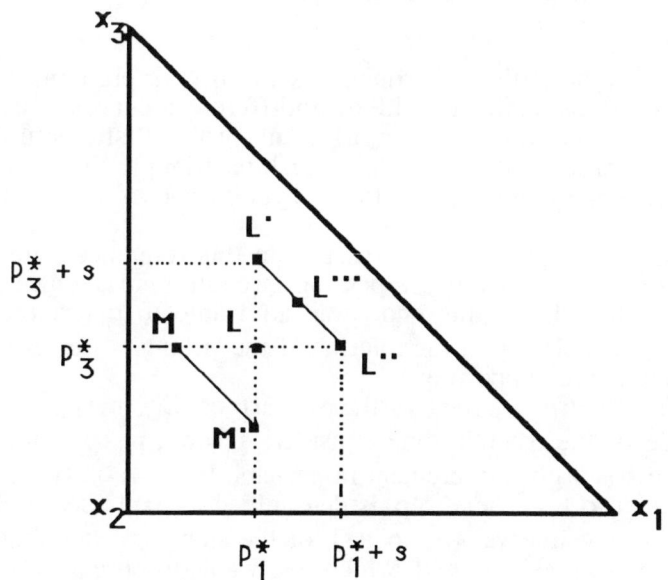

fig. 4. Constructing an indifference curve : the basic principle of the "Closing In" method.

To see where it cuts L'L", take any point like L''' on L' L".
Either $L \lesssim L'''$ or $L''' \lesssim L$. In the first case, the curve cuts L'L" between L" and L''', in the second case, the complementary statement holds. Assume the first case obtains. Then, take any point on L"L''' and start again on the latter segment the same operation conducted above on L'L". A sufficient number of iterations, assuming continuity, will lead to a satisfactory approximation of the point being searched, which we will call L_s^*.

Of course, a careful analyst has to check that the subjects under investigation effectively abide by F.S.D.. But it is much simpler to check F.S.D. with the "Closing In" method (it can be checked directly on the data collected) than the "betweenness" hypothesis with the fixed lotteries-single indexing, for example. This latter check would require, indeed, using the "Closing In" method or some equivalent method! This is why checking this basic hypothesis is simply not done in the experimental studies mentioned above.

This represents a considerable methodological advantage of our method and a serious methodological problem to the other methods mentioned above.

3.2. Choices to be put forward to subjects

The aim of the experiments is to observe preferences allowing the analyst to estimate a field of indifference curves "covering" as completely as is possible the different probabilistic situations, i.e. covering the area of the Marschak-Machina triangle. This implies first that the reference lotteries be sufficiently well chosen across the triangle area.

It also implies that, starting from this reference point, as many points of the indifference curve passing through this reference point as is possible be found. To this end, it is advisable to determine a lottery $L=(p_1^*, p_3^*)$ sufficiently in the interior of the triangle. Let us call C_L the indifference curve supporting L.

To determine the Northeast part of C_L, between L and the hypotenuse of the triangle, one considers $L'=(p_1^*, p_3^*+s)$, and $L''=(p_1^*+s, p_3^*)$, where s is a given increment in probability (fig. 4). Then, the lottery L_s equivalent to L at the s-step, is determined as explained in 3.1. above. Determining the interval $[p_1^*, p_1^*+s]$, or the step s, is then tantamount to determining the precision with which one wants to observe C_L (figure 4). The limits here are plainly the time one can devote to the experiment, as well as the patience and the acuity of perception of the subjects investigated.

A similar procedure can be used to estimate the Southwest part of C_L. Again, one can obtain as many points as one is ready to give different values to s, with again the limits already mentioned. One slight difficulty appears on this Southwest side of C_L. When the value assigned to S leads to a situation akin to the one shown on figure 5, one starts with the comparison between L and M*. By using the F.S.D.-hypothesis already emphasized above, one can determine wether the equivalent lottery lies on MM* or on M*M'.

For every given reference lottery L, the order in which the subjects are confronted to the choices can be the same, but it might be useful to investigate the indifference curves with varying the order.

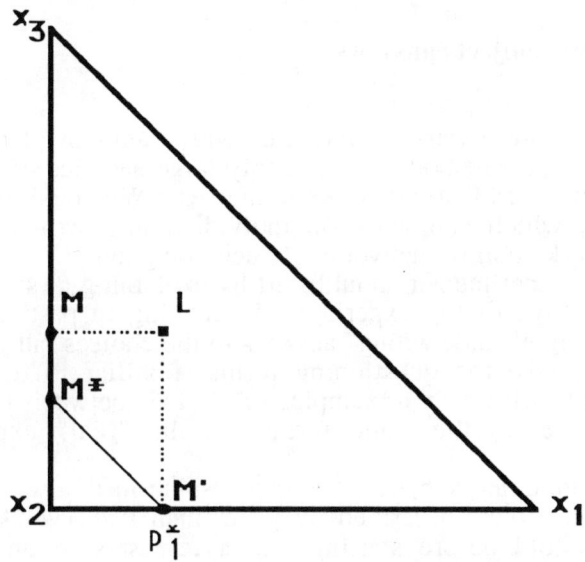

fig. 5. A special case : Here, the equivalent lottery to
L can belong to the boarderline segment [MM*]

Alternatively, one can use a variable step by having recourse to a coefficient λ which can change (table 1) between one alternative and the next one, the idea being then to determine the value $\lambda = \lambda^*$ for which the subject reverses his or her preference between L and L_S. In practice, one determines λ_0 and λ_1 within $]0,1[$ such that the choice between L and L_S for $\lambda < \lambda_0$ is reversed when $\lambda > \lambda_1$, with $\lambda_1 - \lambda_0 \leq \pi$, where π is some value regarded as satisfactory with respect to the precision of the results. λ^* is then taken midway between λ_0 and λ_1.

Table 1

Loterie	Probability of $x_3 = 10.000$ FF	Probability of $x_2 = 2.000$ FF	Probability of $x_1 = 0$
L	p_3^*	p_2^*	p_1^*
L_S	$p_3^* + \lambda s$	$1 - p_1^* - p_3^* - s$	$p_1^* + (1-\lambda)s$

$\lambda \in]0,1[$

4.2. Collecting subjects answers.

It is unnecessary to underline which amount of time would be needed to use our method on reasonably large samples of subjects when working with traditional questionnaires. We designed therefore "Maclabex", which can work on individual microcomputers and will hopefully work soon on networks of such computers.

The experimenter should start by explaining to subjects what the generic objective of the experiment is, making in particular clear that there aren't "right" and "wrong" answers to the choices put forward. Then, in order to make the questioning format familiar to the subject, the program starts with a few examples of choices between lotteries like L and L_S above, in the same format as the "real" experiment (see Appendix).

To motivate subjects, one can assume in a now "classical" way the "isolation effect" described by Kahneman and Tversky [1979], i.e. subjects are told before starting that a few sets of answers will be randomly selected at the end of the experiment and endowed with "real" money. One could point out here[1] that this "motivational trick" assumes an "isolation effect" which is quite close to the independence axiom. Such a remark will be disturbing only if the results of the experiment are validating the expected utility hypothesis, i.e. if the test is *positive*, because one could then object to a circular reasoning (in such a case, the experiment should be run again *without* this motivational scheme, which is not essential to the "Closing In" method). But it has to be made clear that it is no unsound methodology, indeed, to run a *negative* test of a

---

[1] This remark was recently again expressed by Pr. Jacques Drèze at a presentation of some experimental results by one of us (Bertrand Munier) at the University of Louvain-la-Neuve.

hypothesis by assuming at the start that this hypothesis - or something close to it - holds in at least one respect and then show that, *notwithstanding* this partial assumption, the behaviors exhibited by the subjects are *not* in line with the implications of the hypothesis tested.

4. Concluding Remarks

Estimating directly individual indifference curves in the Marschak-Machina triangle using the "Closing In" method has two main advantages with respect to the "fixed lotteries-single indexing" method, of which we shortly mentioned two different versions in section 2 above.

4.1. The first advantage of the "Closing In" method over the preceding one is that it eventually becomes possible - and we conjecture here that this is a most relevant characteristic in risk theory - to relate the performance of one given model of decision under risk to one (or possibly several) "zones" of prospects within the Marschak-Machina triangle. The concept of "contingency" of the models of decision under risk could be grounded on this type of results.

4.2. The second advantage is to allow for more precise data in the results of the experiments and - a *most important* epistemological point - for a posteriori better checked working hypotheses in the protocols and more generally speaking in the methodology of these same experiments.

Classifying generalized expected utility models with the help of fixed lotteries and a single index meets thus factual as well as methodological powerful objections, which, we think, the "Closing In" method allows one to avoid.

Groupe de Recherche sur le Risque, l'Information et la Décision
Ecole Normale Supérieure de Cachan, 61, Avenue du Président Wilson
94235 CACHAN cedex   FRANCE

APPENDIX : MACLABEX

To illustrate now the software MACLABEX works in the application of the "Closing In" method, let us take an example, consisting in having to choose between lotteries L (Urn B) and L_S (Urn A). We represent hereunder the successive screens as they sequentially appear on the computer's monitor when using the interactive software MACLABEX. We assume that, following the basic idea of the "Closing In" method, the subject is asked to search for the lottery equivalent to L = (0.20 ; 0.30; 0.50).

SCREEN 1 :

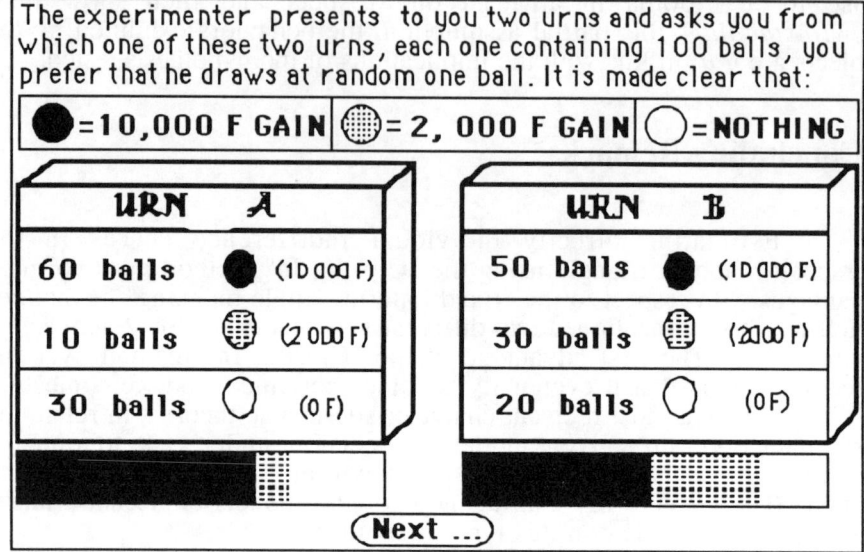

Let us now assume that the subject has clicked on "next": Screen 2 appears. Assume then that the subject prefers the ball to be drawn from Urn B and clicks under the corresponding case (screen 3).

SCREEN 2 :

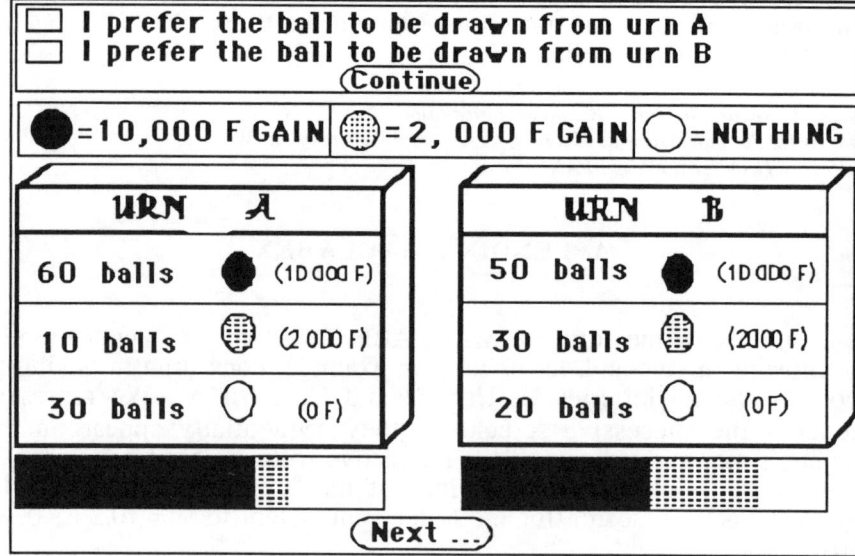

THE 'CLOSING IN' METHOD

SCREEN 3 :

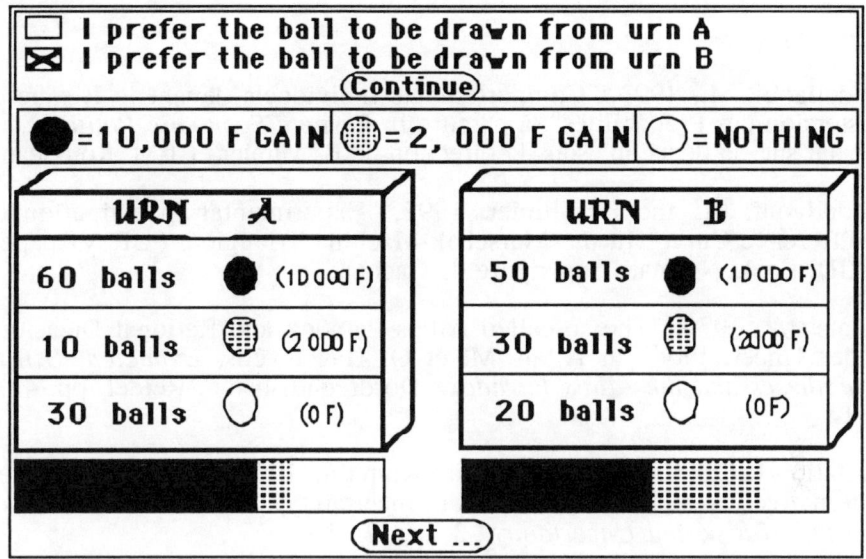

The subject then clicks on "Next" : Screen 4 appears and MACLABEX presents the subject with a new choice entailing a new lottery Ls (urn A) :
SCREEN 4

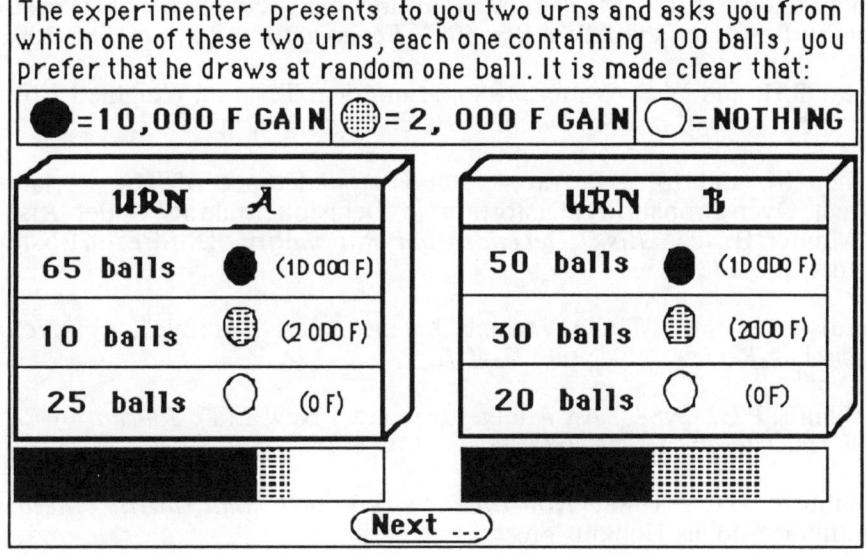

etc...

REFERENCES

Abdellaoui, M., 1993, "Comportements individuels devant le Risque et Distorsion des Probabilités", à paraître in *Revue d'Economie Politique,* n° spécial sur "la décision" sous la direction de B. Munier et J-M. Rousseau.

Abdellaoui, M. and B. Munier, 1992, "Experimental Investigation of Indifference Curves in the Marschak-Machina Triangle", FUR VI paper, GRID, Ecole Normale Supérieure de Cachan.

Allais, M., 1979, "The so-called Allais Paradox and Rational Decisions under Uncertainty", in Allais M. et O. Hagen, eds, *Expected Utility Hypotheses and the Allais Paradox.*, Dordrecht/Boston, Reidel, pp. 473-681.

Battalio, R.C., Kagel, J.H. and J. Komain, 1990, "Testing Between Alternative Models of Choice under Uncertainty : Some Initial Results", *Journal of Risk and Uncertainty* , **3**, pp. 25-50.

Camerer, C.F., 1989, "An Experimental Test of Several Generalized Utility Theories", *Journal of Risk and Uncertainty,* **2**, pp.61-104.

Chew, S.H., 1983, "A Generalization of the Quasilinear Mean with Applications to the Measurement of Income Inequality and Decision Theory Resolving the Allais Paradox", *Econometrica,* **51**, pp.1065-1092.

Chew S.H. and W.S. Waller, 1986, "Empirical Tests of Weighted Utility Theory", *Journal of Mathematical Psychology,* **30**, pp. 55-72.

Cohen M. and J.-Y. Jaffray, 1988, "Preponderance of The Certainty Effect Over Probability Distortion in Decision Making Under Risk", in:Munier B., ed., *Risk, Decision and Rationality*, Dordrecht/Boston, Reidel, pp. 173-188.

Conlisk J., 1989, "Three Variants on the Allais Example", *American Economic Review,* **79**, pp. 392-407.

Fishburn, P.C., 1988, "An Anniversary and a New Era", *Journal of Risk and Uncertainty*, **1**, pp. 267-284.

Fishburn, P.C., 1988, *Non-linear preference and utility theory*, Baltimore, Johns Hopkins press.

Harless D., 1992, "Predictions About Indifference Curves Inside the Unit Triangle, A Test of Variants of Expected Utility Theory", *Journal of Economic Behavior and Organization,* **18**, pp. 391-414.

Harless D. and C.F. Camerer, 1992, "The Utility of Generalized Expected Utility Theories", FUR VI paper, mimeo.

Hey J. and Ch. Orme, 1992, "Circles, Triangles and Straight Lines: Estimation of Betweenness-satisfying Non-Expected Utility Preference Functionals Using Experimental Data", FUR VI paper, mimeo.

Kahneman, D. and A. Tversky, 1979, "Prospect Theory : An Analysis of Decision under Risk", *Econometrica,* **47**, pp. 263-291.

Loomes G.C. and R. Sugden, 1982, "Regret theory: An Alternative Theory of Rational Choice under Uncertainty", *Economic Journal* , **92**, pp.805-824.

Machina, M.J., 1987, "Choice under Uncertainty: Problems Solved and Unsolved", *Journal of Economic Perspectives,* **1**, pp.121-154.

Munier, B., 1989, "New Models of Decisions under Uncertainty", *European Journal of Operational Research*, **38**, pp. 307-317.

Munier, B., 1992, "Expected versus Anticipated Utility : Where do we Stand ?", *Fuzzy Sets and Systems,* **49** (1), pp. 55-64.

Munier, B. and M. Abdellaoui, 1992, "Expected Utility Violations : An Appropriate and Intercultural Experiment", in Chikan, A., ed., *Progress in Decision, Utility and Risk Theory,* Dordrecht/ Boston, Kluwer Acad. Publishers, pp. 175-182.

Quiggin, J., 1982, "A Theory of Anticipated Utility", *Journal of Economic Behavior and Organization* , **3**, pp.324-343.

Rothschild, M. and J. Stiglitz, 1971, "Increasing Risk : II. Its Economic Consequences", *Journal of Economic Theory,* **3**, 66-84.

Segal, U., 1989, "Anticipated Utility : A Measure Representation Approach", *Annals of Operation Research* , **19**, pp. 359-373.

Wakker, P., 1993, "Separating Marginal Utility and Probabilistic Risk Aversion", *Theory and Decision*, **36**, (forthcoming).

GAINS AND LOSSES IN NONADDITIVE EXPECTED UTILITY*

Rakesh Sarin & Peter Wakker

University of California, Los Angeles
Los Angeles, CA
and
Medical Decision Making Unit
University of Leiden (AZL)
Leiden, The Netherlands

1. INTRODUCTION

In a seminal paper, Schmeidler (1989) proposed a nonadditive expected utility theory, called Choquet expected utility (CEU). For decision under uncertainty CEU provides a greater flexibility in predicting choices than Savage's subjective expected utility (SEU). The key feature of Schmeidler's theory is that the probability of a union of two disjoint events is not required to be the sum of the individual event probabilities. Schmeidler's theory and its subsequent developments (e.g., see Gilboa, 1987, Wakker, 1989, Chapter VI) do not, however, make a distinction between gains and losses with respect to the status quo. These theories typically assume that the consequence of a given decision alternative is described by the final wealth position.

In recent years, a body of empirical literature (see Kahneman and Tversky, 1979) has convincingly demonstrated that people's attitudes towards gains and losses are distinctly different. For example, people are risk averse when consequences represent a gain relative to the status quo, and are risk seeking when these represent a loss relative to the status quo. Recently, Kahneman and Tversky (1992) have introduced cumulative prospect theory (CPT), an extension of their original prospect theory, that generalizes nonadditive expected theories to permit differential attitudes towards gains and losses. Similar forms were proposed in Starmer and Sugden (1989) and Luce and Fishburn (1991).

---

* The support for this research was provided in part by the Decision, Risk, and Management Science branch of the National Science Foundation.

In Sarin and Wakker (1992a) a simple approach was used to obtain a transparent axiomatization of CEU. The idea of this approach is to use unambiguous events, such as those generated by a random device, to calibrate decision weights for general events. In this paper we show that the same approach can also be utilized to obtain a simple and transparent axiomatizion of CPT. The main result in this paper is obtained by modifying the cumulative dominance axiom P4 of Sarin and Wakker (1992a).

Section 2 presents two decision problems. The first, a variation of the classical Ellsberg paradox, shows the desirability of extending expected utility; it motivated the development of CEU. The second illustrates the desirability of extending CEU to CPT.

Section 3 derives the CEU model, along the lines developed in Sarin and Wakker (1992a). The latter paper gave a fully developed axiomatic derivation of CEU, where for unambiguous acts expected utility was maximized. Here we simplify the derivation by assuming expected utility for unambiguous acts from the start. That leads to a transparent derivation of CEU.

Section 4 presents the main result of this paper, a new derivation of CPT, and Section 5 contains a discussion.

2. EXAMPLE

Consider a "known" urn that contains 50 yellow and 50 white balls, and an "unknown" urn that contains an unknown proportion of yellow and white balls, totaling 100 balls. In a first scenario, the subjects are offered a choice between the following two options.

Option 1: Bet on known urn, win $200 if yellow ball is drawn; win $0 otherwise.

Option 2: Bet on unknown urn, win $200 if yellow ball drawn; win $0 otherwise.

A majority of subjects chooses option 1 in the above scenario. A typical rationale offered for this choice is that the probability of winning in option 1 is 0.5, while the probability of winning in option 2 is vague or ambiguous. The preference for the known urn is observed even when the subjects are given freedom to specify the color of the ball on which they bet, and even with real money awards. This preference for betting on the known urn is termed ambiguity aversion in the literature and has been observed in many empirical studies in a variety of different settings; e.g., see Ellsberg (1961), Curley and Yates (1985), Einhorn and Hogarth (1985), Kahn and Sarin (1988).

Since the subjects exhibit symmetric preferences within the known urn and the unknown urn by being indifferent between betting on white or yellow colored balls, the observed preference for option 1 cannot be explained by a standard application of subjective expected utility theory. This is because in either urn, under SEU, the subjective probability of drawing a yellow ball equals the probability of drawing a white ball, and is 0.5. If psychological attributes such as regret, suspicion, or disappointment are incorporated to describe the consequence, then SEU could indeed explain the observed choice. We do not pursue this line of reasoning in the present paper.

CEU theory is consistent with the observed preference for option 1. This is because CEU permits the decision weight associated with the superior event (yielding $200) to be less than 0.5 when the ball is drawn from the unknown urn.[1] Here, by symmetry, the decision weight of drawing the yellow ball (if this is the superior event), and for drawing the white ball (if this is the superior event), are both below 0.5, so they add up to less than 1. This is where the nonadditive theories generalize SEU. Thus subjects reveal in scenario 1:

decision weight of yellow ball (superior event) from unknown urn
    < 0.5

In the second scenario, the subjects are offered a choice between the following two options.

Option 1: Bet on known urn, lose $200 if white ball is drawn; lose $0 otherwise.

Option 2: Bet on unknown urn, lose $200 if white ball drawn; lose $0 otherwise.

A majority of subjects now chooses option 2. So here subjects exhibit a preference for betting on the unknown urn, i.e., they show a preference for ambiguity. Under CEU, this preference implies

decision weight of yellow ball (superior event) from unknown urn
    > 0.5.

---

[1] In general, CEU does allow decision weights to differ from objective probabilities, such as those generated by the known urn. For simplicity we assume here that they coincide. This assumption does not affect our subsequent reasoning.

Since the decision weight for the same event (yellow ball) as superior event cannot simultaneously be smaller and larger than 0.5, the above example demonstrates that CEU is unable to accommodate the observed modal preference pattern. CPT, however, does permit the above preference pattern by allowing decision weights to differ in the gain and loss scenario.

3. CHOQUET EXPECTED UTILITY

To bring to the fore the transparency of the axiomatization method adopted in this paper, we first give an elementary, somewhat informal, derivation of CEU. Subsequently we summarize this more formally. The approach in this paper follows Sarin and Wakker (1992) who use unambiguous events to calibrate ambiguous events.

The decision problem is to choose an act from the available set of acts when the outcome of each act is uncertain. An act is denoted

$$(A_1, x_1; \cdots; A_n, x_n)$$

which means that the act yields an outcome x_i if an event A_i obtains. Events $A_1, \cdots, A_n$ are mutually exclusive and collectively exhaustive. The decision maker does not know which event A_i will eventually obtain and therefore does not know which outcome x_i will result from the act.

Preferences between acts are denoted by the symbol $\succcurlyeq$ (with $\preccurlyeq, \sim, \succ, \prec$ as usual). We assume throughout that preferences are complete (every pair of acts is comparable) and transitive. We also assume that all acts have a finite number of outcomes (i.e., acts are simple) and that outcomes in acts $(A_1, x_1; \cdots; A_n, x_n)$ are rank-ordered so that

$$x_1 \succcurlyeq \cdots \succcurlyeq x_n.[2]$$

A crucial assumption in our analysis is that there exist physical devices such as roulette wheels, random number tables, dice, etc., that can be used to generate events with known or generally agreed upon probabilities. Such events are called unambiguous events. An act whose outcomes are generated using unambiguous events alone is called an unambiguous act. We assume that the decision maker maximizes expected utility with respect to these unambiguous acts. The unambiguous acts are usually described through the probability distribution they generate over the outcomes. So we write

---

[2]Preferences over outcomes are derived from acts that have constant outcomes under all events.

$(P(A_1),x_1;\cdots;P(A_n),x_n)$ for $(A_1,x_1;\cdots;A_n,x_n)$, or $(p_1,x_1;\cdots;p_n,x_n)$,

where p_i is the probability of event A_i.

We now turn our attention to general events relevant to the decision problem, such as: interest rates fall, remain the same, or increase. Likelihood comparisons of events are defined in terms of preferences over gambles on the events. That is, an event A is defined as more likely than an event B if a person will prefer to bet on A rather than on B. For unambiguous events, the likelihood relation is represented by probabilities. We use these probabilities to calibrate the likelihood of ambiguous events. This of course requires that for each ambiguous event A, we can find a matching unambiguous event B of equal likelihood, i.e., such that the person is indifferent between betting on A or on B. Then we can assign to event A the number P(B), the probability of event B. We call this assigned number the *capacity* of A, denoted v(A). In this manner we can use the probabilities of unambiguous events to calibrate capacities for ambiguous events. Note that at this stage it cannot be concluded that the capacity satisfies conditions such as additivity $(v(A \cup B) = v(A)+v(B))$, and indeed, in the models of this paper it will not. We will ensure a weaker condition, i.e., *monotonicity* (if $A \supset B$ then $v(A) \geq v(B)$). This is accomplished by simply requiring that a person prefers betting on a larger set (e.g., {cold, warm, hot}) to betting on a smaller set (e.g., {cold, warm}) that is included in the larger set.

Schmeidler and Gilboa introduced a decision model, Choquet expected utility (CEU), that allows for nonadditivity of capacities. In CEU "cumulative" events, i.e., events describing the receipt of an outcome α or a superior outcome, play a central role. For an act $(A_1,x_1;\cdots;A_n,x_n)$, the cumulative events are events of the form

$$A_1 \cup \cdots \cup A_i,$$

for $1 \leq i \leq n$. In CEU, an act is preferred to another if all its cumulative events are more likely, i.e., if the receipt of an outcome α or a superior outcome is at least as likely under the first act as under the second, for all outcomes α. Notice that if each act comes associated with a probability distribution, then this condition merely requires a preference for first order stochastically dominating acts. One could therefore view it as stochastic dominance for the case of uncertainty.

We are now ready to show that the conditions discussed informally so far lead to the CEU representation. Consider an arbitrary ambiguous act $(A_1,x_1;\cdots;A_n,x_n)$. Take an unambiguous act $(p_1,x_1;\cdots;p_n,x_n)$ that is "matching" in the sense that

$$p_1 + \cdots + p_i = v(A_1 \cup \cdots \cup A_i) \text{ for each } i.$$

This matching unambiguous act is constructed by recursively eliciting the capacities of cumulative events $A_1, A_1 \cup A_2$, etc. By cumulative dominance, the ambiguous and unambiguous acts are equivalent. We know that the evaluation of the unambiguous act is given by its expected utility, $\sum_{i=1}^{n} p_i U(x_i)$. It is useful to rewrite this as[3]

$$\sum_{i=1}^{n}((p_1+\cdots+p_i)-(p_1+\cdots+p_{i-1}))U(x_i),$$

which is identical to

$$\sum_{i=1}^{n}(v(A_1\cup\cdots\cup A_i)-v(A_1\cup\cdots\cup A_{i-1}))U(x_i).$$

The latter value is defined as the *Choquet expected utility* (*CEU*) of the act $(A_1,x_1;\cdots;A_n,x_n)$. Let us compare this formula with EU. Both forms take a weighted mean of the utility values $U(x_i)$. In CEU, the decision weights, which we denote as π_i below, are the marginal capacity contributions of events A_i to the more favorable events $A_1,\cdots,A_{i-1}$. That is, if we define

$$\pi_i = v(A_1\cup\cdots\cup A_i) - v(A_1\cup\cdots\cup A_{i-1})$$

for all i, then we can write CEU as

$$\sum_{i=1}^{n}\pi_i U(x_i).$$

Let us now summarize, somewhat more precisely, the assumptions and results presented so far. The conditions (R1)-(R3), presented first, are not necessary, and mainly concern richness assumptions, plus an expected utility assumption in (R1). The conditions (A1)-(A3), presented next, are all necessary for the CEU representation, and also sufficient, given the other conditions. Throughout, $\succcurlyeq$ denotes a preference relation over a set of "conceivable" acts.

(R1) All simple probability distributions $(p_1,x_1;\cdots;p_n,x_n)$ are conceivable. Preferences over these are evaluated by expected utility

$$\sum_{i=1}^{n}p_i U(x_i).$$

---

[3]Throughout this paper we adopt the standard mathematical convention that, for i=1, $p_1+\cdots+p_{i-1}=0$ and $A_1\cup\cdots\cup A_{i-1}=\emptyset$.

We formally define $A \succcurlyeq B$ if there exist outcomes $\alpha \succ \beta$ such that

$$(A,\alpha;A^c,\beta) \succcurlyeq (B,\alpha;B^c,\beta)^4,$$

and assume:

(R2) For each ambiguous event A, there exists an unambiguous event B such that $A \sim B$.

We want to be able to compare all pairs of events A,B, so we assume:

(R3) There exist outcomes $\sigma \succ \tau$ such that, for each event A, $(A,\sigma;A^c,\tau)$ is conceivable.

Next we turn to the necessary conditions.

(A1) $\succcurlyeq$ is complete and transitive.

Define, in condition (R2) above, $v(A)=P(B)$.[5] The following condition will imply monotonicity of the capacity with respect to set inclusion

(A2) $A \supset B$ implies $A \succcurlyeq B$.

Note that, in the preference $(A,\sigma;A^c,\tau) \succcurlyeq (B,\sigma;B^c,\tau)$, (A2) can be reformulated as the requirement that the decision maker should appreciate replacement of the outcome τ by the preferred outcome σ in $A-B$.

Cumulative dominance means:

(A3) If the event of receiving outcome α or a superior outcome is at least as likely under act f as under act g, for all outcomes α, then $f \succcurlyeq g$.

Cumulative dominance implies that $(A,\alpha;A^c,\beta) \succcurlyeq (B,\alpha;B^c,\beta)$ for some outcomes $\alpha \succ \beta$ if and only if this holds true for all outcomes $\alpha \succ \beta$. A consequence of this condition is that the likelihood ordering on events is independent of the particular outcomes that have been chosen, and can be derived from the outcomes $\sigma \succ \tau$ in (R3). Cumulative dominance also

---

[4] The cumulative dominance axiom, defined formally below, will ensure that the ordering $A \succcurlyeq B$ is independent of the particular choice of outcomes $\alpha \succ \beta$; A^c denotes complement.

[5] The cumulative dominance axiom will also ensure that this number is independent of the particular choice of event B.

implies that v(A) is independent of the choice of the unambiguous event B~A because, if C is another unambiguous event such that A~C, then

$$(B,\alpha;B^c,\beta) \sim (A,\alpha;A^c,\beta) \sim (C,\alpha;C^c,\beta)$$

so that, by transitivity of $\sim$ and EU, $P(B) = P(C) = v(A)$. Further, cumulative dominance implies monotonicity of the capacity, because, for $A \supset B$, and unambiguous events C,D with C~A, D~B, the following preferences hold:

$$(C,\sigma;C^c,\tau) \sim (A,\sigma;A^c,\tau) \succcurlyeq (B,\sigma;B^c,\tau) \sim (D,\sigma;D^c,\tau).$$

The weak preference above was implied by (A2). Finally, as can be seen from the result below, the capacity v represents the likelihood ordering $\succcurlyeq$ on the events.

Now we present the result developed in this section.

THEOREM 3.1. Suppose (R1)-(R3) hold. Then CEU holds if and only if (A1)-(A3) hold. □

This seems to be the most transparent characterization of CEU presently available in the literature. The CEU of an act $(A_1,x_1;\cdots;A_n,x_n)$ is given by

$$\sum_{i=1}^{n}(v(A_1\cup\cdots\cup A_i)-v(A_1\cup\cdots\cup A_{i-1}))U(x_i).$$

Uniqueness results are standard. From the definition of the capacity it immediately follows that the capacity is uniquely determined. The utility function for the CEU form is the same as for the EU form for the unambiguous acts, so is unique up to scale and location.

4. A DERIVATION OF CUMULATIVE PROSPECT THEORY

In prospect theory or its extended version, cumulative prospect theory, outcomes are not described as final states of well-being, but rather as deviations relative to the "status quo" outcome. The latter is denoted as θ. To highlight this interpretation, Tversky and Kahneman use the term prospect instead of act. We follow this terminology from now on. We call outcomes $\alpha \succ \theta$ gains, and outcomes $\alpha \prec \theta$ losses. For convenience of notation we shall "collapse" the equivalence class of the status quo, i.e., we assume that all outcomes equivalent to the status quo are in fact identical to the status quo.

The key idea of cumulative prospect theory is that risk attitudes towards gains usually differ from risk attitudes towards losses, and therefore the capacity for gains, denoted v^+, may differ from the capacity for losses, denoted v^-. This means, obviously, that two different elicitations should be carried out, one with gains involved, and one with losses. So we now write, for events A,B, $A \succcurlyeq^+ B$ if there exists a gain $\alpha \succ \theta$ such that $(A,\alpha;A^c,\theta) \succcurlyeq (B,\alpha;B^c,\theta)$.

It turns out to be more convenient and natural to elicit the likelihood ordering for losses, denoted $\succcurlyeq^-$, from bets against events instead of bets on events. Further comments on this will be given in Section 5. Thus we define $A \succcurlyeq^- B$ if there exists a loss $\alpha \prec \theta$ such that $(A,\alpha;A^c,\theta) \preccurlyeq (B,\alpha;B^c,\theta)$. If a person avoids a loss contingent on event A in favor of a loss contingent on event B, then it seems natural to say that he considers event A as more likely to occur than event B.

It is now natural to proceed as follows, modifying the approach to CEU in order to accommodate the CPT theory. First, we assume that R1 (all simple probability distributions available) and A1 (weak ordering) of the previous section hold. In addition we can, and will, assume throughout that $U(\theta)=0$.

(R2') For each ambiguous event A, there exists an unambiguous event B such that $A \sim^+ B$, and an unambiguous event C such that $A \sim^- C$.

Again, we ensure likelihood comparability of all events by:

(R3') There exist outcomes $\sigma \succ \theta \succ \tau$ such that, for each event A, $(A,\sigma;A^c;\theta)$ and $(A^c,\theta;A;\tau)$ are conceivable.

Now we define $v^+(A) = P(B)$, and $v^-(A) = P(C)$ for B and C as in (R2'). Monotonicity of the capacities will again be implied by the following condition:

(A2') $A \supset B$ implies $A \succcurlyeq^+ B$ and $A \succcurlyeq^- B$.

Cumulative dominance in (A3) is now modified to cumulative gain-loss dominance in a natural way:

(A3') For all prospects f,g we have:

$f \succcurlyeq g$ whenever
$\{s \in S: f(s) \succcurlyeq \alpha\} \succcurlyeq^+ \{s \in S: g(s) \succcurlyeq \alpha\}$ for all gains $\alpha \succ \theta$
and
$\{s \in S: f(s) \preccurlyeq \beta\} \preccurlyeq^- \{s \in S: g(s) \preccurlyeq \beta\}$ for all losses $\beta \prec \theta$.

This condition says that prospect f is preferred to prospect g if:

a gain α or a superior gain is *at least* as likely under prospect f as under prospect g, for all gains α,

and

a loss β or a greater loss is *at most* as likely under act f as under act g, for all losses β.

Clearly, f is a more attractive prospect than g if under f greater gains are more likely and greater losses are less likely. Again, this condition, when restricted to gains prospects, implies that $\succcurlyeq^+$ and the gains capacity v^+ are well-defined, and that v^+ is monotonic with respect to set inclusion; a similar conclusion holds for its restriction to loss prospects with $\succcurlyeq^-$ and v^- replacing $\succcurlyeq^+$ and v^+.

We now show that the conditions above lead to the CPT representation for a subclass of the prospects, the "prospects that can be matched" with an unambiguous prospect. Consider an arbitrary ambiguous prospect $(A_1,x_1;\cdots;A_n,x_n)$. Suppose that $x_1 \succcurlyeq \cdots \succcurlyeq x_{k-1}$ are gains, $x_k = \theta$ (this can always be obtained by adding $A_k = \emptyset$ if necessary, or by collapsing the events that yield θ) and $x_{k+1} \succcurlyeq \cdots \succcurlyeq x_n$ are losses. That is,

$$x_1 \succcurlyeq \cdots \succcurlyeq x_{k-1} \succ x_k = \theta \succ x_{k+1} \succcurlyeq \cdots \succcurlyeq x_n.$$

Suppose we can find an unambiguous prospect $(p_1,x_1;\cdots;p_k,x_k;\cdots;p_n,x_n)$ that is "matching" in the sense that

$$p_1+p_2+\cdots+p_i = v^+(A_1\cup\cdots\cup A_i) \quad \text{for each } i<k,$$

and

$$p_n+p_{n-1}+\cdots+p_j = v^-(A_n\cup\cdots\cup A_j) \quad \text{for each } j>k.$$

Thus for gains, the cumulative events $A_1\cup\cdots\cup A_i$ match with respect to $\sim^+$, but for losses the "decumulative" events $A_n\cup\cdots\cup A_j$ match, now with respect to $\sim^-$. By (A3'), the two prospects are equivalent, so that the evaluation of the ambiguous one is given by the expected utility of the unambiguous one, i.e., by $\sum_{i=1}^{n} p_i U(x_i)$. We suppress the term $p_k U(\theta)$ which is 0, and rewrite the sum as

$$\sum_{i=1}^{k-1}((p_1+\cdots+p_i)-(p_1+\cdots+p_{i-1}))U(x_i) +$$

$$\sum_{j=k+1}^{n}((p_n+\cdots+p_j)-(p_n+\cdots+p_{j+1}))U(x_j),$$

which is identical to

$$\sum_{i=1}^{k-1}(v^+(A_1\cup\cdots\cup A_i)-v^+(A_1\cup\cdots\cup A_{i-1}))U(x_i) \;+$$

$$\sum_{j=k+1}^{n}(v^-(A_n\cup\cdots\cup A_j)-v^-(A_n\cup\cdots\cup A_{j+1}))U(x_j).$$

The latter value is defined as the *Cumulative prospect theory value (CPT)* of the prospect $(A_1,x_1;\cdots;A_n,x_n)$.[6] Defining decision weights

for $i<k$: $\pi_i^+ := v^+(A_1\cup\cdots\cup A_i) - v^+(A_1\cup\cdots\cup A_{i-1}))$,

and

for $j>k$: $\pi_j^- := v^-(A_n\cup\cdots\cup A_j) - v^-(A_n\cup\cdots\cup A_{j+1})$,

the CPT value is rewritten as

$$\sum_{i=1}^{k-1}\pi_i^+ U(x_i) + \sum_{j=k+1}^{n}\pi_j^- U(x_j).$$

Again, like expected utility and CEU, the form resembles a weighted mean of the utility values, with the zero term related to $U(\theta)$ suppressed. Now the decision weights for gains are derived from cumulative events and the gains-capacity, and decision weights for losses are derived from decumulative events and the loss-capacity. Unlike the weights in CEU, the weights in CPT need not sum to one. We have now obtained the main result:

THEOREM 4.1. *Suppose R1,R2',R3' are satisfied. Then on the set of prospects that can be matched, CPT holds if and only if A1, A2', and A3' hold.* □

We derived CPT above for the matchable prospects. A prospect can be matched if and only if the sum of the decision weights of the nonneutral outcomes is less than or equal to one. A simpler way to behaviorally test that a prospect can be matched is provided by the following condition, that is necessary and sufficient for matchability. Let $(A_1,x_1;\cdots;A_n,x_n)$ be a prospect with $x_{k-1} \succ x_k = \theta \succ x_{k+1}$. Take any unambiguous event B such that $B \sim^+ A_1\cup\cdots\cup A_{k-1}$. Now the prospect can be matched if and only if

---

[6]Also if the prospect is not matched by an unambiguous prospect, we call this value the CPT value of the prospect.

$B^c \succeq^- A_n \cup \cdots \cup A_{k+1}$. Note that any prospect yielding only gains, or only losses, can always be matched. This shows in particular that Theorem 4.1 gives a CPT representation for any prospect that only yields gains, and for any prospect that only yields losses. Of course, in the case in which there are only gains, or only losses, the CPT representation reduces to the CEU representation.

It is straightforwardly verified that all prospects are matchable if one assumes the "reflection property[7]" of Tversky and Kahneman (1992) and if furthermore superadditivity[8] of the capacities is satisfied; these are two common properties.

In general, it is possible that some prospects may not be matchable. As an extreme example, think of the case in which CPT holds, but v^+ assigns value 1 to an event A, and v^- assigns value 1 to the complement of A. Then, for $\alpha \succ \theta \succ \beta$, the prospect $(A,\alpha;A^c,\beta)$ yields decision weight $\pi^+ = 1$ for the outcome α, and also decision weight $\pi^- = 1$ for the outcome β. This prospect obviously cannot be matched, since for an unambiguous prospect the decision weights (=probabilities) cannot sum to more than one. In such cases the CPT representation may not hold. An elaborated example is presented in the Appendix.

In the absence of matchability, it is still possible to obtain a CPT representation by assuming an additional condition. To explain one such condition, we write, for any prospect f, f^+ for the prospect that results if all losses in f are replaced by the neutral outcome, and f^- for the prospect that results if all gains in f are replaced by the neutral outcome. Now suppose $f^+ \sim g^+$, and $f^- \sim g^-$, for two prospects f,g. It is a necessary condition for CPT that these two equivalences, separately in the gain and loss domain, imply the equivalence $f \sim g$.[9] This is the *double matching* condition of Tversky and Kahneman (1992). By means of this additional condition, a CPT representation can be obtained for all prospects f for which an unambiguous prospect g can be found such that $f^+ \sim g^+$, and $f^- \sim g^-$. Such prospects f are called *doubly matchable*. Note that all prospects are doubly matchable if the utility function is unbounded from both sides.

PROPOSITION 4.2. Suppose all conditions of Theorem 4.1 (R1, R2', R3', A1, A2', A3') hold. CPT holds for all doubly matchable prospects if and only if double matching is satisfied.

---

[7]*Reflection* means that $v^+ = v^-$.
[8]A capacity v is *superadditive* if $v(A \cup B) - v(A) \geq v(B) - v(A \cap B)$ for all events A,B.
[9]This follows mainly because $CPT(f) = CPT(f^+) + CPT(f^-)$.

PROOF. Theorem 4.1 has given a CEU representation (denoted CPT^+ below) for prospects yielding merely gains, and a CEU representation (denoted CPT^- below) for prospects yielding merely losses. For unambiguous prospects, CPT^+ and CPT^- coincide with EU. For a doubly matchable prospect f, and g the doubly matching unambiguous prospect, this ensures that $CPT^+(f^+) = EU(g^+)$, and $CPT^-(f^-) = EU(g^-)$. By double matching f~g, and f can be evaluated by $CPT(g) = EU(g^+) + EU(g^-) = CPT^+(f^+) + CPT^-(f^-) = CPT(f)$. □

5. DISCUSSION

In Theorem 4.1 and in Proposition 4.2, we have derived a CPT representation that relies heavily on the availability of unambiguous prospects. The introduction of unambiguous events simplifies the derivation and the elicitation of the model. If the CPT model holds true but the matchability conditions fail, then the elicitation procedures based on the calibration with respect to unambiguous events can still be carried out. That is, for each ambiguous event A, unambiguous events B and C can be found such that $A \sim^+ B$ and $A \sim^- C$. Thus $v^+(A) = P(B)$, and $v^-(A) = P(C)$ can still be inferred.

There are two differences between the CEU and CPT models. First, the decision weights for gains in the CPT model are independent from those for losses. This provides a greater flexibility in predicting choices. For example, in Section 2 a preference for the known urn in the first (gain) scenario and a preference for the unknown urn in the second (loss) scenario is consistent with CPT by taking $v^+(Y) < 1/2$ and $v^-(W) < 1/2$; the latter implies that the decision weight for yellow in the second scenario, $(1 - v^-(W))$, is greater than 1/2.

The second difference between CEU and CPT concerns the way in which the capacities are used to calculate decision weights. Consider a prospect $(A_1, x_1; \cdots; A_n, x_n)$. In CEU one takes differences $v(A_1 \cup \cdots \cup A_j) - v(A_1 \cup \cdots \cup A_{j-1})$ to obtain the decision weight π_j for event A_j. So here cumulative events are used. In CPT, the computation for decision weights for gains follows a similar scheme, using the gains capacity v^+. In the loss domain however, one uses a difference $v^-(A_n \cup \cdots \cup A_j) - v^-(A_n \cup \cdots \cup A_{j+1})$ to obtain the decision weight π_j^- of event A_j. The decision weight π_j^- is the difference between the capacities of the events "x_j or worse loss" and "strictly worse loss than x_j".[10] So here "decumulative" events are used. This also explains the definition of the likelihood relation $\succcurlyeq^-$ for losses through bets against events, rather than bets on events.

---

[10]For simplicity of presentation assume here $x_j \succ x_{j+1}$.

We note, however, that CEU is a special case of CPT. This can be seen by setting $v^+(A) = v(A)$, and $v^-(A) = 1 - v(A^c)$, for all events A. In the latter case, the decision weight for a loss x_j under CPT is

$$v^-(A_n \cup \cdots \cup A_j) - v^-(A_n \cup \cdots \cup A_{j+1}) =$$
$$1 - v(A_1 \cup \cdots \cup A_{j-1}) - (1 - v(A_1 \cup \cdots \cup A_j)) =$$
$$v(A_1 \cup \cdots \cup A_j) - v(A_1 \cup \cdots \cup A_{j-1}),$$

which is exactly the decision weight resulting from CEU. In other words, the CPT model reduces to CEU if $v^-(A) = 1 - v^+(A^c)$ for all events A.

We now briefly comment on the conditions that we used to derive CPT. We assumed expected utility maximization for unambiguous prospects. Our main results follow, by identical procedures, if one assumes Quiggin's (1982) rank-dependent utility for the unambigious prospects, or even, for CPT, if one assumes CPT for the unambiguous prospects. In other words, if CPT is satisfied on a domain that is sufficiently rich, then by condition (A3'), CPT spreads over the other prospects. Our cumulative gain-loss dominance condition seems to be a generalization of stochastic dominance to the case of uncertainty.

Next we turn to the matchability condition that seems to be the Achilles heel of our development. There is, however, an intuition behind this condition. Recall that, in our example in Section 2, the decision weight for the gain seemed to be reduced for the ambiguous prospect. For an ambiguity-neutral person the decision weight would have been 0.5. But for the modal preference in the example, the decision weight is less than 0.5, i.e., some decision weight is shifted to the neutral outcome, leading to ambiguity aversion. Similarly, in the loss domain the decision weight for the loss is shifted toward the neutral outcome, leading to ambiguity seeking behavior. We conjecture that for a prospect that involves both gains and losses, the shifts of decision weights from tails to the middle occur jointly. Should this occur, then the decision weights for nonneutral outcomes will sum to less than one. In this case the matchability condition will be satisfied.

APPENDIX

EXAMPLE A1. This example shows that the CPT representation in Theorem 4.1 does not necessarily hold for prospects that cannot be matched by an unambiguous prospect.

Suppose outcomes are real numbers, and the utility function U is the identity function. The neutral outcome θ is 0. M is a positive real number. A denotes an ambiguous event (say rain tomorrow). We study the ambiguous prospect $g = (A, M; A^c, -M)$. To meet condition (R3'), we also include the prospects $(A, M; A^c, 0)$, $(A^c, M; A, 0)$, $(A^c, 0; A, -M)$, and

$(A,0;A^c,-M)$. The set of all conceivable prospects consists of these five ambiguous prospects, and the set of all simple probability distributions over IR.

We elicit
$$v^+(A) = v^+(A^c) = 0.6 = v^-(A) = v^-(A^c)$$
by the equivalences
$$(A,M;A^c,0) \sim (0.6,M;0.4,0) \sim (A^c,M;A,0)$$
and
$$(A,0;A^c,-M) \sim (0.4,0;0.6,-M) \sim (A^c,0;A,-M).$$
So the decision weights for the prospect $(A,M;A^c,-M)$ sum to 1.2, i.e., to more than one, and the prospect is not matchable. Suppose that $g \sim M/10$. We can represent the preference relation by a function V that assigns expected value to all unambiguous prospects, further
$$V(A,M;A^c,0) = V(A^c,M;A,0) = 6M/10,$$
$$V(A,0;A^c,-M) = V(A^c,0;A,-M) = -6M/10,$$
and
$$V(g) = M/10.$$

All values except the last coincide with CPT values. The CPT value of g can be calculated, however, it is 0, so it differs from the V value, and does not provide a proper measure to represent preferences.

The preference relation does satisfy all conditions in Theorem 4.1. The only problem that might be expected concerns condition (A3'). In view of the increase of value of g as compared to the CPT model, it could be feared that there exists an unambiguous prospect f (for all ambiguous prospects f the condition is satisfied) such that f and g satisfy all conditions in (A3'), but still $g \succ f$. However, this never occurs. To satisfy the conditions in (A3'), f should assign a probability of at least 0.6 to an outcome at least as high as M. The remaining probability of 0.4 must be assigned to outcomes at least as good as $-M$. So the CPT value of f is at least $2M/10$, and $f \succcurlyeq g$ follows.

The prospect $(0.5, \frac{6M}{5}; 0.5, \frac{-6M}{5})$ shows that double matching is violated in the example. If outcomes would be restricted to $[-M,M]$, then also double matching would be satisfied; then g would not be doubly matchable. □

REFERENCES

Curley, S.P. & J.F. Yates (1985), `The Center and Range of the Probability Interval as Factors Affecting Ambiguity Preferences,´

Organizational Behavior and Human Decision Processes 36, 273–287.

Einhorn, H.J. & R.M. Hogarth (1985), 'Ambiguity and Uncertainty in Probabilistic Inference,' *Psychological Review* 93, 433–461.

Ellsberg, D. (1961), 'Risk, Ambiguity and the Savage Axioms,' *Quarterly Journal of Economics* 75, 643–669.

Gilboa, I. (1987), 'Expected Utility with Purely Subjective Non-Additive Probabilities,' *Journal of Mathematical Economics* 16, 65–88.

Kahn, B.E. & R.K. Sarin (1988), 'Modeling Ambiguity in Decisions under Uncertainty,' *Journal of Consumer Research* 15, 265–272.

Kahneman, D. & A. Tversky (1979), 'Prospect Theory: An Analysis of Decision under Risk,' *Econometrica* 47, 263–291.

Luce, R.D. & P.C. Fishburn (1991), 'Rank- and Sign-Dependent Linear Utility Models for Finite First-Order Gambles,' *Journal of Risk and Uncertainty* 4, 29–59.

Quiggin, J. (1982), 'A Theory of Anticipated Utility,' *Journal of Economic Behaviour and Organization* 3, 323–343.

Sarin, R.K. & P.P. Wakker (1992a), 'A simple Axiomatization of Nonadditive Expected Utility,' *Econometrica* 60, 1255–1272.

Sarin, R.K. & P.P. Wakker (1992b), 'A General Theory for Quantifying Beliefs,' *Econometrica*, forthcoming.

Schmeidler, D. (1989), 'Subjective Probability and Expected Utility without Additivity,' *Econometrica* 57, 571–587.

Starmer, C., & R. Sugden (1989), 'Violations of the Independence Axiom in Common Ratio Problems: An Experimental Test of Some Competing Hypotheses,' *Annals of Operations Research* 19, 79–101.

Tversky, A. & D. Kahneman (1992), 'Advances in Prospect Theory: Cumulative Representation of Uncertainty,' *Journal of Risk and Uncertainty* 5, 297–323.

Wakker, P.P. (1989), '*Additive Representations of Preferences*, A New Foundation of Decision Analysis.' Kluwer Academic Publishers, Dordrecht.

AN OUTLINE OF MY MAIN CONTRIBUTIONS TO RISK AND UTILITY THEORY:

Theory, Experience, and Applications

GENERAL OVERVIEW

Maurice ALLAIS

> *By itself logical thought cannot provide us with knowledge on the world of experience ; all we know about reality comes from experience and leads to it.*
>
> Albert Einstein *

INTRODUCTION

The purpose of this paper is to present an overview of my most significant contributions to the theory of utility and risk, published between 1952 and 1988.

Basically they take place respectively into three periods, 1950-1955, 1974-1979 and 1982-1988, during which I worked most actively on this theory.

First Period : 1950-1955

The first period of my work on risk from 1950 to 1955 originated in the confrontation between the conclusions reached in the second edition of *The Theory of Games* by von Neumann-Morgenstern (published in 1947), and the very different results I had obtained from my own reflections on the theory of games well before, in 1937.

This confrontation led me on to discuss the postulates of the *"Theory of Games"* within the framework of my seminar at the National Centre for Scientific Research (C.N.R.S.) during the academic year of 1950-1951. Almost all of my students were attracted by the developments of the *Theory of Games,* whereas my own contesting point of view was in opposition to their convictions.

In September 1951 at the *European Congress of the International Society of Econometrics at Louvain,* I presented an initial paper entitled *"Theoretical Notes on the Uncertainty of the Future and on Risk",* which outlined the basis for a positive theory of utility and risk, and, with regard to this analysis, showed the quite unacceptable character of the postulates expressed in the theories of von Neumann, Morgenstern, and Marschak.

With the assistance of Prof. Darmois and, under the auspices of the C.N.R.S., I organized an international conference in Paris, in May 1952, on *"The Foundations and the Applications of the Theory of Risk"* among whose participants were Kenneth J. Arrow, Georges Darmois, Bruno de Finetti, Maurice Fréchet, Milton Friedman, Ragnar Frisch, Jacob Marschak, Edmond Malinvaud, Pierre Massé, Paul A. Samuelson, Leonard J. Savage, Herman Wold and myself. Unfortunately Oscar Morgenstern was not able to participate.

At this colloquium I presented two papers, *"Foundations of a Positive Theory of Choice involving Risk"* and *"A Generalization of the Theories of General Economic Equilibrium and of Maximal Efficiency to the Case of Risk".* These two papers were published in the collective volume, *Econométrie,* published by the C.N.R.S. in its series, *Colloques Internationaux* [1]. The substance of these two papers was drawn from certain developments of my 1951 Louvain paper, but developed further.

During that Colloquium, the neo-Bernoullian formulation of the *Theory of Games* was defended in various forms by de Finetti, Friedman, Marschak, Samuelson and Savage, and my contrary position led to very heated debates [2].

At the end of the colloquium I wrote a third paper, *"Foundations of a Theory of Choice Involving Risk, and a Criticism of the Postulates and Axioms of the American School"*. This paper was added to the Colloquium volume [3].

This third paper integrated into *one unified whole,* on the one hand my first paper, entitled *"Foundations of a Positive Theory of Choice Involving Risk",* and on the other hand, a *Critical analysis of neo-Bernoullian theories,* whilst also taking into account the third annex to my 1951 Louvain paper and the discussions which took place at the Paris Colloquium.

Extracts from the third paper were published in French in *Econometrica* in 1953 under the title (translated into English)*"The Behaviour of Rational Man in the Presence of Risk. A Criticism of the Postulates and Axioms of the American School".*

In order to determine the actual behaviour of "rational" people when faced with random choices, I organized a survey in 1952, and submitted a *questionnaire* to over one hundred persons. This Questionnaire was published in the *Journal of the Statistics Society in Paris* in March 1953, together with a general commentary on its subject.

From 1952 to 1955 I was a consultant to the *Algerian Bureau of Mining Research.* In that capacity, and by applying my general theory of risk, I was led to write various studies regarding mining research, and I presented a synthesis of those studies in a general paper of 1954 : *"Method of Appraising Economic Prospects of Mining Exploration over Large Territories - Algerian Sahara Case Study"* [4].

Second Period : 1974-1979

In 1970, I received a letter from Ole Hagen informing me of his work on the theory of risk, and acquainting me with some of the difficulties he had encountered in his relations with Karl Borch of the *Norwegian School of Economics and Business Studies* in Bergen with regard to his adherence to the position I had adopted in 1952. This letter constituted a point of departure for subsequent correspondence on this subject, and for numerous very fruitful meetings in Paris.

This is how the project was progressively elaborated for the book which has finally published in 1979 by *Reidel Publishing Cy* under the title : *Expected Utility Hypotheses and the Allais Paradox. Contemporary Discussions of Decisions under Uncertainty with Allais' Rejoinder* (ed. Maurice Allais and Ole Hagen). The final decision on this publication was taken in 1974 following Werner Leinfellner's decisive support for the project.

This volume contains both the English translation of my general paper of 1952, *The Foundations of a Positive Theory of Choice*

Involving Risk and a Criticism of the Postulates and Axioms of the American School, and a new memoir of synthesis, written from 1974 to 1977, *The So-Called Allais Paradox and Rational Decisions under Uncertainty,* presenting the essential results of the analysis of the replies to the *1952 Questionnaire,* and notably my reply to the criticism which was voiced in opposition to my theory such as it appeared in my 1952 general paper.

Third Period : 1982-1988

The third period, from 1982 to 1988, followed the organization of an International Conference in Oslo in 1982, on the initiative of Werner Leinfellner and Ole Hagen. The Oslo Conference was succeeded by International Conferences in Venice in 1984, Aix en Provence in 1986, and Budapest in 1988.

During this third period, I was induced both to deepen and enlarge on all my preceding analyses ; not only my critical analysis of contemporary theories, but also, and especially, my general theory of random choice and its illustration.

An Analysis of my contributions

Rather than following chronological order, it seems to me to be preferable, in this general overview, to comment briefly on the contributions I have made to six principal fields :

- cardinal utility and its determination ;

- the theory of probability ;

- the theory of random choices ;

- the generalization on the theories of general economic equilibrium and maximum efficiency in cases of risk ;

- a criticism of contemporary theories ;

- the applications of the theory of risk and utility to economic policies.

For each of these fields I will indicate the main lines along which my analyses have run, and how they were interrelated over time.

Finally, I shall briefly show how my contributions are related to the dominant ideas of the day and to their evolution, and what was my own scientific philosophy regarding the general approach of contemporary theories [5].

I

CARDINAL UTILITY AND ITS DETERMINATION

1.1.- *General Properties of Cardinal Utility, 1941-1955*

a - A la Recherche d'une Discipline économique. L'économie pure (The Quest for a Discipline of Economics. Pure Economics, 1943)

In my 1943 book I presented a thorough analysis of the concept of cardinal utility [6]. This analysis is essentially based on the following principles :

- For each subject there exists a utility function, cardinal utility, that represents *the intensity of his preferences.*
- Cardinal utility *may be defined on the basis of our introspection,* either by considering the variations of ordinal utility, that are deemed to be psychologically equivalent or by considering the smallest perceptible variations of that utility.
- Cardinal utility admits *a maximal value that corresponds to satiety.*
- At a first approximation, cardinal utility may be considered to be a *log-linear function of the capital of the considered subject.*
- The properties of cardinal utility are *entirely analogous* to those shown by Weber, Fechner and their successors *for the case of the psycho-physiology of sensations* [7].
- The theory of the dynamics of disequilibrium and of general economic equilibrium, the theory of supply and demand, and the theory of maximal efficiency may be completely elaborated solely by conside-

ring ordinal utilities, *but considering cardinal utility generally permits a simplification of the exposition and renders it more suggestive.*
 - Except for the case of independent goods, it is impossible to determine cardinal utility from the consideration of observed choices.

b - Notes théoriques sur l'incertitude de l'avenir et le risque (Theoretical Notes on the Uncertainty of the Future and on Risk) (September 1951)

In my 1951 Louvain paper I based my analysis of the theory of random choices on the consideration of the concept of cardinal utility.
In *Appendix I* of that paper, *"Definition and properties of cardinal utility"*, I gave a summary of the main points of my 1943 analysis, and in *Appendix II, "Examination of the logarithmic hypothesis"*, I examined the loglinear hypothesis of Daniel Bernoulli, its justifications and its implications [8].

c - The Foundations of a Positive Theory of Choice Involving Risk and a Criticism of the Postulates and Axioms of the American School (1952)

In my 1952 paper, I based all my analyses upon a consideration of cardinal utility and its properties, as I had outlined in my 1943 book and in my 1951 paper.

d - La Psychologie de l'Homme Rationnel devant le Risque.
La Théorie et l'Expérience (The Psychology of Rational Behavior in the Presence of Risk, Theory and Experience (1952)

The survey that I organized in 1952 was based upon the *Questionnaire* that has been published in 1953 under the title, *La Psychologie de l'Homme Rationnel devant le Risque. La Théorie et l'Expérience*. The Questions VI of this Questionnaire were designed to show that cardinal utility was not, as Savage had claimed, *"a myth"*, and that it was indeed possible to determine it on the basis of suitable questions [9].

1.2 - Axiomatic Principles and Empirical Analysis, 1974-1977

The analysis that was performed in 1974-1975 of the answers to *Questions* VI of the *1952 Questionnaire* completely confirmed my previous analyses by showing that *for all the subjects analysed, there does actually exist, an index of psychological value* (cardinal utility) which may be determined independently of any consideration of random choices, and that, in a large domain, that index varies approximately as the logarithm of the argument.

The bases for my theoretical analysis were presented in my 1977 paper *"The So-Called Allais' Paradox and Rational Decisions under Uncertainty"* [10], and the results of the empirical analysis are indicated in its Appendix C [11].

a - Axiomatic bases

My previous reflections on, and my analysis of, the empirical data have caused me to admit two axioms. According to the first, *the axiom of homogenity,* cardinal utility is a *function of the relation* DC/C *of the relative variations of capital*; and according to the second, *the axiom of invariance,* this function is invariant, i.e. it is *the same whatever subject is concerned* [12].

b - The cardinal utility function and the log-linear approximation

In October-December 1975 I found a method which permitted a representation of the function of cardinal utility for *positive* values of DC according to a general formula that admitted a maximum corresponding to satiety [13]. However, since that analysis was relatively complex and required extensive discussion, for lack of space I had to limit myself in my 1977 paper to the log-linear approximation.

My 1975 general formula could only be presented seven years later, in my 1984 Venice paper *"Determination of Cardinal Utility According to an Intrinsic Invariant Model"*.

However, in my 1977 paper, the log-linear approximation permitted *a satisfactory representation as a first approximation* of the cardinal utility of all the subjects that I had studied [14].

1.3.- The Invariant Function of Cardinal Utility 1982-1988

The third period, 1982-1988 was marked by the publication of two new papers on cardinal utility : the paper I gave in Venice in 1984, and the one given in Budapest in 1988.

a - Determination of Cardinal Utility according to an Intrinsic invariant Model (1984)

My 1984 Venice paper outlines, on the one hand, the theoretical method that I have adopted in October-December 1975, and, on the other, the empirical results I obtained. This paper is in fact only a highly abridged résumé of the 200-page general paper, *l'Utilité cardinale et sa détermination - Hypothèses, méthodes et résultats empiriques,* I gave at Venice which presents thorougly the procedure followed, the empirical results and their interpretation.

The essential results are as follows :
- It is possible to represent the cardinal utility for *all* the individuals studied (19 in 1952, and 5 in 1975) *by the same non-loglinear formulation.*
- The formulation of the cardinal utility function was deduced *solely by considering the individuals questioned in 1952.* It follows that to find this formula verified also by the individuals questioned in 1975 is *very remarkable indeed.*
- The formulation obtained is approximately log-linear over a very extended interval of variations [15]. It is rigorously log-linear in the neighborhood of the origin, and it admits an asymptotic value for the very high values of the argument.

This formulation differs from *the 1977 overall log-linear approximation* in two respects : *a cash balance effect near the origin, and a satiety effect for very high values of the argument* [16].
- The curve representing cardinal utility has exactly the same shape as the one found for luminous sensation [17].

All these results are very striking and highly suggestive [18, 19]

b - Cardinal Utility - History, Empirical Findings, and Applications (1988)

In my Budapest paper I deduced, on the basis of a *New Questionnaire,* drawn up in August 1987, the values for the function of cardinal utility, assumed to be invariant *for negative values of the virtual variations of capital.*

The method rests on the consideration of equivalent psychological intervals corresponding to negative and positive variations of capital, *so that negative values of cardinal utility may be deduced from its positive values corresponding to my Venice paper.*

The method applied is *technically far simpler* than that corresponding to the method in the 1984 Venice paper, although it did turn out that the subjects involved had *far greater difficulty* in elaborating their responses that had been the case with *Questions VI* in the *1952 Questionnaire*.

The essential result of this analysis is that cardinal utility declines *very rapidly* for the negative virtual variations of capital [20].

This is the first time in the literature that a consistent estimate of cardinal utility could be made for all the positive and negative values of the argument independently of any consideration of random choices.

II

THEORY OF PROBABILITY

My theory of random choices and of risk is based essentially on two concepts : *the concept of cardinal utility,* which I have just commented, and *the concept of probability.* From 1952 to 1988 I was thus led on to analyse and deepen this concept, and its theoretical analysis.

During a first period, 1952-1955, I confined myself to the distinction between objective probability and subjective probability [21]. After 1974, however, my analysis became progressively refined in basing itself on the one hand on distinguishing *four fundamentally different concepts* : mathematical frequency, empirical frequency, objective probability, and the coefficient of likelihood ; and on the other hand on *a critical analysis* of the existing literature [22].

The main papers I published on this subject from 1974 to 1988 are : *Frequency, Probability and Chance* (1982), the subject of my introductory address to the Oslo Conference ; *The Concept of Probability* (1984) ; and, *Some remarkable Properties of the*

Determination of a Bounded Continuous Distribution by its Moments (1986).

On the 5th of October 1988 I gave to the Dusseldorf Academy of Sciences a paper presenting a synthesis of my probability theory, *Phénomènes Aléatoires et Modèles Fréquentiels - Réalité et Théories - Prolégomènes pour une révision des théories actuellement admises* (Random Phenomena and Frequential Models - Reality and Theories - Prolegomena for a Revision of the Admitted Theories).

2.1 - *Frequency, Probability and Chance (1982)*

My 1982 Oslo paper presents a very brief outline of the guiding ideas which have inspired my work on the theory of probability and risk since 1974.

It presents a critical analysis of : - the concept of probability in the literature ; - the concepts of mathematical frequency, of empirical frequency, of objective probability, and of likelihood ; - the concepts of chance and determinism ; - the simulation of chance ; - the analysis of time series ; and the simulation of chance by almost periodic functions.

It is accompanied by two technical Appendices, *"Empirical Frequencies and Mathematical Frequencies - Illustration"*, and *"Simulation of Chance by Almost Periodic Functions"*, abridged versions of my two other papers presented at the 1982 Oslo conference.

An extended and revised version of this paper and of its two appendices was published in French in 1983 in the *Journal de la Société de Statistique de Paris* under the title, *"Frequence, Probabilité et Hasard"*.

Two of the main *guiding ideas* of these papers should be emphasized :

-There is a profound difference in kind between the empirical random processes and the deterministic frequential models which correspond to them. The calculations which are actually presented in the treatises on *Probability Theory* do not take into account any element of chance, any probability, nor any concept of that sort. They depend exclusively upon calculations of frequencies in situations *where all possible cases are, at least implicitly, assumed to be realized simultaneously. They are thus totally deterministic ;* and they do not correspond at all to the semantics used, nor, *a fortiori,* to the interpretation which almost inevitably generally results from them [23, 24].

-Under very general conditions it is possible to demonstrate that the distribution of values of an almost periodic function, the sum of periodic functions whose periods are incommensurable, is very close to the normal distribution *(Theorem T)*. *This theorem shows that the most absolute determinism can seem to present all appearances of what one generally refers to as chance* [25].

2.2 - Random Phenomena and Frequential Models (1988)

After a new reflection of six years my paper *Phénomènes aléatoires et modèles fréquentiels. Réalité et Théorie. Prolégomènes pour une révision des théories admises (1988)* (Random Phenomena and Frequential Models - Reality and Theory - Prolegomena for a Revision of the Admitted Theories) analyzes thoroughly *the underlying contradictions of the currently admitted probability theories,* and it presents the conditions of a satisfying theory of random phenomena. The guiding ideas of this paper are as follows :

The analysis of random phenomena and their comparison with frequential models lead us to ask a double question :
- How is it possible that on the empirical level individual events which are *essentially unpredictable* may be distributed, at least approximately, according to *predictable* empirical laws ?
- How can *random* phenomena be represented by *totally deterministic* frequential models ?

In fact, *it is the deterministic nature of what is known as randomness which explains the deterministic nature of the asymptotic limits of empirical distributions and the adequation of their representation through the distributions of deterministic frequential models.*

2.3 - Other Papers

From 1976 to 1988 I wrote several other papers which I hope to publish as soon as possible [26].

All these papers, which deal with very different questions, present contributions to a critical analysis of the currently accepted ideas and to the bases of a positive theory of probability and chance. I hope to present an exposition of them in a volume entitled *"Frequency, Probability and Chance"* which is to be published by *Kluwer Academic Publishers.*

III

A POSITIVE THEORY OF CHOICES INVOLVING RISK

From 1950 to 1988 I endeavoured to develop a positive theory of random choices which was *both explanatory and predictive, exempt from any arbitrary hypothesis, and based uniquely upon experiment.* This elaboration took place in three periods, 1950-1955, 1974-1977 and 1982-1988.

3.1.- The Foundations of a Positive Theory of Choice Involving Risk (1952)

The first part of my general paper of 1952 , *Foundations of a Positive Theory of Choices involving Risk - A Critique of the Postulates and Axioms of the American School,* is essentially based on the one hand on my reflections of 1937 upon the trade-off to be sought between mathematical expectation and the probability of ruin [27], and on the other hand upon my analysis of the concept of cardinal utility drawn from my work of 1943 [28].

That paper analyses both the properties of fields of random choices as well as the psychological elements which intervene in choices involving risk. These psychological elements may be separated into two classes : - *fundamental elements* (the psychological distortion of monetary values, the subjective distortion of objective probabilities, the weighting of psychological values according to their probabilities, the taking into account of the form of the probability distributions of psychological values) ; - and *secondary elements* (the costs of distributions of psychological values, the costs of any game, the pleasure of the game considered in itself, the size of the minimal perceptible variation of psychological value, the delay between undertaking a risk and the drawing, etc.). For me, the *pure theory of risk* is limited to the consideration of the four fundamental elements.

What essentially distinguishes this theory from the other conceptions of the epoch is the consideration, *not only of the mathematical expectation of psychological values, but also, and above all, of the whole probability distribution of psychological values around their mean.* This means the consideration : - of the greater or lesser *propensity to security or to risk* which is the result of the distribution of psychological values about their mean ; - of the *psychological complementarity* among the various components of a random prospect ; - and of the *very strong preference for security on the part of all the subjects in the neighborhood of certainty* [29].

The theory is based on the existence, *independent of the consideration of any random choice,* of psychological values (cardinal utilities) and probabilities ; and, this existence being allowed, on an analysis of the properties of the fields of random choices.

The theory rests essentially on three axioms : that the fields of choices are assumed to be *ordered* ; that they are assumed to satisfy the *axiom of absolute preference* [30] ; and that random prospects are assumed to be compounded, according to the fundamental laws of total probabilities and compounded probabilities.

It is expressly assumed that any series of random prospects for the future, considered at a given moment, is reduced to a *unique prospect,* and *it is that unique prospect which is considered in the preference function.* This is an *absolutely essential condition for a correct analysis* of the preference function [31].

The index of preference for each individual is thus a function of the cardinal utilities corresponding to the different eventualities considered, as well as of the associated probabilities. The expression of this index of preference is subordinate to *one single restrictive condition of coherence :* to satisfy the axiom of absolute preference.

It follows that *even by confining oneself to fundamental factors,* it is *impossible* to represent individual psychologies by a unique formulation. *The only psychological factor common to all individuals is a strong preference for security in the presence of certainty* (the certainty effect), although this preference may vary in degree from one individual to the next.

3.2 - The So-Called Allais Paradox and Rational Decisions under Uncertainty (1977)

In my 1977 paper, three absolutely fundamental new axioms were introduced, the *axioms of the homogeneity and invariance* of the index of psychological value, and the *axiom of cardinal isovariation.* The two first axioms have already been discussed above [32]. As for the third, it implies that if all the component cardinal utilities of a given random prospect increase by the same amount, the cardinal utility of this prospect increases by the same amount [33, 34].

From the axiom of cardinal isovariation it follows that the cardinal utility of a random prospect is equal to the sum of the mathematical expectation of the cardinal utilities increased by a function of the moments of the cardinal utilities with respect to their mean. The first term corresponds to *Bernoulli's formulation* while the second term represents the *psychological value of risk.*

In my 1977 paper, my discussion of the St. Petersburg Paradox, with regard to the theory of the ruin of players, provides a particularly significant illustration of the trade-off between mathematical expectation and the probability of ruin.

3.3.- Three Theorems on the Theory of Cardinal Utility and Random Choice (1985)

My 1985 paper presents three theorems on cardinal utility and random choices, the demonstration of which rests upon the properties of invariance, in any linear transformation, of cardinal utility and the neo-Bernoullian index of utility [35].

The proofs of these three theorems are, in fact, quite elementary and obvious, but their implications are profound, both for the determination of the preference function relative to random choices as well as for the neo-Bernoullian formulation.

3.4.- General Theory of Random Choices in Relation to the Invariant Cardinal Utility Function and the Specific Probability Function. The (U, θ) Model. A General Overview (1986)

The object of my 1986 paper, is to illustrate my general theory of random choices (presented in 1952 and completed in 1977) by a model that can easily bring out the implications of my general theory.

This model, *the (U, θ) Model,* is essentially based upon the consideration of the cardinal utility function (determined independently of any consideration of random choices and corresponding to my Venice 1982 paper), and upon the entire distribution of cardinal utilities.

This paper bases itself upon a hypothesis which, according to the available empirical data, appears to be *approximately verified within a very wide domain : the linearity of the cardinal utility of a random prospect in relation to the component cardinal utilities,* a hypothesis which I presented in my 1952 paper, but did not develop at that time [36].

It follows from this hypothesis that the cardinal utility of a random prospect depends *solely* on two functions : the *invariant function of cardinal utility* $u(1+X/U_0)$, and a *specific function* $\theta(F)$ of the function of the decumulative distribution $F(u)$ of cardinal utilities. The quantity U_0 represents the value of the capital of the considered subject such as it is estimated by him, and X represents its eventual variation.

While the cardinal utility function $u(1+X/U_0)$ is assumed to be *the same for all subjects,* the function, $\theta(F)$, which is *representative of the greater or lesser preference for security or for risk,* varies from one subject to another, but it remains constant whatever random perspective P may be considered.

Knowing the psychological capital U_0 and the specific probability function $\theta(F)$ of a subject, permits a *complete determination* of the cardinal utility of a random prospect and of its monetary value *in the most complex cases and in a very wide domain of variation of the utilities, and it permits a prediction of all the decisions of this subject in relation to all the random choices that he might consider.*

The empirical data permit the determination of the function $\theta(F)$ for each subject, and they prove *the existence of a general preference for security in the neighborhood of certainty for all subjects, when large sum are concerned* (the "certainty effect"). In fact, the function $\theta(F)$ varies very slightly, but it is not the same when small sums are involved[37].

This formulation is applied to the analysis of the properties of the field of choices in the case of discrete random prospects P of order three, and is applied in particular to the case of the presentation of a general theory of the *Allais Paradox* which highlights the essential elements that determine the answers to the questions that correspond to it : the psychological capital U_0 of subjects, and their greater or lesser propensity for security or risk as it is represented by the specific probability function $\theta(F)$.

The model thus permits us to discuss the conditions corresponding to the *Allais' Paradox, not only qualitatively, but quantitatively.* It shows that, with regard to people who have an average psychological capital while at the same time having a strong preference for security in the neighborhood of certainty when large sums are concerned, the *Allais' Paradox* is verified [38].

This is the first time in the literature that a theory of random choices permits us, at one and the same time, to represent, account for, and predict, *both qualitatively and quantitatively,* an individual's random choices, and especially those relative to the *Allais' Paradox*. It therefore constitutes *a big step forward* in the theory of random choices.

Naturally, the hypothesis of the linearity of the cardinal utility of a random prospect *with respect to the component cardinal utilities* is only a simplifying hypothesis, but it seems to be largely confirmed by the empirical evidence in a very wide domain of variation of the component of cardinal utilities [39].

IV

GENERALIZATION OF THE THEORIES OF ECONOMIC EQUILIBRIUM AND OF MAXIMAL EFFICIENCY TO THE CASE OF RISK

In my 1952 paper, *"La Généralisation des Théories de l'Equilibre Economique Général et du Rendement Social au cas du Risque"* (The Generalization of the Theories of Economic Equilibrium and of Maximal Efficiency to the Case of Risk), published in the Colloquium volume edited by the C.N.R.S., I showed how it was possible to take into account the uncertainty of the future, of random fields, and of operations relating to the composition of risks (a transposition, in the case of randomness, of production functions concerning the operations of transforming physical goods) to extend the theories of economic equilibrium and maximal efficiency to the case of random choice. Extracts from this paper were published in french under the same title in the journal *Econometrica* in 1953.

The chosen approach was to consider a particular model which was elaborate enough to allow all the important circumstances to appear in it, and thus to enable the different effects to be discussed. Such an approach may be easily generalized.

The model is based both : - on the consideration of fields of choice, which permits an explicit expression, in a simple fashion, which lends itself readily to theoretical analysis, of the greater or lesser propensity for risk or security ; - and on the consideration of production functions which represent the composition of risks according to the principles of the probability calculus. The considered model includes two goods : a sure good (A), and a random good (B), whose values are assumed to be normally distributed. The fields of choice are such that each index of preference is a function of the mathematical expectation and of the standard deviation corresponding to the considered random prospects. In fact the lines of indifference which correspond to the trade-off between the sure good (A) and the random good (B) have a configuration which is entirely different to the one corresponding to the arbitrage between sure goods.

The generalization of the theory of equilibrium is based on the determination of the prices of the sure good and the random good considered according to the double condition that each operator maximizes his index of preference, and that the global supply and demand for goods (A) and (B) are equalized by the price. *The model shows how it is possible to generalize the theorems of equivalence between situations of equilibrium and situations of maximum efficiency.*

The considered model assumes that there are neither insurances nor lotteries ; but, with regard to the results obtained in this particular case, the analysis is extended *to the general case in which the existence of insurances and lotteries is taken into account.* The discussion rests upon the distinction between risks *which cannot be globally eliminated* (the risk of accidents, fire, sickness, etc...), and globally non-existent risks (lotteries).

With respect to the whole literature on the economics of risk, this paper, although relatively short, presents considerable scientific interest. Resting as it does on an entirely original approach, it provides, *for the first time in the literature,* a discussion in depth of the circumstances which present themselves in an economy in which random goods exist [40].

V

A CRITICAL ANALYSIS OF CONTEMPORARY THEORIES

My critical analysis of contemporary theories has developed over the course of three periods.

The first period, from 1950 to 1952, was marked by my general paper of 1952, *Fondements d'une Théorie Positive des Choix comportant un Risque et Critique des Postulats et Axiomes de l'Ecole Américaine* (The Foundations of a Positive Theory of Choice Involving

Risk and a Criticism of the Postulates and Axioms of the American School), and by the poll that I carried out on the basis of the *1952 Questionnaire* [41]. During this period I developed the essential elements of my risk theory and prepared the way for an empirical analysis.

The second period, from 1974 to 1977, was highlighted by my 1977 paper [42], which is fundamentally based upon the analysis of a great number of the answers to the *1952 Questionnaire.*

In *the third period,* from 1982 to 1988, I brought my initial analysis to bear, not only upon the neo-Bernoullian theories, but also upon the more recent theories which, while abandoning the principle of independence, *have nevertheless attached themselves to the same current of thought,* and which, for that reason, may be called *neo-neo-Bernoullian theories.*

5.1.- Critical Analysis of the Neo-Bernoullian Theories, 1950-1952

In their *Theory of Games,* in 1947, von Neumann and Morgenstern presented both a method for determining cardinal utility, and a rational rule of behavior. Both rest upon the consideration of an index which we may call *a neo-Bernoullian index of utility.* The von Neumann-Morgenstern theory proves the existence of such an index from a system of postulates, and they identify it with cardinal utility in the sense of Jevons. According to them, to be rational every subject must maximize the mathematical expectation of that index. Following von Neumann and Morgenstern, this rule of behavior was extolled by other authors, Marschak, Savage, Samuelson, ..., but on the basis of different systems of postulates.

This position appeared to me to be unacceptable because, *directly or indirectly, it amounts to neglecting the distribution of psychological values about their mean,* which is precisely what for me represents *the fundamental element in the theory of risk.*

In the *second part* of my 1952 paper, *"Fondements d'une théorie positive des choix comportant un risque et critique des postulats et axiomes de l'Ecole Américaine"* (Foundations of a Positive Theory of Choice involving Risk, and a Criticism of the Postulates and Axioms of the American School), I presented a criticism of the neo-Bernoullian theories of the American school (von Neumann and Morgenstern, Marschak, Samuelson and Savage). This criticism is based in very large part on the positive theory of random choices outlined in the first part of the paper, and which I had already proposed in my 1951 Louvain paper. It is also founded on the observations I presented during the 1952 Colloquium, of which the principal ones were published in the *Proceedings* of that Colloquium. The main lines of that analysis are as follows :

-Two very different concepts were considered in the discussions during the 1952 Colloquium on the theory of choice involving risk : - *a cardinal index of preference* (or psychological value) of a sure gain (cardinal utility) whose existence is *independent* of the consideration of any random choice, but which ought to be considered to explain behavior with respect to risk ; - and *a neo-Bernoullian index* of such a gain whose existence is only proven from the postulates of the neo-Bernoullian theories. These two indices are both defined up to a linear transformation.

-*The existence of a neo-Bernoullian index* is proven by the neo-Bernoullian school on the basis of various axiomatic systems that differ from author to author (von Neumann-Morgenstern, Marschak, Savage, Samuelson, ...). It follows from these systems that the neo-Bernoullian index, corresponding to a random prospect that assures well determined gains with given probabilities, is equal to the mathematical expectation of the corresponding neo-Bernoullian indices[43].

But in such complex cases as those corresponding to concrete economic applications, *no method for determining the neo-Bernoullian index has been specified.*

- Two very different theses were defended successively by the neo-Bernoullian school : - the first *identifies* the two concepts corresponding to the index of cardinal preference and the neo-Bernoullian index (this is the position taken by von Neumann-Morgenstern in their 1947 *Theory of Games)* ; - the second thesis *denies the real existence of a cardinal index of preference,* and it limits itself to the consideration of the only neo-Bernoullian index (such is Savage's position, for example).

The first position was *totally abandoned* by the supporters of the American school during the 1952 Colloquium, as a result of the criticisms I forwarded. Against the first thesis, I pointed out that such a position would mean considering as irrational every subject which took the distribution of cardinal indices of preference around their mean into account in its choices. *This argument could not be refuted,* and the discussion centred from then onwards on the sole neo-Bernoullian principle of maximizing the mathematical expectation of the neo-

Bernoullian indices, *my opponents contending that cardinal utility had no real existence.*

It follows from this that *if the existence of an index of cardinal preference can be proved, the Bernoullian formula becomes indefensible, even in the eyes of my opponents,* since it cannot be considered irrational to take into account the distribution of the cardinal indices of preference.

-My position was, and remains that :

a) There exists an index of cardinal preference. *It can only be determined directly, independently of any consideration of random prospects.*

b) The cardinal index of preference (or psychological value) corresponding to the monetary value of a random prospect is, in general, *a nonlinear function of the cardinal indices of preference* corresponding to the gains considered and to their probabilities. This means that the psychological value of a random prospect depends not only upon the mathematical expectation of the cardinal indices of preference associated with different gains, but also upon their distribution about their mathematical expectations.

c) One cannot qualify as irrational a subject whose behavior cannot be reduced to maximizing mathematical expectation of the cardinal indices of preference associated with the gains of a random prospect.

d) It is possible that a rational subject might behave by maximizing this mathematical expectation, but *in this case* the neo-Bernoullian index of the neo-Bernoullian theories *necessarily identifies* itself with the index of cardinal preference up to a linear transformation.

e) One cannot admit, as de Finetti claimed (and as many economists still maintain today), that the neo-Bernoullian index takes into account *both* the curvature of the index of cardinal preference and the consideration of the distribution of gains [44].

-From the moment my opponents denied all reality to the cardinal index of preference, I found myself compelled to meet them on their own ground ; and, to this effect, I was led on to present a certain number of counter-examples *independent of any hypothesis as to the existence of a cardinal index of preference* [45]. One of these counter-examples has become celebrated in the Anglo-Saxon literature as the "*Allais Paradox*" [46].

-As a matter of fact, it is easy to see what is the source of the errors committed by the American School. The neo-Bernoullian principle of maximizing the mathematical expectation of the neo-Bernoullian indices corresponding to the gains considered, in effect presupposes *the independence* of the different terms of this mathematical expectation. Now there is *an indisputable complementarity effect* which should not be neglected [47].

In fact, the complementarity effect is strongest the closer one approaches certainty, and all my examples were designed to show this effect, which merely translates the preference of all subjects for security in the neighborhood of certainty.

5.2.- The 1952 Questionnaire

Following the 1952 International Colloquium on random choices, I organized a poll at the end of that year [48]. This poll was based upon a *Questionnaire* which was published in 1953, together with a short introduction, in the *Journal de la Société de Statistique de Paris* under the title, *"La psychologie de l'homme rationnel devant le risque - La théorie et l'expérience"* (The Psychology of Rational Man in the Presence of Risk - Theory and Experience) [49].

All the Questions of this *Questionnaire* have found their origin in the discussions of the 1952 Colloquium [50] - They can take place in four groups :

    a - Questions I and X : Determination of the general characteristics of the psychology of subjects with respect to risk,

    b - Questions VI (Questions 631 to 634 and 651 to 654) : Determination of the cardinal index of preference,

    c - Questions II to V : Tests of the replies to assess their conformity to the neo-Bernoullian formula,

    d - Questions VI, VIII and IX : Determination of the neo-Bernoullian index for series of different questions.

The aim of Questions VI was *to determine the function of cardinal utility from the intensity of preferences such as may be released by introspection* [51, 52].

Questions II (21 and 22) *(Tests IA and IB)* relate to small sums, and tend to make the preference for security or risk evident in subjects who may be considered rational [53].

Questions III (31 to 38) *(Tests IIA, IIB, IIC and IID)* aim to *test the validity* of the fifth axiom of Savage's 1952 paper (which later became "The Sure Thing Principle"). *Test IIC* (Questions 35 and 36) corresponds to the *Allais' Paradox* [54].

Questions III bis (39 and 39 bis) *(Test III)* are designed to test *Samuelson's principle of substitutability* [55].

Questions IV (41-42 and 43-44) (Test IV) have the object of demonstrating that there is a very strong preference for security in the neighbourhood of certainty [56].

Questions V (51-52 and 53-54) (Test V) are designed to test the preference for security in the presence of certainty [57].

Questions VII, VIII and IX aim to show that the neo-Bernoullian indices *deduced from series of different questions are totally different,* as I argued during the 1952 Colloquium discussions [58].

Questions IX permit the determination of sure gains deemed to be equivalent to different gains of probability 1/2, to which there corresponds a neo-Bernoullian index $B_{1/2}$. The aim of *Questions VII* was to determine what sure gains could be judged equivalent to a gain of 200 million francs subject to different probabilities, to which there corresponds a neo-Bernoullian index B_{200}. *Questions VIII* permit the determination of the neo-Bernoullian index $B_{0.01}$ corresponding to sure gains deemed to be equivalent to a gain of 10.000 francs [59] with different probabilities. Finally, from *Questions II, 75 and 83,* it is possible to deduce what sure gains can be judged to be equivalent to the probability equal to 9/10 of winning various gains, and consequently to determine a fourth neo-Bernoullian index $B_{9/10}$. As a matter of fact, *the analysis of the responses shows that these four indices in general differ completely from each other.*

A thorough study of indices $B_{1/2}$ and B_{200} shows that they differ *very significantly in the case of all the subjects,* and correspond to a *100 % rate of violation of the neo-Bernoullian formula* [60].

5.3.- The So-Called Allais Paradox and Rational Decisions under Uncertainty (1977)

As for my criticism of the neo-Bernoullian theories, my paper of 1977 takes its place as a continuation of my 1952 paper, and states my position more precisely and completely, taking into account the criticism addressed to this paper and the responses to my 1952 *Questionnaire* [61].

In fact, *it is based essentially* on the results of the analysis of responses to my *1952 Questionnaire,* the aim of which was to highlight the behaviour of the subjects studied with respect to random choice [62].

The analysis of the answers to the 1952 poll permitted to obtain three essential results :

- *The direct determination of the cardinal index of preference* (cardinal utility) for different subjects from appropriate questions *independent* of any consideration of random choice [63].
- *The general inconsistency of the responses to the questions stated* (Questions II, III, IV and V) *with the neo-Bernoullian formulation* [64].
- *The impossibility of determining a neo-Bernoullian index for each subject* susceptible of representing his behaviour *with regard to a series of different questions* in the hypothesis of the validity of the neo-Bernoullian formulation.

Hence the criticism of the neo-Bernoullian theories which I presented in 1952 *is found to be entirely justified* [65].

Relative to my position of 1952, this analysis confirmed that the neo-Bernoullian theories are unfounded *because they fundamentally neglect* [66] :
- *the greater or lesser propensity for risk* resulting from the distribution of psychological values around their mean.
- *the general complementarity* of the different eventualities of a random prospect contradicting the independence principle of these theories.
- *the very strong preference for security of all the subjects in the neighborhood of certainty*.

All these empirical results show that the postulates on which the *contemporary theories of risk rest, founded on the neo-Bernoullian principle of independence, are not justified ; and that it is impossible to qualify as irrational the choices that are made in the neighborhood of certainty by almost all the subjects, in violation of the neo-Bernoullian principle* [67].

5.4.- The Foundations of the Theory of Utility and Risk (1984)

My 1984 paper, *The Foundations of the Theory of Utility and Risk* presents a critical analysis of :
- all theories of probabilities [68].
- recent developements in the theory of random choices, both in the theoretical considerations and in empirical studies.
- the problems in the philosophy of science which correspond to the theory of probability and to the theory of random choices.

The First Part presents a critical analysis : - of the concepts of chance, mathematical frequency, empirical frequency, objective and subjective probability ; - of the comparative meaning of the principles of Laplace, Bayes and R.A. Fisher ; - of the concepts of chance and determinism ; - and of the concepts of determinism and causality.

The *Second Part* presents a critical analysis - of the concepts of cardinal utility and of neo-Bernoullian utility [69] ; - of Arrow-Pratt's concept of risk aversion ; - of the theories of random choice of, respectively, Daniel Bernoulli, von Neumann and Morgenstern, Savage, and Allais, and their comparative significance. It also presents a brief analysis of recent theoretical and empirical contributions to the theories of random choice, of utility, and of risk [70].

The Third Part, finally presents some comments : - on the future of *the analysis of expected utility* of neo-Bernoullian theories ; - on the role and the functions of axiomatisation ; - on the concept of rationality ; - and lastly on the permanence of problems and the evolution of ideas in the literature.

Considered as a whole, this paper has the essential advantage of placing my theory of random choice *in relation to the prevailing currents of thought i*n the contemporary literature, and of making clear *the central questions* under discussion.

5.5.- The Allais Paradox (1985)

One of the counter-examples to the neo-Bernoullian theories which I presented in 1952 [71] has become famous as the *"Allais' Paradox"*. This Paradox has given grounds for innumerable discussions, and since 1952 it has never ceased to be commented on in all publications on the theory of random choice, particularly in the United States.

At the request of the editors of the the *"New Palgrave",* I have drafted a synthetic analysis of the *"Allais' Paradox"* and of the discussions to which it has given rise. In fact the *Allais' Paradox* is actually only paradoxical in appearance, and it corresponds simply to a very profound reality, *the very strong preference for security in the neighborhood of certainty, and this for all the subjects* (the certainty effect).

Just as the *St. Petersburg Paradox* led Daniel Bernoulli to replace the principle of maximizing the mathematical expectation of monetary values by the Bernoullian principle of the maximization of cardinal utilities, the *Allais' Paradox* leads to completing the Bernoullian formula of mathematical expectation of cardinal utilities by a specific term *characteristic of the propensity towards risk,* taking into account their general distribution.

In reality, there is nothing paradoxical in the Paradox of St. Petersburg, nor in the Allais' Paradox. Both correspond to fundamental psychological realities : - the non-identity of monetary values and psychological values ; - and the psychological importance of the distribution of cardinal utilities around their mean [72].

5.6.- Critical Analysis of the Theories of the Literature in Connection with the Model (U, θ) (1986)

In my 1986 paper, *The general theory of random choices in relation ot the invariant cardinal utility function and the specific probability function, The (U, θ) Model, A general overview* [73], I presented a critical analysis of three theories in the literature, those of Quiggin, 1982, Yaari, 1984, and Segal 1984, each of which, leads to a mathematical formulation analogous to that of the (U, θ) Model, although they differ profoundly as to their inspiration, their conception, and their interpretation.

These three theories, which are very profoundly influenced by the neo-Bernoullian theories, and which seek simply to generalize them, are characteristic in many respects of the tendencies of contemporary theories : an excessive mathematical abstraction and of an insufficient concern with empirical data. *As a matter of fact their postulates do not have any general value, and, as I have shown, they are invalidated by observational data* [74].

5.7.- A New Neo-Bernoullian Theory : The Machina Theory. A Critical Analysis (1986)

In 1982, Mark Machina presented a new theory, *The generalized expected utility analysis,* which in its inspiration and its approach appears to me as a *new neo-Bernoullian theory.*

This theory [75] rests upon the consideration of a new index : the neo-Bernoullian local index, called *"local utility",* and on two Hypotheses (I and II). Like the neo-Bernoullian theories, and despite the fact that it does not admit the independence axiom, Machina's theory rests, as he emphasizes himself, upon the same *"basic concepts, tools and results",* and it rejects the consideration of a cardinal utility defined independently of any random choice.

The object of my 1986 paper *"A New Neo-Bernoullian Theory: The Machina Theory - A Critical Analysis",* is to clarify some very important points relative to Machina's theory of local utility, the mathematical presentation of which is *relatively complex* and generally misunderstood. It is to display *the actual implications* of this theory, and to show how it encounters *major objections*. These objections bear, in the case of discrete or mixed distributions, on the very existence of the local utility index, and, in all cases, on the significance and the implications of Machina's Hypotheses I and II.

On the whole, the critical analysis I present and which is based notably on the theory of moments, *goes very largely beyond the relatively restricted framework of the Machina theory*. As a matter of fact, this analysis has the advantage of focusing attention on some *fundamental aspects* of the theory of random choice, and on the impossibility of a correct representation and a correct explanation of the facts from the *"basic concepts, tools and results" of neo-Bernoullian theories* [76].

VI

APPLICATIONS

On the whole, all my applied works have been based on my general theory of random choice as outlined in my general paper of 1952, *The Foundations of a Positive Theory of Choice Involving Risk and a Criticism of the Postulates and Axioms of the American School,* and on the general principle that the policy to be enacted should rest *upon a reasonable trade-off between the mathematical expectation of anticipated gains and the probability of ruin.*

It has always been possible for me to treat all the concrete cases I have been induced to study in a *very simple fashion* without it being necessary, as in the case of neo-Bernoullian theories, to build up axiomatic theories so complex and so detached from reality that they are truly inapplicable and of no use at all in the field of the real world [77].

6.1.- The Trade-off between the Mathematical Expectation and the Probability of Ruin - My Analysis of 1937

At the origin of all my studies on the theory of choice under uncertainty is a study I made in 1937. It was basically concerned with a method, suggested by a friend, that could be adopted for placing bets at the races. With regard to its main lines, the method consisted of playing those horses which have been most recommended by the press as a whole.

Taking as a point of departure the data published in a journal called *"La Veine" ("Luck")*, and after a close initial examination of the racing forecasts and the actual results, I found that the proposed method permitted me to be sure of a mathematical expectation which was significantly positive.

The problem which arose then was the choice of a rational strategy. *Playing for high stakes* would assure me of substantial winnings *on average* ; but, my resources being *limited,* I risked losing them rapidly and being unable to continue to bet if an unfavourable course of events should ensue. *Playing for small stakes* would practically eliminate the risk, but then the winnings would also be limited. I then realized that the most reasonable strategy had to be based on a trade-off between these two alternatives, i.e. on a trade-off between mathematical expectation and the probability of ruin [78, 79].

It was the result of this reflection which led me to contest the neo-Bernoullian formulation advocated in the 1947 second edition of the *Theory of Games* [80].

6.2 - The Trade-off between the Cost of Security and the Cost of Failure (1954)

During the 1954 Uppsala meeting of the Econometric Society I was led to present a short comment *on the trade-off between the cost of security and the cost of failure in the case of the building of the protective Dutch dykes.*

This case gives a good illustration of the solutions to practical problems *such as those which decision makers usually face.* In fact, for such purposes it is not necessary to have read the innumerable papers that present very abstract, and *usually inapplicable,* mathematical theories designed to handle the theory of random choices.

In the case considered, it was sufficient to submit to the government a table with two columns, the first corresponding to the probability of failure, and the second corresponding to the cost of the installations envisaged as a function of that probability of failure, leaving it to the government to choose the line which appeared to be politically optimal.

Naturally, the techniques for estimating the figures of each case in each column can present considerable difficulties and require long study, but from the point of view of the theory of random choice, identifying the choice that appears to be politically optimal is always relatively simple.

6.3.- The Trade-off between the Mathematical Expectation and the Probability of Ruin in the Case of Mining Research (1955)

From 1952 to 1955 I was a consultant to the Algerian Bureau of Mining Research. In this capacity I was led to prepare several papers [81] a synthesis of which appeared in my paper, *"Evaluation des Perspectives Economiques de la Recherche Minière sur de Grands Espaces - Application au Sahara Algérien" (Method of Appraising Economic Prospects of Mining Exploration over large Territories - Algerian Sahara Case Study).*

This paper was presented in 1955 at both the *Congress of the Society of Mineral Industries,* in Paris, and the *Congress of the International Institute for Statistics,* in Petropolis, Brazil. Internationally, it had a considerable impact upon the experts in mining research.

Upon the suggestion of Jacob Marschak, the English translation of this paper was published in 1957, in the journal *Management Science* [82]. For this paper I was awarded, in May 1958, the *Lanchester Prize* of the *John Hopkins University* and of the *American Society for Operational Research* for the best study of operational research published in 1957.

The purpose of this paper, which was a résumé of a general work on operational research that the Algerian Mining Exploration Board had asked me to make, was to present reasonable forecasts, *before any actual exploration,* as to the economic prospects offered by mining research in the *non-sedimentary* part of the Sahara (the surface of which covers about one million km^2) [83], and to determine an optimal economic strategy for this research [84]. *A priori, this was a perfectly insolvable problem.* A statistical analysis of empirical data, however, showed that it could in fact be solved.

The analysis presented in that paper is based both upon the elaboration of a probabilistic model and the application of this model to the case study using the available empirical data.

The probabilistic model compares mining exploration to a veritable lottery in which the tickets cost hundreds of millions of francs and the prizes may yield hundreds of billions of francs [85]. It is based upon the fact that statistical mining distributions obey certain very well-determined laws in a quite remarkable manner : lognormal law for the value of mineral deposits, Poisson's law for the probability of discovery, and the normal law for dimensionless parameters such as the standard deviation of distributions [86].

As unlikely as this proposition may seem at first sight, it is a fact that *everything happens as if* the laws of probability relating to mineral deposits were *the same* for each million km^2, *whatever the non-sedimentary geological nature of the terrains considered may be*. This result is deduced from the consideration of the countries already explored, and it permits to determine the laws of distribution for the countries still unexplored [87].

The analysis effected thus permits to determine the law of distribution for the global value of mineral deposits likely to be discovered in the non-sedimentary Sahara [88], and to calculate the probability for profitable exploration, and its variation as a function of the prospected area [89].

My entire study has been inspired by the theoretical and empirical research into risk which I pursued in 1950-1952, *my guiding idea being the search for a reasonable trade-off between the mathematical expectation of expected gains and the probability of ruin, with which I could advise the Algerian Mining Exploration Board* [90]. The essential conclusion was that exploration should be pursued throughout the whole of the non-sedimentary Sahara, *as any reduction in the scale of exploration would lead to unacceptable levels of probability of ruin.*

6.4.- Applications of Allais' General Theory of Random Choice - Illustration by the (U, θ) Model - 1986

Three illustrations of my general theory of random choice have been presented within the framework of the (U, θ) Model : the analysis of the *Allais' Paradox,* the purchase of insurance policies, and the purchase of lottery tickets.

a - The Theory of the Allais' Paradox and its Empirical Applications (1986)

In my Aix-en-Provence paper, *"The General Theory of Random Choices in relation to the Invariant Cardinal Utility Function and the Specific Probability Function. The (U, θ) Model",* my general theory of random choices was successfully applied to the theoretical analysis of the *Allais' Paradox* and to the empirical study of the responses provided by four significant subjects [91]. In view of the numerous highly *restrictive* hypotheses that are entailed, the results that were obtained were quite remarkable [92].

b - The Purchase of Insurance Policies and Lottery Tickets (1988)

The application of the (U, θ) model in my 1988 Budapest paper, *Cardinal Utility - History, Empirical Findings, and Applications,* to the theoretical analysis of the purchase of insurance policies and lottery tickets appear particularly *suggestive in clearly bringing out the psychological elements that determine the choices actually made,* and, in particular, *the necessity* of knowing the function of cardinal utility throughout its whole domain of variation, and especially for negative values.

6.5.- Applications to the Problem of Transfers (1988)

In my 1988 Budapest paper I showed that knowing the values of the function of cardinal utility throughout its domain of variation permits two particularly suggestive applications, the first relating to the *transfers of resources,* and the second relating to the optimal distribution of taxes [93].

In both cases the three essential hypotheses made are :
- that the function of cardinal utility is *actually the same* for all subjects once one considers the relative values ΔU/U of psychological capital *(the hypothesis of invariance).*
- that the functions of cardinal utility *are actually comparable from one subject to the next* once these utilities are defined according to the same scale, i.e. the same values at the origin and with regard to satiety.
- and that, lastly, the collective function of well-being may be taken to be equal to the sum of cardinal utilities thus defined of the different subjects.

VII

MY CONTRIBUTIONS
TO THE THEORY OF UTILITY AND RISK,
AND PREVAILING IDEAS

7.1.- My Contributions to the Theory of Utility and Risk

My 1952 paper, *The Foundations of a Positive Theory of Choice Involving Risk and a Criticism of the Postulates and Axioms of the American School,* and my *1952 Questionnaire,* have certainly constituted a decisive step in the critical analysis of contemporary theories of utility and risk.

Under one form or another, directly or indirectly, almost all the critical studies published since 1952 have taken up the developments of my 1952 paper once more, and all of them have taken as their point of departure the *"Allais Paradox"*, and they endeavoured to explain it.

In any case, and whatever position one may adopt on the substance of the debate, my research has contributed to a considerable clarification of some very complex questions, and discussions on the "Allais' Paradox" have everywhere stimulated reflection and further research [94].

I have nevertheless never ceased to encounter powerful opposition in as much as my position appears to be incompatible with the prevailing ideas of the day, and with the universal acceptance of the *"Expected Utility Theory".*

It is a fact that the more ideas tend to diverge from the beaten paths, and from commonly admitted theories, the more difficulties they encounter to be accepted, such is the power of dogmatism and deeply rooted prejudices. Is not the essence of error to believe itself to be the truth ? Cannot the history of science to a great extent be reduced to the history of the errors committed by competent men ?

The dominating position held by neo-Bernoullian concepts remained absolute in the decade following the 1952 Paris Colloquium ; and in his 1957 review of my 1952 paper, *Foundations of a Positive Theory of Choice Involving Risk and a Criticism of the Postulates and Axioms of the American School* [95], Georges Morlat could still write [96]:

"It could be an authentic bet on the part of the Revue of Political Economy to have solicited to review this work a man who, having stood at Allais' side for years throughout the controversy opposing him to the "American School", is today well convinced that the thesis of Jimmy L. Savage in his "Foundations of Statistics" constitutes a fundamental acquisition of logic worthy of serving as a rule of behaviour for all reasonable people - a man, so to say, and to say as Allais might, who has "gone over to the other side". "If there is only one man left, I will be he !" Allais assured us four years ago. It is not improbable that that will soon be the case".

The opposition I have encountered has been going on for a very long time now, and it still continues. I can only return here to the comments I offered in 1983 at the end of my 1984 paper, *The Foundations of the Theory of Utility and Risk* [97].

It is truly striking that in the reviews which were published of the 1979 work *"Expected Utility Hypothesis and the Allais Paradox"* (M. Allais and O. Hagen, ed.), no mention was made of the *fundamental contribution* constituted by the analysis of the responses to the *1952 Questionnaire* in the *Appendix C* of my 1977 paper.

Often too many authors still omit citing my work, maybe when it disturbs them, even when they are perfectly aware of it [98].

For many people incapable of providing a well-founded refutation, their sole weapon is to remain silent. It may not be a very estimable method, but it is often a highly effective one.

But this is only a rear-guard action ; and, *sooner or later, the errors of the neo-Bernoullian theories will end up by being clear for all to see*. For the last twenty years, in fact, a change of opinion has been making itself more and more manifest, and *it continues to grow*.

Here I can only thank all those who have never ceased supporting me with their help since 1970 : Ole Hagen, Werner Leinfellner, Bertrand Munier, and so many others.

7.2.- The Approach of Contemporary Theories and my Scientific Philosophy

In reality, what separates me from a large number of contemporary theories is a profoundly different conception regarding scientific method.

For almost forty years, the literature of contemporary economics has been developing in a totally mistaken direction, owing to the *development of completely artificial mathematical models totally detached from reality* ; and, in fact, it is increasingly dominated by *a mathematical formalism which fundamentally represents an immense regression.*

However, if mathematics constitute an instrument of which mastery is extremely valuable, they are not and never can be more than an instrument. No-one could ever be a good physicist or a good economist for the sole reason of having some knowledge of or ability in mathematics.

Indeed, it is no longer necessary today to justify the utility and the necessity of rigorously edified models from perfectly specified axioms. But, however, *it cannot simply be considered sufficient for a theory to rest upon a rigorous axiomatisation in order to be scientifically valid.* Whatever necessary such an axiomatisation may be, it is in reality only secondary with regard to the critical analysis of the axioms on which it rests and the confrontation of their implications with regard to the data of experience. Paradoxically, from the scientific point of view, incomparably more care is taken today over the mathematical elaboration of models than over the discussion of their structure, and of their results *from the point of view of analyzing the facts.*

Contemporary economic literature offers us innumerable examples of the aberrations that may occur once one neglects the essential principle that theories are not worth more than their agreement with observed facts, and that *the only source of truth is experience.* It is a fact that a major part of the contemporary theoretical literature is progressively passing under the control of pure mathematicians more preoccupied by mathematical theorems than by analyzing real facts, and we are witnessing a new scholastic totalitarianism based upon *a priori* abstract concepts that are detached from all reality, the kind of *"mathematical charlatanry"* that Keynes already denounced in his *Treatise on Probability.*

We cannot repeat it forcefully enough, for the economist as for the physicist, the essential objective is not the use of mathematics for itself, but as a means of exploring and analyzing the real phenomena ; and it follows that the theory must never be dissociated from its applications.

My conviction is that logical deduction, if not constantly linked to the study of reality, only leads to sterility. *The only source of knowledge is, and cannot be anything but, experience.* My scientific work was thus more and more inspired by the necessity of only admitting theories to the extent to which they are capable of representing the observed facts and of being verified by empirical data. The fundamental criterion of a theory's scientific validity is its confirmation by empirical data, and *submission to the data of experience is the golden rule which dominates all scientific disciplines. This rule applies just as much to economic science as to the natural sciences.*

There is science only where regularities exist which can be submitted to analysis and prediction. To a very great extent, therefore, as in the physical sciences, the elaboration of economic science appears to me to have to rest upon the search for relations and quantities which are invariant in time and space.

In this elaboration, the use of mathematics, while it is indispensable in so far as it is an instrument of logical deduction, is in itself of only secondary interest. *What is really essential is the formulation of hypotheses that lend themselves to models which may be confronted with experimental facts.*

Such are the principles that have inspired all my works. All of them arise from a profound unity of conception and a deep concern for synthesis. All are based on a quantitive analysis of facts from models, be they descriptive or explicative. All combine a critical analysis of the existing literature and an econometric analysis of the data of experience.

All my works rest upon the conviction, confirmed by experience, that no real progress in economic science can be derived from purely abstract reasoning, but only from the association of theoretical analysis and the econometric analysis of observed facts. In all these works, I believe that I have freed myself from standard conceptions and from the beaten tracks *by introducing new concepts and by formalising new theories that are better able to represent reality as it is* [99].

NOTES

Introduction

(*)*Comment je vois le monde* (How I see the world), 1939, Flammarion, p. 165.
(**) My most significant contributions to the theory of utility and risk published between 1952 and 1988 will be published by Kluwer under the title *Scientific Papers on Risk and Utility Theory - Theory, Experience, and Applications* (1000 p.).
(1) *Econometrie*, 1952, p. 127-140, and 81-109.
(2) id., p. 26, 34-35, 37-40, 47-48, 110-120, 151-157, 160-162, 194-197, 212-213, 228, 233, and 245-247.
(3) id., p. 257-332.

(4) English translation of my 1954 paper, *Evaluation des Perspectives Economiques de la Recherche Minière sur de Grands Espaces - Application au Sahara Algérien,* published in the american review, *Management Science.*
(5) My notations have varied over the course of my publications. In this regard see especially the note added (p. 699) to the indices of proper names and subjects of my two papers published in Allais and Hagen, 1979, *Expected Utility Hypotheses and the Allais Paradox.*

1.- Cardinal Utility and its Determination

(6) p. 156-177 ; 227-288 ; 233-234 ; 263-264 ; 281-282 ; 416-419. In this book I called ordinal utility and cardinal utility, respectively, *"satisfaction"* and *"satisfaction absolue".*
(7) See in particular p. 163-165. There I reproduced the curve of *psychophysiological sensation as a function of luminous excitation,* a curve which I used again in my 1984 Venice paper, § 4.4 and *Chart XXV.* In fact the cardinal utility curve I have found is practically identical to the psychophysiological curve (1984, p. 118-119).
(8) The english translation of my 1943 analysis will be published under the title, *Absolute Satisfaction,* in Allais and Hagen, 1992, *Cardinal Utility,* Kluwer.
My Louvain 1951 analysis exists only on a mimeographed form.
(9) The complete analysis of the answers to the *1952 Questionnaire* was not performed until 1974. See below, § 5.2.
(10) *The So-Called Allais' Paradox and rational Decisions under Uncertainty,* 1977, § 23.
(11) id., § C.5 to C.9, § C.20 to C.23, and *Charts I to VI.*
(12) id., § 23.2.1.
(13) id., § C.21
(14) id., § C. 5 to C.10, and the associated Charts.
(15) *Determination of Cardinal Utility According to an Intrinsic Invariant model,* 1984, *Chart IX.*
(16) id., 1984, *Chart IX,* and, *Cardinal Utility - History, Empirical Findings, and Applications,* 1988, *Chart I.*
(17) id., 1984, § 4.3, and *Charts III and XXV.*
(18) In my 1986 Aix-en-Provence paper (§ 3.4 below), I presented a table of values for the invariant cardinal utility function as well as interpolation formulae that permit its calculation (Tables B.1 and B.2 corresponding to the maximal value M = 1.9, that corresponds to satiety.

Table I of my 1988 paper (§ 1.3.b below) gives the values for the cardinal utility function when M = 1.

(19) It is appropriate to emphasize here a remarkable fact. Together with his answers to the *1952 Questionnaire* (§ 1.1.d above), Marschak transmitted to me the values of his *"utility function"* deduced, according to his indications from the consideration of the Questions of the *Questionnaire*. Taking into account the value of his capital, as I could estimate it on the basis of his answers, his index of utility is practically identical with the function of cardinal utility of my 1984 Venice paper, (§ 1.3.a above).

On this point, see Allais, *Analyse sommaire des réponses au Questionnaire de 1952 faites par les économistes étrangers participants au Colloque de 1952* : K.J. Arrow, B. de Finetti, M. Friedman, J. Marschak, L.J. Savage* (12 p., October 1975, revised and completed, 1988).

* Brief analysis of the answers to the 1952 Questionnaire of the foreign economists who participated to the 1952 Colloquium.

(20) Diagram VII C of my 1988 paper.

This paper is only a highly abridged version of a much more extensive paper which has been published in the journal, *Theory and Decision (vol. 3 , Nr. , pp. -)* under the title *"Cardinal Utility - Theory, Experience and Applications"*.

2.- Theory of Probability

(21) *The Foundations of a Positive Theory of Choice Involving Risk and a Criticism of the Postulates and Axioms of the American School,* 1952. See the *Introduction* above.

(22) *The So-Called Allais' Paradox and Rational Decisions under Uncertainty,* 1977, Appendix D, and, *Frequency, Probability and Chance,* 1983.

(23) Thus the term, *random variables,* assigned to mathematical variables that are distributed according to some statistical law, is *particularly inappropriate.*

(24) 1983, id., Appendix A.

(25) 1983, id., Appendix B.

(26) These still unpublished papers are the following :
- *Les fondements de la théorie des probabilités,* 1976, (The Foundations of Probability Theory) ;
- *Régularités présentées par les décimales des nombres irrationnels définis à partir de la suite des nombres entiers,* 1982, (Regularity

Properties of the Decimal Figures of Irrational Numbers Defined from the Sequence of Integers) ;
- *Sur la théorie des tests,* 1982, (On the Theory of Tests) ;
- *Formulation fréquentielle du théorème de Bayes,* 1982, (A Frequential Formulation of Bayes's Theorem) ;
- *Analyse critique de quelques points fondamentaux de la littérature sur la théorie des probabilités,* 1983, (A Critical Analysis of Some Fundamental Points in the Literature of Probability Theory) ;
- *La théorie axiomatique de Kolmogorov et la théorie fréquentielle de Richard von Mises au regard de la réalité concrète,* 1983, (Kolmogorov's Axiomatic Theory and Richard von Mises's Frequential Theory, Confronted by Concrete Reality) ;
- *Processus aléatoires empiriques et théorie axiomatique - La liaison expérience - théorie et le principe de correspondance,* 1983, (Empirical Random Processes and Axiomatic Theory - The Link Experience - Theory and the Principle of Correspondence) ;
- *Sur les travaux de la littérature en liaison avec le Théorème (T),* 1984 (On the Literature dealing with the T-Theorem) ;
- *Extension du théorème central limite au cas de variables non indépendantes,* 1984, (An Extension of the Central Limit Theorem to the Case of non-independent Variables) ;
- and, *Sur la détermination d'une distribution continue bornée par une infinité dénombrable de moments,* 1987, (On the Determination of a Continuous Bounded Distribution by a Denumerable Infinity of Moments).

3.- *A Positive Theory of Choice Involving Risk*

(27) § 6.1 below.
(28) § 1.1.a above.
(29) *"Certainty effect"* des théories contemporaines.
(30) According to this axiom if one compares two random prospects, and if one of them offers greater gains than the other in all possible cases, it is preferred to the other.
(31) Many confusions in the contemporary theories arise from the neglect of this condition.
(32) § 1.2.a above.
(33) In fact, I had already introduced the axiom of cardinal isovariation in another form in my 1952 monograph, *Foundations of a Positive Theory of Choice involving Risk and a Critique of the Postulates and Axioms of the American School,* § 69.b.

(34) It should be emphasized that the formulation that had been proposed in 1738 by Daniel Bernoulli for the cardinal utility of a random prospect satisfies both these axioms.
(35) The proof of these theorems assumes, *as it results from all the available empirical evidence,* that for each subject there exists a well determined index of cardinal utility that is defined up to a linear transformation.

By the first theorem, the preference function with regard to random choices should not have any expression, and it is expressed in the form of a function of the component cardinal utilities which is *invariant under any linear transformation.*

According to the second theorem, the postulate of cardinal isovariation (§ 3.2, above) is actually only a special consequence of the first theorem.

According to the third theorem, cardinal utility and the neo-Bernoullian index, if it exists, are *identical,* up to a linear transformation.
(36) My 1952 paper, id., § 41, relation IV.
(37) My 1986 paper, § 1.5.2.
(38) The responses of four of the subjects, who were particularty interesting, de Finetti, Malinvaud, Saint Guilhem and Jacquelin, are analysed.
(39) Some questions with which we deal in §§ 3.1, 3.2, 3.3 and 3.4 above have been developed in four papers which will be published shortly : - *Le Paradoxe de Saint-Pétersbourg et la ruine des joueurs,* 1976, (The Saint-Petersburg Paradox and the Ruin of Gamblers ; - *New Applications of the Allais (U, θ) Model,* 1987 ; - *The Preference Function relating to Random Prospects as a Function of Moments,* 1987 ; - and, *On the Variation of Preference Functionals,* 1987.

4.- Generalization of the Theories of Economic Equilibrium and Maximal Efficiency to the Case of Risk

(40) See particularly my remarks in the paper read by M. Arrow at the 1952 Paris Colloquium in the corresponding book, *Econométrie,* p. 47-48.

5.- A Critical Analysis of Contemporary Theories

(41) See § 1.1.d above.
(42) See § 1.2 above.

(43) To explain the *Saint-Petersburg Paradox,* Daniel Bernoulli, in his 1738 paper, considered *the mathematical expectation of cardinal utilities,* but without attaching any normative value to it.
(44) On this point see my observations during the 1952 Paris Colloquium, volume of the Colloquium, *Econométrie,* 1953, General Observations, § 3, p. 346-347 ; and my 1984 paper, *The Foundations of the Theory of Utility and Risk,* § 2.4.1.
(45) See my 1952 paper, *The Foundations of a Positive Theory of Choice Involving Risk and a Criticism of the Postulates and Axioms of the American School.*
(46) 1952, id., § 63 and 1977, *The So-Called Allais' Paradox and Rational Decisions under Uncertainty,* § 36.
(47) See, in particular, 1952, id., § 63 and 64.
(48) See my 1977 paper, § 3,6.
(49) As I stated at the end of this paper, I intended to follow this publication with a paper expliciting *the principles* followed in the writing of the various questions and *their implications,* and which would present the first results obtained in the analysis of the answers to the *Questionnaire.*
The main lines of that paper were presented in my lecture of November, 19, 1952 before the Statistical Society of Paris. Unfortunately, I was then absorbed by other very pressing obligations and had to postpone this publication and the intended paper was never published.
(50) See the volume of the 1952 Paris Colloquium, *Econométrie,* CNRS, 1953, (note 1 above).
(51) In point of fact, *Questions 631-634* only provided limited information, and only *Questions 651-654* were well chosen. Unfortunately, they were too few and they only covered a *too limited* interval of relative variation regarding the sums considered, from 1 to 10. As a result there were difficulties in using the answers.
When I decided in 1975 to undertake a confirmatory poll, I considered a total interval of relative variation from 1 to 1000, (see my 1984 paper, *Determination of Cardinal Utility According to an Intrinsic Invariant Model,* § 2.2).
(52) I recall here that if there is a cardinal utility, the neo-Bernoullian formulation is not necessarily invalidated (§ 5.1 above).
(53) For small sums the neo-Bernoullian formulation implies that the utility of a random prospect be equal to the mathematical expectation of the nominal values considered.

(54) *The Foundations of a Positive Theory of Choice Involving Risk and a Criticism of the Postulates and Axioms of the American School,* 1952, § 63 ; *The so-called Allais' Paradox and rational Decisions under Uncertainty,* 1977, § 36 ; and *The General Theory of Random Choices in relation to the Invariant Cardinal Utility Function and the Specific Probability Function. The (U, q) Model,* 1986, § 2.2.3.2 and A.4.

The theoretical formulation underlying Tests II A (Questions 31-32), II B (Questions 33-34), and II D, (Questions 37-38) is identical to that of the *Allais' Paradox.* Only the sums and probabilities which are implied differ.

(55) The corresponding analysis is provided in my 1952 paper, § 64 and 71 ; and in my 1977 paper, § A.6.2.

(56) Let X_1 and X_2 be the responses to *Questions 41 and 42.* A neo-Bernoullian psychology should imply that $X_1 > X_2$, with the difference $X_2 - X_1$ being very small. Actually, we find that, in general X_2 is significantly larger than X_1.

Let X_3 and X_4 be the responses to *Questions 43 and 44.* A neo-Bernoullian psychology would imply that they should be practically equivalent. We find, however, that, in general, X_3 is far larger than X_4.

For the analysis of these questions, see my observations during the 1952 Paris Colloquium in *Econométrie,* 1953, p. 245-247, § 4.2, and in my 1977 paper, § A.4.

(57) A neo-Bernoullian psychology would imply in both cases that if situation A is preferred to situation B, situation C should be preferred to situation D. Experience shows that this is not so for a great number of subjects.

(58) See my observations during the 1952 Paris Colloquium, *Econométrie,* 1953, p. 160-162 and p. 246-247, § 3.

(59) The monetary unit considered in the *1952 Questionnaire* is the franc of 1952. One hundred francs of 1952 are approximately equivalent to one dollar of 1985.

(60) On the indices $B_{1/2}$ and B_{200} see : *The So-Called Allais' Paradox and Rational Decisions under Uncertainty,* 1977, Appendix C, Sections III and IV.

The answers to Questions VII and IX are also used in my 1986 paper, *The General Theory of Random Choices in relation to the Invariant Cardinal Utility Function and the Specific Probability Function. The (U, q) Model,* § 3.1 and A.3.

(61) 1977, id., § 32 to 38.

(62) A brief summary of the main results is presented in *Appendix C* of my 1957 paper. See also § 6 above.
(63) See my 1987 paper, § 23, B.1, C.5 - C.9, C.18, C.20- C.23.
(64) id., 1977, § 22 and *Appendix C,* note 15.
(65) id., 1977, § 22-23, 28, C. 19 and C.23.
(66) id., 1977, § 18, 35.2, 36.1, 36.2 and § 36.3.
(67) Regarding these results, my 1977 paper offers : - *a critical analysis* of the fundamental concepts of the neo-Bernoullian theories, § 27-31 ; - *an answer* to the criticisms that have been made of my work, § 32-38 ; - *a general interpretation* of my analysis regarding the theory and the empirical results, and *a comparison* of the axiomatic foundations of my theory with those of the von Neumann-Morgenstern theory, § 39-41 ; - and an analysis of the von Neumann-Morgenstern theory of choice, *Appendix A.*
As for the properties of fields of random choices, and from *the axiomatic point of view, the crucial difference* between my theory and the neo-Bernoullian theories is found in *the substitution of the axiom of absolute preference and of the axiom of cardinal isovariation for the axiom of independence* of the neo-Bernoullian theories, or for the equivalent axioms such as, for example , von Neumann-Morgenstern's axioms 3Ba and 3Bb (see § 40). In fact, the *axiom of cardinal isovariation* is *identically* satisfied by the neo-Bernoullian formulation.
Finally, my 1977 paper offers a *new proof* of the identity, up to a linear transformation, of the neo-Bernoullian index, *if it really exists,* with cardinal utility *(Appendix B1).*
(68) Not only in the field of economics, but also in the field of physics, *especially from the point of view of determinism and quantum theory.*
(69) In my 1985 paper, "*Three Theorems on the Theory of Cardinal Utility and Random Choice",* founded on the definition, up to a linear transformation, of cardinal utility, and its implications, I offered a *fourth proof* of the identity, up to a linear transformation, of the neo-Bernoullian index, *when it exists,* and of cardinal utility. On these four proofs, see also the note 29 of my 1986 paper *A New Neo-Bernoullian Theory : The Machina Theory - A Critical Analysis.*
(70) On the *theoretical plane* : - the theory of local utility of Mark Machina ; - Camacho's principle of *"long run success"* ; - the formulation by G. Bernard, Kahneman and Tversky ; - the analysis by Robin Pope of the role of time in random choices ; - and, *on the empirical plane* : the contributions of Roman Krzysztofowicz, of

Mark Cord and Richard de Neufville, and of Hector Munera and Richard de Neufville, *who are placing themselves on the lines of my early work* and who, all, invalidate the neo-Bernoullian theories.

(71)*The Foundations of a Positive Theory of Choice Involving Risk and a Criticism of the Postulates and Axioms of the American School,* 1952, § 63.

(72) Apart from my 1985 paper, *The Allais Paradox,* I have analysed this so-called paradox on different occasions, see in particular my 1977 paper, § 36, § 2.2., 3.2 and A.4.

(73) Section A.5

(74) See my 1986 paper, § A.5.11, p. 274, and § A.5.9, p. 273.

It should be emphasized that the axiomatic systems upon which Quiggin's, Yaari's and Segal's theories are based are refuted by empirical evidence because the functions θ(F) they consider *are not the same* when very large or very small sums are implied.

(75) I had already given a brief analysis of the Machina's theory in my 1984 paper, *The Foundations of the Theory of Utility and Risk,* § 2.3.1.

(76) On the critical analysis of the neo-Bernoullian theories I have three papers to be published : - *Les Tests de compatibilité des choix avec le principe néo-Bernoullien,* (Tests of the Compatibility of Choices with the Neo-Bernoullian Principle, 13 p. October 1975) ; - *Analyse sommaire des réponses au Questionnaire de 1952 faites par les économistes étrangers participant au Colloque de 1952 : K.J. Arrow, B. de Finetti, M. Friedman, J. Marschak, L.J. Savage,* (A Brief Analysis of the Responses to the *1952 Questionnaire* made by the Foreign Economists attending the Paris 1952 Colloquium, 12 p., October 1975), and *The Psychological Structure of Choices Involving Risk* (approximately 400 pp. and 300 Charts). Only a short extract of this memoir has been presented in the *Appendix C* of my 1977 paper.

6.- Applications

(77) One can only wonder about the applications of a theory such as Savage's *because the probabilities and the neo-Bernoullian index, the existence of which he proves on the basis of his postulates, remain unknown.*

(78) On this questions, see my 1977 paper, *The So-Called Allais' Paradox and rational Decisions under Uncertainty,* § 1.

(79) After having adopted the principle of a reasonable strategy, and as a precaution, I decided to proceed on the basis of a new analysis of the data over a longer period of three months. According to this new analysis, the mathematical expectation was no more significantly positive, and I gave up trying to apply the suggested method.

Without the tax on parimutuel winnings, at that time, about 20%, the method would have proved quite advantageous.

(80) One can only regret here that so few theorists of risk have ever, themselves, taken, or even considered taking, any *real* risks.

(81) Their list is given in *Appendix VIII* to my 1955 paper. Whatever the interest of some of these papers from the point of view of risk theory, they are only disponible on a mimeographied form.

(82) A more complete version was published in 1957 by the Bureau de Recherches Minières de l'Algérie (22, avenue Président A. Freger (Hydra) Bermandreis), in the form of a book of 101 pages. The main body of the text is the same as that of my 1955 paper, but it contains much more charts, all very stimulating.

In fact, I had the intention of publishing a more extensive work that would bring together my 1955 paper and the greatest part of the twenty two papers listed in the *Appendix VIII* of my 1955 paper, some of which are of great scientific interest. But, too absorbed by other works, I was never able to realize this publication.

(83) That is to say, excluding deposits of hydrocarbons.

(84) See the Summary, § 1-13 ; The Introduction, Section 1 ; and the Conclusions, Section VI of my 1955 paper.

All these pages are essential for the comprehension of the paper.

(85) The franc considered in this paper is the franc that preceded the French monetary reform of 1959 (See note 59 above).

(86) My 1955 paper, Section II, and Section III, § 17.

(87) id., Introduction, § 17, § 19-20, and § 36.

(88) id., § 26-34;

(89) id., § 34-35.

(90) id., § 34 and 35, It results from that analysis that the probability of ruin, that is, of expenses exceeding the overall value of the potential deposits, was about 1/3.

(91) Voir § 3.4 and note 38 above.

(92) § 3.3.2 of my 1986 paper.

This analysis has been completed in 1987-1988 by the analysis of the answers relating to the *Allais' Paradox* made by all the subjects mentioned in the *Appendix C* of my 1977 paper.

(93) Section III,2 of my 1988 Budapest paper.

7.- My Contributions to the Theory of Utility and Risk, and Prevailing Ideas

(94) My theory of random choices and risk is, in fact, only a part of a much larger structure bearing upon all economic phenomena.

My contributions to fundamental economic analysis have dealt essentially with five closely interrelated and complementary domains within which I have not ceased working since 1941 : - the theory of maximal economic efficiency ; - the theory of capital ; - the theory of random choices, of utility and of probability ; - the theory of monetary dynamics ; - the theory of chance, of exogenous influences, and of time series.

The theoretical analysis has naturally led me to applications, and the study of concrete questions has brought me to think about the theoretical fundamentals from which satisfactory answers can be obtained.

General overviews of my works are given in my 1978 Memoir, *Contributions to Economic Science,* and in my 1989 book, *Autoportraits,* (Self-portraits).

(95) Published by the *Imprimerie Nationale* in 1955 as a volume, 56 p.

(96) *Revue d'Economie Politique,* 1957, pp. 378-380.

(97) § 3.1 and 3.5, and notes 149**, 150, 166, 167, 167* and 172.

(98) For example, I can only be surprised (and this is an understatement) that in two very recent papers, *Choice under Uncertainty : Problems Solved and Unsolved, (Economic Perspectives,* 1987, p. 121-154), and *Expected Utility Hypotheses, (The New Palgrave, A Dictionary of Economics,* 1987, Vol. 2, p. 232-239), Machina does not cite any of my papers presented at the Conferences at Oslo, Venice and Aix-en-Provence in which he participated as well.

I believe that although on the scientific plane, one may agree or disagree with certain points of view, it is contrary to scientific deontology to be silent about them whereas quite obviously they bring significant contributions (see also my quotation of Robin Pope, in my 1986 paper, *The general theory of random choices in relation to the invariant cardinal utility function and the specific probability function. The (U, θ) Model,* note 15, p. 276).

(99) The above text has been entirely written *before* the Nobel Prize in Economic Science was awarded to me in October 1988.

REFERENCES

1943 *A la Recherche d'une Discipline Economique - Première Partie - L'Economie Pure*
Première édition, Ateliers Industria, 1943, 852 p. et Annexes, 68 p.
Deuxième édition, 1952, publiée avec le concours du Centre National de la Recherche Scientifique, sous le titre : *Traité d'Economie Pure,* Imprimerie Nationale, 5 vol., in 4°, 984 p. Cette seconde édition ne diffère de la première que par l'addition d'une "Introduction à la deuxième édition" (63 p.)
Troisième édition, publiée avec le concours du Ministère de la Recherche Scientifique, Editions Clément Juglar, 1994, avec une nouvelle "Introduction".

1951 *Notes théoriques sur l'incertitude de l'avenir et le risque,* Congrès Européen de Louvain de la Société Internationale d'Econométrie, 72 p.

1952 a "La Généralisation des Théories de l'Equilibre Economique Général et du Rendement Social au Cas du Risque" (Mémoire présenté au Colloque International de Paris du Centre National de la Recherche Scientifique sur les "Fondements et Applications de la Théorie du Risque en Econométrie", Paris, 12-17 mai 1952, in : *Econométrie,* Collection des Colloques Internationaux du Centre National de la Recherche Scientifique, Vol. XL, Paris, 1953, p. 81-120.

1952 b "Fondements d'une Théorie Positive des Choix comportant un Risque" (Mémoire présenté au Colloque International de Paris du Centre National de la Recherche Scientifique sur les "Fondements et Applications de la Théorie du Risque en Econométrie" , Paris, 12-17 mai 1952), in: *Econométrie,* Collection des Colloques Internationaux du Centre National de la Recherche Scientifique, Vol. XL, Paris, 1953, p. 127-140.

1952 c "Fondements d'une Théorie Positive des Choix comportant un Risque et Critique des Postulats et Axiomes de l'Ecole

Américaine" (Mémoire d'ensemble rédigé à la suite des débats du Colloque International de Paris), *Actes du Colloque,* ibid°., p. 257-332.
Ce mémoire a été republié en 1955 avec quelques additions mineures dans un numéro spécial des *Annales des Mines* et sous la forme d'un volume séparé par l'Imprimerie Nationale (56 p. in 4°).

1952 c* "The Foundations of a Positive Theory of Choice Involving Risk and a Criticism of the Postulates and Axioms of the American School", traduction anglaise de 1952 c publiée dans Allais et Hagen, 1979, *Expected Utility Hypothesis and the Allais' Paradox ; Contemporary Discussions of Decisions under Uncertainty with Allais' Rejoinder*, Dordrecht/Boston, Reidel.

1952 d "La Psychologie de l'Homme Rationnel devant le Risque. La Théorie et l'Expérience", *Journal de la Société de Statistique de Paris,* janvier-mars 1953, p. 47-73.

1952 e "L'Extension des Théories de l'Equilibre Economique Général et du Rendement Social au Cas du Risque", *Econometrica,* Vol. 21, n° 2, avril 1953, p. 269-290.

1952 f "Le Comportement de l'Homme Rationnel devant le Risque. Critique des Postulats et Axiomes de l'Ecole Américaine", *Econometrica,* Vol. 21, n° 4, octobre 1953, p. 503-546.

1952 g "Observations", *présentées lors du Colloque de 1952 de Paris,* in : *Econométrie,* CNRS, 1953, p. 26, 34-35, 37-40, 47-48, 110-120, 151-157, 160-162, 194-197, 212-213, 228, 233, 245-247.

1954 a "Evaluation des Perspectives Economiques de la Recherche Minière sur de Grands Espaces - Application au Sahara Algérien" (Etude faite pour le Bureau de Recherches Minières de l'Algérie, 1953-1954), *Bulletin de l'Institut International de Statistique,* Tome XXV, 4, Rio de Janeiro, 1957, p. 89-140, et : *Revue de l'Industrie Minérale,* Paris, janvier 1956, p. 329-383. Traduction anglaise :
"Method of Appraising Economic Prospects of Mining Exploration over large Territories - Algerian Sahara Case Study", *Management Science,* Vol. 3, n° 4, juillet 1957.
(*Prix Lanchester* de l'Université John Hopkins et de la Société Américaine de Recherche Opérationnelle, 1958).
Une édition française plus complète a été publiée en un volume sous le même titre : *Evaluation des Perspectives Economiques de la Recherche Minière sur de Grands Espaces*

- *Application au Sahara Algérien,* par le bureau de Recherche Minière de l'Algérie, Alger, 1957, 101 p.

1954 b "Observations sur le Choix entre la Sécurité et son Coût relativement à la Construction de Digues Protectrices en Hollande", Intervention à la suite de la Communication de Van Dantzig, "Economic Decisions Problems for Flood Protection", Congrès de la Société Européenne d'Econométrie, Uppsala, 1954.

1955 "Observations sur la Théorie des Jeux",*Travaux du Congrès des Economistes de Langue Française,* 1954, Editions Domat-Montchrestien, 1955, p. 143-163.

1957 a "Sur la Théorie des Choix Aléatoires", *Revue d'Economie Politique,* 1953, n° 3, p. 381-390.

1957 b "Test de Périodicité - Généralisation du Test de Schuster au cas de Séries Temporelles Autocorrelées",*Comptes-Rendus de l'Académie des Sciences,* Tome 244, 13 mai 1957, n° 20, p. 2469-2471.

1959 "Test de Périodicité - Généralisation du Test de Schuster au cas de Séries Temporelles Autocorrélées", Vol. 1 des *Studi in Onore di Corrado Gini,* Istituto di Statistica della Facoltà di Scienze Statistische Demografiche ed Attuariali, p. 1-14.

1961 "Généralisation du Test de Schuster au Cas de Séries Temporelles Autocorrélées dans l'Hypothèse d'un Processus de Perturbations Aléatoires d'un système Stable", *Bulletin de l'Institut International de Statistique, 1962,* Tome 39, 2è livraison, p. 143-194.

1977 a *Expected Utility Hypothesis and the Allais' Paradox ; Contemporary Discussions of Decisions under Uncertainty with Allais' Rejoinder,* Maurice Allais and Ole Hagen editors, Reidel Publishing Company, Dordrecht, 1979, 714 p.
Contributions personnelles :
1. "Foreword" (p. 3-11)
2. "The Foundations of a Positive Theory of Choice Involving Risk and a Criticism of the Postulates and Axioms of the American School" (p. 25-145, traduction anglaise du mémoire "Fondements d'une théorie positive des choix comportant un risque et critique des postulats et axiomes de l'école américaine, Vol. XL, *Econométrie,* Colloques Internationaux du Centre National de la Recherche Scientifique, Paris, 1953).
3. "The So-called Allais' Paradox and Rational Decisions under Uncertainty" (p. 434-698)

1977 b   "On the Concept of Probability", *Rivista Internazionale di Scienze Economiche e Commerciali*, novembre 1978, n° 11, p. 937-956.
1978   *Contributions à la Science Economique - Vue d'ensemble 1943-1978*, Paris, Centre d'Analyse Economique, 176 p.
1982   "Frequency, Probability and Chance", in : *Foundations of Utility and Risk Theory with Applications*, Bernt F. Stigum et Fred Wenstop, eds., D. Reidel Publishing Compagny, Dordrecht, 1983, p. 35-84.
1983 a   "Sur la Distribution Normale des Valeurs à des Instants régulièrement Espacés d'une Somme de Sinusoïdes", *Comptes-Rendus de l'Académie des Sciences*, Tome 296, Série 1, p. 829-832.
1983 b   "Fréquence, Probabilité et Hasard, avec deux Appendices :
         1. Fréquences empiriques et fréquences mathématiques - Illustration. 2. Le Théorème (T) - La simulation du hasard par des fonctions presque périodiques, *Journal de la Société de Statistique de Paris*, 2è et 3è trimestres 1983, p. 70-102 et 144-221.
1983 c   "The Foundations of the Theory of Utility and Risk", in: *Progress in Decision Theory*, O. Hagen et F. Wenstop, eds., D. Reidel Publishing Company, Dordrecht, 1984, p. 3-131.
1984 a   "L'Utilité Cardinale et sa Détermination - Hypothèses, Méthodes et Résultats empiriques", *Second International Conference on Foundations of Utility and Risk Theory*, Venise (5-9 juin 1984).
1984 a* "The Cardinal Utility and its Determination - Hypotheses, Methods and Empirical Results", (traduction anglaise de 1984a), *Theory and Decision, vol. , N°. , pp. -)*
1984 b   "Determination of Cardinal utility according to an Intrinsic Invariant Model", in : *Recent Development in the Foundations of Utility and Risk Theory*, L. Daboni, A. Montesano, and M. Lines, eds., D. Reidel Publishing Company, 1986. p. 83-120. Ce mémoire est une version *très abrégée* de 1984 a.
1985 a   "Three Theorems on the Theory of Cardinal utility and Random Choice", *Essays in Honour of Werner Leinfellner*, Gerald Eberlein and Hal Berghel, éd., pp. 205-221, Theory and Decision Library, D. Reidel Publishing Company, Dordrecht, 1987.
1985 b   "The Allais Paradox",*The New Palgrave. A Dictionary of Economics*, Vol. 1, p. 78-80, MacMillan, 1987.

1986 a   "The General Theory of Random Choice in Relation ot the Invariant Cardinal Utility Function and the Specific Probability Function. The (U, θ) Model. A General Overview", in: *Risk, Decision and Rationality* , Bertrand Munier, éd., Reidel Publishing Company, Dordrecht, 1987, p. 231-289.

1986 b   *The General Theory of Random Choices in Relation to the Invariant Cardinal Utility Function and the Specific Probability Function. The (U, θ) Model,* Version *très étendue et révisée* de 1986 a (sera publiée prochainement)

1986 c   "A New Neo-Bernoullian Theory : The Machina Theory - A Critical Analysis, in: *Risk, Decision and Rationality,* Bertrand Munier édit., D. Reidel Publishing Company, Dordrecht, 1987, p. 347-403.

1987   "Some Remarkable Properties of the Determination of a Continuous Distribution by its Moments", in:*Risk, Decision and Rationality* , Bertrand Munier, éd., D. Reidel Publishing Company, 1987, p. 557-561.

1988 a   "Cardinal Utility. History, Empirical Findings and Applications. An Overview", Fourth International Conference on the Foundations and Applications of Utility, Risk, and Decision Theory, Budapest, juin 1988, in : A. Chikàn, ed., Kluwer Publishing Company, 1991.
Theory and Decision, Vol. 91, p. 99-140, 1991.

1988 b   *Cardinal utility - History, Empirical Findings, and Applications*
Version très étendue et révisée de 1988 a (sera publiée prochainement).

1988 c   "Phénomènes Aléatoires et Modèles Fréquentiels. Réalité et Théorie. Prolégomènes pour une Révision des Théories Admises", Conférence du 5 octobre 1988, Rheinisch Westfälische Akademie der Wissenschaften, 40 p.

1989   *Autoportraits,* Montchrestien, Paris, 150 p.

1994   *Cardinal Utility,* Maurice Allais et Ole Hagen, Kluwer.

1994   *Scientific Papers on Risk and Utility Theory. Theory, Experience, and Applications,* Kluwer Publishing Company, 1000 p.

1994   *Cardinal Utility and Random Choice Theory,* Kluwer
Ce volume incluera : 1943, *Satisfaction absolue,* 1984 a*, 1986 b et 1988 b.

4. MULTIPLE CRITERIA DECISION-MAKING UNDER

UNCERTAINTY

Practical decision-making seldom happens with nicely defined utility functions and well-perceived event probabilities. When it comes to chosing among strategies in business organizations, it is frequently necessary to begin by *constructing* the preferences of the decision-maker, in other words, to *design* several indices, each with a probability distribution, with the aim of establishing either a global utility function or some equivalent scheme able to guide the decision-maker in determining the direction in which he or she would like to move. Direct optimization may turn out to be impossible and may have to be replaced by some compromise-seeking device. Multi-Criteria Decision Making thus often appears as the operational tool of "bounded", or "procedural" rationality, as defined and advocated by H.A. Simon.

The next step is to design a support system enabling the decision-maker(s) to implement the selected strategy within the relevant organizational context. This organizational context may not be neutral with respect to the first phase of the analysis, i.e. it may have an impact on the attributes chosen, or on the procedure chosen to aggregate them, as well as on the design of the support to be elaborated.

The three papers in this section are devoted to this type of question, and thus deal with several *prescriptive* aspects of decision-making. Hence, they not only deal with Multiple-Criteria Decision making (MCDM) but also with Multiple-Criteria Decision Aid (MCDA). They do so in a context of risk or uncertainty, which this type of approach too often overlooks. As such, they quite naturally fit into this volume.

In the first paper, Zaras and Martel address the question of how to aggregate the multiple attributes of an alternative when these attributes are described under risk, i.e., are lotteries. They observe that, in the traditional analysis of the Keeney-Raiffa type, assessing a partial utility function for each attribute is not an easy task, and they look for a less demanding procedure. They suggest using the different available concepts of Stochastic

Dominance (from first up to third order, with varying definitions). But they want to go beyond this suggestion, and provide the reader with some properties of such a procedure.

They are able to show that, under given assumptions on the attributes and for a given class of von Neumann-Morgenstern preferences (roughly, for preferences exhibiting some type of "reflection effect") there are cases where verifying certain Stochastic Dominance relations allows one to state that an alternative a is "transparently" preferred to an alternative b, and there are other cases which are "non-transparent", calling for additional explanations from the decision-maker. They then design a two-stage procedure and use B. Roy's rule of aggregation to build an outranking binary relation. From this "global" relation, a set of preferred solutions can be determined.

In the second paper, Quingsan Cao and Jean-Pierre Protzen suggest a different answer to the same problem. They first remark that all aggregation procedures rest on similar general common-sense considerations. They argue that beyond the traditional aggregation procedures using "algebraic quantifications", the method of "logic substitution", based on Yager's fuzzy multiple objective functions, provides an alternative way of aggregating attributes.

Cao and Protzen then raise the question of extending both types of procedures to evaluation under uncertainty. If uncertainty reflects not only objective facts, but also imprecisions of logical judgment (which is the view of the authors), then an evaluator should use fuzzy numbers to measure attributes' performances and fuzzy functions to aggregate these fuzzy performance measurements. Whether to use an "algebraic" or a "'logical" aggregation function "is a matter of the evaluator's opinion", each method having advantages and disadvantages. The authors appear to favor the second method, which leaves a larger scope for personal reasoning and deliberation.

In contrast to the preceding papers, the contribution by Claude Pellegrin is devoted to an application of MCDA in an explicitly organizational context. More specifically, the problem is to harmonize flexibility in business decisions - which calls for some decentralization of decisions in the organization - and security preserving behavior of the organization, the example here being reliability of technology. To this effect, the author suggests modelling costs and downtime parameters, on the one hand, and reliability parameters on the other hand. Using some of his previous results, Pellegrin shows how a graphical representation can be turned into an interactive decision-aid support. The advantages of this graphical support scheme are shown to be both organizational (coordinating decisions taken by possibly different executives of the organization) and economic (maintaining an efficient operation of the plant).

MULTIATTRIBUTE ANALYSIS BASED ON STOCHASTIC DOMINANCE

Kazimierz ZARAS[*]

Jean-Marc MARTEL[**]

This paper presents a multiattribute analysis using Stochastic Dominances. These Dominances are proposed in relation with Separate Utility Models for gains and for losses. Two classes of utility functions, DARA-INARA, will be suggested for each of these domains on each attribute. These models allow us to identify the "transparent" category of stochastic dominances and to establish for each of these attributes the preferences of a decision maker. In practice, the essential characteristic of a multiattribute problem is that we have several conflicting attributes. Consequently, the Multiattribute Stochastic Dominance relationship risk being poor, thus resulting in uselessness to the decision maker. This is why we propose to weaken the unanimity condition of classic dominance. We will use Roy's Preference Aggregation Rule which allows us to build a global outranking relation. Very often we can build a global outranking relation based only on the "transparent" category of stochastic dominances, because this category is satisfied in a high percentage of cases.

---

[*]   Université du Québec en Abitibi-Témiscamingue.
[**] Faculté des sciences de l'administration, Université Laval.

I INTRODUCTION

The aim of most theoretical works in multiattribute utility theory is to investigate possibilities for simplifying the task of multiattribute utility assessment. Keeney and Raiffa (1976) showed that if certain independence hypotheses are verified, it is possible to decompose the utility function using one-attribute utility functions and scaling constants.

Nevertheless, even if it is available, the assessment of each of the one-attribute utility functions isn't the easiest task. This is essentially why in the one-attribute context, the concept of stochastic dominance was developed.

Huang et al. (1978) showed, in the case of the probability independence and the additive multiattribute utility function, that the necessary condition for the multiattribute stochastic dominance is to verify stochastic dominances on the level of each attribute. In practice, the essential characteristic of a multiattribute problem is that we have several conflicting attributes. Consequently, the Multiattribute Stochastic Dominance relationship risk being poor results in uselessness to the decision maker. It seems to be reasonable to weaken this unanimity condition and to accept a majority attribute condition. We suggest that one use Roy's Preference Aggregation Rule which was proposed in the non-stochastic context (see Jacquet-Lagreze, 1973).

A link between the stochastic dominance and the preferences is well known for the class DARA (Decreasing Absolute Risk Aversion) utility functions (Bawa, 1975). In this paper, the stochastic dominance is based on the concept of the generalized stochastic dominances (Zaras, 1989) and on two classes of utility functions, DARA and INARA (Increasing Absolute Risk Aversion), to define the preference aggregation rule in multiattribute stochastic context.

The paper is structured as follows. The problem is formulated in section II. Section III presents the results emanating from stochastic dominance conditions for each attribute. In Section IV these results are used to build the global outranking relations. The method, thus developed, is described in Section V using a step by step procedure, and is then applied, in Section VI, to solve one example taken from a concrete context.

II FORMULATION OF THE PROBLEM

Our problem belongs to the class of the problems which can be represented by the A, A, E model (Alternatives, Attributes, Evaluations).

Then we consider:
1. a finite set $A = \{a_1, a_2, ..., a_m\}$ of alternatives;
2. a set $A = (X_1, X_2, ..., X_n)$ of attributes which are probabilistically independent and also satisfy the independence conditions allowing us to use the additive utility function form;
3. a set $E = \{X_{ik}\}_{m \times n}$ of evaluations, where X_{ik} is random variable with probability function $f_i(x_{ij})$, which can thus be associated to the performance of each alternative a_j with respect to the attribute X_i. If the interval of variation of the random variables associated with the attribute X_i is represented by $[x_{io}, x_i^o]$, where x_{io} = the worst value obtained for the attribute X_i, and x_i^o = the best value, the performance of the alternative a_j is modelled such that:

$$\sum_{x_{ij} \in [x_{io}, x_i^o]} f_i(x_{ij}) = 1 \text{ for a discrete attribute scale, and}$$

$$\int_{x_{io}}^{x_i^o} f_i(x_{ij}) dx_{ij} = \int_{x_{io}}^{x_i^o} dF_i(x_{ij}) = \int_{x_{io}}^{x_i^o} d\overline{F}_i(x_{ij}) = 1$$

for a continuous attribute scale, where $F_i(x)$ and $\overline{F}_i(x)$ represent respectively cumulative and decumulative distribution functions.

These attributes are defined such that a larger value is preferred to a smaller value ("more is better") and the probability functions are known.

Next, the comparison between two alterna-tives, $a_j, a_j' \in A$ leads to the comparison of two vectors of probability distributions $\{f_1(x_{1j}), ..., f_n(x_{nj})\}$ and $\{f_1(x_{1j}'), ..., f_n(x_{nj}')\}$. On the one hand, taking into account our hypothesis of independence, we accepted that this multiattribute comparison can be decomposed into n one-attribute comparisons. On the other hand, as these comparisons will be accomplished from the stochastic dominances and the classes DARA-INARA utility functions, they will be expressed in terms of "a_j is at least as good as a_j'" in relation to each attribute and for all pairs $(a_j, a_j') \in A \times A$.

Finally, we use concordance analysis, based on Roy's Preference Aggregation Rule, to conclude on the global outranking relation. These outranking relations are used to solve the problem by either choosing the best alternative or ranking the set of alternatives.

III PARTIAL PREFERENCES BETWEEN TWO ALTERNATIVES UNDER RISK

As indicated above, the context examined is one in which the performance of each alternative, with respect to each attribute, is expressed by a probability distribution.

Using stochastic dominance, it is unnecessary to make completely explicit the decision maker's utility function in order to pronounce on the proposition that, from his point of view, "alternative a_j is at least as good as a_j'" with respect to attribute X_i.

A decision under risk is made to choose between two alternatives, a_j and a_j', on attribute X_i in a closed interval $[x_o, x^o]$

where

$$x_o = \min [\min \{x_{ij}\}, \min \{x_{ij}'\}],$$
$$x^o = \max [\max \{x_{ij}\}, \max \{x_{ij}'\}] \quad (1)$$

and $x_{ij} \in X_{ij}, x_{ij}' \in X_{ij}'$.

If $0 < x_o < x^o$, then we have strictly positive prospects, or if $x_o < x^o < 0$, then we have strictly negative prospects. To come to a clear conclusion on the proposition "a_j is at least as good as a_j'", it is necessary to establish the type of pairwise stochastic dominance relation between alternatives a_j and a_j'. Two dominance groups can be suggested: the FSD/SSD/TSD group, and the FSD/SISD/TISD1/TISD2 inverse stochastic dominances group (see appendix I for the definition). By definition, TSD is more general than FSD and SSD thus:

$$FSD \subseteq SSD \subseteq TSD$$

and TISD1 or TISD2 is more general than FSD and

SISD thus: $\quad (2)$

$$FSD \subseteq SISD \subseteq TISD1 \text{ or } TISD2 .$$

Consequently, if FSD is satisfied, all of Stochastic Dominances will have been verified.

If the means $\mu(F_j) \neq \mu(F_j')$ and FSD are not verified, SISD can be complementary to SSD, and they fulfil the following equations:

$$SSD \cup SISD = SSDG$$
$$SSD \cap SISD = \phi \quad (3)$$

where SSDG denotes the Second Degree Generalized Stochastic Dominance.

If $\mu(\overline{F}_j) \neq \mu(\overline{F}_j')$ and SISD are not verified, TISD1 and TISD2 can be complementary to TSD, and they fulfil the following equations:

$$TSD \cup TISD1 \cup TISD2 = TSDG$$
$$TSD \cap TISD1 \cap TISD2 = \phi \quad (4)$$

where TSDG denotes the Third Degree Generalized Stochastic Dominance. These two Stochastic Dominance groups can be applied in relation to two Separate Models for gains and for losses.

In the domain of the gains, we assume a class of concave utility functions DARA, and in the domain of the losses, a class of convex utility functions INARA. By allowing concavity or convexity of utility functions in either domain for each pair of alternative a_j, a_j', we distinguish between "transparent" and "non-transparent" categories of stochastic dominances as are given in the table 1.

TABLE 1: Situations In Which "a_j Can Be At Least As Good As a_j'".

	$x_o < x^o < 0$	$0 < x_o < x^o$
F_j FSD F_j'	(*)	(*)
F_j SSD F_j'	(?)	(*)
F_j TSD F_j'	(?)	(*)
$\overline{F}_j$ SISD $\overline{F}_j'$	(*)	(?)
$\overline{F}_j$ TISD1 $\overline{F}_j'$	(*)	(?)
$\overline{F}_j$ TISD2 $\overline{F}_j'$	(*)	(?)

For the situations indicated by (?) in table 1, the conclusion concerning the proposition "a_j is at least as good as a_j'" is not clear and it is classified as non-transparent. In fact, the non-transparent category of Stochastic Dominance (SD_{NT}) includes not only (?) situations but also all mixed situations where gains and losses are combined (i.e. $x_o < 0 < x^o$). The cases indicated by an (*) on table 1 are considered transparent (SD_T) and they are based on the rules given in appendix II. For example, these rules are obeyed by a Decision Maker with particular Separate Utility Models. These particular models assume the family of concave-exponential utility functions for gains and the family of convex-power utility functions for losses.

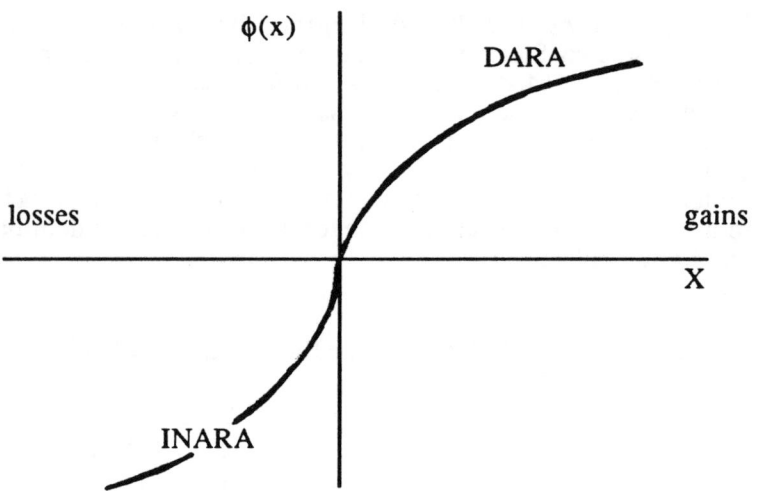

Figure 1: Dara-Inara Utility Model

DARA Utility Functions

$$U_D = \{\phi(x)/\phi'(x) > 0, \phi''(x) \leq 0, \phi'''(x) \geq 0\} \quad (5)$$

where $\phi'''(x) \phi'(x) \geq (\phi''(x)^2)$

INARA Utility Functions

$$U_I = \{\phi(x)/\phi'(x) > 0, \phi''(x) \geq 0, \phi(x)''' \leq 0\}$$

(6)

where $\phi'''(x) \geq 0$ and $\phi'''(x) \phi'(x) \leq (\phi''(x)^2)$

IV THE SYNTHETICAL OUTRANKING APPROACH

In our approach, two complexity levels are distinguished in the expression of the decision-maker's pairwise alternative preferences with respect to each attribute X_i:
1. Clear - if SD are transparents (SD_T)
2. Unclear - if SD are non-transparents (SD_{NT})

The following question arises: is it always necessary to clarify all the cases in which the decision-maker's preferences are unclear in order to make use of a multicriterion decision aid for the statement on alternatives ranking ? It will soon be clear that this depends on the level of concordance threshold p required by the decision-maker in the construction of the outranking relations according to Roy's rule.

The lower that this level is, the more useful it could be to delineate the unclear situations. Our objective is to reduce the number of questions put down by a Decision Maker for a multicriterion decision aid.

Given the level of concordance threshold desired by the decision-maker, the value of the concordance index can be decomposed into two parts:

1. Explicable concordance

This results from cases in which the expression of the decision-maker's preferences is clear:

$$C_E(a_j, a_j') = \sum_{i=1}^{n} w_i \, d_i^E(a_j, a_j')$$

(7)

where $d_i^E(a_j, a_j') = \begin{cases} 1 \text{ if } F_{ij} \, SD_T \, F_{ij}' \\ 0 \text{ otherwise} \end{cases}$,

w_i = relative importance accorded the i-th attribute, with $\sum_{i=1}^{n} w_i = 1$.

2. Non-explicable concordance

This corresponds to the potential value of the cases in which the expression of the decision-maker's preferences is unclear

$$C_N (a_j, a_j') = \sum_{i=1}^{n} w_i \, d_i^N (a_j, a_j') \qquad (8)$$

where $d_i^N (a_j, a_j') = \begin{cases} 1 \text{ if } F_{ij} \text{ SD}_{NT} \text{ } F_{ij}' \text{ and } F_{ij}' \text{ SD}_{NT} \text{ } F_{ij} \\ 0 \text{ otherwise} \end{cases}$

The explanation of the unclear cases may be beneficial if the following two conditions are verified:

If $C_E (a_j, a_j') < p$

and $C_E (a_j, a_j') + C_N (a_j, a_j') \geq p$ \qquad (9)

where p is the concordance threshold.

If it is the case, then this explanation can lead to a value of the concordance index such that the concordance test is satisfied for the proposition that "alternative a_j globally outranks the alternative a_j'".

If the explained concordance index is superior or equal to concordance threshold p, then it is unnecessary to explain the unclear relations. Moreover, if concordance threshold p is equal to 1, then Multiattribute Stochastic Dominance MSD_n is fulfilled.

If $C_E (a_j, a_j') \geq p$, then $a_j \text{ S } a_j'$

i.e. $(a_j, a_j') \in S(p)$ \qquad (10)

where S(p) = set of alternative pairs $(a_j, a_j') \in A \times A$ such that an outranking relation on the concordance threshold level p is verified.

In particular if $p = 1$, we have that $a_j \text{ MSD}_n \text{ } a_j'$, i.e. $F_{ij} \text{ SD}_T \text{ } F_{ij}$, for all attribute X_i, $i = 1,..., n$, and $MSD_n \subseteq S(1)$.

If we wish to obtain a more complete network relations between alternative pairs, we can decrease the value of the concordance threshold. If we order the relative importance accorded to each attribute in the following manner:

$$w_{(1)} \leq w_{(2)} \leq , ..., w_{(n)},$$

then for $p = 1 - w_{(1)}$ we have that: (11)

$$a_j \, MSD_{n-1} \, a_j' \text{ if } F_{ij} \, SD_T \, F_{ij'}, \, \forall \, X_i \in A\backslash X_{(1)}$$

Then we obtain a partial Multiattribute Stochastic Dominances for all attributes, except the attribute whose relative importance is minimal. Then we can build the global outranking relation based on partial Multiattribute Stochastic Dominances for n and n-1 attributes.

$$MSD_n \cup MSD_{n-1} \subseteq S(1-w_{(1)})$$

We can continues this procedure for n-2 attributes if the decision maker agrees to do so.

V. STEP BY STEP PROCEDURE

In the first stage of the suggested procedure, we have a classical statement of the multicriterion problem, which is followed by the establishment of the set of feasible alternatives, and a list of criteria and construction of scales. In the second stage, the verification of independent conditions is considered as well as the identification of the reference point, which may be the current wealth position or could depend on how prospects are expressed (Currin and Sarin, 1989). The notion of a reference point is as a neutral level by the Decision Maker (D.M.) and it is considered quite natural to assign the value 0 to such a level. Next, the distributional evaluations of the alternatives on each attribute will be made (for example by experts).

The initial stage of our analysis starts from the identification of the types of stochastic dominances on each attribute for each pair of alternatives. For the same pair of alternatives we calculate the explicable concordance index and the non-explicable concordance index. For multicriterion decision aid the concordance threshold value p is determined with the D.M. and this value gives us information about the minimal number of attributes which should be in concordance with the proposition that "alternative a_i is at least as good as the alternative a_j'".

Next, we can build the outranking relations using only the explicable concordance index. If the concordance test is not verified, we check if the sum of non-explicable concordance value index and explicable concordance value index is greater than or equal to the desired concordance threshold. If this is the case, the explanation of unclear relations between considered alternatives may be beneficial. Then, we obtain the list of the relationships to explain between alternatives on each attribute. This list can be reduced in a significant manner if we check the impact of an unclear relation on the global (inverse) ranking of the alternatives; we use inverse ranking as a precaution. The explanation of an unclear relation is necessary only if it can change the ranking. This procedure is presented in Figure 2.

VI. EXAMPLE

In this example, the objective is to model the decision-maker's preferences over ten projects which are expressed in the form of probability distributions (see table 2) for each of the four following attributes:
— X_1: personal resources effort
— X_2: discounted profit
— X_3: chances of success
— X_4: technological orientation

It is assumed that the first and last attributes have the same importance 0.09. The most important is the second attribute, 0.55, and the importance of the attribute X_3 is assumed to be 0.27.

To apply this approach, it is first necessary to establish the types of pairwise stochastic dominance relations for each pair of alternatives using each attribute. Table 3 shows that the relations between all alternative pairs are explained by all the possible stochastic dominance conditions except for TISD2.

It is assumed that the reference points equal to zero are at the origin of the ten attribute scales. The explicable concordance was calculated for the FSD/SSD/TSD group of stochastic dominances, and the non-explicable concordance for the SISD/TISD1 group of inverse stochastic dominances. The values of the explicable and non-explicable concordance indexes appear in table 4. The Multiattribute Stochastic Dominance (MSD_n) is verified only for a concordance threshold value of $p = 1.0$.

MULTIATTRIBUTE ANALYSIS BASED ON STOCHASTIC DOMINANCE

STEP BY STEP PROCEDURE

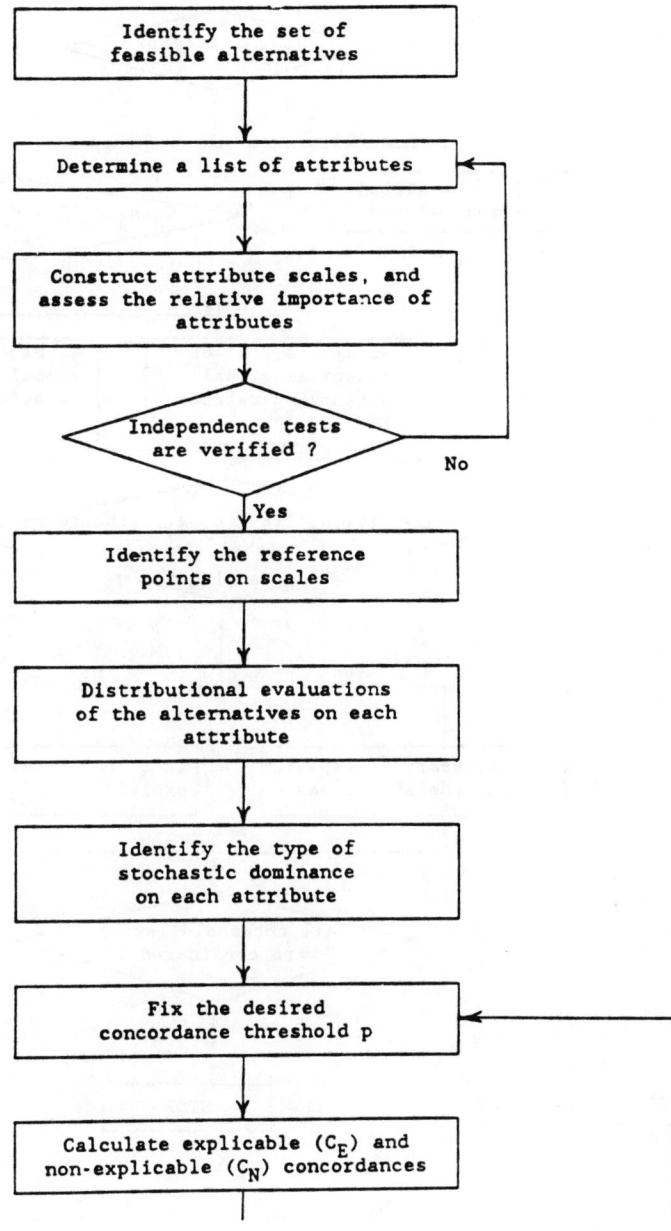

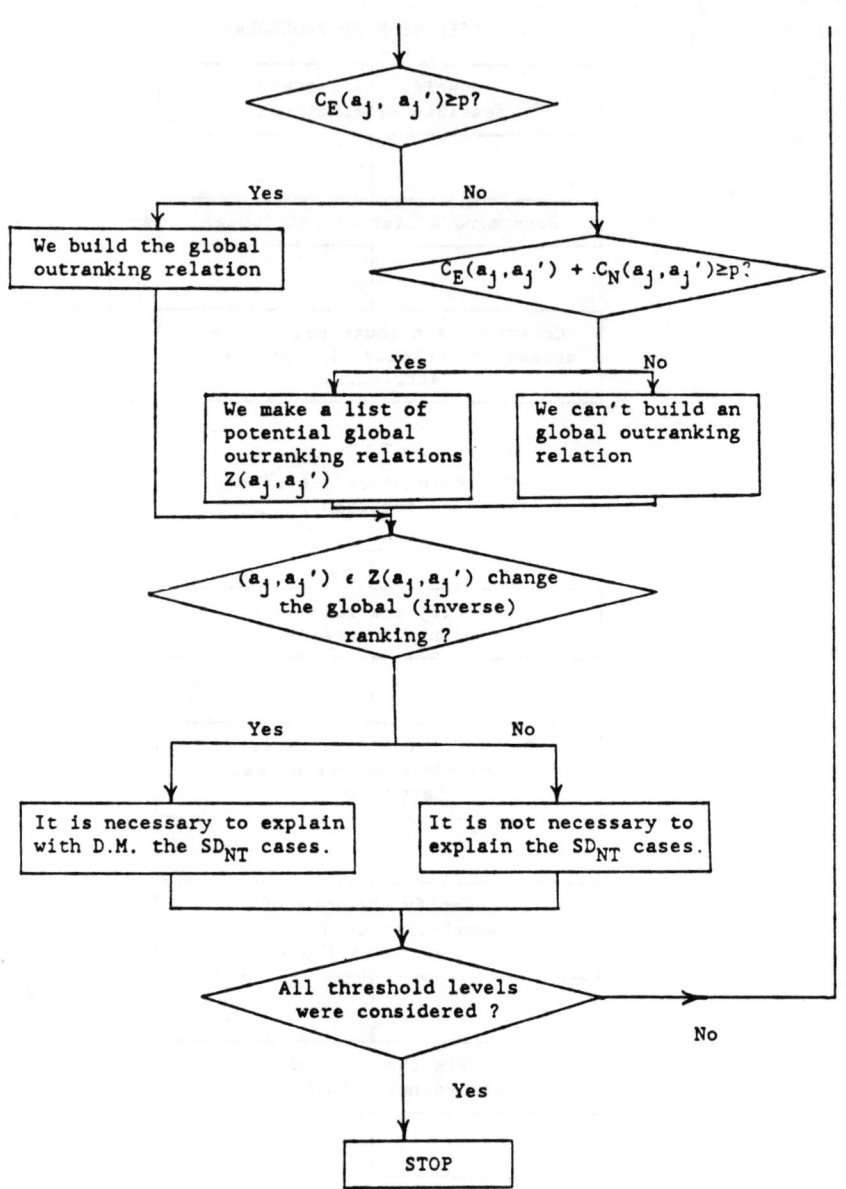

Figure 2: Step by step procedure

MULTIATTRIBUTE ANALYSIS BASED ON STOCHASTIC DOMINANCE

TABLE 2: Distributional Evaluations

Projects	x_1										x_2										x_3										x_4									
	1	2	3	4	5	6	7	8	9	10	1	2	3	4	5	6	7	8	9	10	1	2	3	4	5	6	7	8	9	10	1	2	3	4	5	6	7	8	9	10
1		3/7	1/7		2/7					1/7		2/7	1/7		2/7							1/7	3/7			1/7		1/7	1/7				3/7		2/7					1/7
2	1/7		2/7	1/7	2/7		1/7	1/7																	1/7	1/7		1/7	2/7	3/7								1/7	4/7	1/7
3			3/7	1/7	1/7	1/7	2/7						1/7		1/7	1/7									1/7		1/7	4/7	3/7								1/7	4/7	2/7	
4		1/7			1/7	1/7	1/7	2/7	1/7	3/7	1/7		1/7	1/7			1/7	3/7	1/7										3/7	1/7							1/7	3/7	1/7	3/7
5					1/7	1/7	1/7	1/7	1/7	2/7		1/7	1/7	2/7	1/7	1/7		3/7	1/7					1/7	1/7	2/7	2/7	2/7	1/7	1/7				1/7		1/7	1/7	1/7	3/7	1/7
6						1/7	1/7	2/7	2/7	1/7		3/7	1/7	1/7			1/7	2/7							2/7	1/7	1/7	2/7	1/7						1/7	1/7	1/7	2/7	1/7	1/7
7	1/7		3/7		1/7	1/7	1/7				3/7	3/7	1/7	1/7							2/7	1/7		4/7		2/7	2/7				2/7	1/7		1/7	1/7	1/7		3/7	1/7	
8	1/6	2/6		1/6	2/6	1/6		1/6				1/6					1/6	3/6		1/6	1/6		1/6			1/6						1/6		1/6		2/6	1/6	1/6		1/6
9					2/6	1/6	2/6	1/6								1/6	4/7										2/7								1/7	2/6	1/6	1/6	1/6	1/6
10	1/5	1/5	2/5				1/5					1/6																									2/6	1/6	1/6	1/6

TABLE 3: Observed Dominances

X1

	1	2	3	4	5	6	7	8	9	10
1	x	-	-	-	-	-	-	FSD	-	-
2	FSD	x	-	-	-	-	-	FSD	FSD	FSD
3	FSD	FSD	x	-	FSD	-	SSD	FSD	FSD	FSD
4	FSD	FSD	FSD	x	FSD	SSD	FSD	FSD	FSD	FSD
5	FSD	FSD	SISD	-	x	-	SSD	FSD	SISD	-
6	FSD	FSD	FSD	-	FSD	x	SSD	FSD	FSD	FSD
7	SISD	SISD	-	-	-	-	x	FSD	-	SISD
8	-	-	-	-	-	-	-	x	-	-
9	FSD	FSD	FSD	-	-	-	SSD	FSD	x	FSD
10	SSD	-	FSD	-	FSD	-	-	FSD	-	x

X2

	1	2	3	4	5	6	7	8	9	10
1	x	-	-	-	-	-	SISD	FSD	-	-
2	FSD	x	FSD	FSD	FSD	FSD	FSD	FSD	FSD	FSD
3	FSD	-	x	FSD	FSD	FSD	FSD	FSD	FSD	FSD
4	FSD	-	-	x	-	FSD	FSD	FSD	FSD	FSD
5	FSD	-	-	SSD	x	-	FSD	FSD	-	-
6	TSD	-	-	-	-	x	-	FSD	-	-
7	-	-	-	-	-	-	x	-	-	-
8	SSD	-	-	-	-	SSD	SSD	x	SSD	SISD
9	FSD	-	-	-	TISD	SISD	FSD	FSD	x	-
10	-	-	-	-	-	-	-	-	-	x

X3

	1	2	3	4	5	6	7	8	9	10
1	x	-	-	-	-	-	FSD	FSD	-	TSD
2	FSD	x	-	SSD	-	SSD	FSD	FSD	FSD	TSD
3	FSD	FSD	x	SSD	SSD	SSD	SSD	FSD	FSD	FSD
4	FSD	-	-	x	-	-	FSD	FSD	FDS	FSD
5	FSD	SSD	-	SSD	x	FSD	FSD	FSD	FSD	FSD
6	FSD	-	-	SSD	SSD	x	-	FSD	FSD	FSD
7	-	-	-	-	-	-	x	FSD	-	-
8	-	-	-	-	-	-	FSD	x	FSD	SSD
9	SSD	-	-	-	-	-	-	FSD	x	FSD
10	-	-	-	-	-	-	SISD	FSD	FSD	x

X4

	1	2	3	4	5	6	7	8	9	10
1	x	-	FSD	-	-	-	-	SSD	-	-
2	FSD	x	-	-	FSD	FSD	FSD	FSD	SSD	-
3	FSD	FSD	x	FSD	FSD	FSD	FSD	FSD	FSD	-
4	FSD	-	-	x	FSD	FSD	FSD	FSD	FSD	-
5	FSD	FSD	-	-	x	-	FSD	FSD	FSD	-
6	FSD	-	-	-	-	x	SSD	FSD	SSD	-
7	-	-	-	-	-	-	x	-	-	-
8	-	-	-	-	-	-	-	x	-	-
9	TISD1	-	-	-	-	-	SSD	FSD	x	-
10	SSD	-	-	-	-	-	-	-	-	x

TABLE 4: Explicable And Non-Explicable Concordances

C_E / C_N	1	2	3	4	5	6	7	8	9	10
1	X	-	-	-	-	-	0,27 / 0,64	1,0	- / 0,09	- / 0,27
2	1,0	X	0,64 / -	0,82 / -	0,64 / -	0,91 / -	0,91 / 0,09	1,0	0,91 / -	1,0
3	1,0	0,3 / -	X	0,91 / -	0,91 / 0,09	0,91 / -	1,0	1,0	1,0	0,91 / -
4	1,0	0,18 / -	0,09 / -	X	0,18 / -	0,73 / -	1,0	1,0	1,0	0,45 / -
5	1,0 / -	0,36 / -	- / 0,09	0,82 / -	X	0,64 / -	1,0	1,0	0,91 / 0,09	0,36 / 0,55
6	1,0	0,09 / -	0,09 / -	0,27 / -	0,36 / -	X	1,0	1,0	0,45 / -	0,36 / 0,55
7	0,09 / 0,64	- / 0,09	-	-	-	-	X	1,0	0,09 / -	- / 0,36
8	-	-	-	-	-	-	-	X	-	-
9	0,91 / 0,09	0,09 / -	0,09 / -	-	-	0,55 / -	0,91 / -	1,0	X	0,36 / -
10	0,73 / -	-	0,09 / -	0,55 / -	0,09 / 0,55	0,09 / 0,55	0,64 / 0,36	1,0	0,09 / -	X

We can build the graph (Fig.3) which shows us MSD_4 considering only the explicable concordance when the threshold p is equal to 1. To be more careful, the graph is built from the last to first level of ranking, i.e. inverse ranking. Next, for the same threshold where p is equal to 1, we try to explain, together with the Decision Maker, the "non-transparent" stochastic dominances which can give us more detailed ranking.

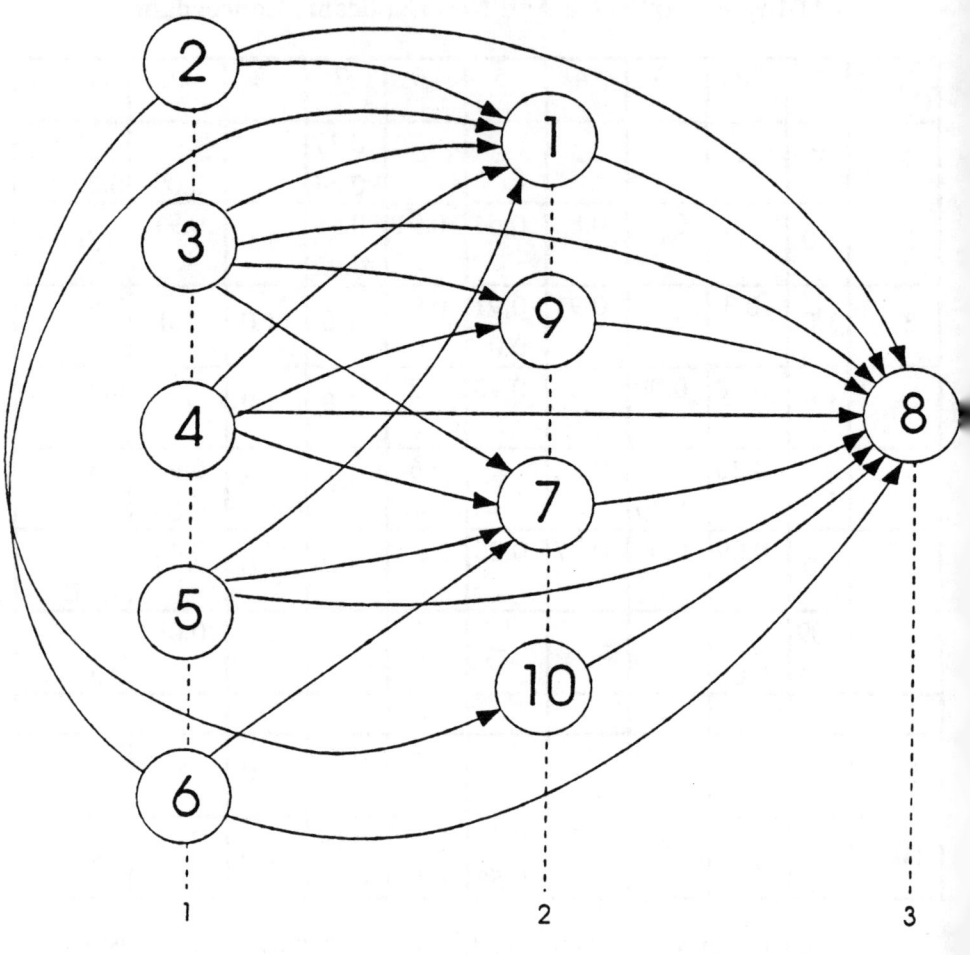

Figure 3: Concordance threshold p = 1 ==» MS

D.M.: In our example, we have to explain at least five relations with

On <u>attribute</u> 1 (personal resources effort)
choose between:

Project 5 $\begin{cases} 3; .142 \\ 6; .286 \\ 7; .286 \\ 9; .286 \end{cases}$ and Project 9 $\begin{cases} 5; .333 \\ 6; .167 \\ 7; .333 \\ 8; .167 \end{cases}$;

Project 3 $\begin{cases} 5; .428 \\ 6; .143 \\ 7; .143 \\ 8; .286 \end{cases}$ and Project 5 $\begin{cases} 3; .142 \\ 6; .286 \\ 7; .286 \\ 10; .286 \end{cases}$;

Project 10 $\begin{cases} 2; .143 \\ 3; .143 \\ 4; .286 \\ 7; .286 \end{cases}$ and Project 7 $\begin{cases} 1; .143 \\ 5; .428 \\ 6; .143 \\ 8; .143 \\ 10; .143 \end{cases}$.

Assume that for the D.M.:

Project 5 $>_1$ Project 9, Project 5 $>_1$ Project 3 and Project 7 $>_1$ Project 10, on attribute 1.

On <u>attribute</u> 3 (chances of success)
choose between:

Project 10 $\begin{cases} 1; .167 \\ 2; .333 \\ 6; .267 \\ 7; .333 \end{cases}$ and Project 7 $\begin{cases} 3; .428 \\ 4; .143 \\ 5; .143 \\ 6; .286 \end{cases}$

Assume Project 10 $>_3$ Project 7.

On <u>attribute</u> 4 (technological orientation) choose between:

$$\text{Project 9} \begin{cases} 2; .167 \\ 4; .167 \\ 6; .333 \\ 8; .167 \\ 10; .166 \end{cases} \quad \text{and} \quad \text{Project 1} \begin{cases} 3; .428 \\ 5; .286 \\ 8; .143 \\ 10; .143 \end{cases}$$

Assume Project 9 $>_4$ Project 1.

After these explanations, we obtain a four level graph with projects 3, 4 and 5 on the first hierarchical level (ranking) (Fig. 4).

To obtain more detailed ranking we can also reduce the value of the concordance threshold to $p = 0,91 = 1 - w_{(1)}$. In this case we have partial Multiattribute Stochastic Dominances MSD_4 and MSD_3. We can build the graph (Fig. 5) which shows us MSD_4 and MSD_3 considering only the explained concordance. At this threshold level, we have to explain, with the D.M., the relation between project 1 and project 7 on the attribute two (see Table 4).

As we can see, in proceedings of this manner we reduce significantly the number of questions to ask to T.M. concerning his preference. In our example, ten projects and four attributes, we have only six binary relations to explicate with Decision Maker.

MULTIATTRIBUTE ANALYSIS BASED ON STOCHASTIC DOMINANCE

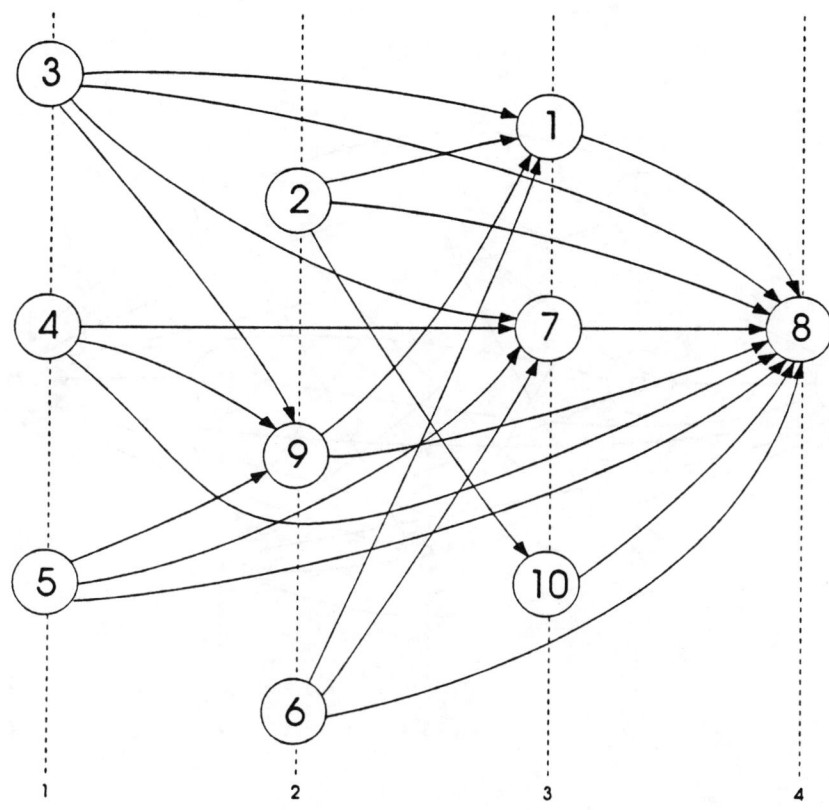

Figure 4: Concordance threshold p = 1, plus explanations

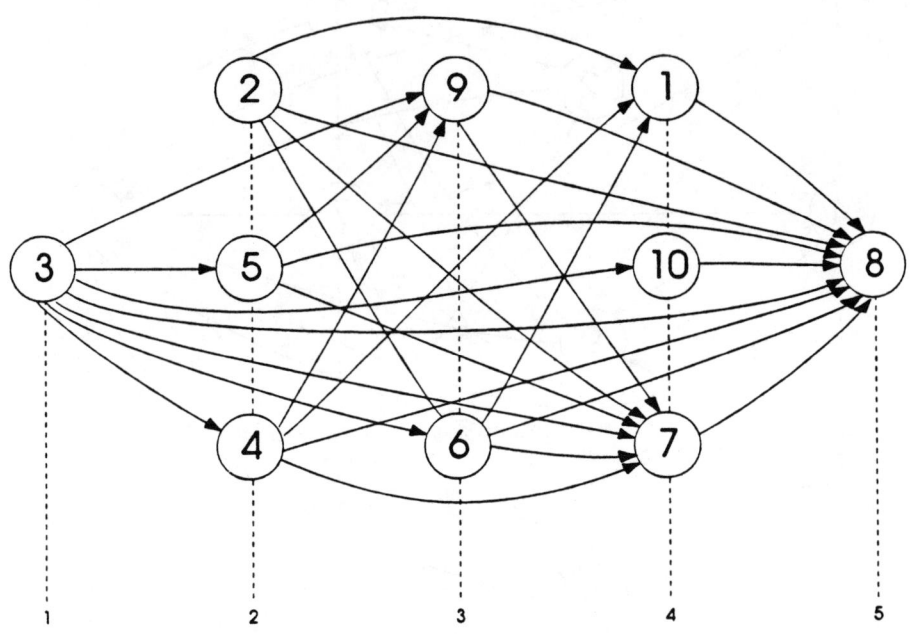

Figure 5: Concordance threshold p = 0.91==» MSD$_4$ U MSD$_3$

CONCLUSION

We have presented, in this article, an approach based on Separate Utility Models for gains and for losses. We assumed the general shape of the DARA-INARA classes of utility functions for each attribute. These models allowed us to identify the "transparent" and "non-transparent" stochastic dominances and to establish the preferences of decision maker in all alternative pairs where it was possible.

The number of "non-transparent" stochastic dominances is minimized, in this model, if the reference point is the origin or an extreme value of the attribute scale.

In the construction of the overall outranking relation using Roy's rule, we suggest two steps. First, adopting the Stochastic Dominance concept on each attribute for a reduced number of alternative pairs requiring some information on decision maker's preference. Second, to try to explain "non-transparent" stochastic dominance relations, when it is beneficial, together with Decision Maker.

REFERENCES

Bawa, V.S., "Optimal Rules for Ordering Uncertain Prospects", Journal of Financial Economics, Vol. 2, 1975, (95-121).

Currin, I.S. and R.K. Sarin, "Prospect Versus Utility", Management Science, 35 1989, (22-41).

Huang, C.C., Kira, D. and I. Vertinsky, "Stochastic Dominance Rules for Multiattribute Utility Functions", Review of Economic Studies, Vol. 41, 1978, (611-616).

Jacquet-Lagrèze, E., "Le problème de l'agrégation des préférences: une classe de procédures à seuil", Mathématiques et Sciences Humaines, Vol. 13, 1973.

Keeney, R.L. and H. Raiffa, Decisions with Multiple Objectives: Preferences and Value Tradeoffs, Wiley, 1976.

Zaras, K., "Dominances stochastiques pour deux classes de fonctions d'utilité: concaves et convexes", RAIRO: Recherche Opérationnelle, Vol. 23, 1, 1989. (57-65).

APPENDIX I

Definition 1

F_i FSD F_j if and only if $F_i \neq F_j$ and

$H_1(x) = F_i(x) - F_j(x) \leq 0$ for all $x \in [x_o, x^o]$

Definition 2

F_i SSD F_j if and only if $F_i \neq F_j$ and

$H_2(x) = \int_{x_0}^{x} H_1(y) dy \leq 0$ for all $x \in [x_o, x^o]$

Definition 3

$\overline{F}_i$ SISD $\overline{F}_j$ if and only if $\overline{F}_i \neq \overline{F}_j$

$\overline{H}_2(x) = \int_{x}^{x_0} H_1(y) dy \geq 0$ for all $x \in [x_o, x^o]$

Definition 4

F_i TSD F_j if and only if $F_i \neq F_j$ and

$H_3(x) = \int_{x_0}^{x} H_2(y) dy \leq 0$ for all $x \in [x_o, x^o]$

Definition 5

$\overline{F}_i$ TISD1 $\overline{F}_j$ if and only if $\overline{F}_i \neq \overline{F}_j$ and

$\hat{H}_3(x) = \int_{x_0}^{x} \overline{H}_2(y) dy \geq 0$ for all $x \in [x_o, x^o]$

Definition 6

$\overline{F}_i$ TISD2 $\overline{F}_j$ if and only if $\overline{F}_i \neq \overline{F}_j$ and

$\overline{H}_3(x) = \int_{x}^{x_0} \overline{H}_2(y) dy \geq 0$ for all $x \in [x_o, x^o]$

APPENDIX II

Rule 1

If $H_1(x) \leq 0$ for all $x \in [x_o, x^o]$

then $E_i(x) - E_j(x) \geq 0$ for all $\phi(x) \in U_1$

where $U_1 = \{\phi(x)/\phi'(x) > 0\}$

Rule 2

If $H_2(x) \leq 0$ for all $x \in [x_o, x^o]$

then $E_i(x) - E_j(x) \geq 0$ for all $\phi(x) \in U_2^1$

where $U_2^1 = \{\phi(x)/\phi'(x) > 0, \phi''(x) \leq 0\}$

Rule 3

If $\mu(F_i) \leq \mu(F_j)$ and $H_3(x) \leq 0$ for all $x \in [x_o, x^o]$

then $E_i(x) - E_j(x) \geq 0$ for all $\phi(x) \in U_3^1$

where $U_3^1 = \{\phi(x)/\phi'(x) > 0, \phi''(x) \leq 0, \phi'''(x) \geq 0\}$

and $\phi'(x)\phi'''(x) \geq (\phi''(x))^2$

Rule 4

If $\overline{H}_2(x) \geq 0$ for all $x \in [x_o, x^o]$

then $E_i(x) - E_j(x) \geq 0$ for all $\phi(x) \in U_2^2$

where $U_2^2 = \{\phi(x)/\phi'(x) > 0, \phi''(x) \geq 0\}$

Rule 5

If $\hat{H}_3(x) \geq 0$ for all $x \in [x_o, x^o]$

then $E_i(x) - E_j(x) \geq 0$ for all $\phi(x) \in U_3^2$

where $U_3^2 = \{\phi(x)/\phi'(x) > 0, \phi''(x) \geq 0, \phi'''(x) \leq 0\}$

Rule 6

If $\overline{H}_3(x) \geq 0$ for all $x \in [x_o, x^o]$

then $E_i(x) - E_j(x) \geq 0$ for all $\phi(x) \in U_3^3$

where $U_3^3 = \{\phi(x)/\phi'(x) > 0, \phi''(x) \geq 0, \phi(x)''' \geq 0\}$

and $\phi'(x)\phi'''(x) \leq (\phi''(x))^2$

AGGREGATION AND UNCERTAINTIES IN DELIBERATED EVALUATION

Quingsan Cao
and
Jean-Pierre Protzen

Department of Architecture
University of California, Berkeley

Performance evaluation is often encountered by designers, planners and other decision makers. Deliberated evaluation is a systematic evaluation method consists of 1)deliberating a complex evaluation task into aspects, 2)aggregating an overall evaluation from its aspects' evaluations, and 3)materializing an aspect evaluation as a function of objectively measurable physical variables. This method leads to a mapping, as a model of evaluation processes, from objective measures of an evaluated object to its subjectively assessed performance measure. The main purpose of this method is "objectification" that means the evaluation conducted by one evaluator being fully understandable and reproducible by others.

This paper presents some new developments of the deliberated evaluation method, especially in the methods of aggregating multiple-aspect performance measures. This paper, using fuzzy arithmetic, also addresses the problem of subjective uncertainty embedded in the evaluation process.

1. Deliberated performance evaluation

In this paper, the word performance refers to the aptness of an object for certain objectives. It is equivalent to "utility", "quality", "value", etc. The result of evaluation helps decision making such as selecting a plan or design among many others. Deliberated evaluation as a method for performance measurement has two main purposes: 1) *Objectification*: to describe somebody's evaluation system in explicit terms so that others can understand how this evaluator arrived in his/her judgment and the same judgment can be arrived under the same situation by others (may be a machine, although they may not share the basis for evaluation); 2) *Rationalization*: to encourage and help the evaluator to analyze and think more systematically in comprehending information and achieving judgments through the process of evaluation. The deliberated evaluation method provides a vehicle to explicitly describe the criteria specified by an evaluator such that other evaluators can obtain the same evaluation result given the same situation. However, the method does not, and is not intended to, guarantee a "correct" evaluation or an "optimal" decision. The correctness and optimality subject to criteria that may vary from evaluator to evaluator and situation to situation.

The deliberated evaluation method consists the following procedures:
1. Deliberation: analyze a complex evaluation task and divide it into aspects and sub-aspects;
2. Materialization: explicitly describe an aspect (sub-aspect) evaluation measure as a function of physical variables.
3. Aggregation: aggregate multiple aspect performance measures into an overall performance measure;

These procedures result in an evaluation pyramid structure. It forms a mapping between physical variables and the overall performance measure of the evaluated object, through evaluations of aspect performance at various levels in between. The existence of such a mapping relies on the assumption that the measurable properties completely determine the performance of an object. Although this assumption may cause some controversies in fundamental philosophy, it is vital for design practices. It is the physical properties, measurable objectively, of a designed object that can be manipulated by a designer to adjust the object's performance.

Some preliminary assumptions and rules of the method have been addressed long time ago (Musso and Rittel, 1967). However, many issues involved require further study, such as the variety of measurement scales, the forms of aggregation functions, the construction of transformation functions, and the issue of subjective uncertainty (Cao, 1992). This paper, in Section 2, discusses the methods to construct aggregation functions that facilitate aggregation process. Section 3 addresses the problem of subjective uncertainty embedded in the evaluation process.

2. Aggregation functions

An aggregation function specifies the relationship between the performance measure of overall object (aspect) and the performance measures of its aspects (sub-aspects). It may have various forms as long as it satisfies a set of fundamental assumptions (Cao and Protzen, 1992):
1. *Closed operator*: The aspect performances and the overall performance use the same measurement scale.

2. *Uniqueness*: The overall (aspect) rating is completely determined by its aspect (sub-aspect) ratings.
3. *Preservation of extremes*: If all of the independent variables have the maximum (minimum) rating the function has the same rating.
4. *Monotonicity*: An aggregation function is a monotonically non-decreasing function of each independent variable.

An aggregation essentially involves three factors:
1. Quantity of satisfied aspects.
2. Quality of the satisfaction of each aspect.
3. Importance of each aspect.

These factors can be summarized into the validity of the following statement:

At least q important aspects are satisfied,

or briefly,

Q WEs are in X.

Q stands for the amount of at least q, a quantitative criterion parameter. W stands for important, Es stands for aspects, and X stands for satisfied. For example, the statement can be: "The majorities of the aspects are satisfied." with the quantity Q being the majority, or "At least one of the aspects are satisfied." with Q being at least one. The construction of an aggregation function is now equivalent to measuring the validity of this statement. There are two different methods to measure the validity of the statement and thus to derive different aggregation functions: algebraic quantification and logic substitution.

2.1. Algebraic quantification

The algebraic quantification method starts from measuring the *quantity* of satisfied aspects augmented by the quality and the importance of each aspect's satisfaction. Then, the augmented quantity (r), a p-norm function of performance measures (x_i) of all aspects weighted by their relative importance factors (w_i),

$$r = \left(\sum_{i=1}^{n} w_i x_i^p\right)^{1/p}, \quad p \in R^+$$

is compared with an *expected* quantity (r_q) to form an aggregation function as:

$$x = F(x_1, ..., x_n) = Q(r)$$

where Q is a monotonically non-decreasing function such that

$$F = Q(r) = 1, \quad \text{if } r > r_q.$$

The function Q can be interpreted as an expectation function of the evaluator about the quantity of satisfied aspects.

Specifically, when the parameter p in the p-norm function becomes one (1.0), this aggregation function coincides with the fuzzy quantifier with non-fuzzy cardinality of a fuzzy set (Zadeh, 1983) which is also referred to as the algebraic quantifier (Yager, 1983). Function Q is the fuzzy quantifier. The arithmetic mean of the aspect performance measure

$$r = \sum_{i=1}^{n} w_i x_i$$

is the non-fuzzy cardinality of the fuzzy set of satisfied aspects. The aspect performance measure (x_i) is the membership of the aspect in the set.

An interesting special case is the geometric mean, the limit of the p-norm function when the value of p approaches zero (0),

$$r = \prod_{i=1}^{n} x_i^{w_i}$$

Another interesting special case of the p-norm function is the 2-norm ($p=2$),

$$r = \sqrt{\sum_{i=1}^{n} w_i x_i^2}$$

which has a geometric meaning as the length of a vector with components, x_i. Furthermore, the maximum function is also called infinity norm as a special case of p-norm in mathematics.

2.2. Logic substitution

Another method of constructing an aggregation function is to use logic substitution according to the theory of fuzzy set, similar to that of constructing a multiple objective decision function (Yager, 1984). With the help of the concept of fuzzy set, the original statement "Q WEs are in X." is equivalently translated to:

Q E_i in W are in X

where Q E_i stands for at least q aspects. W is the fuzzy set of important aspects. X is the fuzzy set of satisfied aspects. The logic substitution method consists of three steps:

1) Linguistic substitution:

Without changing validity, equivalently substitute the original statement "Q WEs are in X." by a composite of elementary components, *e.g.*,
There exists a (crisp) set C_q such that:
there are Q E_is in C_q and W, and for all E_is in C_q, if E_i is in W then E_i is in X.
It can be written as:

$$\bigcup\nolimits_{C_q^k \subset E} \left[(QE_i \in W \cap C_q^k) \cap \bigcap_{i=1}^{n} (E_i \in W \cap C_q^k \Rightarrow E_i \in X) \right]$$

2) *Algebraic substitution*:
   Substitutes the validity of each component ($E_i \in W$ or $E_i \in X$) of the composite by the membership value (w_i or x_i) of the corresponding element (E_i) to the corresponding fuzzy set (**W** or **X**). The membership value of an element to a fuzzy set is a real number on the interval [0, 1]. In this case, it is nothing but the performance measure or importance factor of an aspect.
3) *Arithmetic substitution*:
   Derive the validity of the composite, as a function of that of its components, by defining a corresponding arithmetic function to substitute each type of logic operations involved in the composite, including *conjunctive* ($\cap$), *disjunctive* ($\cup$) and *implication* ($\Rightarrow$).

Combining the three steps, the validity of the original statement "Q WEs are X" can be measured as:

$$F = S_{k=1}^{n_q}\left\{ T_1\left[Q(r_k), T_{3i=1}^{n}\left(I\left(T_2(c_i^k, w_i), x_i \right) \right) \right] \right\}$$

where n is the total number of elements (E_is in E) and n_q is the total number of all possible sets C_q that contains at least q elements. The T_1, T_2 and T_3 are functions associated with the conjunctive operator with different subscripts indicating possibly different forms, the I is a function associated with the implication operator, and the S is a function associated with the disjunctive operator. This equation is a more general form than the general competitive decision function derived by Yager, and Table 1 lists some special forms of it (Yager, 1984).

The quantity $r^k (=|T_2(c_i^k, w_i)|)$ is the cardinality of the fuzzy set $W \cap C_q^k$, which measures the number of important (**W**) aspects in C_q^k. $Q(r^k)$ is a quantifier that represents the quantity criterion in the statement. It is a monotonically non-decreasing function that has its range on [0, 1]. There can be different formulas that define the cardinality of a fuzzy set, such as the non-fuzzy cardinal and the fuzzy cardinal (Zadeh, 1983). The non-fuzzy cardinality can be interpreted as the quantity of aspects in the set and calculated as

$$r_k = \left| T_2(c_i^k, w_i) \right|_{i=1}^{n} = \sum_{i=1}^{n} T_2(c_i^k, w_i).$$

The function Q depends on the original quantified linguistic statement. For instance, if the quantified statement is "at least half of the **W** aspects are in C_q", the quantifier function Q will be a monotonically non-decreasing function such that $Q_2(r_2) = 1$, when $r_2 \geq 0.5$. In another case, if the statement is "at least one of the **W** aspects is in C_q", the quantifier function Q will be a monotonically non-decreasing function such that $Q_1(r_1) = 1$, when $r_1 \geq 1$.

To investigate different types of aggregation functions, a case study has been conducted based on a survey result (Cao, 1992). The aggregation

functions examined include the p-norm function ($n=6$, $0 \leq p \leq 5$) and four aggregations listed in Table 1. ($n=6$, $q=0, ..., 6$). The results of this case study (Cao and Protzen, 1992) indicated that
1. An aggregation function can, indeed, closely describe the evaluator's natural aggregation process with a high correlation, when the format is properly selected.
2. The algebraic quantifier and the logic substitution approaches work equally well, when the values of parameters are properly selected. However, a) the algebraic quantification method is simple and easy to implement with minimal amount of computation; b) the aggregation functions obtained with logic substitution method provide more logic insights about the evaluators' aggregation process. For instance, it reveals that most of the evaluators are looking for the majority, instead of all, of the aspects being satisfied.

Table 1. Special cases of the general aggregation function.

	All aggregation functions have $I(u,v) = u^v$.	
	$T(u,v) = u \wedge v = Min(u,v)$	$T(u,v) = u \cdot v$
$S(u,v) = Max(u,v)$	$Max_{k=1}^{n_q} = \left(Q(r_k) \wedge Min_{i=1}^{n} x_i^{c_i^k \wedge w_i} \right)$	$Max_{k=1}^{n_q} \left(Q(r_k) \prod_{i=1}^{n} x_i^{c_i^k \cdot w_i} \right)$
$S(u,v) = Min(u,v)$	$\left(\sum_{k=1}^{n_q} Q(r_k) \wedge Min_{i=1}^{n} x_i^{c_i^k \wedge w_i} \right) \wedge 1$	$\left(\sum_{k=1}^{n_q} Q(r_k) \prod_{i=1}^{n} x_i^{c_i^k \cdot w_i} \right) \wedge 1$
Q: $q=n$	$Min_{i=1}^{n} x_i^{w_i}$	$\prod_{i=1}^{n} x_i^{w_i}$
Q: $q=1$	$Max_{i=1}^{n} x_i^{w_i}$	
Q: $q=0$	$F \equiv 1$	

3. Subjective uncertainty

3.1. Sources of uncertainties

Following the deliberated evaluation method, an evaluator often faces some uncertainties when he/she attempts to explicitly express an evaluative judgment. The uncertainties may have many different sources.

First of all, an evaluator's judgment or rating of a particular object's performance depends not only on the object but also depends on the evaluator's background references, such as experience, education and expectation. These background references are changing from time to time and so will be the evaluator's judgment that reflects the evaluator's (implicit) interpretation of the performance measurement scale. This change should be described by the change of transformation function used for materialization in the deliberated evaluation. The transformation functions explicitly describe the evaluator's interpretation of the performance measurement scale. Secondly, an evaluator's rating on performance depends on the variation of the object itself. The objective characteristics of an object and thus its performances are often subject to dynamic changes. For example, room temperature, humidity, and ventilation conditions in a room are all constantly varying in some range. Therefore, the precise performance of the room in terms of thermal comfort is also varying. Although, the conditions, theoretically, can be specified and controlled, it is not practical or not even meaningful in many real situations where an evaluation needs to be conducted. This objective uncertainty caused by dynamic variation is most commonly handled by statistical measures with the probability theory that treats the measurements as random variables.

Besides the changing reference and the objective uncertainty mentioned above, there is still another factor that causes the uncertainty when someone tries to describe his/her judgment, that is the uncertainty of the judgment itself. It is reasonable to believe that a subjective judgment has its natural uncertainty that may often be referred to as hesitation. In other words, no matter how well the objective conditions be controlled, there is still some uncertainty, or hesitation, when an evaluator is making a judgment even at a single moment that is not subject to the changes of the background references. From now on, we will refer to this phenomenon by the term *subjective uncertainty*.

In order to achieve the purpose of objectification, the subjective uncertainties need to be properly addressed in the deliberated performance evaluation method. In other words, the uncertain preference on a rating scale should be faithfully recorded and properly processed. This task calls for a new mathematical tool that can deal with entities, numbers or sets of numbers, that are not defined crystal clear.

3.2. Fuzzy performance measurements

A fuzzy number can be used to directly describe a subjective (quantitative) assertion, a number with uncertainty. We refer to a fuzzy number describing a performance measurement with uncertainty as a fuzzy performance measurement or rating. Using a fuzzy number as a "rating" on a continuous scale, an evaluator can describe his subjective judgment better than using a regular number, since a fuzzy number allows the evaluator to express his preference with described uncertainty. A fuzzy rating is a more faithful representation of the judgment than a regular rating. It simply specifies (Kaufmann and Gupta, 1985)

"What is the smallest value given to this uncertain number? What is the highest? Further, if we were authorized to give one and only one value, what value should we give?"

In addition, considering each linguistic label on a discrete scale, such as "bad", "neutral" or "good", as a fuzzy set defined on a continuous scale with a membership function, the discrete scale and the continuous scale can be mapped onto each other with some uncertainty described by the membership functions. Then each linguistic label becomes a fuzzy rating on the continuous scale defined by its membership function.

3.3. Aggregation of fuzzy performance measurements

For the case of using regular numbers as performance measurement, we have discussed many types of aggregation functions in the previous section. These functions consist of arithmetic operations on the independent variables, crisp performance measurements. The operations include summation, subtraction, multiplication, maximum and minimum. Within the frame of fuzzy arithmetic (Kaufmann and Gupta, 1985), there is no difficulty to apply these same operations to fuzzy performance measurements. The independent variables are the fuzzy measurements of aspect performances, and the function value is then the fuzzy measurement of the overall performance. Therefore, the uncertainty described by the membership function of a fuzzy measurement, as part of the information, is carried through the aggregation process.

Although the result, a fuzzy performance measurement, does not have a precise value in the regular sense, it carries more information than a crisp measurement (a regular number) could. It contains the information about the uncertainties that the evaluator has when judging the performance. Among different objects, the overall ratings should be compared as fuzzy numbers. It might seem becoming more ambiguous compared with ratings expressed in regular numbers, however it reveals more information and describes the truth more faithfully, since a subjective judgment itself is not and, probably, can never be crystal clear.

In the process of materialization, a transformation function needs to describe the relationship between a set of physical variable that do not contain subjective uncertainty and a fuzzy performance measure that has uncertainty. It has to be a function that maps a set of crisp variables onto a fuzzy number. In other words, the functions need to be such that for each given vector of the independent variables on its domain, the function will have a unique fuzzy number on its range. Unlike the fuzzy arithmetic, used in aggregation functions, that carry through and process uncertainty of independent variables, a fuzzy transformation function "generates" uncertainty. We need to define such a fuzzy function and we will refer to it as a fuzzy function. The uncertainty generated by a fuzzy transformation function should describe the uncertainty occurred to an evaluator in the process of making numerical judgments.

Let's consider, at first, the transformation functions with only one independent variable. Similar to the rating assignment, an evaluator needs to establish a membership function for a fuzzy transformation function, the performance rating as a function of physical measurement, R(x). That is to specify a range of confidence at each level of presumptions ($0 \le \mu \le 1$). However, in this case of a fuzzy transformation function, the evaluator needs to specify two continuous functions (aspect ratings as functions of the corresponding physical measurement) as the upper and lower bounds of a range of confidence ($[A_\mu(x), B_\mu(x)]$) at all levels of presumptions ($0 \le \mu \le 1$), instead of two numbers as the upper and lower ends of an interval of confidence. A range of confidence is a band shaped area on the plane of the (aspect) performance rating vs. the physical measurement as illustrated in Figure 1.

The same concept can be generalized to the case of multiple-variable transformation functions with little more effort. For instance, in the case of two independent variables, the range of confidence at a particular presumption level is the space bounded by the two surfaces, $r = A_\mu(x_1, x_2)$ and $r = B_\mu(x_1, x_2)$, in the three-dimensional space, with the independent variables in two of the dimensions and the performance rating in the third. The most likely function value is also a 3-D surface, $r = R(x_1, x_2)$, which spans within the confidence range at any presumption level as illustrated in Figure 2. For a fuzzy function of three independent variables, just like a regular function, the geometric interpretation is not very clear.

As discussed above in this section, we can improve our stands in front of the problem of subjective uncertainty by using the tools of fuzzy numbers, fuzzy arithmetic and fuzzy functions. Introducing these tools, we are simply admitting the fact of uncertainty and faithfully record, process and present it, so that the result is more meaningful although it seems less precise. We trade off the arbitrary precision for faithfulness. In other words, in the price of "loosing" precision that does not exist we preserved the information of the uncertain preference that truly exists.

In order to have fuzzy numbers fit into the frame of deliberated performance evaluation, some of the fundamental assumptions (Cao, 1992) about the measurement scales, the aggregation functions and the transformation functions made for the deliberated evaluation method needs modification. The modifications are fairly straight forward.

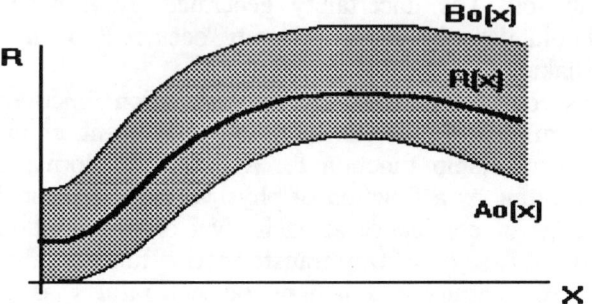

Figure 1. A single variable fuzzy transformation function.

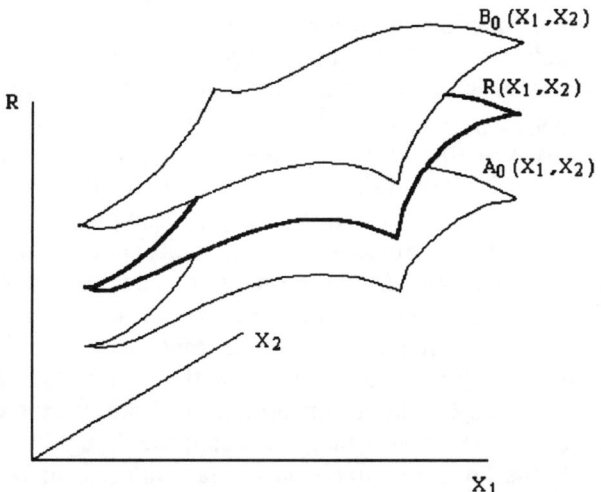

Figure 2. A two variable fuzzy transformation function.

4. Conclusions

The method of deliberated evaluation provides a procedure to model and describe an evaluation process. It allows one evaluator's evaluation process and thus the result be understood by others such that the others, even if not agree, can reconstruct the same evaluation. It also provides a means in reproducing evaluations. An expert's evaluation process, after being studied carefully, can be described explicitly with the deliberated evaluation system and be reproduced by other evaluators, a computer for instance.

This paper presented two methods to construct aggregation functions to be used in the aggregation phase of the deliberated evaluation. The selection of aggregation function and the method to construct it is a matter of evaluators' opinion. The logic substitution provides a means to construct an aggregation function based on logical reasoning of aggregation criteria. It often is based on or leads to a better understanding of the aggregation process. Algebraic quantification provides another means to construct aggregation functions. It is intuitively more straight forward. It is often more simple computationally. A few types of aggregation functions have been examined with survey data in a case study to confirm the above conclusions.

In this paper, we have proposed to use fuzzy numbers as fuzzy performance measurement and to use fuzzy arithmetic aggregate fuzzy performance measurements. We have also defined a fuzzy function to describe the generation of the subjective uncertainties in the process of making numerical judgment on perceived performance. These fuzzy analysis tools allow evaluators to explicitly describe and process the subjective uncertainties embedded in the performance evaluation. However, how does the theoretical benefits out weigh the additional practical efforts introduced is yet to be evaluated through experiments in practice. The problems, such as decision making based on a fuzzy performance evaluation, are left for future studies.

References:

Cao, Q. and J.P. Protzen, 1992: "Deliberation and Aggregation in Computer Aided Performance Evaluation," in A. Tzonis and I. White (edts.): *Automation Based Creative Design (ABCD): Current Issues in Computer and Architecture*, Elsevier North-Holland Excerpta Medica.

Cao, Q., 1992: "Deliberated Performance Evaluation and Application in Comfort Assessment," Ph.D. dissertation, University of California at Berkeley, Department of Architecture, Berkeley California, May, 1992.

Kaufmann, A. and M. M. Gupta, 1985: *Introduction to Fuzzy Arithmetic*, Van Nostrand Reinhold Company, New York.

Musso, A. and H. Rittel, 1967: "Measuring the Performance of Buildings," Report of a Pilot Study, Washington University, St. Louis, Missouri, September, 1967.

Yager, R. R., 1983: "Quantified Propositions in a Linguistic Logic," *International Journal of Man-Machine Studies*, 1983, 9, pp. 195 - 227.

Yager, R. R., 1984: "General Multiple-Objective Decision Functions and Linguistically Quantified Statements", *International Journal of Man-Machine Studies*, 1984, 21, pp. 389 - 400.

Zadeh, L. A., 1983: "A Computational Approach to Fuzzy Quantifiers in Natural Languages", *Computers and Mathematics with Applications*, 1983, vol. 9, No. 1, pp. 149 - 184.

MULTICRITERIA DECISION MODEL

AND DECISION MAKING PROCESS

IN AN ORGANIZATION :

An Application in Industrial Management

C. Pellegrin
IAE de LYON
University of Lyon III
France

This contribution is part of the Multicriteria Decision Aid approach (Roy 1990). A graphical multicriteria decision model to support the decision making process in industrial preventive maintenance is developed. Three different readings of the graphical procedure are proposed in order to show how the decision model, as designed, generates informations able to aid the agents involved in the decision process to make "collective sense" of their experience and to help take decisions in conformity with the goals of the maintenance organization.
" The objective of multicriteria approaches is to help us to make better decisions, but what is the meaning of *better* ? " [Roy 1990]. This question leads B. Roy to distinguish between two attitudes, Multiple Criteria Decision Making (MCDM) and Multicriteria Decision Aid (MCDA), the latter aiming at helping the actors taking part in the decision process " either to shape, and/or to argue, and/or to transform preferences, or to make a decision in conformity with the goals".
The present contribution is based on a research related to the development of tools supporting decision making in industrial preventive maintenance. Its purpose is to use a graphical multicriteria decision model developed in such a case [Pellegrin 1992 a,b] in order to show how the decision model, *as designed,* generates informations able to :
. bring to actors involved in the decision process a representation of the preventive maintenance organization in which their actions are inserted,
. aid to create learning and innovation processes,

increase the consistency between a decision related to a particular action of preventive maintenance with a set of actions aiming at improving the flexibility of the productive system.

In the first part we present the decision problem related to this particular maintenance action and we exhibit a graphical multicriteria procedure of decision making. We propose, then, three different readings of this tool and we conclude, finally, by showing how this tool is able to participate in a process aiming at developing, confronting and formalizing the professional knowledges of the maintenance organization.

1. A multicriteria decision problem

Expanding the flexibility of productive systems, that is, their ability to quickly adjust to any changes in relevant factors like product, process, loads and machines failures, is become paramount in manufacturing. *For the maintenance organization, this means to be able to improve the availability, reliability and maintainability of plants.* We are going to consider, in this paper, a particular contribution of the preventive maintenance towards achieving this objective, namely, the on-condition maintenance.

The practice of the periodic on-condition maintenance surveillance is based on an assumption : the gradual wear and deterioration process of the productive equipment is described by an indicative parameter and this quantity under control is measured periodically. When an inspection detects that this quantity exceeds a alarm threshold, a preventive intervention is launched in order to avoid a breakdown of the plant.

A key concept for modelling the issues of such an inspection process is the delay time of a fault arising in the plant : the delay time h is the time interval between the initial time t when the alarm threshold is exceeded and the time a repair is considered essential (failure or reaching an unacceptable threshold). It was found possible by Christer and Waller in 1984 [Cf Christer 1992] " to obtain estimates of delay time and thereby construct useful and influential models of inspection processes ".

We briefly summarize, below, the assumptions of the decision problem, the criteria defining the efficiency of this maintenance policy and the main result allowing to construct the graphical procedure (cf Pellegrin 1992a for the proof).

Assumptions on the maintenance procedure

(a) Inspections are performed with periodicity T in order to measure the value of the indicative parameter. Each inspection brings about a cost c_i and a downtime d_i .

(b) A preventive intervention is immediately launched when an inspection detects that a predetermined alarm threshold is exceeded, that is, when a "damage state" arises in the plant. Each preventive intervention causes a cost c_p and a downtime d_p.

(c) If the measured parameter exceeds a predetermined unacceptable threshold then the plant is considered as failed and a breakdown repair is required. A breakdown repair causes a cost c_b and a downtime d_b. It is here assumed that $c_i + c_p < c_b$ and $d_i + d_p < d_b$; otherwise the decision problem is trivial.

(d) A damage state present within the plant at an inspection will be identified.

(e) Any repair, after the detection of a damage state or after a failure, restores the item to its original condition, that is, the condition parameter returns to its initial "as-new" value.

Assumptions on the modelling of the wear and deterioration process

(f) The elapsed time, from when the equipment is in its original condition to when a damage state arises, is denoted by t and the delay time, i.e, the elapsed time between the occurrence of a damage state and the time a repair is considered as essential, is denoted by h.

(g) The variables h and t are, in addition, assumed stochastically independent.

(h) Let f and F be respectively the p.d.f. and the c.d.f. of the delay time h, then, then failure rate function $x \rightarrow f(x) / [1 - F(x)]$ is assumed to be non decreasing (Increasing Failure Rate Hypothesis).

Efficiency of an on-condition maintenance inspection policy

Let T be the inspection interval and define a cycle as the time interval from the start of operations from a new or just repaired state to the completion of the next repair.

Suppose the damage state arises between the (i-1)-th inspection and the i-th inspection, i.e., the damage state arises at t so that $(i-1)T \leq t < iT$, then :

- either the delay time is great enough, i.e. h is more than iT-t, then the damage state is detected at the i-th inspection and the cycle (so called preventive cycle) ends with a preventive intervention,

- or the delay time is too small, i.e., h is less than iT-t, then a failure occurs at t+h and the cycle ends with a breakdown repair.

Now, three kinds of criteria can be considered for the choice of the inspection interval T :

. **a reliability measure** : to choose the period T so that the probability P(T) of a preventive cycle exceeds a given value (the focus is on the reliability of the plant) ;

. a cost criterion : to minimize the average cost per time unit C_T, i.e., the ratio [Expected cost due to inspections, preventive repair, breakdown repair] / [average cycle time length]

. a availability criterion : to minimize the average downtime per time unit D_T, i.e., the ratio [Expected downtime due to inspections, preventive repair, breakdown repair] / [average cycle time length]

(The availability criterion is similar to the cost criterion and only the criteria C_T and P(T) will be considered in the sequel).

For example, if T is chosen close to 0, the reliability measure is maximized but the inspection may be costly (cost or downtime due to inspections). On the other hand, if T is infinite, that means, to choose a breakdown maintenance policy, i.e., repair on failure only. In this case $P(\infty) = 0$ and the cost criterion is $C_\infty = c_b / [E(t) + E(h) + d_b]$ where E(.) denotes the expected time until a damage state arises and the expected delay time respectively.

And we can say : *an on-condition maintenance surveillance with periodicity T is economically feasible if $C_T \leq C_\infty$ and, in this case, $100.(C_\infty - C_T)/C_\infty$ is the percentage cost saving which ensues from such an inspection policy of periodicity T.*

The following proposition enables us to build a graphical procedure for the inspection decision making .

Proposition (Pellegrin 1992a)

Let T be the inspection interval and denote by

y = P(T) the corresponding reliability measure, i.e., the probability of avoiding a breakdown,

x = S(T) the average number of inspections until a damage state arises, i.e., S(T) is an indicator of the frequency of inspections,

F the function expressed as P(T) = F(S(T)).

Then, under the above assumptions, there is a positive function Y so that :

for any given value m, the percentage cost saving that could result from the choice of an inspection interval T is at least 100.m % if the periodicity T may be chosen to satisfy the condition :

$$P(T) \geq a_m S(T) + b_m - c_m Y(S(T)) \quad (1)$$

where a_m, b_m and c_m are depending only on input cost and downtime parameters, and, on E(t) and E(h) previously defined.

We can give the following interpretation :

" for any given value m, there is a curve C_m, defined by the right hand term in the above relation (1), so that, if a part of the curve F lies above the curve C_m and if the inspection interval T corresponds to a point (S(T), P(T)) on this part then the cost saving $(C_\infty - C_T)/C_\infty$ is at least m".

Figure 1 illustrates the graphical procedure.

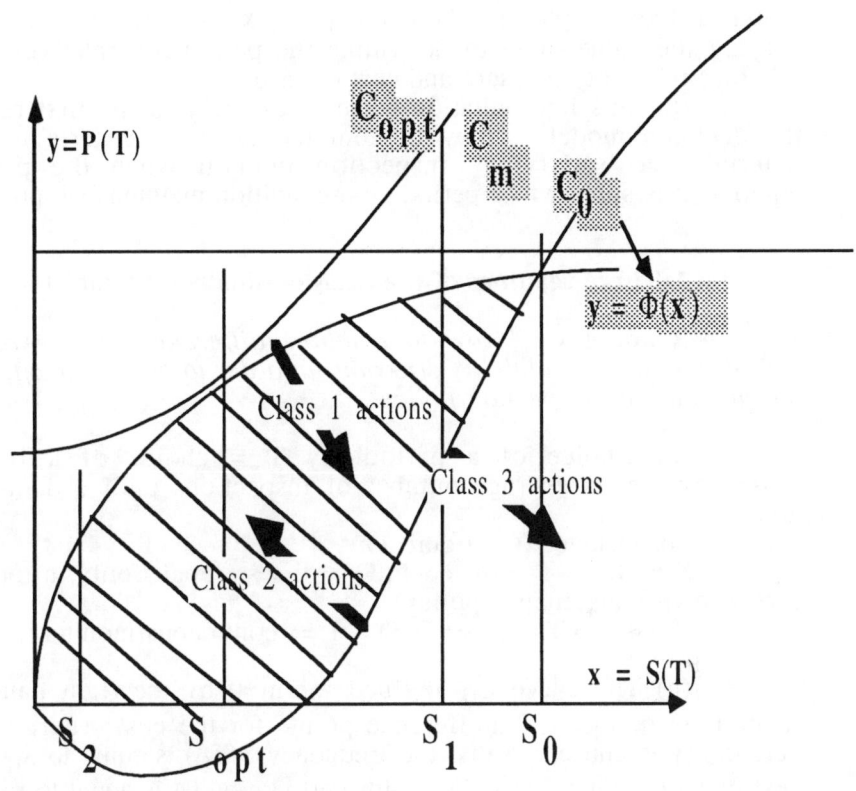

T = inspection interval
P(T) = reliability measure
S(T) = average number of inspections before damage state
▨ = limit gain in cost reduction (economical efficiency)

Fig 1 : Graphical procedure for inspection decision making

We are going now to state precisely this first reading but also to propose two other readings of this tool in order to present the model as a metaphor of the capacity of the maintenance organization to respond to any changes in its environment.

This graphical procedure may be implemented as an interactive graphical tool, by plotting the curve $y = F(x)$ and the curve C_m, and by varying the value of m to determine the periodicity relatively to both criteria : reliability measure and cost criterion.

But this interpretation corresponds only to the first reading of the decision model : "how to combine different criteria to help to determine a "satisfying" inspection interval when the productive equipment is subject to a periodic on-condition maintenance policy".

2. Three readings of the decision model (cf figure 1)

Reading 1 : *"How to combine different criteria (reliability measure, cost or availability criterion) in order to assess the efficiency of an on-condition inspection policy".*

(a) Choice of a periodicity T = choice of a inspection frequency, i.e., a average number of inspections until a damage state arises.

For instance (see figure 1):
$S = 0 \Leftrightarrow T = \infty \Leftrightarrow P(T) = 0 \Leftrightarrow$ repair only after failure (breakdown maintenance policy)
$S = \infty \Leftrightarrow T = 0 \Leftrightarrow P(T) = 1 \Leftrightarrow$ continuous monitored system

(b) The curve C_0 (defined for m=0 by the right hand of the relation 1) defines a "indifference point" for the cost criterion : if the periodicity is chosen so that the frequency $S(T_0)$ is equal to S_0 then the cost of an on-condition policy with periodicity T_0 is equal to the cost of a breakdown policy. Besides, the cost of an inspection policy is less than the cost of a breakdown maintenance if the periodicity T is chosen so that $S = S(T)$ is between 0 and $S(T_0)$, i.e, T is greater than T_0.

(c) The area of the region bounded by the curve F and the curve C_0 shows the limit gain in cost reduction that could result from the choice of such a periodic inspection policy.

(d) The curve C_0 cuts the curve F in two points and defines S_1 and S_2 so that the cost reduction $(C_\infty - C_T)/C_\infty$ is at least equal to m if the inspection interval is chosen so that $S(T)$ is between S_1 and S_2.

(e) The curve C_{opt} defines the optimal inspection frequency S_{opt} and the optimal gain according to cost criterion.

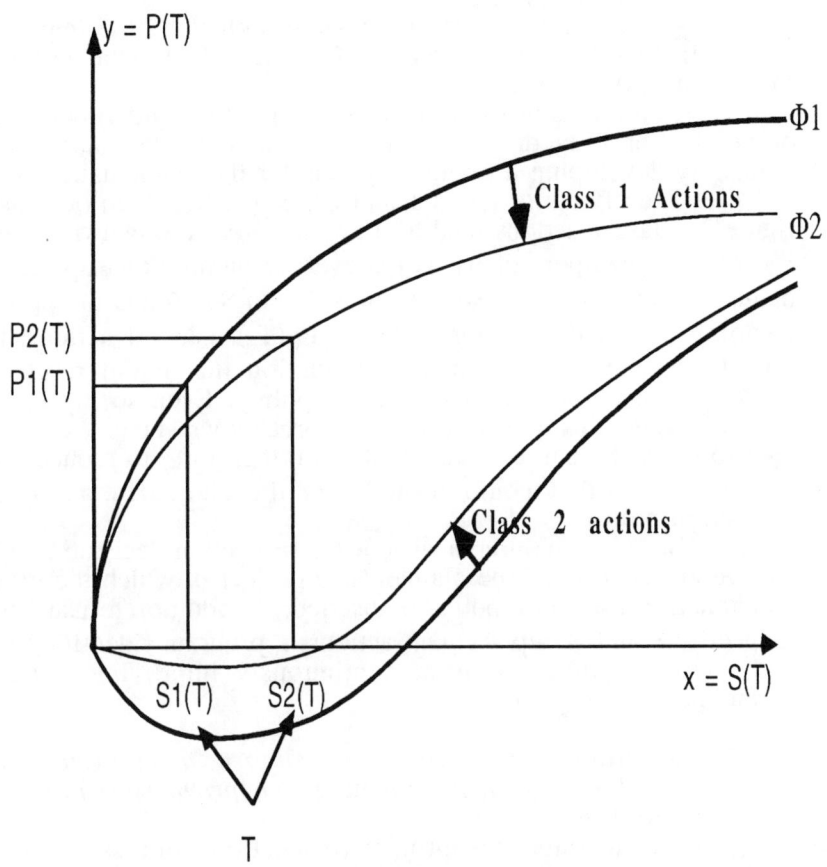

Fig 2 : Class 1 and Class 2 actions

Reading 2 : " *A representation of actions launched by the maintenance organization for facing up to failure risk"*

But the on-condition maintenance is only a part of a preventive maintenance program to face up to failure risk. We can distinguish two kinds of actions, namely Class 1 actions and Class 2 actions.

Class 1 actions aim at :
- either preventing misuse failures on the basis of analysis and improvement of plant working conditions (use conditions, cleaning and lubrication operations ...),
- or reducing inherent weakness failure by the improvement of the intrinsic reliability of plants (for example by the use of Failure Modes and Effects Analysis).

Class 2 actions aim at reducing cost and downtime due to preventive or breakdown repairs by improving the maintainability of plants, by developing training programs for the maintenance agents.

The effects of Class 1 and Class 2 actions can be illustrated by figure 2. Class 1 actions tend to draw the curve F downwards from F_1 to F_2 (for a given periodicity T, the average number of inspections until a damage state arises, increases from $S_1(T)$ to $S_2(T)$ and the probability of avoiding a breakdown from $P_1(T)$ to $P_2(T)$). Class 1 actions, therefore, tend to reduce the gain in cost reduction that could result from the choice of an on-condition inspection policy. Even so, by reducing the cost of inspections and preventive or breakdown repairs, class 2 actions tend to draw the curve C_0 upwards and, therefore, to reduce the gain in cost reduction that could result from the choice of an on-condition inspection policy.

In short, the graphical tool for inspection decision making gives us a representation of the maintenance project in which the on-condition maintenance inspection policy is inserted : in addition to usual preventive inspection[1] and/or replacement actions, a program (identified by class 1 and class 2 actions) aims at continuously improving reliability and maintainability of plants.

Reading 3 : *"Needing to choose a maintenance action consistent with a set of actions aiming at improving the flexibility of the productive system".*

The maintenance project (inspection policies, Class 1 and 2 actions, replacement policies, ...) aims at giving to the productive system the capacity to continue operating effectively despite risk due to machines breakdowns. In fact, the maintenance project contributes to an objective become paramount in manufacturing system : to expand its flexibility, i.e., its ability to quickly adjust not only to machines failures but also to any changes in other factors like product, process or loads. One of the important issues in this respect is to make the system more reactive (by reducing work in process and, particularly, the buffers which protect against the outcomes of machine failures) and, as a consequence, to make the productive system more sensitive to disturbances due to machine failures.

---

[1] not only on-condition inspection policies (here considered)

In fact, this set of actions (Class 3 actions on figure 1) aiming at improving the reactivity of the productive system leads to increase cost and downtime due to failures, and, therefore, tend to draw the curve C_0 downwards.

In short, this reading of the decision model expresses the need to choose a maintenance action consistent with a set of actions aiming at expanding the flexibility of the productive system.

3. Conclusion : the tool and its contribution to Multicriteria

Does such a tool help the agents involved in the decision process "either to shape, and/or to argue, and/or to transform (their) preferences or to make decisions in conformity with the goals" ? Obviously, only an empirical study could answer this question. However it is possible to identify in this decision-aiding tool two classes of mechanisms able to help the maintenance agents making "collective" sense of their experience and to help taking decisions in conformity with the goals of the maintenance organization.

The first class concerns what we call the **proposition function** *for the maintenance process.*

- We have, first, a symbolic representation of the technical / economic debate (reading 1) : to take into account only the curve F related to the reliability measure for the choice of the inspection interval or to take into consideration curves C_0 and C_m related to the economical point of view .

- We have also (reading 2) an "indirect" representation of the class 1 and class 2 actions who are likely to be substituted to the on-condition maintenance policy : either by drawing curve F downwards or by drawing curve Co upwards. Choosing Class 1 and 2 actions appears thus, *via this tool*, as an alternative choice of the on-condition maintenance

Other mechanisms that it is possible to point out, via this tool, are related to **the co-ordination function** *of actions of the maintenance organization.*

Readings 2 and 3 introduce what we call a "double-loop regulation" of potential actions of maintenance agents by pointing out to the need, first to take into consideration Class 1 and 2 actions and, second, to choose a local maintenance action consistent with a set of actions aiming at expanding the flexibility of the productive system. Figure 3 illustrates this "double-loop regulation".

This "double-loop" control may raise again the question of choice regarding the on-condition maintenance itself.

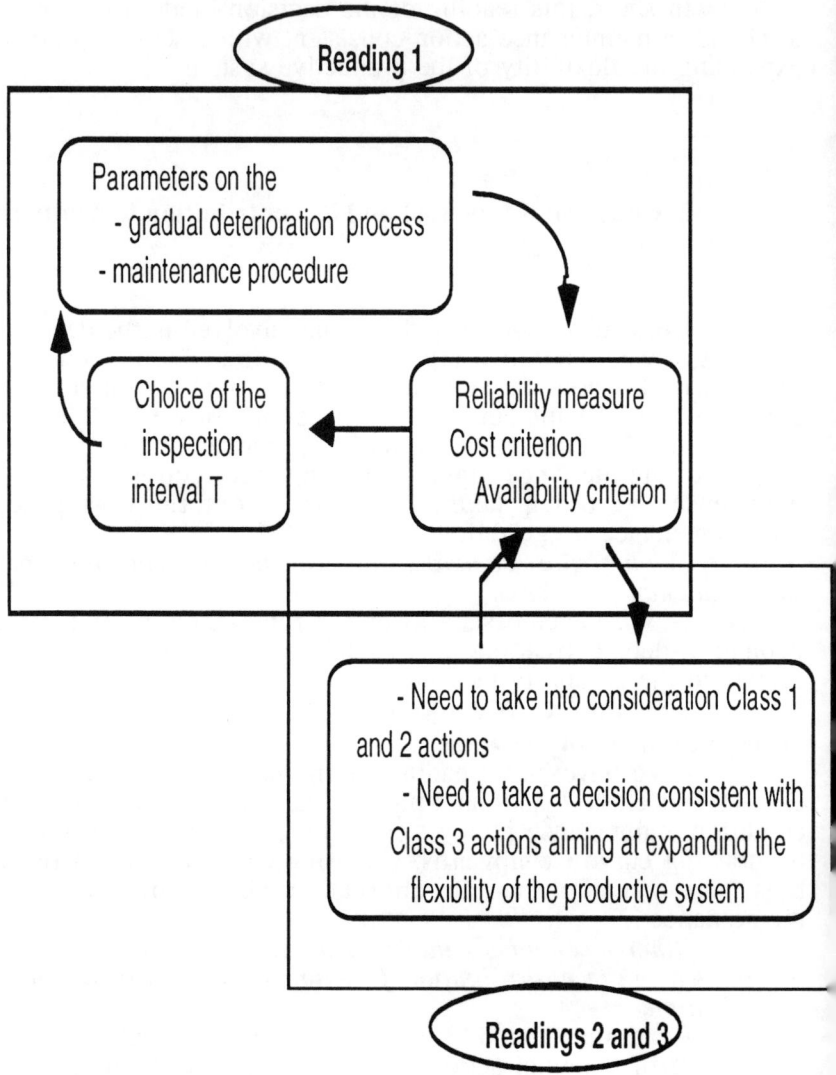

Fig 3 : Graphical decision procedure and "double-loop regulation"

But it has to be observed that this "double-loop" control depends on agents involved in the decision process because readings 2 and 3 contain the preliminary assumption that Class 1, 2 and 3 actions are known. It also depends on how the tool is implemented in the decision-making process, i.e., on the way the tool is used in order to facilitate formalization and sybergy with professional knowledge that maintenance agents possess.

REFERENCES

Christer, A. H., 1992, "Prototype modelling of irregular condition monitoring of production plant", *IMA Journal of Mathematics Applied in Business and Industry*, 3, 219-232.

Pellegrin, C., 1992a, "Graphical procedure for an on-condition maintenance policy", *IMA Journal of Mathematics Applied in Business and Industry,* 3, 177-191.

Pellegrin, C., 1992b, "Choice of a Periodic On-Condition Maintenance Policy", *International Journal of Production Research*, vol 30, n° 5, 1153-1173.

Roy, B., 1990, "Decision-aid and decision-making", *European journal of Operational Research*, 45, 324-331.

5. PRODUCTION, FIRMS AND MARKETS

One very intriguing question, which up to now has not been sufficiently explored, is to find out what changes in economic models and in management science procedures need to be introduced if one wants to draw out all of the consequences of the research on risk behavior to which the previous chapters have been devoted. The three papers of this section deal with applying risk research to agricultural management and financial economics.

The first paper, by Eirik Romstad and Per Kristian Rørstad, deals with a decision problem in agriculture which is well known: namely, when risk affects production and thus profit can be broken down into two different parts. One part is related to the fact that, whatever the climatic conditions during the year, the production and profit response to some decision of the farmer, for example the choice of a level of an input factor, is risky ; the other part being that the farmer doesn't know in advance what the climatic conditions will be during the winter and the spring. Traditionally, production functions (or profit functions) are estimated by pooling all past data, without distinguishing between states of climatic conditions, the result being, as the authors show, that sub-optimal decisions are made by the farmer.

Romstad and Rørstad suggest writing the decision problem, when uncertainty also bears on the climatic conditions, as a game in extensive form in which Nature would be the first player and the farmer would only play second. They further suggest estimating, for each possible climatic state, a contingent production function, whenever this turns out to be possible from the data structure. They finally show that the farmer's problem can be solved by minimizing a Bayesian loss function where probabilities are estimated from past climatic data. They solve a "real world" case using their method and show that their results are quite encouraging. Note that what they do is somewhat akin to minimizing an expected regret in the sense of Loomes and Sugden (1982).

The two other papers of this section depart from the agricultural sector and deal rather with financial market questions.

The chapter by François Quittard-Pinon and Jacques Sikorav provides a very compact and effective synthesis of the methodology used to value non-marketed contingent assets along the lines of Black and Scholes in the early 1970' s. They compute original formulas for the market equilibrium values of these assets, using the three main features of the methodology : a) modelling the movement of the underlying asset to capture both time and uncertainty; b) constructing a riskless portfolio with equivalent payments, c) using the No Arbitrage equilibrium condition to value the asset considered in a) with the equilibrium value of the asset considered in b).

Finally, the paper by Alain Chateauneuf, Robert Kast and André Lapied also deals with the very same question of asset valuation in a financial market. It also follows the lines of authors like Harrison and Kreps in their well-known paper relating Arbitrage Pricing Theory to general equilibrium. It follows as well the lines of Arrow in his celebrated 1953 paper on "Le rôle des valeurs boursières....". Like Quittard-Pinon and Sikorav, Chateauneuf, Kast and Lapied remind the reader that standard financial theories assume that the value of an asset is the sum of the values of the assets in a portfolio which would yield the same payments in all states.

However, the last three authors remark that this is at odds with observed datas in many cases. The divergence is generally attributed to transaction costs, as is too often argued when a theory is invalidated by empirical observations. But Chateauneuf, Kast and Lapied stress that, even if we were to accept this explanation, we would not account for all available data, especially data related to close-to-maturity values. They conclude that this remark calls for a different rule of asset valuation than the linear rule and show that, in the case where markets are "slack", i.e., not perfectly "tight" in Duffie's sense (they offer more than one possible price for a given asset), market equilibrium does not "reveal" a single probability distribution, but a capacity in Choquet's sense. In this case, the valuation of an asset is not the expected value of its cash flows (as in Arrow' s case), but the Choquet integral of these same cash flows in the continuous case (or, in the discrete case, the sum of these cash flows weighted by differences between cumulative capacity to the left and cumulative capacity to the right of the considered value). A particularly interesting feature of this model is captured when one assumes that the assets of a portfolio are non-comonotonic (i.e., there can be hedging effects in a broad sense between the assets). In such a case, the value of a portfolio can be larger than the sum of its constituent assets.

This means that the financial notion of "risk" used in the model of the authors has been enriched with respect to the one used in standard theory, and made quite closer to the real world perception of risk, to the extent that the *specific manner* in which assets affect the variation of value of portfolio also does enter the representation of "risk".

This very enlightening enrichment is due to non-expected utility theory, for the Choquet integral is a representation of the Quiggin-Allais-Segal-Wakker Functional in the Rank Ordered Model of lotteries valuation.

EXPECTED PROFITS AND INFORMATION

UNDER UNCERTAINTY

Eirik Romstad & Per Kristian Rørstad
Department of Economics and Social Sciences
Agricultural University of Norway
Ås, Norway

The traditional way of obtaining production functions is to pool all available data for a given product and to estimate the production function with the required properties given these data. The purpose of this paper is two-fold:
(i) To show that when decisions about input factor use have to be made prior to the realization of profits and realized profits are stochastic, the traditional approach may lead to sub-optimal input factor use.
(ii) To devise an alternative approach to reduce the sub-optimality of the input factor use under the conditions outlined in (i).

The suggested approach is applicable whenever the profit response to input factor use entail stochastic elements, which for example is the case regarding yield response in rain fed agriculture. The basic principle of the suggested approach is to classify production data into various states, and estimate state specific production functions based on these data. The resulting input factor use from this approach will under the mentioned conditions be less sub-optimal than the input use derived from the traditional approach.[1] An important side effect of the proposed approach is that it provides the decision maker with more information regarding the nature of the stochastic elements affecting production and thus profits.

In the next section a model for finding expected ex ante optimal input factor use under these conditions is presented, with special emphasis on

---

[1] The expected profits from the suggested approach can of course never exceed the expected profits from perfect foresight, but under the type of conditions for which the approach is applicable, perfect foresight is not possible.

presenting the conditions under which the proposed approach may prove beneficial compared to the traditional approach. The succeeding section provides an application using simulated data on fertilization in Norwegian grain production. Finally, the informational benefits of the suggested approach are discussed.

THE MODEL

Assume that profits as a function of input factor entail considerable stochastic elements, and that it is not possible in advance − when decisions about input factor use are made − to know the exact profit responses to various levels of input factor use. Consequently, it is impossible to determine the optimal input factor use. Also assume that it is possible − on the basis of historical data − to classify production outcomes ex post into various states. Two approaches stand out when it comes to detecting types of outcomes:

(i) *The residual method:* If the traditional regression approach to estimate the production function(s) yields residuals that are not "white noise" − and in particular if the residuals for some level of input factor use are multi-modally distributed − this is a strong indication that it may be possible to estimate state specific production functions.

(ii) *The decision maker's "notion" method:* In some cases the decision maker may have an idea about various states that could arise. This is for instance the case in rain fed agriculture. Most farmers know that depending upon the growing conditions, of which the amount and distribution of rain through the growing season are important stochastic elements, yield response to various fertilizer levels may vary.

Both methods imply that the decision maker may be better off by a decision tree approach to choose the level of input factor use. This is also indicated by Figure 2. Assume that the decision maker: (a) seeks to maximize expected profits and (b) knew what state would emerge in the next production period. The state dependent optimal input factor use is then given by:

$$\left\{ \substack{MAX \\ x|\theta} \right\} E[\pi(\mathbf{p},\mathbf{v})] = \left\{ \substack{MAX \\ x|\theta} \right\} \{ \mathbf{p}\, f_\theta(x) - \mathbf{v}\, x \}, \theta \in \Omega \qquad [1]$$

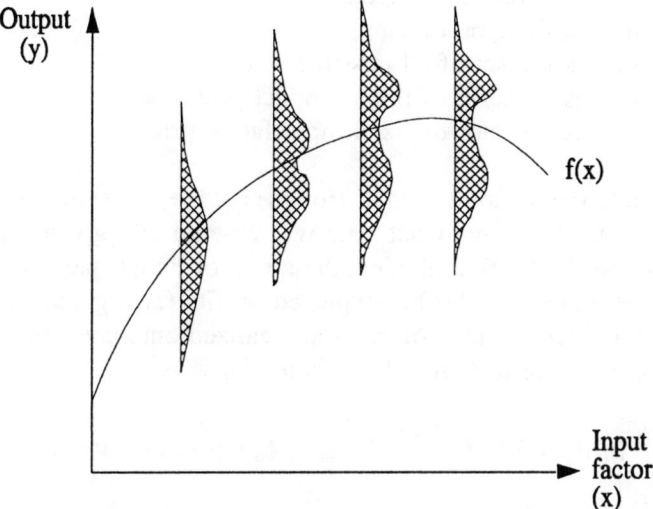

Figure 1: Production function based on pooled data (shaded areas indicate the distribution of output around the pooled estimated production function.

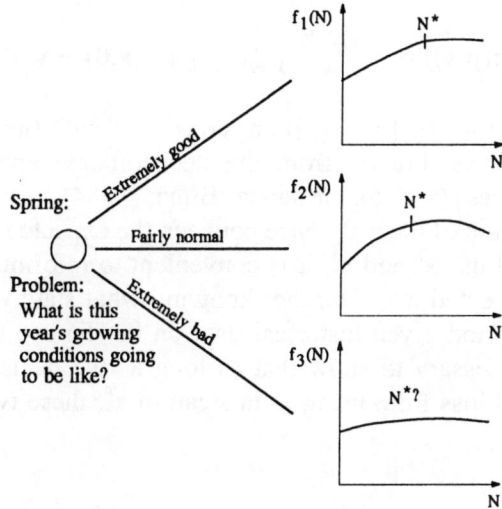

Figure 2: Yield functions under 3 types of growing conditions (N^* indicates ex-post optimal fertilization for a given set relative prices, under each of the 3 growing conditions).

where: x   is a vector of inputs,
        θ   is the type of state,
        Ω   is the set of all possible states
        p   is a vector of fixed product prices, and
        v   is a vector of fixed input factor prices.[2]

Let x^θ denote the solution of [1]. However if the decision maker is not able – ex ante – to determine what state will emerge in a given production period, he/she needs to find the combination of input factors, x^*, that irrespective of θ maximizes his/her expected profits for a given production period. If θ is a discrete index of previous realized outcomes, the decision maker's problem can be formulated the following way:

$$\left\{ \begin{array}{c} MAX \\ x \end{array} \right\} E[\pi(p,v)] = \left\{ \begin{array}{c} MAX \\ x \end{array} \right\} \Sigma_{\theta \in \Omega} \phi_\theta [\, p\, f_\theta(x) - v\, x\,] \qquad [2]$$

where: ϕ_θ is the probability of any state θ, $\theta \in \Omega$.

In case the amount of historical data is large, it may be possible for the decision maker to formulate the problem in terms of a probability distribution $\phi(\theta)$ over the possible states, Ω, i.e.

$$\left\{ \begin{array}{c} MAX \\ x \end{array} \right\} E[\pi(p,v)] = \left\{ \begin{array}{c} MAX \\ x \end{array} \right\} \int_{\theta \in \Omega} [\, p\, f(x,\theta) - v\, x\,]\, d\theta \qquad [3]$$

Both formulations ([2] and [3]) are consistent with the expected profit approach that follows directly from the decision tree approach for state contingent outcomes (see for instance Bunn, 1984). For purposes of obtaining information of the difference between the expected profits from the optimal input level use x^θ and x^*, it is convenient to reformulate [2] and [3] in terms of the expected loss from not knowing what state will occur in the next production period given historical data on θ. To use this formulation to find x^*, it is necessary to show that as long as the decision maker only views the expected loss from using x^* in stead of x^θ, these two formulations are identical.

---

[2] Allowing for random prices or letting prices be determined by aggregate supply and demand for inputs and products, would yield the same qualitative results, but would make notation more messy and is therefore omitted.

LEMMA 1: When the loss function is linear, the solution of MAX $E[\pi(x^*|p,v)]$ is equivalent to the solution of MIN $\{E[\pi(x^\theta|p,v)] - \pi(x^*|p,v)]\}$.

PROOF [3]: Assume given historical information on θ, and let $\pi_\theta(\cdot)$ denote the state dependent profits. The following identity then holds:

MAX $E[\pi(x^*|p,v)]$
$\equiv$ MAX $\{E[\pi(x^\theta|p,v)] - E[\pi(x^\theta|p,v)] + E[\pi(x^*|p,v)]\}$
$\equiv$ MAX $\{E[\pi(x^\theta|p,v)] - E[\pi(x^\theta|p,v) - \pi(x^*|p,v)]\}$
$\updownarrow$
MAX $\Sigma_{\theta\in\Omega}\ \phi_\theta\ \pi_\theta(x^*|p,v)$
$\equiv$ MAX $\{\Sigma_{\theta\in\Omega}\ \phi_\theta\ \pi_\theta(x^\theta|p,v)$
$\qquad - \Sigma_{\theta\in\Omega}\ [\phi_\theta\ \pi_\theta(x^\theta|p,v) - \phi_\theta\ \pi_\theta(x^*|p,v)]\}$

$\qquad\qquad \Sigma_{\theta\in\Omega}\ \phi_\theta\ \pi_\theta(x^\theta|p,v)$ is constant given information on θ,
$\qquad\qquad \Rightarrow \Sigma_{\theta\in\Omega}\ \phi_\theta\ \pi_\theta(x^\theta|p,v) \equiv K$

MAX $\Sigma_{\theta\in\Omega}\ \phi_\theta\ \pi_\theta(x^*|p,v)$
$\equiv$ MAX $\{K - \Sigma_{\theta\in\Omega}\ [\phi_\theta\ \pi_\theta(x^\theta|p,v) - \phi_\theta\ \pi_\theta(x^*|p,v)]\}$
$\equiv K -$ MAX $\{\Sigma_{\theta\in\Omega}\ [\phi_\theta\ \pi_\theta(x^\theta|p,v) - \phi_\theta\ \pi_\theta(x^*|p,v)]\}$

$\qquad\qquad -$ MAX $f(x) =$ MIN $f(x)$

MAX $\Sigma_{\theta\in\Omega}\ \phi_\theta\ \pi_\theta(x^*|p,v)$
$\equiv K +$ MIN $\{\Sigma_{\theta\in\Omega}\ [\phi_\theta\ \pi_\theta(x^\theta|p,v) - \phi_\theta\ \pi_\theta(x^*|p,v)]\}$

$\therefore$

As any constant K in the above functional form does not affect the minimization or maximization problem, MAX $E[\pi(x^*|p,v)]$ yields the same solution as solving MIN $\{E[\pi(x^\theta|p,v)] - \pi(x^*|p,v)]\}$.

Q.E.D.

Thus it is possible to formulate the decision maker's discrete state problem in θ as a Bayes' risk decision problem:

$$\left\{\begin{matrix}\text{MIN}\\x^*\end{matrix}\right\} R(x^*,\theta) = \left\{\begin{matrix}\text{MIN}\\x^*\end{matrix}\right\} L(x^*|p,v,\theta) =$$
$$\left\{\begin{matrix}\text{MIN}\\x^*\end{matrix}\right\} \{E[\pi(x^\theta|p,v)] - \pi(x^*|p,v)]\}$$
$\updownarrow$

[4a]

---

[3] The proof is only undertaken for the discrete state case of θ. The continuous case proof follows basically the same steps and yields the same qualitative results.

$$\{{\textstyle{MIN \atop x^*}}\} \; \Sigma_{\theta \in \Omega} \; \{\phi_\theta \, [\; p \; f_\theta(x^\theta) - v \; x^\theta \;] - \phi_\theta \, [\; p \; f_\theta(x^*) - v \; x^* \;]\} \qquad [4b]$$

A similar expression can be formulated for the continuous time problem. Both formulations resemble the regret theory formulation used by Loomes and Sugden (1982).

AN APPLICATION: FERTILIZATION IN NORWEGIAN GRAIN PRODUCTION

The shape of yield curves and thus what constitutes profit maximizing fertilization have been heavily discussed in Norway these last 2-3 years.[4] Bakken, Botterweg and Romstad (1992) started to approach these problems in a fashion consistent with the theory section of this paper. The application provided here is an extension of the approach indicated by Bakken et al., and is based on simulated data for barley on clay soils.[5] For demonstrational purposes, only one controllable input factor is considered – fertilizer-N.

The Traditional Approach

Several production functions were estimated using all of the simulated data. Based the distribution of the residuals as well as statistical properties

---

[4] The main reason that yield curves for the production of grains have gained so much attention in Norway is that some research that has been undertaken indicates that taxing fertilizer Nitrogen with 100-300 % is the most cost-effective way of reducing pollution from Norwegian agriculture. These reductions may be sufficient for Norway to meet its obligations within the North Sea treaty.

[5] Unfortunately only some of the data material have been processed by the time this paper is written, but on the basis of these data, a data set was created for 15 different growing seasons and for the N-fertilization levels 10 kg to 200 kg per hectare, with increments of 10 kg per hectare. The formulas used to create the simulated data are consistent with functional relationships suggested by Holm, Sødal and Vestøl (1989) and Vagstad (1991). Source data used to create the simulated data set are at the courtesy of the Centre of Soil and Environmental Research.

like estimated F-values for the functions and T-values for the estimated parameters, a quadratic specification was chosen[6], i.e.:

$$y = f(N) = ß_0 + ß_1 N + ß_2 N^2 + \varepsilon \qquad [6]$$

Estimating [6] using OLS yielded the following parameter estimates (standard errors in parentheses): $ß_0 = 2411.6$ (120.5), $ß_1 = 28.249$ (2.643) and $ß_2 = -0.09453$ (0.01222). Data points and the predicted values from [6] are shown in Figure 3.

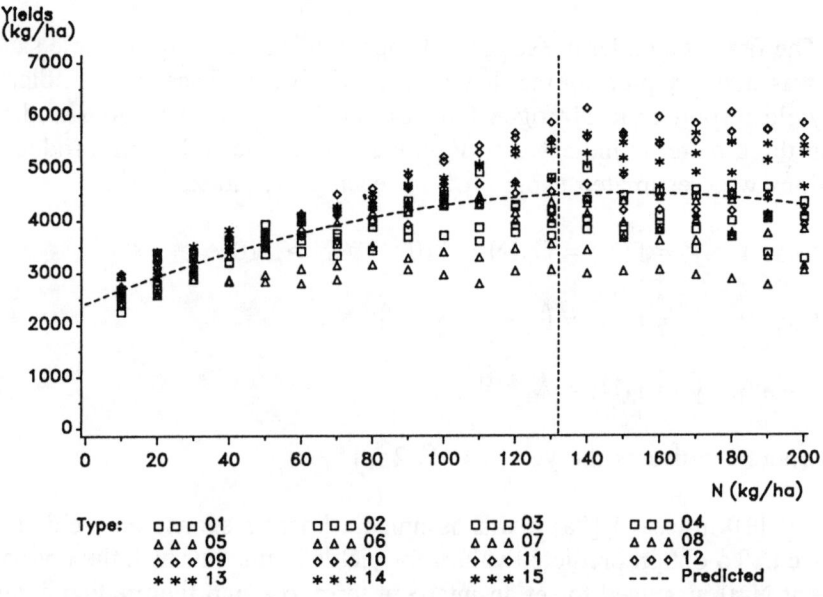

Figure 3: Yield response and N (estimated model: $\hat{y} = 2412 + 28.249 N - 0.0945 N^2$).

From the predicted and observed values it is easy to see that the estimated function have heteroscedastic residuals. Heteroscedasticity causes no problems regarding the unbiasedness of the estimated parameters, but the standard errors become inflated (Judge, Hill, Griffiths, Lütkepohl and Lee,

---

[6] One weakness with polynomial production function specifications is that they often overestimate the profit maximizing input use (Ackello-Ogutu, Paris and Williams, 1985).

1982). In the estimated model, however, lack of significance of the estimated parameters is no problem.

At a grain price of 0.29 ECU per kg and an N price of 0.96 ECU per kg, the privately expected profit maximizing fertilization level using the estimated model is 131.8 kg per hectare (indicated by the vertical line in Figure 3). At this fertilization level, the expected profits are 1163 ECU per hectare.

The Proposed Approach

The first step under the suggested approach is to identify possible states. This was done by plotting the data on a yearly basis. These plots indicated that yield responses to Nitrogen fertilization for a given year followed one of the three patterns indicated in Figure 2. Thus the following production functions were estimated using OLS for each year, indexed by i:

Case 1: $\hat{y}_i = f_i(N) = \hat{G}_i (N - 110)^{\delta_i} \quad \forall \, N > 110$ [7a]

Case 2: $\hat{y}_i = f_i(N) = \hat{\beta}_{i0} + \hat{\beta}_{i1} N + \hat{\beta}_{i2} N^2$ [7b]

Case 3: $\hat{y}_i = f_i(N) = \hat{A}_i N^{\hat{\lambda}_i}$ [7c]

where i indicates the year, $i \in \{1,2,..,15\}$.

For $N \leq 110$ in case 1 [7a] it was assumed a linear response on yields from Nitrogen. To obtain predicted values for yields in this interval, the observed value at N=0 was used to set an intercept term, α_{i0}, and the predicted value from [7a], evaluated at N=111 used to find the parameter α_{i1}. A temporary specification of the first case thus becomes:

$$\left. \begin{array}{l} \hat{y}_i = f_i(N) = \alpha_{i0} + \alpha_{i1} N, \quad \forall \, N \leq 110 \\ \hat{y}_i = f_i(N) = \hat{G}_i (N - 110)^{\delta_i}, \quad \forall \, N > 110 \end{array} \right\} \quad [8]$$

One problem with [8] is that it is not guaranteed that the first order derivatives are the same where the segments are joined, resulting to a non-existing first order derivative at this point. Similar problems exist when using von Liebig specifications (Paris and Knapp, 1989; Berck and Helfand, 1990), which [8] bears some resemblance to. One advantage of the Cobb-

Douglas type specification (used for N > 110), is that the first order derivative changes rapidly as N → 110⁺. Letting N → $\tilde{N}^+$, $\tilde{N}$ > 110, it was therefore possible to make the first order derivatives of the two segments the same, yielding a small change from the value of the parameter α_{i1}. More specifically the new parameters for the slope of the linear segment, γ_{i0} and γ_{i1}, are found by:

$$\gamma_{i1} = [\hat{G}_i (\tilde{N}_i - 110)^{\delta_i} - y_i(0)]/\tilde{N}_i = \hat{\delta}_i \hat{G}_i (\tilde{N}_i - 110)^{(\delta_i - 1)} \quad [9a]$$

$$\gamma_{i0} = \hat{G}_i (\tilde{N}_i - 110)^{\delta_i} - \gamma_{i1} \tilde{N}_i \quad [9b]$$

where $y_i(0)$ is the actual yield in year i at N=0

This procedure ensures differentiability at N = $\tilde{N}_i$. The revised specification of [8] thus becomes:

$$\left. \begin{array}{l} \hat{y}_i = f_i(N) = \gamma_{i0} + \gamma_{i1} N, \quad \forall N < \tilde{N}_i \\ \hat{y}_i = f_i(N) = \hat{G}_i (N - 110)^{\delta_i}, \quad \forall N \geq \tilde{N}_i \end{array} \right\} \quad [10]$$

If $p \cdot \gamma_{i1} < v$, the possibility of the optimal fertilization level being zero is checked[7], as this implies that the value of the marginal product is less than the marginal costs for N ∈ [0,$\tilde{N}_i$).

To figure out which equation ([7b], [7c] or [10]) to use in a given year, the size and distribution of the residuals around the implied profit maximizing fertilization level were tested. In borderline cases between any of the specifications, expected profits at the inferred optimum fertilization levels were also checked, and the specification yielding the highest profits was chosen for that year. The chosen states, and thus the year specific yield function, gave good predictions of the observed yield levels for that year (Figure 4 on the next page shows the observed values as well as predicted values for two given years).

As the growing conditions in a specific year is not known in advance, optimal fertilization level was found using the following reformulation of [4b]:

---

[7] This check includes testing if the expected profits for any fertilization level above $\tilde{N}_i$ kg per hectare exceeds the profits at zero fertilization.

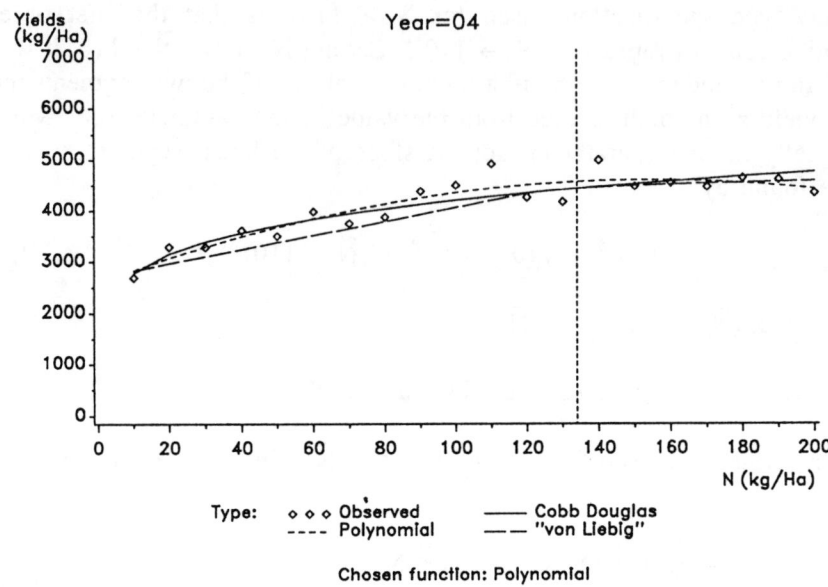

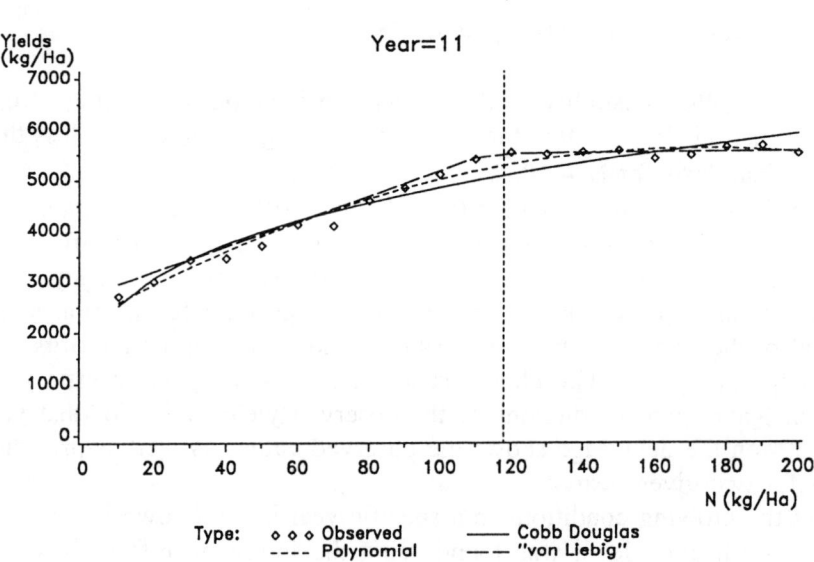

Figure 4: Observed and predicted values for two chosen years (vertical lines indicate the year specific profit maximizing fertilizer level).

$$\{\mathop{\text{MIN}}_{N^*}\} \; \Sigma_{i \in T} \; \{[\; p \; f_i(N^i) - v \; N^i \;] - [\; p \; f_i(N^*) - v \; N^* \;]\} \qquad [11]$$

where: T is the set $\{1,2,...,15\}$,

N^i is the ex post (perfect information) optimal fertilization level in year i, and

N^* is the 15 year fertilization level that minimizes the difference in expected profits obtained from the ex post optimal fertilization levels and a constant fertilization regime.

The results from the simulations based on [11] are shown in table 1:

Table 1: *Profit maximizing fertilization levels, yields and resulting profits from the traditional and revised approach.*[a]

Approach	Profit maximizing behavior:		
	Fertilization levels (kg N/ha)	Expected yields (kg/ha)	Expected profits (ECU/ha)
Traditional	131.8	4492.9	1163.20
Revised	129.0	4490.9	1165.25
Difference	− 2.8	− 2.0	2.05

a. Grain price: 0.29 ECU per kg, Nitrogen price: 0.96 ECU per kg

The differences in suggested profit maximizing fertilization levels, resulting yields and profits are not very large. Moreover, these differences may be deemed insignificant when the uncertainties regarding the estimated parameters are taken into consideration. There are two reasons for these small differences:

(i) In the simulated data only one of the years were found to be "type one" [10], the remaining years were "type two" [7b] (see Figure 2 for a reference to year types).

(ii) For the "type one" year, the "kink" ($\tilde{N}$) occurs in the interval of 110 to 130 kg of Nitrogen per hectare, which does not differ much from the profit maximizing fertilization level found using the traditional approach.

For data were a larger percentage of the years would fall in groups "one" [10] or "three" [7c], and the "kink" is further away from the profit maximizing fertilization level indicated by the traditional approach, these differences would be larger.

INFORMATIONAL BENEFITS OF THE PROPOSED APPROACH

As indicated in the previous section, the differences in fertilization levels and profits were small between the two approaches. On these particular data the benefits of the suggested approach may therefore appear to be minor. Such a view represents a gross over-simplification of the problem at hand. A major advantage of the proposed approach is that it provides information regarding the value of perfect information in each year.

The expected value of perfect information (EVPI) indicates the potential benefits the decision maker may get from obtaining more information (Bunn, 1984). In this case study the difference between the year specific maximum profits and the profits that are derived using a fixed fertilization regime is a proxy for this measure.

Figure 5 shows how this difference is distributed through a bar chart. The mean estimated difference is 17.52 ECU per hectare, with a standard deviation of 19.97 and a maximum difference of 61.29 ECU per hectare. This indicates that the potential benefits of collecting more information may be considerable. The shaded portions of the bars indicate that the loss of profits from the fixed fertilization regime is caused by too little fertilizer being applied. The converse holds for the non-shaded

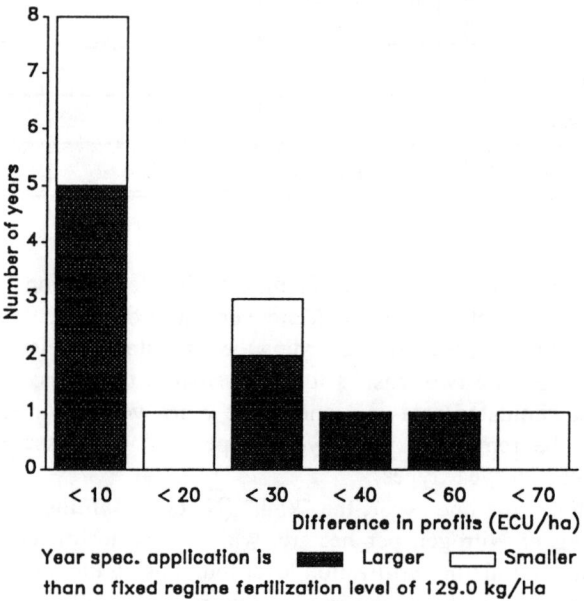

Figure 5: Bar diagram of the difference between the year specific maximum profit levels and the profits obtained from a fixed fertilization regime.

areas. In the case of fertilization it could be interesting to have a closer look at split fertilization, in particular if the farmer is able to predict what kind of growing season the current year will become by the time eventual additional fertilizers are to be applied. Such an approach implies lower first time application rates of fertilizers.[8]

CONCLUSIONS

The suggested approach is applicable whenever profits are stochastic, and it is possible − ex post − to group data into various profit states. Most likely the suggested approach will cause profits to increase. The most significant advantage of the approach is that it provides a measure for the expected value of perfect information, which indicates potential benefits of gathering more information or postponing decisions until more information is available.

The application using simulated data from grain production demonstrates that the potential benefits of the suggested approach may be large, and indicates that other approaches along the same lines may prove beneficial.

More research along these lines are needed. In particular regarding more sophisticated methods to identify states and selection of the state dependent production functions from the functional forms being estimated. The somewhat low increase in the expected profits using the suggested approach may be attributed to these phenomena.

REFERENCES

Ackello-Ogutu, C., Q. Paris & W.A. Williams (1985): "Testing a von Liebig Crop Response Function against Polynomial Specifications", *American Journal of Agricultural Economics*, Vol. 67, pp. 873-880.

Bakken, L., P. Botterweg & E. Romstad (1992): "Agriculture and Pollution: Risky Approaches to Uncertainties", in Central Bureau of Statistics (coordinator) *Seminar on Uncertainty in Management of Natural Resources*, pp. 175-180.

Berck, P. & G. Helfand (1990): "Reconciling the von Liebig and Differentiable Crop Production Functions", *American Journal of Agricultural Economics*, Vol. 72, pp. 985-996.

---

[8] An additional benefit of split application could be reduced pollution from grain production, in particular if the first time application rate is considerably lower than what is indicated as being the fixed regime profit maximizing fertilization level when all fertilizers are applied in early spring.

Bunn, D.W. (1984): *Applied Decision Analysis*, McGraw-Hill, New York.

Holm, Ø., D.P. Sødal & J.Å. Vestøl (1989): *Arealavrenning fra landbruket. En modellstudie med vekt på endret regional produksjonsfordeling og endret arealintensitet*, SEFO-report no. 12, Ås, Norway.

Judge, G.G., R.C. Hill, W.E. Griffiths, H. Lütkepohl & T-C Lee (1982): *Introduction to the Theory and Practice of Econometrics*, John Wiley & Sons, New York.

Loomes, G. & R. Sugden (1982): "Regret Theory: An Alternative Theory of Rational Choice Under Uncertainty", *Economic Journal*, Vol 92, pp. 805-824.

Paris, Q. & K. Knapp (1989): "Estimation of von Liebig Response Functions", *American Journal of Agricultural Economics*, Vol. 71, pp. 178-186.

Vagstad, N.H. (1990): *Miljøoptimal gjødsling: Nitrogen som miljø- og produksjonsfaktor i jordbruket, spesielt i kornproduksjonen*. Report from the Centre of Soil and Environmental Research, Ås, Norway.

MARKET PREFERENCES REVEALED BY PRICES : NON-LINEAR PRICING IN SLACK MARKETS.

A. Chateauneuf[1], R. Kast[2], A. Lapied[3]

In Finance, valuation theories are based on observable data : "arbitrage pricing" uses market prices to derive non-marketed assets values. The principle is simple : if the market does not allow arbitrage opportunities (equilibrium prices) and if it is rich enough in the sense that any asset can be replicated by a portfolio of marketed assets (complete markets), then any asset is priced by the formation cost of a replicating portfolio. Black and Scholes [1973] and Merton [1973] used this principle to derive "the prices of options and other derivative securities" from the observed prices of a riskless bond and of the underlying asset. Using the same principle, Ross [1976] offered his APT as an alternative to the classical CAPM.

The No Arbitrage principle and the assumption that there are no frictions enforce linear pricing rule in the following sense : assets are valued by a linear function of their payments (mathematical expectation). The linear pricing theory is built in a context where assets are defined by their payments, other assets characteristics such as hedging properties, liquidity facilities etc... being irrelevant. Conversely in such a context, linear pricing excludes arbitrage possibilities when

---

[1]CERMSEM, Université de Paris I.

[2]GREQE, C.N.R.S., Marseille.

[2]GREQE,Université de Toulon et Groupe Enseignement International des Affaires, Marseille.

We wish to thank many reseachers for their comments, criticisms, and encouragements, particularly Michèle Cohen, Jerome Detemple, Anton Vorst, Heraklis Polemarchakis and Hans Wiesmeth.

there are no transaction costs : the value of a portfolio is the linear combination of the prices of the assets in the portfolio.

In a context with transaction costs, pricing rules may not be linear. Two portfolios yielding the same payments need not have the same formation cost (net of transaction costs) but the difference cannot be used for a free lunch because of transaction costs. This is in accordance with the trend of explanations encountered in the literature on mispricing puzzles such as the violation of the call-put parity[1](see J. Gould and D. Galai [1974] and R. Klenkovski and B. Resnik [1979] for example) or the premium paid for holding a prime and a score on an underlying security[2].

The object of this paper is to investigate the potential of a more general, non-linear, pricing rule adapted to markets with transaction costs. The way we deal with the problem is to depart from the usual pricing methodology which consists in valuating an asset (defined as a random variable) by a functional which is an extension of observed market prices. Alternatively, we use the common evidence that prices rank the assets traded on a market (market prices reveal market preferences), so that the valuation of non marketed assets should be consistent with this ranking. Valuation is defined by a functional which represents this ranking. In the usual methodology, linear pricing rules are obtained under No Arbitrage conditions which imply the linearity and the positivity of the functional which is then represented by a measure (the "risk neutral" distribution, which is unique if markets are complete). With our methodology, the same linear pricing rule can be obtained under conditions on the ranking. These equilibrium conditions, related to the No Arbitrage ones, provide a way to extend the ranking to non-marketed assets. Valuation of assets is then the representation of this extended ranking by a positive linear functional.

This alternative methodology yields a valuation equivalent to the usual No Arbitrage one, in the case of markets without transaction costs. However it opens the possibility to be generalized so as to encompass non-linear pricing rules. This is done by weakening one of the conditions so as to take into account some hedging effects of the combination of assets in a portfolio. Our valuation allows portfolios yielding the same payments to have different formation costs (net of

---

[1] A put has the same payoffs as a portfolio formed with a call with the same characteristics, a short position on the stock and a long position on the riskless bond (see section 2.3, below).

[2] Decomposition of a security into a prime (yielding the dividends plus a strike price at an expiration date) and a score (yielding the excess value to the strike price only) has been marketed. The combination of the prime and the score replicates the payoffs of the security, however the sum of their prices exceeds the security price by an important premium (Jarrow and O'Hara, [1989]).

transaction costs). However transaction costs are invoked to sustain the non-linear pricing rule, because they prevent investors to use the differences in formation costs to construct riskless gains at zero cost.

In the first section of this paper we use our valuation methodology, founded on the ranking of assets by market prices, to derive a linear pricing rule. This is still done in the case of tight markets, tightness is expressed here by a condition on the ranking.

In the second section of the paper we weaken this last condition. We get an existence theorem for valuation in slack (i.e. not tight) markets. Valuation of an asset in slack markets is a non-linear pricing rule : the Choquet integral of its payments. This is a generalization of valuation in tight markets, where valuation of an asset is the mathematical expectation (Lebesgue integral) of its payments.

1. Pricing in tight markets.

Harrisson and Kreps [1979] gave the first microeconomic analysis of the foundation of arbitrage theory. They emphasized the concept of viability as being less stringent than equilibrium and equivalent to some precise No Arbitrage hypothesis. In a static model and under the complete market hypothesis, which we make in all that follows, they show that viability is equivalent to the positivity of the linear value function. Linearity of the value function comes from an other No Arbitrage assumption which is well stressed by Duffie [1988] who calls it " tight markets". Markets are tight if they satisfy the "one good one price" assumption which is implicit in all equilibrium models. In particular it was shown in Ami, Kast and Lapied [1991] that this assumption is fundamental in Arrow's [1953] model. This model obtains the result, common to all modern Finance arbitrage theories, that the price of an asset is the mathematical expectation of its future payments with respect to a specific probability distribution "revealed" by market prices. Arrow's result is more general than Finance models in the sense that he assumes no known distribution on the set of states, on the other hand it only considers a static framework and a finite number of states. Arrow's model and its conclusions can be generalized so as to encompass valuation models in finance[1], notably the famous one by Black and Scholes. These models assume uncertainty to be described by a probability space (S, s, µ) where µ is known. For instance in the Black and Scholes model, µ is such that the process of future random prices (of the underlying security) is a generalized Wiener process with a constant drift and known

---

[1]See, for instance, R. Kast, A. Lapied [1992].

instantaneous variance. In this context, the set Y of assets is the space $L^2(S, s, \mu)$ endowed with the L^2 norm topology.

The relevance of the a priori distribution μ (on which all agents must agree) can be questioned. It has been introduced in dynamic models to describe the stochastic processes of future prices and to give the set of assets a topological structure. In a static model however, uncertainty may be more correctly described by the space (S,s). *In what follows the set Y of assets will be taken to be the space b(S,s,R) of bounded s-measurable functions from S to R.*

Let M ($Y \supseteq M$) denote the set of marketed assets, and assume the characteristic function 1_S of S, belongs to M (the riskless asset paying one unit of money in all states). Let Θ denote the set of portfolios θ which can be built with marketed assets. By definition, a portfolio θ is defined as the list $\theta(y) \in R$, $y \in M$, of quantities of marketed asset y with which portfolio θ is formed, where only a finite number of $\theta(y)$ is different from zero. Such a portfolio θ uniquely yields an asset, say θ^* the payments of which satisfy

$$\theta^* = \sum_{y \in M} \theta(y) \, y.$$

Notice that the set $\{\theta^*, \theta \in \Theta\}$ = Span(M). Span(M) will be referred to as the set of marketable assets and *we assume that the market is complete*, more precisely we assume that Span(M) = Y. Marketed assets $y \in M$ have prices q(y), and the formation cost of a portfolio defined by $(\theta(y))_{y \in M}$, is:

$$K(\theta) = \sum_{y \in M} \theta(y) \, q(y).$$

The No Arbitrage assumptions bear upon portfolios. We now turn to an alternative methodology to valuate non-marketed assets from observed market prices.

1.1. Prices as a ranking revealed by the market.

The value notion which we develop in this section is founded on the idea that asset prices represent a ranking of assets made by the market. The reciprocal is obvious : market prices rank assets according to their values, whatever theory justifies their existence.

As market prices rank marketed assets, if non marketed assets were to have a value, they would be ranked according to this value. Representation of a ranking (an order or pre-order) by a numerical function relies on some properties. In accordance with these properties, the ranking may be represented by a functional on the set of assets : this functional defines the assets values.

Here $x \geq_Y y$ (resp. $>_Y$) means that the value of x is greater (resp. strictly greater) than the value of y, $x \sim_Y y$ means x and y have the same value.

Our first condition imposes that if x has a higher value than y, then it has a higher value than any asset less valued than y (transitivity). Obviously the ranking must be reflexive (x is "equivalent" or has the same value, as x). Furthermore taking any two assets x and y, we must be able to say wether x has a higher, lower or equal value, than y (the ranking is complete).

Condition 1 : *The market ranking $\geq_Y$ defines a complete preorder on the set of assets.*

The second conditions looks a bit more technical, continuity is indeed a necessary condition (Debreu [1952]) for the representation of an order by a numerical function. This condition is a No Arbitrage condition: if an increasing sequence of assets payments converges toward an asset, then the sequences of their values should converge toward the value of their limit. We first express it in a strong form :

Condition 2 : *The market ranking respects monotonic uniform convergence: for any sequence x_n such that $x_n \geq_Y y$ (resp. $x_n \leq_Y y$) and $x_n \downarrow x$ (resp. $x_n \uparrow x$) uniformly, then $x \geq_Y y$ (resp. $x \leq_Y y$).*

Our third condition says that if the payments of an asset are increased, then its value should increase as well :

Condition 3 : *The market ranking is monotonic in the sense that if $x, y \in Y$ and $a \in R_+^*$, then $x \geq y + a 1_S$ (in the usual sense for real valued functions) implies that $x >_Y y$.*

It is easy to show that conditions 1, 2 and 3 imply that if $x \geq y$ (x takes values superior to the values taken by y in each state), then $x \geq_Y y$ (the market ranking is monotonic with respect to the natural order on assets). In particular if $x \geq 0$ then the value of x should be more than the value of an asset paying nothing, we shall see that this is necessarily equal to 0.

It is well known from decision theory, that a preorder satisfying the previous three conditions can be represented by a continuous real function, say v, defined up to an increasing transformation, and such that: $x \geq_Y y$ if and only if $v(x) \geq v(y)$.

1.2. Linear ranking.

An other condition seems quite natural: two portfolios formed by adding the same asset (z) to two equivalent assets (i.e. with the same value), should have the same value, or:

Condition 4 : *If assets x, y are such that $x \sim_Y y$, then for any asset z, $x + z \sim_Y y + z$.*

Although this last condition might look quite innocuous at first view, it implies a particular (but nonetheless common to most Finance models) market situation: there cannot be any arbitrage opportunities left, in the sense that the value of a portfolio is necessarily its formation cost. Indeed, this comes from the fact that we get the same valuation formula as in the case of No Arbitrage, as proved by:

Theorem 1 :
> The ranking on Y is such that there exists a unique additive probability measure Π on (S,s) such that: $\forall x, y \in Y$, $x \geq_Y y \Leftrightarrow E_\Pi(x) \geq E_\Pi(y)$, if and only if conditions 1 to 4 are satisfied. This defines the value of an asset $y \in Y$ as $v(y) = E_\Pi(y)$.

The "only if" part of the proof is straightforward. The "if" part goes in the following way: From conditions 1 and 2 a continuous function representing the ranking exists. From the comment we made on condition 3, it is clear that such a function is increasing. As Y is the set of bounded random variables, define such a function by $v(y) = \inf_{\alpha \in R} \{\alpha 1_S \geq_Y y\}$; then by continuity we have for any $y \in Y$: $y \sim_Y v(y) 1_S$.

It remains to show that $v : Y \to R$ is linear and then use the same result as in theorem 2.

Additivity of v relies on condition 4 : Let x and y be in Y, then we have $x + y \sim_Y v(x+y) 1_S$, $x \sim_Y v(x) 1_S$ and $y \sim_Y v(y) 1_S$.

From condition 4, $y \sim_Y v(y) 1_S \Rightarrow x + y \sim_Y x + v(y) 1_S$. Similarly, because $x \sim_Y v(x) 1_S$, we have :

$x + y \sim_Y v(x) 1_S + v(y) 1_S = [v(x) + v(y)] 1_S$, hence $v(x+y) = v(x) + v(y)$.

From additivity, $v(nx) = nv(x)$ for any positive integer n, furthermore $v(0) = 0$ and $v(-x) = -v(x)$. For any integers n and m, $v(n.\frac{1}{n}x) = nv(\frac{1}{n}x)$, hence $v(\frac{1}{n}x) = \frac{1}{n}v(x)$ and $v(\frac{m}{n}x) = \frac{m}{n}v(x)$. Linearity is obtained through the usual arguments on the construction of real numbers as limits of rational numbers, and using the continuity of v ♦

Notice that here again, only additivity of the probability is obtained. In order to have a representation by a σ-additive probability an other assumption replacing condition 2 is necessary (and sufficient):

Condition 2' : *The market order respects monotonic convergence : for any sequence x_n such that $x_n \geq_Y y$ (resp. $x_n \leq_Y y$) and $x_n \downarrow x$ (resp. $x_n \uparrow x$), then $x \geq_Y y$ (resp. $x \leq_Y y$).*

2. Pricing in slack markets.

When markets are not tight they are slack, this means that two portfolios which give rise to the same payments may have different formation costs. In this case, an asset cannot be identified with its formation cost which then, cannot be its price. The price or the value, of an asset has to be defined in an other way, intuitively it should lie in between the formation costs of the different portfolios replicating this asset. Clearly this cannot happen in equilibrium if there are no frictions in the market because No Arbitrage are necessary equilibrium conditions. The presence of transaction costs, however, will sustain prices violating linearity.

Using the same method as in the previous section the value notion is directly founded on the ranking of assets by the market. Namely we shall define the function v by: $v(y) = \inf_{\alpha \in R} \{\alpha 1_S \geq_Y y\}$. This ranking will allow valuation in slack markets, this is obtained by a weakening of condition 4.

2.1 Non linear ranking.

Linear ranking cannot account for prices which leave differences in formation costs between assets with the same payments. Services or transaction costs could explicitly be taken into account in these payments in order to differentiate assets with different prices. Such an approach would loose the generality of pricing theories based on the definition of assets as random variables (or stochastic processes) representing their payoffs. Another way out is to use more finely the definition of payments. Accordingly, we will focus on the way payments vary (as a function of the states) and take into account some hedging effects in the formation of portfolios.

Let us give some simple examples. For instance a call and the underlying stock vary in the same way, in the sense that, when the selling price of the stock increases (in this case, stock prices are the states) the payment of the call (price at expiration date), increases as well. Conversely payments of a put vary in the opposite way. For instance, assume that the underlying security price is S and can only take two values at the maturity date: K + h and K – h . If K is the exercice price of a call and of a put on this security we have the following payments schemes for the different assets, S, –S, C, –C, P, –P (we assume the riskless interest rate to be 0 and we label assets by their initials with a minus sign to indicate a short position) :

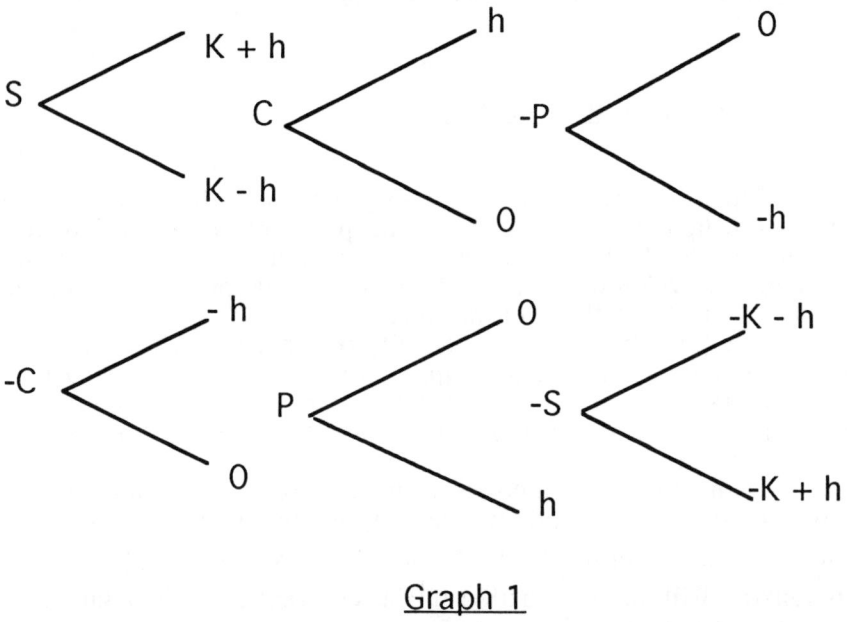

Graph 1

A call and the underlying security, as well as a short position on the put, are said to be comonotonic, this is formalised in the following:

Definition 1 : *Two random variables x and y are comonotonic iff for any s and t in S :*

$$[x(s) - x(t)] [y(s) - y(t)] \geq 0.$$

This definition can be understood as a characterisation of assets which cannot diversify risk away. In order to see this let x, y and z be three assets such that $x \sim_Y y$, z and x are not comonotonic but z and y are comonotonic : roughly speaking z varies in the same way as y while it doesn't with x. Then one can consider portfolio $x + z$ as more diversified than portfolio $y + z$ which is formed of two assets varying in the same way. Clearly $x + z$ can have less variability than x because increases in x can be compensated by decreases in z, therefore z has an hedging effect when used in a portfolio with x. In contrast, because y and z are comonotonic, $y + z$ cannot have less variability than y[1].

For instance assume that there are markets in which more diversified portfolios are at least as valuable as non diversified ones, this can be expressed, for assets x, y and z belonging to these markets and such that $x \sim_Y y$ and z is comonotonic with y, by : $\quad x + z \geq_Y y + z$.

On the other hand assume that there are markets in which assets with similar payment schemes offer services that make them more valuable than heterogeneous ones. For instance, assume that for assets x, y and z belonging to these markets and such that $x \sim_Y y$ and z is comonotonic with x, we have : $x + z \geq_Y y + z$.

In both cases if z is comonotonic with x and with y, assuming $x \sim_Y y$ and adding z to each of them does not modify the way the portfolio payments vary (diversification, say), hence a minimal assumption replacing condition 4 is :

Condition 4' : *If assets x, y and z are such that $x \sim_Y y$ and z is comonotonic with x and y comonotonic with z, then $x + z \sim_Y y + z$.*

Condition 4' weakens condition 4 in the sense that it is limited to comonotonic assets. As we shall see, a portfolio formed with comonotonic assets is valued by the linear combination of the values of the assets forming it. However this does not need to be the case for a portfolio formed with non-comonotonic assets. Hence two portfolios may have different formation costs (exclusive of transaction costs) although they yield the same payments. This will be made more precise later and we shall obtain a valuation formula similar to the previous one (theorem 1), with a capacity replacing the revealed probability.

---

[1]Hedging effect under uncertainty was already discussed in Yaari [1969], Yaari [1987] p 104, and Wakker[1990]. Comonotonicity plays a central role in recent decision theory models such as Yaari [1987] and Schmeidler [1989]. The relationship between comonotonicity and correlation is made precise in the appendix, it is shown that for any distibution the variance of $x + z$ is lower than the variance of $y + z$.

2.2. "Choquet pricing".

The different theories of linear valuation (section 1) are generally referred to as "Arrow pricing" and we saw they define the value of an asset by a mathematical expectation (i.e. Lebesgue integral) as in Arrow [1953]. In the following theory the value of an asset will be the Choquet integral of its payments, this is why we call it "Choquet pricing".

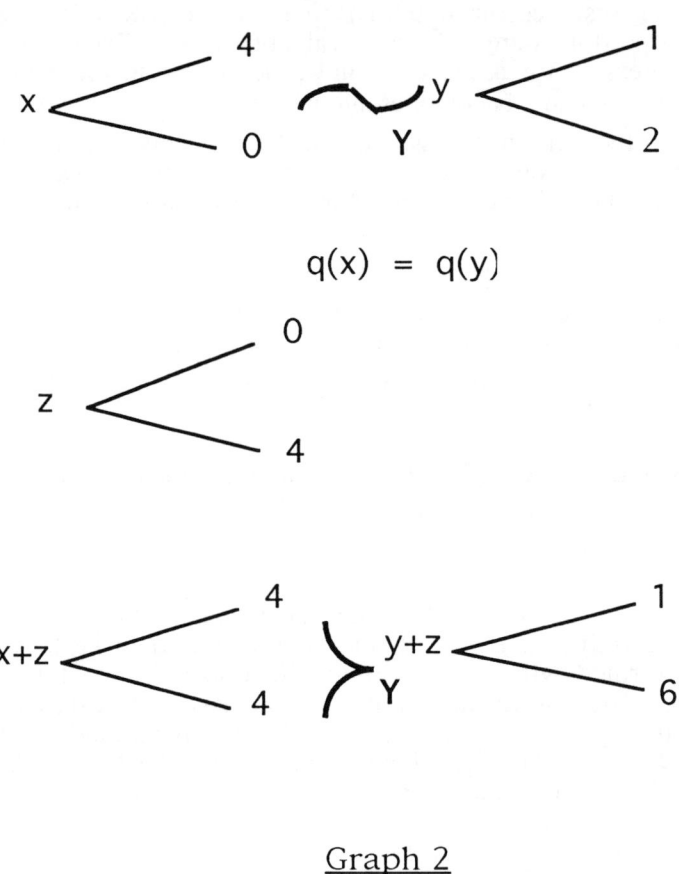

Graph 2

Instead of revealing a probability distribution, market prices will only reveal a capacity :

Definition 2 : *A (normalized) capacity on a probabilisable space (S, s) is a set function $\wp: s \to [0,1]$ satisfying $\wp(S) = 1$, $\wp(\emptyset) = 0$ and monotonicity with respect to inclusion: if $B \supset A$ then $\wp(B) \geq \wp(A)$*[1].

Theorem 2:
> *The ranking on Y is such that there exists a unique normalized capacity $\wp$ on (S,s) such that: $\forall x, y \in Y$, $x \geq_Y y \Leftrightarrow \int_S x \, d\wp \geq \int_S y \, d\wp$ (*), if and only if conditions 1, 2, 3 and 4 'are satisfied. This defines the value of an asset $y \in Y$ as $v(y) = \int_S y \, d\wp$ (*).*

(*) Here $\forall z \in Y$, $\int_S z \, d\wp$ denotes the Choquet integral of z with respect to capacity $\wp$, i.e.:

$$\int_S z \, d\wp = \int_{R_-} (\wp[z \geq t] - 1) dt + \int_{R_+} \wp[z \geq t] dt .$$

In order to simplify notations let us write from now on $1_A = A^*$ for any $A \in s$. The proof goes as follow:

For the "only if" part, define $\wp(A) = v(A^*)$ where v is the Choquet integral as defined in the theorem, for all x in b :

$$v(x) = \int_{R_-} [\wp(x \geq t) - 1] \, dt + \int_{R_+} \wp(x \geq t) \, dt = \int x \, d\wp .$$

Condition 1 is obviously satisfied. It is known (see e.g. Dellacherie [1970] and Schmeidler [1986]) that v is additive for comonotonic assets : if x and y are comonotonic, $v(x + y) = v(x) + v(y)$. From this we see condition 4' is satisfied : if z is comonotonic with x and with y, then $v(x + z) = v(x) + v(z)$ and $v(y + z) = v(y) + v(z)$. If furthermore $x \sim_Y y$, then $v(x) = v(y)$, so $v(x) + v(z) = v(y) + v(z)$ and $v(x + z) = v(y + z)$ which means $x + z \sim_Y y + z$.

Condition 3 comes from the monotonicity of $\wp$:
if $x \geq y + aS^*$ with $a > 0$, then $\wp([x \geq t]) \geq \wp([y + aS^* \geq t])$ $\forall t \in R$, hence $v(x) \geq v(y + aS^*) = v(y) + a$. The last equality holds because S^*, as a constant, is comonotonic with any asset. It implies $v(x) > v(y)$ because $a > 0$, and then $x >_Y y$.

---

[1]Moreover $\wp$ is said to be monotonely sequentially continuous if for any sequence A_n converging monotonely towards A, $\wp(A_n)$ converges monotonely towards $\wp(A)$. It must be clear that an additive probability is a special case of a capacity, a σ-additive probability, a special case of a monotonely sequentially continuous capacity.

Condition 2 is satisfied because of the monotonicity of $\wp$ and the additivity of v for comonotonic assets : assume $x_n \downarrow x$ uniformly (the same proof holds for $x_n \uparrow x$), then $\forall \varepsilon > 0 \; \exists N(\varepsilon) \; \forall n \geq N(\varepsilon)$ $x \leq x_n \leq x + \varepsilon S^*$, hence $v(x) \leq v(x_n) \leq v(x + \varepsilon S^*)$ but the last term of the inequalities $= v(x) + \varepsilon$, which means $v(x_n) \downarrow v(x)$ uniformly.

The "if" part of the proof is the same as that of theorem 1 as far as conditions 1, 2 and 3 are concerned. Define $v(y) = \inf_{\alpha \in R} \{ \alpha 1_S \geq_Y y \}$ and $\wp(A) = v(A^*)$ for any $A \in s$. It is straightforward that v and $\wp$ are monotonic and $\wp(S^*) = 1$.

Condition 4' implies that v is additive for comonotonic assets, indeed let x and y be comonotonic, obviously, $x \sim v(x).S^*$ and $y \sim v(y).S^*$. Then from axiom 4', as y is comonotonic with x and with $v(x).S^*$ (it is a constant), we have : $x + y \sim y + v(x).S^*$ and similarly : $y + v(x).S^* \sim (v(x) + v(y)).S^*$; hence :
$$x + y \sim (v(x) + v(y)).S^*. \quad \text{So} \quad v(x + y) = v(x) + v(y)$$
(comonotonic additivity). The result (v is a Choquet integral with respect to capacity $\wp$) is a direct application of Schmeidler's theorem (p.256 in Schmeidler [1986], see also Chateauneuf[1991]). ♦

Valuation by Choquet's integral instead of Lebesgue's (mathematical expectation) introduces some lack of precision in the measurement of risk by the market : instead of eliciting a probability distribution from observed market prices, it elicits a capacity only. The difference is clearly understood in the case of a finite set of states : asume card(S) = n, elicitation of a probabilty necssitates $n - 1$ prices of linearly independant assets, a capacity generally necessitates $2^n - 2$ prices.

2.3. Applications.

An important consequence of the preceding results is that the value of a long position on an asset (say S) is not the opposite of the value of a short position on the same asset (–S) : $v(S) \neq -v(-S)$. This is because S and –S are not comonotonic so we have :
$0 = v(S-S) \neq v(S) + v(-S)$. In order to understand the meaning of this difference, we can consider a special situation where the value of an asset (v(S)) is the price at which a dealer sells it to individuals. In this situation v(–S) can be interpreted as the price at which the dealer buys asset S from an individual. In this situation prices are imposed by the dealer.

Obviously, in this situation we expect that :
$v(S) — v(—S) > 0$, allowing the dealer to make a profit. This is consistent with condition 4' and even with a more restrictive condition :

Condition 4" : *If assets x , y and z are such that* $x \sim_Y y$ *and z is comonotonic with x , then* $x + z \leq_Y y + z$.

Otherwise stated, if x and z are comonotonic but y and z are not, with v(x) = v(y), then v(x + z) ≤ v(y + z).

This is a special case of our pricing theory, it can be shown[1] that in this case the capacity is concave : ℘(A∪B) + ℘(A∩B) ≤ ℘(A) + ℘(B) and the Choquet integral is the maximum of a family of Lebesgue integrals with respect to a family of probability distribution P such that P ≤ ℘ :

v(x) = Max{ ∫ x dP / P ≤ ℘ }[2] .

An interpretation of this result is the following : if markets were tight, a probability distribution would be determined, the dealer sells at the highest of these tight prices. Obviously he buys at the lowest possible prices and it is indeed the case that :

−v(−x) = Min { ∫ x dP / P ≤ ℘ } .

In this context it is clear that v(x) + v(−x) is positive, this is the gain of the dealer, or the transaction cost an individual has to pay if he had the (strange) idea to buy and sell the same asset. This difference is sufficient to explain two mispricing puzzles which we adress now.

Violation of the famous Put-Call parity is inconsistent with linear valuation founded on No Arbitrage in a market without transaction costs. As many empirical researches have shown[3], violations are observed when a put is introduced in a market for options. A (European) put however, yields the same payments as a portfolio formed with a long European call (on the same security with the same maturity and the same exercise price), a short position in the underlying security and a long position on the riskless asset. More precisely if S is the security price, C the call price with exercise price K, P the put price with the same exercise price and 1 the riskless asset price, under linear pricing one should have:

P = C − S + K because at expiration date the same relation holds for payments (expiration prices are the payments in this case, assuming no dividends). Under linear pricing the value of the asset, here P, is equal to the formation cost of a replicating portfolio, here C − S + K.

This formula has been violated in practice when a put was introduced in an option market, this means that the value of the put may not be equal to the formation cost of the replicating portfolio. These violations are usually attributed to transaction costs, a paradoxical explanation because transaction costs are inconsistent with the "No Arbitrage" assumption of linear pricing. Furthermore if the difference in prices between the put and the replicating portfolio was due to

---

[1] see Schmeidler[1989].
[2] Moreover the Choquet integral satisfies v(x + y) ≤ v(x) + v(y) . This inequality is consistent with assumptions on prices in the presence of transactions costs made by Bensaid et alii [1991] or with bid-ask spread made by Jouiny and Kallal [1991].
[3] See Gould and Galai [1974] and Klemkovski and Resnik [1979] for example.

transaction costs only, this difference should not disappear when the market settles. It does, however as it is likely that shophisticated agents use the call-put parity to price the put, so that after some time the relation does hold. Our non-linear pricing theory justifies that the value of the replicating portfolio, which is a diversified portfolio, differs from the value of the put. The violation is then possible and transaction costs which would prevent arbitragers to use the violation, are not inconsistent with our theory.

"Primes and scores are not originally issued securities but are created through establishment of a trust. The trust accepts shares of common stock in a specified company and issues in exchange a unit of the trust. The trust has a maturity of five years, at which time the outstanding units are re-converted to the underlying stock. Each unit contains a prime and a score. The prime component receives all dividend payments and any increase in the stock price up to a termination value. The score receives any appreciation above the termination value. The termination price is set at the beginning of the trust and has generally been at a 20-25% premium to the current stock price."

This definition is taken from Jarrow and O'Hara [1989] who investigate the relative mispricing of primes and scores to the underlying stock. They "find the surprising result that prime and score prices exceed the price of the underlying stock often by a considerable amount ... and then investigate wether these prices differentials are consistent with arbitrage opportunities."

Now assume the dealer realizes there is a demand for primes and a demand for scores coming from different individuals. He can offer this service by buying the underlying security and by selling separately primes and scores, he will make the profit :

$v(C) + v(P) + v(-S) \geq [v(C) + v(P)] - v(S) \geq 0$.

However no individual could replicate the prime or the score at lower cost given the selling prices of the dealer.

A very similar argument can be put forward for other dichotomized securities. When a security is decomposed into components the payments of which are not comonotonic, our theory is consistent with a difference in the price of the underlying security and the sum of the prices of the dichotomized securities. For instance a mortgage-backed security can be decomposed into interest-only and principal-only components and it is the case that they sell at a premium to the underlying mortgage-backed security. This is in contradiction with linear pricing theories which hold in tight markets, but consistent with our pricing in slack markets.

Conclusion.

In this paper we follow a "Finance" approach, this is to say we describe assets by their flow of payments and we deduce a pricing formula from observed data and assumptions on market structures. The usual No arbitrage pricing theory sets up such a structure, it rules out frictions such as transaction costs and gives no role to the way assets vary relative to each other (no hedging effect). It implies a linear pricing rule which makes prices reveal a probability distribution (unique if furthermore markets are complete). The market structure we consider (slack markets) is less constraining. The pricing rule we obtain is founded on a weakening of the tightness condition : the value of a portfolio depends not only on the assets forming it, but on the way they influence its variability. The pricing rule is not linear, it makes prices reveal a capacity, which is consistent with a family of probability distributions.

The value of an asset is the Choquet's integral of its payments with respect to a capacity. This capacity expresses risks appreciation by the market in the same way as the linear pricing in tight markets reveals a probability. Slack markets introduce an indetermination relative to formation costs of portfolios, this implies an indetermination on the revealed probability distributions on the random states. For instance in a situation where a dealer sets prices, a portfolio formed with non-comonotonic assets can be priced more than an asset yielding the same payments. Then it can be shown that the capacity is concave and the value functional (Choquet integral) is the maximum of the family of mathematical expectations with respect to probability distributions bounded from below by this capacity. Our pricing rule can then be understood as the maximum of a family of linear pricing rules. In the special case when this indetermination disappears because markets are effectively tight, the Choquet's integral reduces to a mathematical expectation with respect to a probability distribution which reveals the market risks appreciation. It must be emphasized that non-linear pricing opens a wide new range of investigations in Finance theory. It is consistent with some puzzling observations of market prices without having to refer to transaction costs, taxes and other valuation of services in an explicit way in the definition of assets payments. Obviously transaction costs are still invoked to sustain prices which would otherwise leave arbitrage opportunities available. Non-linear pricing sheds a new light on the notion of "risk neutral probability" (here capacity) in the sense that it requires less acuity in the assignations of "weights" to the states by the market.

Applications of this theory are the pricing of transaction costs, hedging costs, or services costs by exploiting the differences between the price of an asset and the sum of the prices of assets in a replicating portfolio. From a more theoretical point of view, the methodology used to derive the pricing formula opens a new way of looking at the notion of assets value, and, in an other but related field, to the "representative agent" paradigm and the many puzzles (equity premium and risk premium puzzles) linked to it, this is the object of further researches.

Appendix :

Comonotonicity and covariance.

It is well known since Markowitz theory that diversification should play a role in the valuation of portfolios, at least by agents which minimize the variance of their portfolios. The CAPM is consistent with arbitrage pricing theories and it provides indeed, a linear pricing rule. Our pricing theory refers to diversification (more generally : hedging effects) however we did not assume a given probability distribution. Because Finance has always investigated asset pricing in the context of "risk", i.e. uncertainty described by a set of states measured by a given probability distribution, it will help the intuition to relate comonotonicity of two assets and them having a positive covariance.

Consider a probabilisable space (S, s) in which we assume s contains all singletons, and let b(S, s) be the set of real bounded s-measurable functions. We have the following result relating comonotonicity of two random variables and the sign of their covariance;

Theorem : *Let x and y be two random variables in b(S, s), they are comonotonic if and only if their covariance is positive for any additive probability distribution on (S, s).*

Proof :

For the "if" part assume that for any distribution P, $Cov_P(x,y) \geq 0$. For any s and t in S such that s ≠ t, we need to show that $[x(s) - x(t)][y(s) - y(t)] \geq 0$.

Consider the distribution P(s,t) such that $P(s,t)[\{s\}] = p$ and $P(S,t)[\{t\}] = 1-p$ for some $p \in [0,1]$. For this distribution we have :

$Cov(x,y) = p(x(s)-[px(s)+(1-p)x(t)])(y(s)-[py(s)+(1-p)y(t)]) + ...$

$...(1-p)(x(t) - [px(s) + (1-p)x(t)])(y(t) - [py(s) + (1-p)y(t)])$

$= p(1-p)^2[x(s)-x(t)][y(s)-y(t)]+p^2(1-p)[x(s)-x(t)][y(s)-y(t)]$

$= p(1-p)[x(s) - x(t)][y(s) - y(t)]$

Hence $Cov(x, y) \geq 0 \Rightarrow [x(s) - x(t)][y(s) - y(t)] \geq 0$.

The "only if" part directly derives from the proof of one of Chebichev's theorem done by F. Franklin in the *American Journal of Mathematics*, 1885 !

Assume $\forall s,t \in S$ $[x(s) - x(t)][y(s) - y(t)] \geq 0$, and let P be any additive distribution on (S, s), we have:

$$I = \int_{S\times S}[x(s) - x(t)][y(s) - y(t)] \, P \times P(ds \times dt) \geq 0$$

$$I = \int_S P(ds) \int_S [x(s)y(s) + x(t)y(t) - x(t)y(s) - x(s)y(t)] \, P(dt)$$

$$I = 2[E_P(xy) - E_P(x)E_P(y)] = 2\text{Cov}_P(xy)$$ hence $\text{Cov}_P(xy) \geq 0$. ♦

* * *

References

Ami, D., Kast, R., Lapied, A. [1991]: "Generalizing Arrow pricing to understand financial markets", in *Actuarial approach in financial risk*, second AFFIR international colloquium, 1991, Institute of Actuaries, Vol 4, pp 1-25.

Arrow, K.J. [1953]: "Le rôle des valeurs boursières dans l'allocation optimale des risques", in *Econométrie* 40, pp 41-47, Cahiers du CNRS, Paris.

Bensaid B., Lesne, J.P., Pagès, H., Scheinkman, J.S.[1991] : "Derivative assets pricing with transaction costs", Working paper 91/1, Banque de France.

Black, F., Scholes, M. [1973]: "The pricing of options and corporate liabilities", *Journal of Political Economy*, 81, pp 637-654.

Chateauneuf, A. [1991]: "On the use of capacities in modeling uncertainty aversion and risk aversion", *Journal of Mathematical Economics*.

Debreu, G. [1952]: "Representation of a preference ordering by a numerical function", in *Readings in Mathematical Economics*, P. Newman ed., John Hopkins press, pp. 257-263.

Dellacherie, C. [1970]: "Quelques commentaires sur les prolongements de capacités", Séminaire de probabilitésV Strasbourg, *Lecture Notes in Mathematics* vol. 191, Springer -Verlag, Berlin.

Duffie, D. [1988] :*"Security markets stochastic models"*, Academic Press, New York.

Gould, J.P., Galai, D. [1974] : "Transaction costs and the relationship between put and call prices", *Journal of Financial Economics,* 1, pp. 105-129.

Harrisson, J.M., Kreps, D. [1979] : "Martingales and arbitrage in multiperiod securities markets", *Journal of Economic Theory*, 20, pp 381-408.

Jarrow, R.A., O'Hara, M. [1989] : "Primes and scores: an essay on market imperfections", *The Journal of Finance*, vol. XLIV, n°5, pp. 1263-1287.

Jouini E., Kallal, H. [1991] : " Martingales, arbitrage and equilibrium in securities markets with transaction costs", mimeo CERSEM, Université de Paris I.

Kast, R. , Lapied, A. [1992] : "Fondements microéconomiques de la théorie des marchés financiers", Economica, Paris, [1992].

Klemkosky, R.C., Resnick, B.G. [1979] : "Put- call parity and market efficiency", *The Journal of Finance*, 34, pp. 1141-1155.

Merton, R.J. [1973]: " The theory of rational option pricing", *Bells journal of economics and management science*, 4,pp. 141-183.

Ross, S.A. [1976]: " The arbitrage theory of capital asset pricing", *Journal of economic theory*, 13, pp. 341-360.

Schmeidler, D. [1986]: " Integral representation without additivity", *Proceedings of the American mathematical society*, vol 97, N° 2.

Schmeidler, D. [1989]: "Subjective probability and expected utility without additivity", *Econometrica*, 57, pp. 571-587.

Wakker, P.P. [1990]: "Characterizing pessimism and optimism directly through comonotonicity", miméo Duke University.

Yaari, M.E. [1969]: "Some remarks on measures of risk aversion and their uses", *Journal of economic theory*,1, pp. 315-329.

Yaari, M.E. [1987]: "Dual theory of choice under uncertainty", *Econometrica*, 55, n°1, pp. 95-115.

RISK, TIME, AND FINANCIAL DECISION

François Quittard-Pinon[1]
Jacques Sikorav[2]

I. INTRODUCTION

The notion of risk is linked to the idea of potential damage. So there are of course many kinds of risks. In the financial world the most important are : the default risk, the liquidity risk and the market risk. The default risk is the impossibility of a debtholder to keep his engagement. The liquidity risk is the temporary inability to get money from immobilizations. The market risk is the possibility to face losses, to miss opportunities or even to make profits from very fluctuating prices or rates in financial markets. So this last kind of risk is intrinsically associated with time and it is only this type of risk that we consider in this paper. Financial markets, lato sensu, are the very places where risk, time and financial decision meet.

During the last 20 years this risk has been more and more increasing. Since the denounciation of the BRETTON-WOODS agreements the exchange rates have started to fluctuate as stock prices have always done. Moreover since 1979 and due to the new monetary policy implemented in the U.S.A. the interest rates are now very unstable. Deregulation measures, internationalization of capital markets and the use of very powerful data processing systems have made the intervention in financial markets very easy but risky too.

To cope with this financial risk, there has been a continuous flow of financial innovations both in products and structures. So were born the very successful derivative markets where more and more financial contracts are traded : especially futures and options ones. Banks and financial institutions taylor for their customers very adapted products negociated O.T.C..

To make money in this investment-technology the contracts must be carefully conceived and managed to meet an actual demand. At the heart of this industry there is a huge need to know the equilibrium price of the considered products. The problem has at least two dimensions : for an already traded product what is its fair price ? and for a new one, generally complex what could be its price ? To give this price is actually a challenge both for the financial manager and the financial economist.

---

1 Ecole Normale Supérieure de Cachan, G.R.I.D.
2 Crédit Commercial de France.

It is stimulating to note that up to now, the scientific community has given in time and at least partial but often satisfactory answers to these problems. The best known example is the Black and Scholes option pricing formula, giving the fair price of a European call written on a non-dividend paying stock. Black and Scholes (thereafter B.S.) made their discovery just when the option market took off in the U.S.A.. Another point to note in their formula is the fact that, if risk is measured by the standard deviation of the return of the underlying asset, the B.S. formula gives a biunivoque correspondence between the call price and the risk. It is important to point out, that what you sell or buy is nothing but volatility of the underlying asset : stock, bond, currency, etc... Since then, more sophisticated products have been designed, for instance in the last two years many exotic warrants or equity linked bonds in the Euro-market have been issued. These contingent claims have path-dependent pay-offs which can depend on past prices of the underlying asset during the life of the claims. Asian and lookback options are built like that. So far, the probabilistic approaches have been the only ones to provide, sometimes in closed form, the valuation of these warrants, which is an important feature for practical hedging implementation.

A pattern to the valuation problem is given by the B.S. approach : firstly, model the movements of the financial underlying asset to capture both time and uncertainty - a generally sucessful but not unique way to do it, is to represent price movements by diffusion processes - secondly, try to construct a riskless portfolio, then use an arbitrage argument which in its simpler form asserts that if the market is in equilibrium the return of the riskless portfolio must be equal to the return of the risk-free asset, as given for instance by the monetary market rate. Using Ito's formula this approach generally leads to a partial differential equation in the price of the examined financial asset. HARRISON and PLISKA scrutinizing the B.S. solution implemented a new methodology using martingale theory and gave a very fundamental equation to value many financial instruments. Their main result can be roughly stated as follows : if there is no arbitrage opportunity in the market the discounted prices of financial assets follow martingales with respect to (thereafter w.r.t.) a special probability measure. Under this probability the instantaneous expected return of financial assets are equal to the risk free rate. It is the reason why this measure is called risk-neutral probability. The now fundamental equation for valuation takes the following form :

Q being the risk-neutral probability, given a price process $S(t)$ of a financial asset with a cumulative dividend process $D(t)$, $\delta(t)$ being the discount function and F_t the information filtration, we have in this setting :

$$S(t) = \delta^{-1}(t) E_Q \left[\int_t^\tau \delta(s)dD(s) + \delta(\tau)S(\tau)/F_t \right] \forall\ 0 \leq t \leq \tau.$$

In fact to follow a rigorous approach raises a lot of very technical difficulties. In particular about the existence and unicity of the risk-neutral probability, these questions are related to the notion of complete market. (Cf. [DUFFIE]).

Ignoring these mathematical and economic technicalities we illustrate the power of the so-called martingale approach in pricing explicitly two special financial tools : contingent rebates and guaranteed warrant exposed to exchange rate risk. To achieve this goal we give in the second section of this paper the mathematical tools needed i.e. Girsanov's theorem and some functionnals of the brownian motion noted B.M. thereafter, the third section is devoted to the valuation formulae and the fourth and last section presents our conclusions.

II. MATHEMATICAL TOOLS FOR OUR FINANCIAL ANALYSIS

This section gives the mathematical ingredients necessary to understand the pricing of the options considered in this paper. In the first paragraph we recall useful definitions and some properties of stochastic processes, the second one, recalls what diffusion processes are, the third one, the main results of stochastic calculus i.e. Ito's rule and Girsanov's theorem, the fourth one, the reflected principle for B.M. and the fifth, the laws of some functionals of B.M..

2.1) General definitions and properties

The uncertainty is modelled by a probability space (Ω, A, P), the conjunction of time and risk is modelled by a real-valued stochastic process $X(\omega,t)$ where t stands for time : $\forall\ \omega \in \Omega\ X(\omega,t)$ simply written $X(t)$ is called the sample path of the process. We set F_t^x the tribe generated by $X(s)\ s \in [0,t]$. F_t^x represents the information revealed by X up to time t. A filtration $\{F_t\}_{t \in [0.T]}$ is a non decreasing family of tribes. A process is said to be adapted to the filtration F_t if and only if X(t) is F_t measurable for each $t \geq 0$. (Ω, A, F_t, P) is called a filtered space and in our context is the structure which takes into account : the risk, the time and the information, the one released by the process X if $F_t = F_t^x$. X(t) is generally a representation for stock prices, interest rates or exchange rates.

If $E(|X(t)|)$ exists the stochastic process X(t) ($t \geq 0$) is said to be a martingale (resp. submartingale ; supermartingale) if : $E(X(t)/F_s) = X(s)$ holds $0 < s < t < \infty$ (resp. $E(x(t)/F_s) \geq X(s) ; E(X(t)/F_s) \leq F_s \leq X(s)$).

A random time T is a stopping time if the event $\{T \leq t\}$ is F_t measurable for every $t \geq 0$ and is called an optional time if $\{T < t\}$ is F_t measurable for every $t \geq 0$.

If T is an optional time of the filtration $\{F_t\}$ such that : $P(T < \infty) = 1$, for an $\{F_t\}$ martingale X with a last element, we have : $E(X(T)) = E(X(0))$ (Optional sampling theorem).

A Brownian motion denoted B(t) or B_t in this paper is a stochastic process with :

- continuous sample paths $\forall \omega \in \Omega$
- independent and stationary increments
- nul when t = 0

such that $B(t) - B(s) \sim N(0, \sigma \sqrt{t-s})$ $0 < s < t < \infty$
when $\sigma = 1$ the B.M. is called standard.

The processes B(t), $B^2(t) - t$, $\exp\{aB(t) - 1/2 a^2 t\}$ ($a \in R$) are martingales.

The B.M. is the fundamental martingale with continuous paths.

2.2) Diffusion processes

It is possible to construct a special integral w.r.t. to B.M. called Ito's integral. (Cf. [KARATZAS]). So, let us consider the equation in x : (x(0) given)

$$x(t) = x(0) + \int_0^t f(x(s), s) \, ds + \int_0^t g(x(s), s) \, dB_s$$

The first integral is a usual Rieman integral, the second one being a stochastic integral. f and g are real valued functions (eventually in vector or matrix form). This equation is often written formally :

$$dx = f(x,t)\, dt + g(x,t)\, dB$$

and is called a stochastic differential equation. If the functions f and g verify usual properties (Cf. [KARATZAS]) the solution x exists is unique and is a markovian process with continuous sample paths. It is called a Ito process or diffusion process. The function f is called the drift of the process.

2.3) Ito and Girsanov theorems

The main results of stochastic calculus are given by two fundamental theorems of Ito and Girsanov, now in general use for financial modelling.

ITO's rule

For every real valued function $y(x,t) \in C^{2,1}$, if x follows the diffusion equation :

$$dx = \mu(x,t)\, dt + \sigma(x,t)\, dB.$$

Then y(x,t) is a diffusion and obeys the following S.D.E. :

$$dy = \left\{ y_t + y'_x \mu + 1/2 \text{ trace} \left[y_{xx} \sigma\sigma' \right] \right\} dt + y'_x \sigma dB.$$

A subscript stands for a derivative and a' for a transpose.

GRISANOV's theorem

Let B_t be a n-dimensional B.M.

X an adapted R^n valued process with : $\int_0^T \|X(t)\|^2\, dt < \infty$.

$$\text{Set } Z_t = \exp\left\{ \int_0^t X(s)\cdot dB_s - \frac{1}{2}\int_0^t \|X(s)\|^2\, ds \right\}$$

if $E(Z_T) = 1$ Set Q the probability measure :

$$Q(d\omega) = Z_T(\omega)\, P(d\omega)$$

then the process $\widehat{B}_t = B_t - \int_0^t X(s)\, ds \quad 0 \le t \le T$ is a Q-Brownian motion.

Given the utmost importance of these results in continuous time finance let us give in this context a very simple illustration : assume the price S of a financial asset, say a stock, follows a geometric brownian motion :

$$dS = \mu S dt + \sigma S dB \quad (\mu,\sigma) \; R^+ \times R^+$$

r as usual denoting the risk-free asset return, supposed to be constant over time.

Set : $\overline{S} = S \exp\{-rt\}$ the discounted stock price at rate r . Ito's rule gives :

$$d\overline{S} = (\mu-r) \overline{S} dt + \sigma \overline{S} dB$$

Set : $X(s) = (r-\mu)/\sigma$, Girsanov's theorem gives :

$$d\overline{S} = \sigma \overline{S} d\widehat{B}$$

So the discounted price S is a Q-martingale. The Black and Scholes formula can be easily obtained by a simple calculus of expectation, using the fundamental financial formula of section I. In the next section we shall see other applications of Girsanov's theorem.

2.4) Reflected principle

Let B_t be a standard one dimensional B.M., let us define a passage time T_y to a level y > 0 by : $T_y = \inf\{t \geq 0 / B_t = y\}$

T_y is the first time B_t attains y . Such a passage time for continuous process is a stopping time. The reflected motion of B_t w.r.t. y is defined by :

$$\widetilde{B}_t = B_t \, 1_{t \leq T_y} + (2y - Bt) \, 1_{t > T_y}$$

of course : $P(T_y < t) = P(T_y < t, B_t > y) + P(T_y < t, B_t < y)$

then, one can prove (Cf. [KARATZAS]) that :

$P(T_y < t, B_t < y) = P(T_y < t, B_t > y) = P(B_t > y)$

So the density f(t) of the passage time is :

$$f(t) = P(t - dt < T_y < t + dt) = \frac{|y|}{\sqrt{2\pi t^3}} e^{-\frac{y^2}{2t}} dt .$$

2.5) Computing some functionals of Brownian motion

In this section we compute some functionals of B.M., using the reflection principle, the optimal stopping theorem and of course

Girsanov's theorem. Some of these computations may be found in [KARLIN] and [CONZE].

Set :

$$M_t = \text{Max}\{B_u/u \in [0,t[\}$$

N(z) is the cumulative distribution function of a standard normal distribution.

We consider the risk-neutral probability P under wich the stock price S_t with value S_0 at time 0 obeys the equation :

$$d(\log S_t) = (r - 1/2\ \sigma^2)\ dt + \sigma\ dB$$

r stands for the riskfree rate.

As already noted the two sample paths B_t and $\tilde{B}_t$ have the same probability of occurence. Therefore we can compute :

$$P(\sigma B_t \leq x,\ M_t > y) \quad (y \geq x \text{ and } y \geq 0)$$

$$\begin{aligned}
P(\sigma B_t \leq x,\ M_t > y) &= P(\sigma B_t \leq x,\ T_y < t) \\
y \geq x \quad y \geq 0 \\
&= P(2y - \sigma B_t \leq x,\ T_y < t) \\
&= P(\sigma B_t \geq 2y - x,\ T_y < t) \\
&= P(\sigma B_t \geq 2y - x) \\
&= 1 - N\left(\frac{2y-x}{\sigma \sqrt{t}}\right) \\
&= N\left(\frac{x-2y}{\sigma \sqrt{t}}\right)
\end{aligned}$$

In the case of a Brownian motion with <u>drift</u> we can extend the previous result.

Define $X_t = \mu t + \sigma B_t$ and $M_t^X = \underset{0 < u \leq t}{\text{Max } X_u}$ we have

$$P(X_t \leq x, M_t^X \geq y) = e^{2\mu y/\sigma^2}\ N\left(\frac{x - \mu t - 2y}{\sigma \sqrt{t}}\right)$$

Proof :

« Define $B_t^* = B_t + \frac{\mu}{\sigma} t$, using Girsanov theorem B_t^* is a Q-F$_t$ standard Brownian motion where Q is defined by

$$dP/dQ = \exp\left(\frac{\mu}{\sigma} B_t^* - \frac{\mu^2}{2\sigma^2} t^*\right)$$

we have

$$P(X_t \leq x, M_t^X \geq y) = E_P\left(1_{B_t + \frac{\mu}{\sigma} t \leq \frac{x}{\sigma}, \underset{u}{Max} B_u + \frac{\mu}{\sigma} u > \frac{y}{\sigma}}\right)$$

$$= E_Q\left(\exp\left(\frac{\mu}{\sigma} B_t^* - \frac{\mu^2}{2\sigma^2} t\right) 1_{B_t^* < \frac{x}{\sigma}, M_t^* > \frac{y}{\sigma}}\right)$$

using Girsanov theorem

$$= E_Q\left(\exp\left(\frac{\mu}{\sigma}\left(\frac{2y}{\sigma} - B_t^*\right) - \frac{\mu^2}{2\sigma^2} t\right) 1_{\frac{2y}{\sigma} - B_t^* < \frac{x}{\sigma}, M_t^* > \frac{y}{\sigma}}\right)$$

using the reflected principle

$$= E_Q\left(\exp\left[\frac{\mu}{\sigma}\left(\frac{2y}{\sigma} - B_t^*\right) - \frac{\mu^2}{2\sigma^2} t\right] 1_{\sigma B_t^* \geq 2y-x}\right)$$

$$= E_P\left(e^{2\mu \frac{y}{\sigma^2}} 1_{\sigma B_t + \mu t \geq 2y-x}\right) \quad \text{(Girsanov)}$$

$$= e^{2\mu \frac{y}{\sigma^2}} P(X_t \geq 2y-x+2\mu t)$$

then

$$P(X_t \leq x, M_t^X \geq y) = e^{2\mu \frac{y}{\sigma^2}} N\left(\frac{x-\mu t-2y}{\sigma \sqrt{t}}\right). \gg$$

We can apply this previous result to the valuation of the law of the maximum price reached by a stock during a period of time.

If $M_t^S = \underset{0 \leq u \leq t}{Max} S_u$ we are now able to compute

$$P\left(S_t \leq a, M_t^S > b\right) = \left(\frac{b}{S_0}\right)^{\frac{2r}{\sigma^2}-1} N\left(\log\frac{\left(\frac{aS_0}{b^2}\right) - \left(r - \frac{\sigma^2}{2}\right)t}{\sigma\sqrt{t}}\right)$$

a≤b   b>0

We shall now compute the density function of the first passage time to a simple barrier for a stock S_t.

Setting $T_a = \inf\{t \geq 0, S_t \geq a\}$

$\qquad = \inf\left\{t \geq 0, X_t \geq \log\left(\frac{a}{S_0}\right)\right\}$

$T_a = \zeta_{\log\left(\frac{a}{S_0}\right)}$ where $\zeta_z = \mathrm{Inf}\{s \geq 0, X_s \geq z\}$

We can compute the Laplace transform of ζ_z

$\forall \lambda > 0$, $\zeta_t^{(\lambda)} = \exp\left(\lambda W_t - \frac{\lambda^2}{2}t\right)$ is a P martingale

and $E_P\left(\zeta_t^{(\lambda)}\right) = 1$, $\forall t$

using the optional stopping theorem we know that

$E_P\left(\zeta_{y_z}^{(\lambda)}\right) = 1$

for $\lambda = \bar\lambda\sigma$ we have

$E_P\left(\exp\left(\lambda\sigma W_{\zeta_z} - \lambda^2\frac{\sigma^2}{2}\zeta_z\right)\right) = 1$

$E_P\left[\exp\left(\lambda\left(X_{\zeta_z} - \left(r - \frac{\sigma^2}{2}\right)\zeta_z\right) - \lambda^2\frac{\sigma^2}{2}\zeta_z\right)\right] = 1$

$E_P\left(\exp\left[\lambda z - \left[\left(r - \frac{\sigma^2}{2}\right)\lambda + \lambda^2\frac{\sigma^2}{2}\right]\zeta_z\right]\right) = 1$

Let $\alpha > 0$ and λ solution of $\frac{\sigma^2}{2}\lambda^2 + \left(r - \frac{\sigma^2}{2}\right)\lambda - \alpha = 0$ with

$r - \dfrac{\sigma^2}{2} > 0$.

We have

$$E\left(\exp(-\alpha\,\zeta_z)\right) = \exp\left[-z\sigma^2\left[\sqrt{\left(r-\dfrac{\sigma^2}{2}\right)^2 + 2\sigma^2\alpha} - \left(r-\dfrac{\sigma^2}{2}\right)\right]\right] \quad (R)$$

Using the derivative for $\alpha = 0$ we found that

$$E(T_a) = E(\zeta_z) = \dfrac{\log \dfrac{\alpha}{S_0}}{r - \dfrac{\sigma^2}{2}}$$

One should notice that $E(T_a)$ is increasing with respect to σ. The higher, the volatility, the longer we should wait before the stock reaches the level a ! When $r - \dfrac{\sigma^2}{2}$

it is possible to insert the relation (R) and obtain the density of ζ_z starting with $z_0 = \log S_0$

$$f(t,z,z_0) = \dfrac{z - z_0}{\sigma\sqrt{2\pi t^3}} \exp\left(-\dfrac{\left(z - z_0 - \left(r - \dfrac{\sigma^2}{2}\right)t\right)^2}{2\sigma^2}\right) \quad t > 0$$

III. VALUATION OF SOME EXOTIC CONTINGENT CLAIMS

In this section we compute contingent rebates and guaranteed warrants on foreign stock indexes.

3.1) Computing contingent rebates

In this section we shall examine contingent claims whose values depend on the price attained by a stock over the period $[0,T]$.

i) Let C_0 be an asset with the following pay-off at time T

$$C_T = R\,1_{\left\{\underset{0\le t\le T}{\text{Max}}\, S_t > L\right\}}$$

The owner will receive R at time T only if the value of the stock reached the level L during the period T. Some guaranteed funds use these kind of products to protect against any crash after a rally in the stock market.

Using the risk-neutral valuation methodology we have

$$C_0 = E_P \left(e^{-rT} R \, 1_{\underset{0 \leq t \leq T}{\text{Max}} S_t > L} \right)$$

$$C_0 = e^{-rT} R \, P(T_L \leq T)$$

$$C_0 = e^{-rT} R \, P(M_T^S \geq L)$$

$$C_0 = e^{-rT} R \left[e^{\frac{2\left(r - \frac{\sigma^2}{2}\right) \log\left(\frac{L}{S_0}\right)}{\sigma^2}} N\left(\frac{\log \frac{S_0}{L} - \left(r - \frac{\sigma^2}{2}\right)T}{\sigma\sqrt{T}} \right) + N\left(\frac{\log \frac{S_0}{L} - \left(r - \frac{\sigma^2}{2}\right)T}{\sigma\sqrt{T}} \right) \right]$$

This formula gives the "fair" value of the rebate at time T, and also makes it possible to compute a hedge ratio to derive a self financing strategy of replication of that claim.

ii) Rebate at time T_L

We examine here the case where the amount of the rebate is received when the "knock-out" boundary is first reached. The discounted reward per unit of time is :

$$R \, e^{-rT} \, P(t \leq T_L < t+dt)$$

Therefore the value of the rebate is :

$$C_0 = R \int_0^T e^{-rL} P(t \leq T_L < t+dt) \, dt$$

$$C_0 = R \int_0^T \frac{\log\left(\frac{t}{S_0}\right)}{\sigma\sqrt{2\pi t^3}} \exp\left[-\frac{1}{2\sigma^2 t} \left[\log\left(\frac{L}{S_0}\right)^2 + \left(\left(r - \frac{\sigma^2}{2}\right)^2 + 2\sigma^2 r\right) t^2 - 2\left(r - \frac{\sigma^2}{2}\right) t \log\left(\frac{L}{S_0}\right) \right] \right]$$

We set $\lambda = \sqrt{\left(r - \frac{\sigma^2}{2}\right) + 2\sigma^2 r}$ and $Z_t = \sigma W_\tau + \lambda t$.

Using Girsanov's theorem we have :

$$C_0 = R\left[e^{\left(r-\frac{\sigma^2}{2}-\lambda\right)/\sigma^2 \log\left(\frac{L}{S_0}\right)} N\left(\frac{\lambda T - \log\frac{L}{S_0}}{\sigma\sqrt{T}}\right) + e^{\left(r-\frac{\sigma^2}{2}\times\lambda\right)/\sigma^2 \log\left(\frac{L}{S_0}\right)} N\left(\frac{-\lambda T - \log\frac{L}{S_0}}{\sigma\sqrt{T}}\right)\right]$$

3.2) Valuation of guaranteed warrant

This kind of warrant is designed for investors who want to take positions in a foreign equity market without facing an exchange rate risk. For instance the pay-off for an American investor of a guaranteed call is :

$$X_0 \text{Max}(S_T - K, 0)$$

where - S_T is the level of the CAC 40 index at time T in french francs

- X_0 is the FRF/\$ exchange rate at time 0 when the option starts.

As already mentioned by M. RUBINSTEIN, the irony of this option is that the FRF/\$ exchange rate during the life of the option does not seem to enter in the definition of the pay-off. So how could we hedge the option ? The Girsanov's theorem gives us the answer !

Let us suppose that :

$$\begin{cases} \dfrac{dX_t}{X_t} = \tilde{\mu}\, dt + \tilde{\sigma}\, d\widetilde{W}_t \\[2ex] \dfrac{dS_t}{S} = \mu\, dt + \rho\, \sigma\, d\widetilde{W}_t + \sigma\sqrt{1-\rho^2}\, dW'_t \end{cases}$$

in the historical universe

and that $E\left(d\widetilde{W}_t\, dW'_t\right) = 0$.

r is the US spot rate.

r_f is the FRF spot rate.

Then for an american investor the value of the CAC in US\$ is $X_t S_t$ with

$$\frac{dXS_t}{X_t S_t} = \left(\mu + \tilde{\mu} + \rho\,\sigma\tilde{\sigma}\right) dt + \left(\tilde{\sigma} + \sigma\rho\right) d\widetilde{W}_t + \sigma\sqrt{1-\rho^2}\, dW'_t$$

(Ito's formula) .

If the market is complete and there is not arbitrage opportunity, we know there exists an unique probability, risk-neutral, where the processes :

$$\left(M_t = e^{-rt} X_t S_t\right) \text{ and } \left(N_t = e^{-rt}\left(e^{r_f t} X_t\right)\right) \text{ are Q-Martingales.}$$

But
$$\begin{cases} \dfrac{dM_t}{M_t} = \left(\mu + \tilde{\mu} + \rho\sigma\tilde{\sigma} - r\right) dt + \left(\tilde{\sigma} + \sigma\rho\right) d\widetilde{W}_t + \sigma\sqrt{1-\rho^2}\, dW'_t & (1) \\[2mm] \dfrac{dN_t}{N_t} = \left(\tilde{\mu} + r_f - r\right) dt + \tilde{\sigma}\, d\widetilde{W}_t & (2) \end{cases}$$

As $\widetilde{W}_t$ and W'_t are uncorrelated we might seek Q with the following Radon-Nikodim derivative :

$$\frac{dQ}{dP}\bigg|_{\mathfrak{I}_t} = \exp\left(\lambda \widetilde{W}_t - \frac{\lambda^2 t}{2}\right) \exp\left(v W'_t - \frac{v^2 t}{2}\right)$$

Where λ and v are two positive constants to be determinated.
Using equations (2) and (1) we easily deduce that :

$$\lambda = \frac{r - r_f - \tilde{\mu}}{\tilde{\sigma}}$$

$$v = \frac{1}{\sigma\sqrt{1-\rho^2}}\left[r - \rho\sigma\tilde{\sigma} - \mu - \tilde{\mu} - \frac{\tilde{\sigma}+\rho\sigma}{\tilde{\sigma}}\left(r - r_f - \tilde{\mu}\right)\right]$$

Set
$$Y^1_t = \widetilde{W}_t - \lambda t$$
$$Y^2_t = W'_t - v t$$

$\left(Y^1_t, Y^2_t\right)$ is a 2 dimensional standard brownian motion under Q using Girsanov theorem ! And we have :

$$\begin{cases} \dfrac{dM_t}{M_t} = \left(\tilde{\sigma}+\sigma\rho\right) dY^1_t + \sigma\sqrt{1-\rho^2}\, dY^2_t \\[2mm] \dfrac{dN_t}{N_t} = \tilde{\sigma}\, dY^1_t \end{cases}$$

Using Ito's formula, we have :

$$d(\log S_t) = \left(r_f - \rho\sigma\tilde{\sigma} - \frac{1}{2}\sigma^2\right)dt + \rho\sigma\, dY_t^1 + \sigma\sqrt{1-\rho^2}\, dY_t^2$$

$$d(\log S_t) = \left(r_f - \rho\sigma\tilde{\sigma} - \frac{1}{2}\sigma^2\right)dt + \left[\rho\sigma\, dY_t^1 + \sigma\sqrt{1-\rho^2}\, dY_t^2\right]$$

But $\rho\, dY_t^1 + \sqrt{1-\rho^2}\, dY_t^2$ is a standard Brownian Motion B_t. It is then easy to compute the value of the call C_0 :

$$C_0 = X_0 S_0 \exp\left(-\left(r - r_f + \rho\sigma\tilde{\sigma}\right)T\right) N(d_1) - KX_0 e^{-rT} N(d_2)$$

with $\quad d_1 = \dfrac{\log\dfrac{S}{K} + \left(r_f - \rho\sigma\tilde{\sigma} - \dfrac{\sigma^2}{2}\right)T}{\sigma\sqrt{T}}$

$d_2 = d_1 - \sigma\sqrt{T}$

We have now a formula which from we can deduce a hedge ration with respect to the stock price S_0, but also with respect to the exchange rate X_0, taking into account the correlation beetween the exchange rate and the stock return.

IV. CONCLUSIONS

What are the benefits of the use of stochastic processes in the financial markets over the last two decades ? The answer is obvious. It has been a very strong tool in designing a lot of contingent claims which suited the most the needs of investors and issuers. Options allow to redistribute risk through the security markets and risk-neutral valuation makes its possible to replicate the various pay-off of such instruments.

As far as the financial world goes and as usual there seems to be no limit in the imagination both for "rocket scientists" and for financial engineers the first providing the hedging formulae of the very much sophisticated options taylored by the second in response to a not so easy to tackle market risk. But there is still a lot of applied research to do in order to test and adapt these formulae in a real environment where the assumptions of the underlying models do not fit perfectly.

REFERENCES

Black, F., Scholes, M. (1973) : "The Pricing of Options and Corporate Liabilities". *Journal of Political Economy.* 81 pp. 637-659.

Conze, A., Viswanathan (1991) : "Path Dependent Options : the Case of Lookback Options". *Journal of Finance*, Vol. XLVI december.

Duffie, D. (1990) : "The Theory of Value in Security Markets" (to appear in *"The Handbook of Mathematical Economics"*).
Harrison, J.M., Pliska, S. (1981) : "Martingales and Stochastic Integrals in the Theory of Continuous Trading". *Stochastic Processes and their Applications*, 11, pp. 313-316.
Karatzas, I., Shreve (1988) : *"Brownian Motion and Stochastic Calculus"*. New-York : Springer Verlag.
Karlin, S., Taylor, H. (1975) : *"A First Course in Stochastic Processes"*. Academic Press;
Merton, R. (1973) : "Theory of Rationnal Option Pricing". *Bell Journal of Economics and Management Sciences*, pp. 141-183.
Merton, R. (1990) : *"Continuous Time Model"*. Blackwell.
Rubinstein, M. (1991) : "Two into One". *Risk*.

6. GAMES AND SOCIAL CHOICE

Whereas the previous sections of this volume have covered various aspects of individual choice under risk and uncertainty, the final section covers the multi-person topics of game theory and social choice. The first paper in this section, by Colin Camerer and Risto Karjalainen, consists of an experimental study of the effects of "ambiguity" (i.e., the nonexistence of well-defined probabilities) in the context of individuals playing games of strategy. Although the whole issue of ambiguity for the classical theory of choice under uncertainty goes back at least as far as the seminal work of Ellsberg, it has never been studied in a game-theoretic setting. Yet the strategic prediction of others' actions would seem to be one of the most important sources of ambiguity an individual could face.

In a series of experimental games based on versions of the Ellsberg Paradox and other ambiguous situations, Camerer and Karjalainen find that reaction to ambiguity - in the form of ambiguity aversion - is widespread among subjects, although not strong in degree. These authors go on to discuss the implications of such phenomena for the design of future experiments, as well as for real-world market settings.

The paper by Gilbert Laffond, Jean Laine and Jean-Francois Laslier examines the notion of a "composed tournament." A tournament is a mathematical structure that has seen applications in fields as wide-ranging as statistics, social choice theory, and game theory. For example, it can be used to model the process of ranking by majority choice. A tournament is termed "composed" if it can be broken down into two more "component" tournaments. The authors examine the formal implications of this type of structure, with applications to social choice theory, game theory, and political science.

The final paper in the volume, by Gisèle Umbhauer, treats the topic of strategic information transmission in signaling games, in situations where agents use forward induction. A signaling game is one where at least one of the players' strategy set consists not so much of an "action" in the usual sense, but rather, the transmission of information to the other player. An example is the interaction of a vendor and a customer, where the vendor merely posts a price (which serves as a "signal" of quality), and the customer makes the purchase decision.

The incorporation of forward induction into such games represents an improvement over the standard tool of backward induction, in that it allows the player(s) to interpret "out-of-equilibrium" messages as strategic departures on the part of the sender. In this paper, Umbhauer, considers two alternative forward induction schemes, and examines the game-theoretic implications of each scheme, in particular in connection to the phenomenon of self-enforcing equilibria in signaling games.

Ambiguity-aversion and Non-additive Beliefs in Non-Cooperative Games: Experimental evidence

Colin F. Camerer and Risto Karjalainen[1]

I. INTRODUCTION

In subjective expected utility (SEU), people choose among acts which have different consequences, depending on which of several uncertain states occurs. Choices between acts therefore reveal implicit beliefs about the likelihood of the states, or "subjective probabilities" (Ramsey, 1931; Savage, 1954). In the SEU framework, the (implicit) likelihoods of different states certainly affects choices, but the ambiguity[2] surrounding that likelihood-- the confidence a person has in her judgment of likelihood, or the amount of information on which it is based-- should not affect her choices.

However, there are many experimental demonstrations (beginning with Ellsberg, 1961) that ambiguity <u>does</u> affect choices: Holding the judged likelihood of states constant, people generally prefer to bet on states with less ambiguity. We think many naturally occurring economic phenomena, like brand loyalty for consumer products, and various kinds of risk premia and volatility in financial markets, might be partly explained by ambiguity-aversion (see the review by Camerer & Weber, 1992).

Theorists have suggested several related ways to express attitudes toward ambiguity formally. The method we prefer, and use in this paper, is to allow subjective probabilities to be nonadditive to reflect aversion to ambiguity.

Additivity means that for disjoint events ($p(A \cap B)=0$), $p(A)+p(B)=p(A \cup B)$. Suppose two events A and B are each separately ambiguous, but their ambiguity is cancelled when their union A U B is taken. (For example, A and B might partition events in the world-- either the National (A) or American (B) League team wins the World Series in 1997-- so that P(A U B)=1, but you have no idea whether A or B will occur.) If A and B are ambiguous, it seems intuitive to express an aversion to betting on either of them by lowering both P(A) and P(B). But then P(A)+P(B) < P(A U B), violating additivity. The gap, P(A U B)-P(A)-P(B), measures the degree of ambiguity-aversion.

In this paper we extend research on ambiguity to non-cooperative game theory. This extension is novel, but it seems natural to us because the strategies that players choose in non-cooperative games are simply bets on events (or states); the unique feature of game theory is that choices by one player are precisely the events another player bets on. Since what other players will do might be an ambiguous event, insights from research on decision making under ambiguity may be helpful for understanding decision making in games.

We explore ambiguity in games with four experiments. Three of the experiments are designed to measure the degree of ambiguity-aversion in simple games, and the fourth experiment tries to manipulate the amount of ambiguity. Our experiments generally show a modest, but persistent, degree of ambiguity-aversion.

The research raises many questions, both substantive and methodological. The main substantive question is whether there are important games in which the amount of ambiguity is larger than we observed, or in which the small degree of ambiguity we observed has large effects. (If not, then ambiguity and belief nonadditivity may be relatively unimportant for game theory.) A related topic is whether ambiguity persists over time, as people learn; and if ambiguity decreases as confidence in judgments grows, does it ever rise again (perhaps when surprises occur)? The main methodological question is how nonadditive beliefs can be measured, without having the measurement process affect the beliefs that are reported (as appeared to happen in some of our pilot experiments).

Ambiguity-aversion and SEU

The "Ellsberg paradox" (Ellsberg 1961) is the most well-known demonstration that "ambiguity", or uncertainty about a probability, can affect choices. In the "two-color" form of the paradox, subjects are offered bets on either an unambiguous urn (which contains 50 red balls and 50 black balls) or an ambiguous urn with 100 red or black balls in an unknown mixture of colors. People often strictly prefer to bet on a red draw from the unambiguous urn, instead of a red draw from the ambiguous urn, and the same for a black draw. Such a pattern of preference cannot be reconciled with additive probabilities in both urns.

Ellsberg's two urns draw a distinction between "risk" (known probability) and "uncertainty" (unknown probability; see Knight, 1921), or between the "implications of evidence" (likelihood) and the "weight of evidence" (ambiguity) (Keynes, 1921). Roughly speaking, in the SEU approach only the implications of evidence should matter in forming a decision weight to attach to consequences of states. Ellsberg's thought experiment demonstrates that the weight of the evidence, or its ambiguity, may reduce the revealed decision weight also.

A dozen or so experiments have replicated the Ellsberg paradox or variants of it, in tasks using bingo cages, cards, and bets on natural events (e.g., sports contests). Most of these experiments have used actual money (albeit small amounts). Furthermore, subjects generally do not change their decisions when the conflict between their choices and decision-theoretic principles is pointed out (Camerer & Weber, 1992).

In the Ellsberg urns, ambiguity arises because there is missing information-- the composition of the second urn-- which is relevant to the decision and which could be known, in principle. Frisch & Baron (1988) suggest that the existence of missing, relevant, knowable information is the principal psychological basis for ambiguity. Their definition is useful because it suggests the circumstances under which ambiguity will be high or low. For example, experiments suggest people are reluctant to bet on events which have already occurred, or in domains they know very little about (see Heath & Tversky 1991); in both cases, people know there is missing information that they could know but do not, which undermines their confidence and causes a reluctance to bet.[3]

Approaches to modelling ambiguity-aversion

Theorists have taken several approaches to modelling aversion to ambiguity (reviewed more thoroughly in Camerer & Weber, 1992).

One approach is to assume that utilities for ambiguous events are lower than for unambiguous events, accounting for the reluctance to bet on ambiguous events (Smith, 1969; Sarin & Winkler, 1992).

A dual approach is to assume that ambiguous probabilities are weighted differently, perhaps lowered to reflect the unattractiveness of betting on ambiguous events (Fellner, 1963; Einhorn & Hogarth, 1985; Segal, 1987).

A third approach is to assume probabilities are not unique (i.e., there are multiple priors). If a person has a "second-order" probability distribution of possible probabilities, for example, then ambiguity-aversion is akin to an aversion toward risk-- the risk arising from the distribution of probabilities (sometimes called "epistemic risk").

Further down the same analytical path, nonunique probabilities might be contained in a set (even if elements of the set-- possible probability values-- do not have crisp second-order probabilities). Maximin representation theorems show how preferences can be expressed by expected utilities minimized over the probabilities in the set (Bewley, 1986; Gilboa, 1987; Gilboa & Schmeidler, 1989).

The final approach is to assume that probabilities are not additive. Subadditivity adds an extra degree of freedom which can be used to express the degree of ambiguity of a set of events. The ratio P(A)/P(B) still expresses the relative likelihood of the ambiguous states, or put differently, P(A)/(P(A)+P(B)) expresses a "normalized" likelihood. Then P(A U B)-P(A)-P(B)-- which is forced to be zero under additivity-- expresses the degree of ambiguity of the events. Preferences can then be represented by a special sort of integral (Choquet, 1953-4) over "differences" in sets of subadditive probabilities (Schmeidler, 1989).[4]

To express this formally, suppose unpredictable states are denoted s_i. Then for a particular act f, states can be ranked by the utilities of their consequences, from s_1 to s_n (that is, $u(f(s_1))>...>u(f(s_n))$ where $u(f(s_i))$ denotes the utility of act f's consequence in state s_i). Then the finite Choquet integral is:

$$(1) \quad u(f(s_1))p(s_1) + \sum_{i=2}^{n} u(f(s_i))[p(\cup_{j=1}^{i} s_j) - p(\cup_{j=1}^{i-1} s_j)]$$

Note that if p(.) is additive and the states s_i are mutually exclusive, then the term in brackets reduces to $p(s_i)$ and the Choquet integral (1) reduces to the more familiar SEU expression $\sum u(f(s_i))p(s_i)$.

For aesthetic reasons, and because it is more amenable to measurement, we prefer the nonadditive probability approach, and adopt it here as a method to measure the ambiguity of events in games.

SEU and game theory

SEU forms the foundation of noncooperative game theory. In a game, strategies of players are acts and uncertain states are moves by other players (and random moves by nature). Much of game theory concerns the logic players use to form beliefs about what other players will do. As in SEU, the beliefs of players should certainly affect their choices, but the confidence players have in their beliefs should not (holding those beliefs constant). Furthermore, there are several variables which might affect confidence or ambiguity without affecting beliefs, which should be irrelevant under SEU but might actually affect choices.

Game-theoretic behavior consistent with ambiguity-aversion

There is some scattered experimental evidence which is consistent with the presence of ambiguity-aversion in games. The simplest example is a game studied experimentally by Beard and Beil (1994). We describe the game and their findings because it illustrates our point in the simplest possible game-theoretic framework, and motivates our further experimental work.

The game (their game ii) is shown in Figure 1. Player 1 moves first, left (L) or right (R). Then player 2 moves, left (l) or right (r). The payoffs are chosen so player 2 has a weakly dominant strategy (assuming self-interest), to play r. The game tests whether players perform one level of iterated dominance: If player 1 believes that player 2 will obey dominance, then player 1 should move R; otherwise player 1 could reasonably move L. Put more intuitively, a choice of R by player 1 is a bet on player 2's "rationality" (her propensity to obey the conjunction of dominance and self-interest).

In Beard and Beil's experiments with the game in Figure 1, a substantial proportion of the player 1 subjects (67%) chose L (see also Schotter, Weigelt & Wilson 1994). Assuming SEU and risk-neutrality, a player who chooses L reveals herself[5] to believe that $p(l) \geq .14$. But in fact, in variations of game (ii), the strategy l was chosen by only 2 of 68 player 2's, around 3%. (In game (ii) specifically, player 2s <u>never</u> chose l.)

There are three reasonable explanations for the discrepancy between player 1s' revealed beliefs about $p(l)$-- those who picked L act as if $p(l) \geq .14$-- and the actual frequency of l play (around .03). First, player 1 subjects may simply overestimate the fraction of dominance-violating player 2s; such an overestimation would be interesting to study in further work.[6] Second, it is possible that player 1's have empirically-correct beliefs ($p(l)$ is around .03) but are highly risk-averse. However, the <u>degree</u> of risk-aversion required to explain their choices this way is very high; it requires a certainty-equivalent for a coin flip paying either $3 or $10 to be on the order of $3.21.[7]

A third explanation invokes ambiguity-aversion. The choice by player 2 of r or l is an ambiguous event for player 1 (by the Frisch-Baron definition) because player 1 knows there is missing information-- viz., whether player 2 is purely self-interested and obeys dominance-- which is relevant and

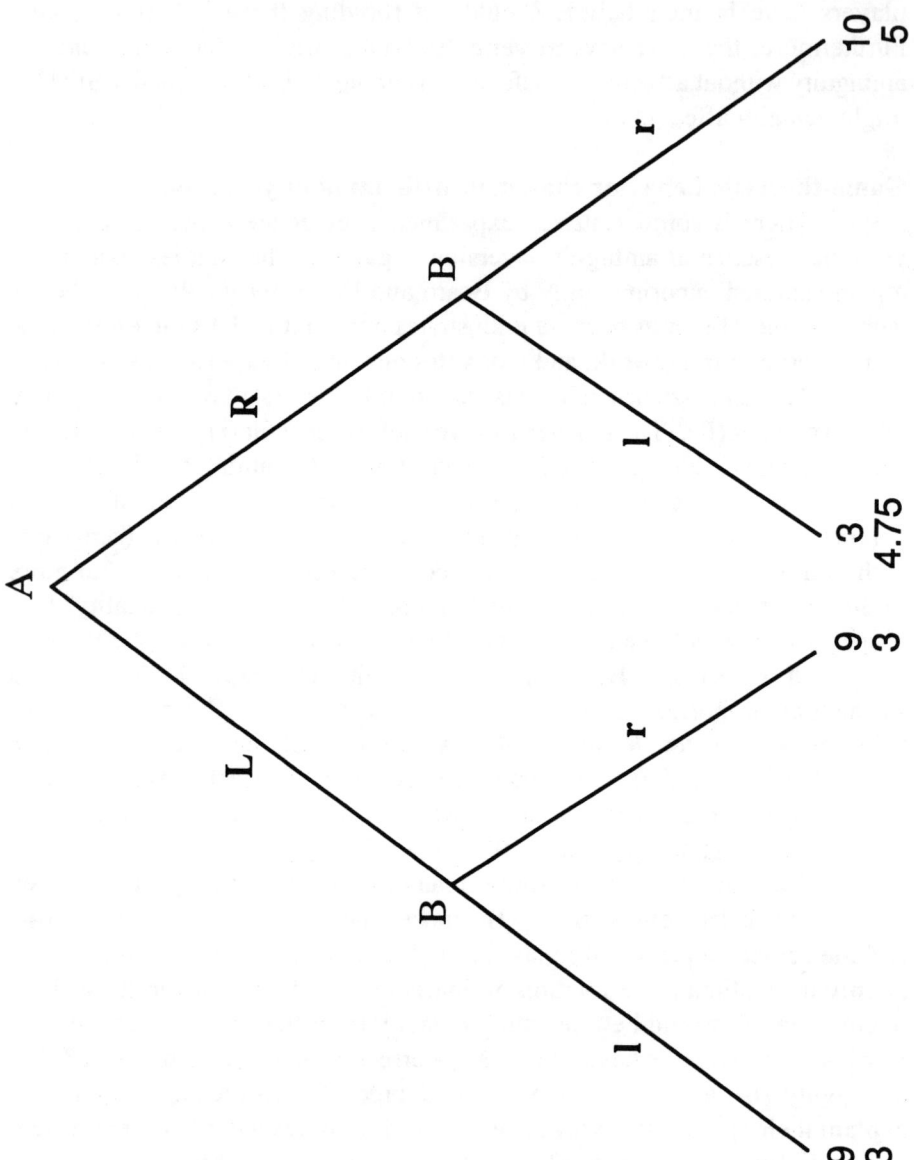

Figure 1. Game (ii) of Beard and Beil [1990].

potentially knowable. Player 1's may be reluctant to bet on either r or l; their beliefs p(r) and p(l) may be subadditive, reflecting their aversion to strategic uncertainty.

In an SEU analysis with additive beliefs, the choice of L yields utility u($9) and the choice of R yields an SEU of p(r)u($10)+p(l)u($3). In an SEU analysis with subadditive beliefs, the choice of R yields a (Choquet) SEU of p(r)u($10)+(1-p(r))u($3). In the nonadditive-SEU analysis the weight on the bad outcome (R,l), is 1-p(r) rather than to p(l). (Under additivity, p(l)=1-p(r).) Therefore, in the nonadditive-SEU analysis p(l) could be close to the empirically correct value of .03 but the player 1's shy away from the riskier strategy R if p(r) is sufficiently low-- it would have to be $\leq$.86-- so that the weight 1-p(r) is placed on the $3 outcome is large. Ambiguity-aversion therefore allows us to rationalize choices of L without assuming either excessive risk-aversion or systematic overestimation of p(l).

A similar phenomenon is reported by Van Huyck et al (1991) in their study of "median effort" coordination games (see also Van Huyck et al, 1993; Cachon & Camerer, 1994). In their game, each player chooses an action (an integer from 1 to 7). A player's payoff depends on her own action choice and on the median action chosen by all the players. Figure 2 shows a payoff matrix. The payoffs are such that each player prefers to choose the median, and players collectively prefer the median to be a higher number (7 is the best).

The median effort game is interesting because strategic uncertainty might prevent players from reaching the Pareto-optimal equilibrium in which everyone picks 7. In experiments, players generally pick a distribution of numbers around 4 or 5 the first time they play the game, creating a initial median of 4 or 5. When the game is repeated, the median in the first round inevitably determines the median in later rounds.

The persistence of the initial median in later rounds is not too surprising, since the best response to a median of X is an action of X (and every combination of X's is a Nash equilibrium) (see also Crawford, 1992). The puzzle is why 4 or 5 is usually chosen initially. A natural explanation is that players have (additive) subjective beliefs which place some weight on the median being 3, 4, 5, etc., and they simply choose the strategy which maximizes their SEU given their beliefs. The structure of the payoff matrix means that diffuse beliefs and risk-aversion favor choosing middle-number strategies, rather than high or low numbers.

We suggest a different interpretation: Suppose beliefs are subadditive.

MEDIAN ACTION

	1	2	3	4	5	6	7
1	1.40	1.50	1.40	1.10	0.60	−0.10	−1.00
2	1.30	1.60	1.70	1.60	1.30	0.80	0.10
3	1.00	1.50	1.80	1.90	1.80	1.50	1.00
4	0.50	1.20	1.70	2.00	2.10	2.00	1.70
5	−0.20	0.70	1.40	1.90	2.20	2.30	2.20
6	−1.10	0.00	0.90	1.60	2.10	2.40	2.50
7	−2.20	−0.90	0.20	1.10	1.80	2.30	2.60

(row label: ACTION)

Figure 2. The payoff table of the median coordination game. The table indicates the payoff for a player for each possible combination of her choice (called "action") and the median choice of all nine players of the game.

Then players may not truly believe that lower numbers will be chosen (i.e., p(1), p(2) etc. may be small), but if players are not sure that higher numbers will be chosen either then the Choquet integral used to compute nonadditive SEU will put large decision weight on low-value outcomes. For example, in valuing the choice of 4, the Choquet integral puts a weight 1-p(2 U 3...U 7) on the lowest-valued outcome from choosing 4 (a payoff of $.50), which results when the median is 1. If beliefs are subadditive, so 1-p(2 U 3 ...U 7) is much larger than p(1), then the lowest-valued outcome receives a large weight, even if subjects do not believe the median is actually likely to be 1 (e.g., p(1) could even be zero).

The standard SEU view is that by choosing 4, players are revealed to put substantial probability on low-valued outcomes. Our point is that if probabilities are not additive, players can put substantial weight on low-valued outcomes without attaching high probability to those outcomes. (Without additivity, weights and probabilities will differ.)

An extreme form of subadditivity is worth noting. Suppose a person is so ambiguity-averse that they attach p=0 to all choices by an opponent. Then the Choquet integral will put all the decision weight on the minimum-outcome for each strategy. Such a person maximizes nonadditive SEU by using a maximin decision rule, choosing the strategy which has the highest minimum-outcome. Thus, nonadditive SEU with p=0 beliefs puts a decision-theoretic underpinning under the familiar maximin decision rule proposed for decision-making under ignorance (Wald, 1950). (In our view, the connection points out the absurdity of maximin in most actual decisions, since maximin is only rational if a person is unwilling to assign any probability weight to any event.)

The experimental results of Beard & Beil (1994) and Van Huyck et al (1991) are consistent with player timidity that could be traced to ambiguity-aversion in strategic situations, but they are also consistent with extreme risk-aversion or with errors in beliefs. The crucial empirical question is whether we can distinguish the standard additive-probability approach and the nonadditive approach empirically. We can distinguish the two, by measuring bounds on subjective probabilities for each of two events A and B which are complementary and exhaustive. Then we can test directly whether p(A) and p(B) add to one; if they add to less than one, we have evidence of ambiguity-aversion.

II. EXPERIMENTAL DESIGN AND RESULTS

We ran four experiments to test for ambiguity-aversion, measure the amount of it, and see if we could control it by altering the timing of moves in a game. The first two experiments estimate rough bounds on the degree of ambiguity-aversion (if any) which subjects exhibit in game-theoretic variants of the celebrated Ellsberg (1961) paradox. A third experiment measures ambiguity-aversion more precisely, in a coordination game. The fourth experiment tries to manipulate the degree of ambiguity-aversion by varying the timing of play.

Experiment 1: A two-color game

In our first experiment we constructed a game-theoretic analogue to Ellsberg's two color problem. We felt that problem was a good place to start our explorations, because the problem is simple and there is so much data from individual choice experiments with which we can compare our game-theoretic evidence.

Figure 3 shows a game tree. The first move, by nature, determines the color of ball, either red or black, which wins for both players. Conditional on nature's move, player 1 then chooses either R or A (if nature drew RED-WIN) or B or A (if nature drew BLACK-WIN). The idea is simpler than the tree indicates: After observing RED-WIN, for example, player 1 can either bet on a chance device which yields a p chance of winning $5 (by choosing R), or bet that player 2 has chosen r (by choosing A). After observing BLACK-WIN player 1 chooses between a q chance of $5 (B) and a bet on player 2 choosing b (A). Player 2 chooses either r or b without knowing either nature's move or player 1's move. Intuitively, player 2 is trying to guess which winning color nature has drawn, and player 1 is betting on whether player 2 has figured out the right color. If player 1 is unsure of player 2's choices, she can opt for the ambiguity of a chance device at each node instead of the ambiguity of another person's decision.

Some details about the experimental setup are worth mentioning. (These details apply to the other experiments unless noted otherwise.) Subjects were University of Pennsylvania undergraduates recruited by posting announcements on campus. Subjects were run in groups of 10-15. They sat in cubicles separated by partitions; instructions were read out loud and subjects completed a short quiz testing their comprehension of the instructions. Only 1-2 subjects were assigned the player 2 role in each group, because the data

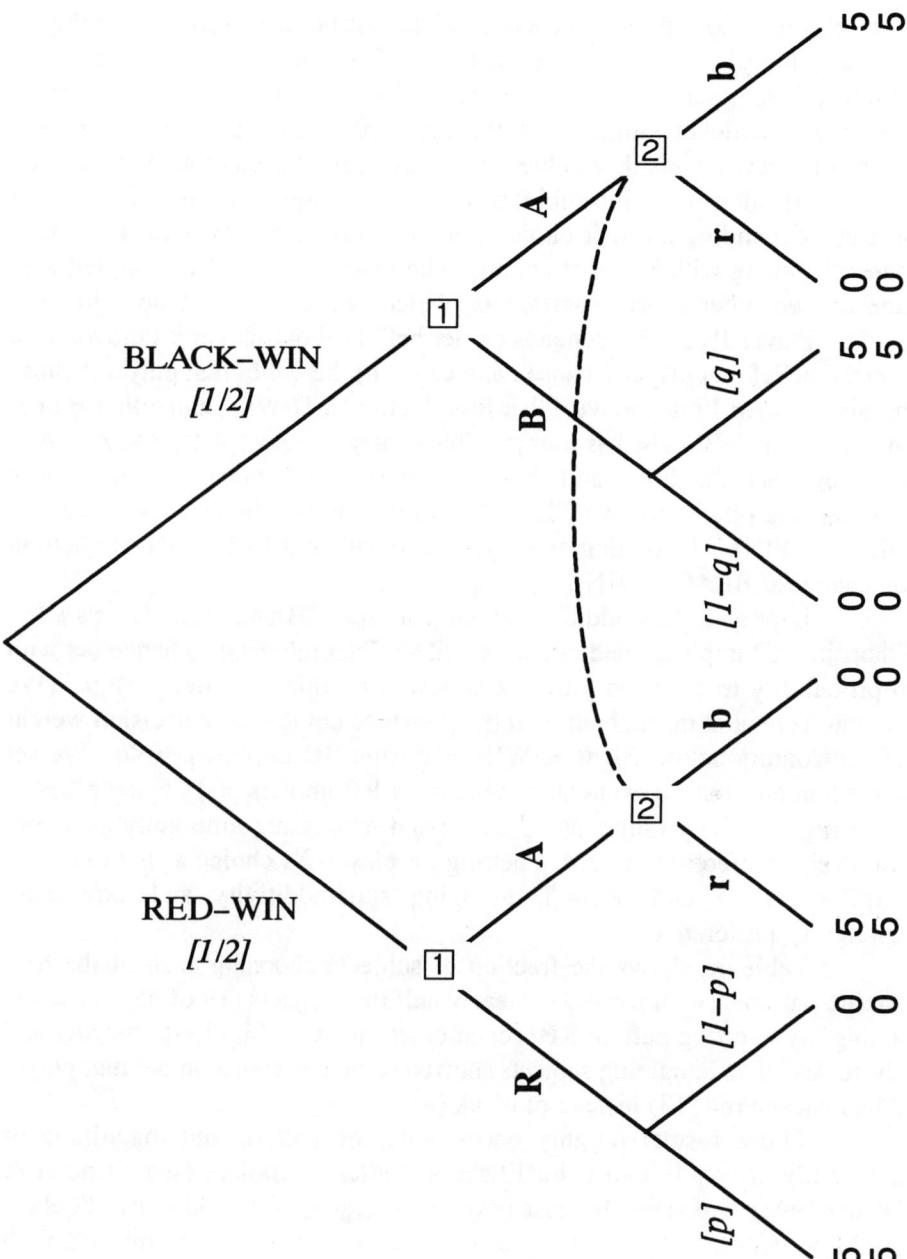

Figure 3. The two–color game. The probabilities in square brackets correspond to moves by nature.

from player 2 subjects are not useful, and there is no reason for the number of player 1 and player 2 subjects to be equal. The chance device was a box of 100 tickets numbered 1-100. A p chance of winning was operationalized by winning if a ticket numbered 1 through 100p was drawn from the box. (Subjects drew tickets themselves, independently of each other.) At the end of the experimental session subjects were paid the amount shown in Figure 3 in cash, depending on their choices, and on player 2's choice or the chance outcome, along with $3 for attending. The sessions were often coupled with one or two other short experiments, which seemed to have no influence.

Player 1's choice depends on her beliefs about player 2's move. Call $p(r)$ the belief that player 2 chose r and call $p(b)$ the belief that player 2 chose b. Since player 1 must move either R or A after RED-WIN, and either B or A after BLACK-WIN, she has four possible strategy choices, RB, RA, AB, AA. If her beliefs are additive, and choices obey SEU, then player 1 could choose RA (betting on chance at RED-WIN and betting on player 2 choosing b at BLACK-WIN), AB (betting on player 2 choosing r at RED-WIN and betting on chance at BLACK-WIN).

If $p+q=1$ then additive beliefs rule out RB and AA. Here's why: Choosing RB implies, conditional on RED-WIN, preferring a chance bet with p probability to a bet on player 2 choosing r, which implies $p(r)<p$. (We assume here, and throughout, that the p-chance device has a decision weight of p.) Conditional on BLACK-WIN, choosing RB implies $p(b)<q$. We set $p=q=.5$ in our first experiment, so preferring RB implies $p(r)<.5$ and $p(b)<.5$, violating additivity (since $p(r \cup b)=1$) and expressing ambiguity-aversion. Similarly, preference for AA-- betting on player 2's choice at both nodes-- implies $p(r)>.5$ and $p(b)>.5$, implying superadditivity and expressing ambiguity-preference.

Table 1a shows the fraction of subjects choosing each of the four choice patterns (with $p=q=.5$). Nearly half the subjects (19 of 45) chose the ambiguity-averting pattern RB; seven others were ambiguity-preferring and chose AA. The remaining subjects showed some preference to bet that player 2 had chosen red (13) instead of black (6).

These results roughly corroborate the pattern and magnitude of ambiguity effects in two-color Ellsberg studies of choices (see Camerer & Weber 1992). However, because $p=q=.5$ the degree of subadditivity of beliefs could be very small. To obtain a tighter bound we ran more subjects with $p=q=.45$. Subjects choosing RB then reveal $p(r)<.45$ and $p(b)<.45$, which suggests a higher degree of subadditivity (and hence, more ambiguity-

strategy	n	(%)
RB	19	(42.2)
RA	6	(13.3)
AB	13	(28.9)
AA	7	(15.6)

Table 1a. Results from the two-color game ($p = q = 0.50$).

strategy	n	(%)
RB	5	(10.9)
RA	7	(15.2)
AB	6	(13.0)
AA	28	(60.9)

Table 1b. Results from the two-color game ($p = q = 0.45$).

choice	A'	B'	C'	%
A	5	5	6	64.0
B	4	0	3	28.0
C	0	1	1	8.0
%	36.0	24.0	40.0	100.0

Table 2. Results from the three-color game.

aversion).

Results from p=q=.45 are shown in Table 1b. There is a large movement of subjects away from the ambiguity-averse pattern RB (only 10.9% remain) toward the ambiguity-preferring pattern AA (60.9%). Thus, it appears that while a large fraction of subjects are ambiguity-averse, consistent with subadditivity of beliefs p(r) and p(b), the degree of subadditivity is small. For most subjects p(r) and p(b) lie (strictly) between .45 and .50.

Experiment 2: A three-color game

Our second experiment created a game-theoretic version of Ellsberg's three-color problem. Our goal was to test robustness of the two-color problem results and also test for links between ambiguity-aversion and violations of Savage's sure-thing principle.

Figure 4 shows the game. Player 2 moves first, choosing either "ZEJ" or "ZOJ".[8] Player 1 then chooses a row from the matrix in the top panel of Figure 4, and a random ticket from 1-100 is drawn. Both players earn the same payoff, shown in the payoff table, according to their choices and the ticket number drawn.

The choice of row A pays $5 if the ticket drawn is 1-30, regardless of player 2's choice. Row B (C) pays $5 if the ticket drawn is 31-100 and player 2 chose ZEJ (ZOJ). Thus, A is a bet on chance while B or C are bets on the conjunction of chance and player 2's choice.

If player 1's beliefs about player 2's choice are additive, then the subjective expected utilities of the three acts are:

row A[9]   p(1-30)u($5)
row B   p[(31-100) ∩ ZEJ]u($5)
row C   p[(31-100) ∩ ZOJ]u($5)

To proceed further, we must make two assumptions. The first is that subjective probabilities for chance events correspond to the relative frequencies of tickets, so p(1-30)=.3 and p(31-100)=.7. (More subtly, all we require is that players believe all tickets are equally likely to be drawn, or that the tickets 1-30 are no more likely to be drawn than average.) The second is that player 2's choice and the random ticket drawing are (perceived to be) independent events, so p[(31-100) ∩ ZEJ]=p(31-100)p(ZEJ). Then we can learn something about the subjective probabilities p(ZEJ) and p(ZOJ) from choices, viz.,

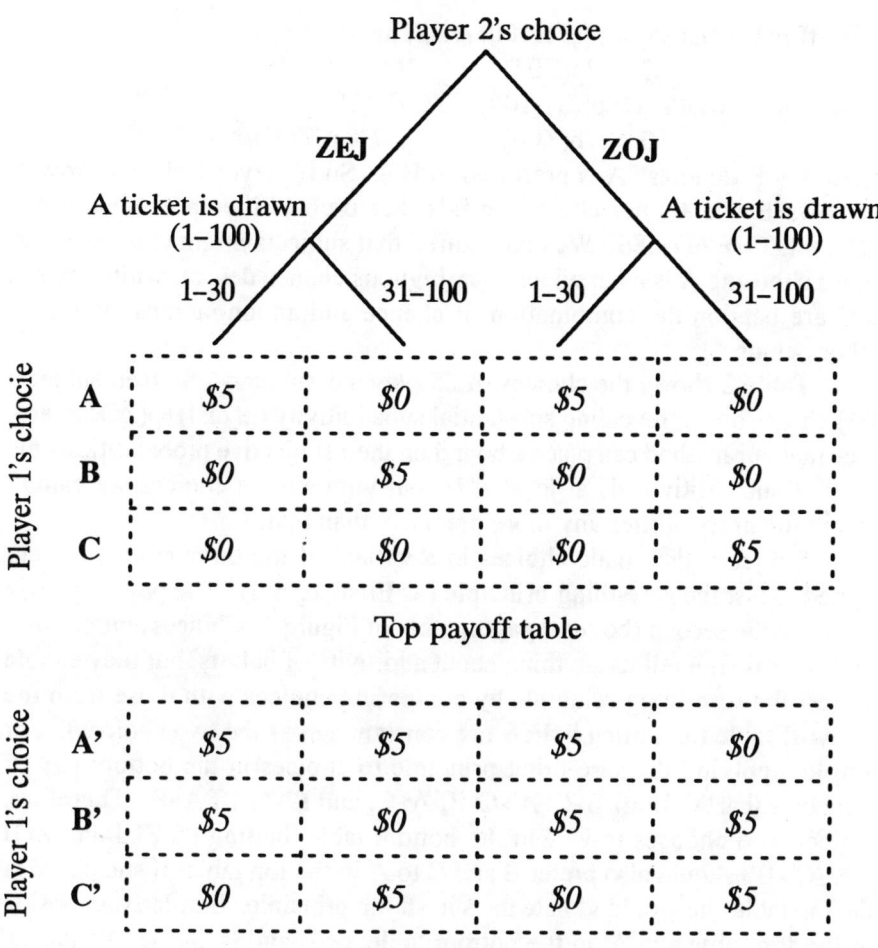

Figure 4. The three-color game.

A ≻ B iff p(1-30)u($5) > p[(31-100) ∩ ZEJ]u($5)
$$.3 > .7p(ZEJ) \text{ or } 3/7 > p(ZEJ)$$
A ≻ C iff p(1-30)u($5) > p[(31-100) ∩ ZOJ]u($5)
$$.3 > .7p(ZOJ) \text{ or } 3/7 > p(ZOJ)$$
(where A ≻ B denotes "A is preferred to B"). So if player 1 chooses row A over rows B and C, her choice reveals that probabilities are subadditive, p(ZEJ)+p(ZOJ)<6/7=.86. We conjectured that subjects might choose row A because choosing A is a bet on an unambiguous chance device, while rows B and C are bets on the combination of chance and an ambiguous choice by another person.

Table 2 shows the choices of 25 player 1 subjects. Sixteen subjects (64%) chose row A, revealing substantial subadditivity (p(ZEJ)+p(ZOJ)<.86). Notice that our method can place a <u>bound</u> on their subjective probabilities-- the degree of subadditivity is at least 1/7-- but with simple choices we cannot estimate the probabilities any more precisely than that.

Subjects also made choices in a variant of the three-color problem designed to test the sure-thing principle (as Ellsberg did). The payoff matrix is shown in the second (bottom) payoff table of Figure 4. Choices among rows A',B' and C' do not tell us anything about additivity of beliefs, but they enable us to test the sure-thing principle by comparing choices with those from the top payoff table (assuming beliefs are constant across the two choices). For example, applying the sure-thing principle to choices in the bottom payoff table shows that A'≻B' iff B≻C, A'≻C' iff A≻C, and B'≻C' iff A≻B. Therefore, a subject who chooses row C' in the bottom table, betting on ZEJ and ZOJ (C'≻A', C'≻B') should also prefer B and C to A in the top table; if she chose A in the top table she would violate the sure-thing principle. Similarly, choosing C in the top table and A' in the bottom table, or B and B' in the two tables, violates the sure-thing principle.

Table 2 shows that only six subjects violated the sure-thing principle (by choosing A in the top table and C' in the bottom table). Of the sixteen who exhibited subadditivity (choosing A in the top panel), six violated STP. Machina & Schmeidler (1992) show a system of axioms on preferences which can explain STP violation, while preserving additivity (see also Sarin & Wakker, 1994). In our study, however, only six subjects violated STP, and all of them violated additivity too. Thus, while the Machina-Schmeidler axioms fill in an important theoretical void, they describe none of these 25 subjects.

Experiment 3: A median effort coordination game

The first two experiments loosely <u>bound</u> the degree of subadditivity revealed by choices of some subjects. We can derive sharper bounds on the degree of subadditivity using the median coordination game first studied by van Huyck et al (1991), which was briefly described above.

In the median coordination game (see Figure 2), subjects choose an action number from 1 to 7 and their payoff depends on the median action chosen, and on the distance between their choice and the median. Subjects prefer to be close to the median, and they prefer the median to be large (7 is the best).

The best way to measure ambiguity-aversion is to measure subadditivity by eliciting measures of each of the subjective beliefs $p(1)$, $p(2)$,...$p(7)$. We thought this was too difficult for subjects and might cause measurement problems (due to "yes-bias", discussed below). To simplify belief elicitation, we partition the set of possible medians into subsets of high and low medians, {1,2,3,4} and {5,6,7}, and we elicited beliefs that the median would fall into each set, denoted $p(1..4)$ and $p(5..7)$.

Here is how the experiment was conducted. Each subject was first instructed about the coordination game (see the Appendix for instructions). Their task was not to play the game, but to bet on whether the actual median, randomly-chosen from a sample of games played by other subjects, would be low or high.

We elicited beliefs in the following way: Subjects were asked whether they preferred to bet on the median being in the set {1,2,3,4} or on a chance device. The chance device was a box containing tickets numbered 1-100. For example, subjects might be offered a bet which paid \$5 if the median was in {1,2,3,4}, or a bet which paid \$5 if the ticket numbered 1 through 62 was drawn from the box. If a subject preferred the median bet, we inferred $p(1..4) \geq .62$; if the subject preferred the chance bet we inferred $p(1..4) \leq .62$. We began with a bet in which the ticket number was randomly chosen (from 1 to 100), then offered a series of such bets in which the winning ticket number threshold (62 in the example just above) was raised or lowered depending on the subject's response, to move the subject toward indifference. (For example, if she preferred betting on the median being {1,2,3,4} to drawing 62 or less, we <u>raised</u> the ticket number to make the drawing more attractive.) We continued until the iterations were less than 2 tickets (.02 in probability). At the end, one of the many trials was chosen at random and the choice the subject made in that trial was played for money. Reaching indifference took

15-25 trials per subject, about 19 trials on average. This iterated-choice method controls for risk-aversion by offering the same dollar prize for both types of bets, and is (myopically) incentive-compatible.[10]

In pilot experiments we used the iterated-choice method to first infer a tight bound on p(1..4) (raising and lowering ticket-number levels for bets on the median being low), then to infer p(5..7) with a subsequent series of choices. We found, much to our surprise, a persistent degree of superadditivity (p(1..4)+p(5..7) greater than one). We conjectured that when asked to bet on the median being {1,2,3,4}, subjects could imagine reasons or ways in which the median would lie in that set, inflating their expressed belief p(1..4). When asked to bet on {5,6,7} they did the same, inflating p(5..7). (In survey research, this kind of "yes bias" is common.[11]) Our pilot results show how fragile measurement can be in a game-- even a simple one-- when beliefs are apparently not well-formed enough to be independent of the procedure used to elicit them.

To avoid "yes bias", beliefs p(1..4) and p(5..7) were elicited together. That is, the computer screen showed both median-vs.-chance bets at the same time. (Notice that asking for probability-equivalents for p(1..4) and p(5..7) at the same time is also a conservative test of ambiguity-aversion, since more subjects would probably give additive beliefs than if p(1..4) and p(5..7) were elicited separately.)

Figure 5 shows a scatterplot of beliefs elicited from n=33 subjects, in a two-dimensional graph with p(1..4) on the x-axis and p(5..7) on the y-axis. Each subjects' pair of elicited beliefs create a data point. If beliefs are additive, points should lie along the downward-sloping dotted line (p(1..4)+p(5..7)=1). Ambiguity-aversion is represented by subadditive beliefs, lying inside the line toward the origin; ambiguity-preference is represented by superadditive beliefs, outside the line and away from the origin.

The data show substantial variation. Several subjects appear to be precisely additive, a few are superadditive, and most (about 60%) are subadditive. The superadditive subjects (to the upper right of the additivity line) might be suspect outliers: The degree of superadditivity is often very large, and the variation across subjects in that region of the graph is much lower than for subadditive subjects.[12] Across subjects, the mean of the summed beliefs is .964 and the standard deviation is .141. A t-test of the hypothesis that the the beliefs are additive yields $t(32)=1.46$ (p=.08, one-tailed). Trimming outliers or computing robust estimates improves power and lowers the p-value a bit. Thus, we can reject additivity, but only at a marginal

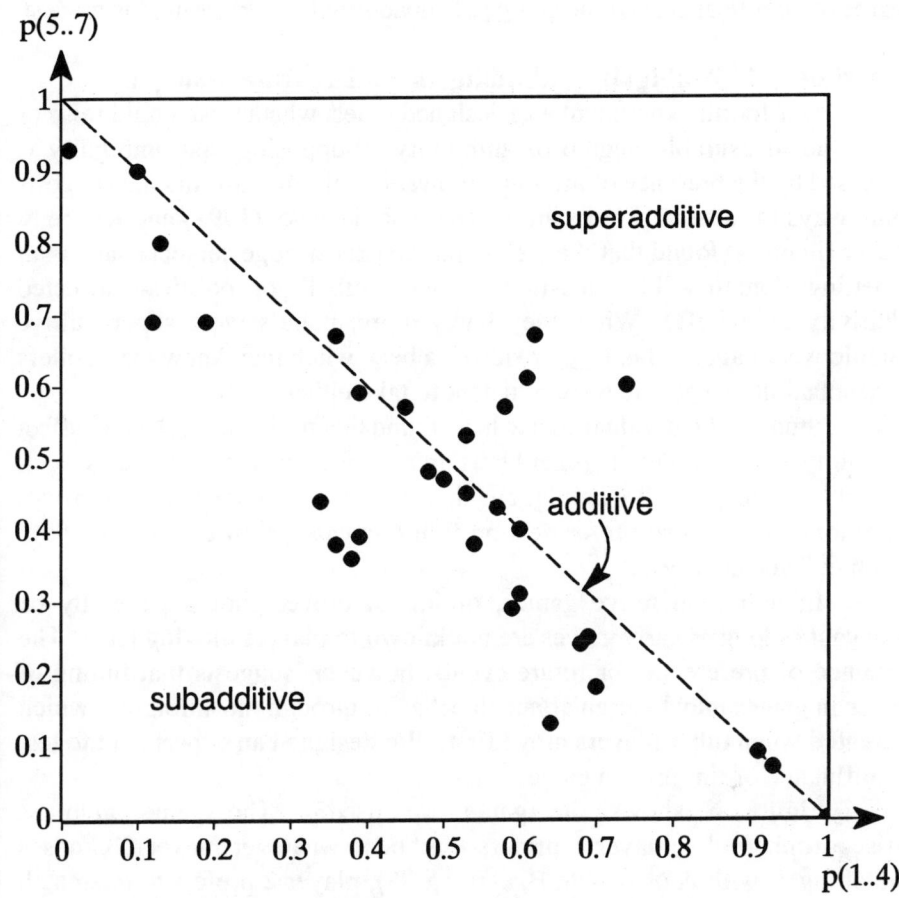

Figure 5. The beliefs of subjects in the median game experiment.

degree of significance, and the degree of subadditivity we measured is modest.

Experiment 4: Ambiguity and timing in a miscoordination game

Our fourth experiment was designed to test whether we could raise or lower the measurable degree of ambiguity. Supposing that ambiguity is increased by the presence of missing, knowable, relevant information suggests some ways to raise it. For example, Heath & Tversky (1991) and Keppe & Weber (in press) found that the (self-reported) knowledge subjects had about a betting domain-- like questions about football, or politics-- affected additivity of beliefs: When they knew more, beliefs were superadditive (people were eager to take either side of a bet); when they knew less, beliefs were subadditive (people were reluctant to take either side).

Studies of individual choice have found that timing does seem to affect ambiguity-aversion. People regard bets on past events (like yesterday's stock market behavior) as more ambiguous than bets on future events (tomorrow's behavior); people also prefer bets on future events (Brun & Tiegen, 1990; Heath & Tversky 1991).

In non-cooperative games, timing of moves should generally be irrelevant as long as early moves are not known to players moving later. The evidence of preference for future-events, however, suggests that timing of moves in games may have an effect on behavior through the ambiguity which is created when other players move first. We designed an experiment to test the influence of timing in a game.

Figure 6 shows the game we used. The game involves "miscoordination": Player 1 prefers to choose whatever player 2 chooses (matching A with A or B with B, earning $5); player 2 prefers to mismatch with player 1. To measure ambiguity-aversion, we included a third move for player 1, denoted G. If player 1 chooses G, then a chance device (drawing a ticket from 100 tickets numbered 1-100) determines whether the outcome is (5,0) or (0,5), regardless of player 2's move.

Denote player 1's beliefs about player 2's move by p(A) and p(B). Assuming that the decision weight attached to the chance device is .5, the SEUs for each move by player 1 are as follows:

$$SEU(A) = p(A)u(\$5)$$
$$SEU(B) = p(B)u(\$5)$$
$$SEU(G) = .5u(\$5)$$

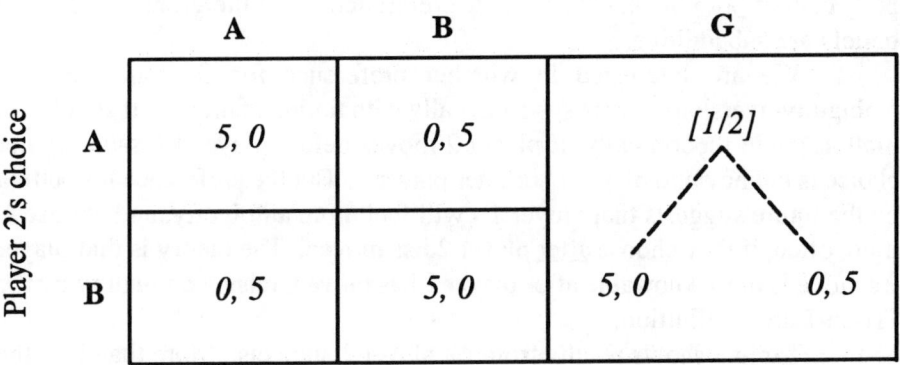

Figure 6. The "miscoordination" game. If player 1 chooses G, a random drawing determines the payoffs to the two players.

		Player 1's choice		
Timing	Ambiguity	A or B	G	% G
Player 2 moves first	high	7	16	69.5
Player 2 moves second	low	9	10	52.6

Table 3. Results from the timing experiment.

Now if player 1 has additive beliefs about player 2's move, then she will either play A (if p(A)>.5) or B (if p(B)>.5); she should never play G since p(A) and p(B) cannot <u>both</u> be less than .5. A preference for G therefore reveals that beliefs are subadditive.

We are interested in whether preference for G-- our index of ambiguity-aversion-- varies systematically with timing of moves. It should not matter, game-theoretically, if player 2 moves before player 1 (assuming her choice is unknown to player 1) or after player 1. But the preference for betting on the future suggests that player 1's will feel more ambiguity, and choose G more often, if they choose <u>after</u> player 2 has moved. The theory is that player 2's move is more knowable after player 2 has moved, raising ambiguity by the Frisch-Baron definition.

Table 3 shows results from 42 player 1 subjects. More than half the subjects chose G rather than A or B (26 of 42, 62%), reflecting ambiguity-aversion. There is a weak effect of timing, in the predicted direction: Slightly more subjects (69.5% vs. 52.6%) chose G when player 2's moved first. (The difference is significant at $p<.13$, one-tailed, test statistic $z=1.13$.)

Like the degree of subadditivity measured in experiment 3, the median coordination game, there is an effect of timing in the miscoordination game but the effect is not significant at conventional levels and is small.

III. DISCUSSION AND IMPLICATIONS

There is widespread evidence from individual choice experiments that people dislike betting on "ambiguous" events (holding judged likelihood constant). Furthermore, ambiguity seems to be enhanced by an awareness that information which is relevant and knowable is missing. Various theories have been proposed to express ambiguity-aversion formally. For measurement purposes, we adopt an approach in which probabilities may be subadditive, so that p(A) and p(B) could add to less than p(A U B) if A and B are ambiguous disjoint events. Smaller values of p(A) and p(B) (compared to P(A U B)) are an expression of the distaste for betting on <u>either</u> A and B because of their ambiguity.

Non-cooperative games are examples of decision situations in which decisions of other players create random states of nature. Since the motives and rationality of other players are a kind of knowable missing information, other players' moves could be seen as ambiguous states.

We conducted four experiments to see if players in noncooperative games were averse to the ambiguity created by other players' choices. Two of the experiments are analogies to famous examples popularized by Ellsberg (1961), involving urns containing two or three colors of balls. In these experiments, we observe that roughly half of the subjects prefer betting on chance devices to betting on <u>either</u> of two possible moves by another player in a game. In one experiment, we found that the <u>degree</u> of ambiguity-aversion was small: For a small majority of subjects the revealed decision weights on two ambiguous complementary events r and b, were both less than .5, but for almost all those subjects the weights were above .45. Thus, our first two experiments found roughly the kind, frequency, and degree, of ambiguity-aversion observed in many experiments which replicated or extended Ellsberg's problems.

A third experiment tried to more precisely measure the <u>degree</u> of ambiguity in beliefs about the median numerical choice of other subjects in a coordination game. We found that a majority of subjects (60%) expressed subadditive beliefs for two complementary events (low median or high median). But the degree of subadditivity was small-- p(low median)+p(high median)=.96 on average-- and the difference from one was only marginally significant.

In a fourth experiment, we changed a feature of the game form, the order of play, which could increase ambiguity but should have no game-theoretic effect. In our game, whether player 1 moves first or second should make no difference (assuming player 2 does not know player 1's choice after 1 movest). However, player 1 subjects were (marginally) more ambiguity-averse when player 2 moved first, consistent with some choice studies showing that people find events which already occurred more ambiguous, and dislike betting on them.

Taken together, our results are certainly supportive of the idea that choices of other players are ambiguous (or, more ambiguous than chance devices). Across the four experiments, from 40 to 65% of the subjects express <u>some</u> degree ambiguity-aversion. We think of the results as an empirical existence proof, which show enough widespread ambiguity-aversion in games to justify more research along these lines. The data shift the burden of proof to critics who think ambiguity-aversion doesn't exist.

We think there are two important lessons in the data; both have implications for future research.

Methodological conclusions

One sort of lesson is methodological. This kind of work is difficult for three reasons. First, we found it difficult to construct even the simplest possible games in which ambiguity-aversion could be clearly revealed by incentive-compatible choices of subjects. Bounding or measuring beliefs required us to generally add chance nodes to game trees, complicating the trees substantially (and perhaps confusing some subjects). A narrower approach, using a particular theory of ambiguity to make specific predictions about choices in games, could be more fruitful.

Second, eliciting "true" beliefs is hard because we suspect that the kinds of well-structured games we used, and the mere act of measuring the ambiguity in beliefs, might reduce the measured ambiguity substantially. We chose games in which ambiguity-aversion would be clearly recognizable; our results may therefore understate the degree of ambiguity in naturally-occurring situations. Furthermore, by eliciting beliefs from choices we might have caused subjects to think harder about their beliefs than they normally would, effectively reducing their ambiguity because thought processes reduce the amount of relevant, knowable information (a la the Heisenberg uncertainty principle in physics). Better methods for extracting beliefs more unobtrusively, in a wider variety of games, would therefore be useful.

Third, in most games the effects of ambiguity-aversion are very similar to risk-aversion: Both lead people to overweight low-value payoffs compare to high-value ones (whether through subadditivity of probabilities or concave utility over outcomes). Games should be carefully constructed, as we tried to, to distinguish the two kinds of aversion. One way to distinguish ambiguity- and risk-aversion is to search for variables that affect the amount of ambiguity without affecting the distribution of outcomes (such as our fourth experiment on the order of play variable). Another way is to presume that ambiguity is reduced throughout repeated play of a game and see whether ambiguity-averse choices are reduced too (since risk-aversion, a property of preferences rather than information, should remain constant across repeated plays, except for tiny wealth effects).

Substantive lessons

The other major lesson from the data is substantive. The degree of ambiguity-aversion expressed by most subjects is modest in size. (A substantial minority are ambiguity-neutral, consistent with SEU.) We think that ambiguity is likely to be important in some natural settings, but our evidence suggests that we should look hard for settings in which ambiguity-aversion is larger than we observed, or for ways in which a small degree of ambiguity-aversion (like p(A)+p(not-A)=.95) could have important economic consequences. We have a few tentative ideas about how a little ambiguity could have big economic effects.

For example, in games with multiple equilibria, precedent often plays a strong role in "locking in" an equilibrium, perhaps a Pareto-dominated one (like the median-effort games in which the empirical equilibrium is 4 or 5 rather than the Pareto-efficient choice of 7). In some cases, a small degree of ambiguity in beliefs could be enough to tip the balance toward an initially poor equilibrium, which is locked in by the force of inertia or precedent. Behavior in early periods, when ambiguity is highest, can therefore matter in the long run, even after experience has reduced ambiguity substantially.

A second possibility is that ambiguity in beliefs may increase, rather than decrease, when aggregated across several stages of a game or across multiple players. If so, then small amounts of ambiguity about a single stage or player could lead to much larger ambiguity about the entire game. To give a numerical illustration, in some models ambiguity is expressed by assuming a set of beliefs rather than a unique distribution of belief. (For example, in the set-of-belief approach applied to the two-color Ellsberg problem, p(red) and p(black) would lie in the interval [0,1] with p(red)=1-p(black).) In the set-of-probability approach the amount of ambiguity corresponds to the size of the set. When constructing beliefs over two stages of a game, or over joint choices by two other players, ambiguity could increase with aggregation.

For example, suppose each of two players are assumed to move A or B with an ambiguous (additive) probability p(A) in [L,H] (with H>L of course). What is the distribution of probability of the two players' joint moves? Assuming the players move independently (for simplicity), one way to compute the probabilities is to multiply all elements of the sets-of-beliefs. Then p(A,A) is somewhere in $[L^2,H^2]$, p(A,B) and p(B,A) are somewhere in [L(1-H),(1-L)H], and p(B,B) is in $[(1-H)^2,(1-L)^2]$. Suppose we take H-L to be the size of the initial belief set. Then a little algebra shows that for any values of H and L, either p(A,A) or p(B,B) has a bigger belief set than p(A) does.[13] In this sense ambiguity is increased, not diminished, by aggregation across players. Since the choice studies all deal with single-player "games", and our new experiments use two-player single-stage games, we have no evidence of how the aggregation of ambiguous beliefs works. Any evidence would be useful.

A third way a little ambiguity could have a big effect is in competitive markets where ambiguity-aversion (or -preference) works like a transaction tax (or subsidy).[14] If demand and supply are highly elastic, then even if the effects of ambiguity-aversion on prices are small, the effect on the volume of trade could be large. The market for initial public offerings (IPOs) of common stock might be an example (see Yoo, 1990). IPOs are more ambiguous than "seasoned" issues because firms that make initial offers are, by definition, not yet publicly traded and usually there is less public information about their activities and prospects. (Recall the Frisch-Baron recipe for producing ambiguity: Make people aware that missing, relevant, knowable information exists.) As a result, IPOs usually rise in price immediately after their shares are issued, around 10%. This rise could be interpreted as a risk premium paid to investors for tolerating ambiguity. But perhaps the bigger effect is that the volume of IPOs issued fluctuates dramatically, creating "hot" and "cold" IPO markets, in response to relatively small changes in the risk premiums.

REFERENCES

Beard, T. R., and R. O. Beil Jr., 1994, "Do People Rely on the Self-interested Maximization of Others?", *Management Science*, 40, pp. 252-262.

Bewley, T. F., 1986, "Knightian Decision Theory: Part I", Cowles Foundation discussion paper no. 807, New Haven CT.

Brun, W. and K. Tiegen, 1990, "Prediction and Postdiction Inferences in Guessing", *Journal of Behavioral Decision Making*, 3, pp. 17-28.

Cachon, G. and C. F. Camerer, 1994, "Focal Principles, Loss-avoidance and Forward Induction in Experimental Coordination Games", University of Chicago Graduate School of Business working paper.

Camerer, C. F., and T.-H. Ho, 1994, "Violations of the Betweenness Axiom and Nonlinearity in Probability", *Journal of Risk and Uncertainty*, 8, pp. 167-196.

Camerer, C. F. and M. Weber, 1992, "Recent Developments in Modeling Preferences: Uncertainty and Ambiguity", *Journal of Risk and Uncertainty* 5, pp. 325-370.

Choquet, G., 1953-4, "Theory of Capacities", *Annales de l'Institut Fourier*, 5, pp. 131-295.

Crawford, V., 1992, "Adaptive Dynamics in Coordination Games", University of California, San Diego Department of Economics working paper 92-02.

Dow, J., Madrigal, V. and S. R. C. Werlang, 1989, "Preferences, Common Knowledge, and Speculative Trade", working paper, London Business School.

Dow, J. and S. R. C. Werlang, 1992, "Uncertainty Aversion, Risk Aversion and the Optimal Choice of Portfolio", *Econometrica*, 60, pp. 197-204.

Einhorn, H. J. and R. M. Hogarth, 1985, "Ambiguity and Uncertainty in Probabilistic Inference", *Psychological Review*, 92, pp. 433-461.

Ellsberg, D., 1961, "Risk, Ambiguity, and the Savage Axioms", *Quarterly Journal of Economics*, 75, pp. 643-669.

Frisch, D. and J. Baron, 1988, "Ambiguity and Rationality", *Journal of Behavioral Decision Making*, 1, pp. 149-157.

Gilboa, I. and D. Schmeidler, 1989, "Maxmin Expected Utility with a Non-unique Prior", *Journal of Mathematical Economics*, 18, pp. 141-153.

Heath, F. R. and A. Tversky, 1991, "Preference and Belief: Ambiguity and Competence in Choice under Uncertainty", *Journal of Risk and Uncertainty*, 4, pp. 5-28.

Keppe, H.-J. and M. Weber, 1994, "Judged Knowledge and Ambiguity-aversion", *Theory and Decision*, forthcoming.

Keynes, J. M., 1921, *A Treatise on Probability*. London: MacMillan.

Knight, F., 1921, *Risk, Uncertainty, and Profit*. Boston: Houghton Mifflin.

Machina, M. and D. Schmeidler, 1992, "A More Robust Definition of Subjective Probability", *Econometrica*, 60, pp. 745-780.

Milgrom, P. and N. Stokey, 1982, "Information, Trade, and Common Knowledge", *Journal of Economic Theory*, 26, pp. 17-27.

Ramsey, F., 1931, "Truth and Probability", in *The Foundations of Mathematics and Other Logical Essays*, London: Routledge & Kegan Paul, 1931, pp. 156-198. Reprinted in H. E. Kyburg & H. E. Smokler (Eds.), *Studies in Subjective Probability*. New York: Wiley, 1964, pp. 61-92.

Sarin, R. and P. Wakker, 1994, "A General Result for Quantifying Beliefs", *Econometrica*, 62, pp. 683-685.

Sarin, R. and R. L. Winkler, 1992, "Ambiguity and Decision Modeling: A Preference-based Approach", *Journal of Risk and Uncertainty*, 5, pp. 389-407.

Savage, L. J., 1954, *The Foundations of Statistics*. New York: Wiley.

Schmeidler, D., 1989, "Subjective Probability and Expected Utility Without Additivity", *Econometrica*, 57, pp. 571-587.

Schotter, A., Weigelt, K. and C. Wilson, 1994, "A Laboratory Investigation of Multiperson Rationality and Presentation Effects", *Games and Economic Behavior*, 6, 445-468.

Segal, U., 1987, "The Ellsberg Paradox and Risk-aversion: An Anticipated Utility Approach", *International Economic Review*, 28, pp. 175-202.

Tversky, A. and D. Kahneman, 1992, "Advances in Prospect Theory: Cumulative Representations of Uncertainty", *Journal of Risk and Uncertainty*, 5, pp. 297-323.

Van Huyck, J. B., Battalio, R. B. and R. O. Beil, Jr., 1993, "Asset Markets as an Equilibrium Selection Mechanism: Coordination Failure, Game Form Auctions, and Forward Induction", *Games and Economic Behavior*, forthcoming.

Van Huyck, J. B., Battalio, R. B. and R. O. Beil, Jr., 1991, "Strategic Uncertainty, Equilibrium Selection Principles, and Coordination Failure in Average Opinion Games", *Quarterly Journal of Economics*, 106, pp. 885-910.

Wald, A., 1950, *Statistical Decision Functions*. New York: John Wiley & Sons.

Yoo, K. R., 1990, "A Theory of Underpricing of Initial Public Offerings", working paper, MEDS Department, Northwestern University.

ENDNOTES

1. Graduate School of Business, University of Chicago, and Division of Social Sciences, California Institute of Technology; Department of Operations and Information Management, The Wharton School, University of Pennsylvania.

2. Vagueness, confidence, weight of evidence, Knightian uncertainty, and second-order uncertainty are all terms used by different authors which are roughly synonymous with "ambiguity".

3. Some readers may find it useful to conceptualize ambiguity-aversion in the following way: When players have asymmetric information, it is rational to hesitate to accept a bet offered by someone else, because that person might be better-informed. In the experiments, subjects just extend their intuition about betting in situations of asymmetric information, to situations where they do lack information but where nobody else is better informed (e.g., the Ellsberg urns).

4. The nonadditive approach and the sets-of-probabilities approach are closely related (Camerer & Weber, 1992, p. 352; Gilboa & Schmeidler, 1989). If the nonadditive probabilities are convex (i.e., $P(A \cup B) \geq P(A) + P(B) - P(A \cap B)$) then their core (defined as in cooperative game theory) is a set of probabilities; the Choquet integral over the unique nonadditive probability is the same as the minimum expected utility over the probabilities in set. Thus, the nonadditive probability is a unique, compressed way of expressing an SEU which corresponds to the minimum SEU over a set.

5. That is, $L > R$ iff $u(L) > u(R)$ iff $u(\$9) > p(l)u(\$3) + (1-p(l))u(\$10)$. If player 1 is risk-neutral, $u(x) = ax + b$ ($a > 0$) and simple algebra shows that $L > R$ implies $p(l) \geq 1/7 = .14$.

6. For example, in several variants of <u>expected</u> utility (in which probabilities are objectively known), subjects are assumed to weight probabilities nonlinearly. Putting a decision weight of .14 on an objective probability of .03 could be consistent with such theories (Tversky & Kahneman 1992; Camerer & Ho 1994).

7. For example, suppose player 1 has empirically correct beliefs, p(l)=.03, and is indifferent between L and R. Fitting a hyperbolic absolute risk-aversion (HARA) utility function yields a certainty-equivalent for a coin flip between $3 and $10 of $3.21.

8. Studies in the 1950s showed that nonsense syllables like these have few prior associations and are therefore close to "ethically-neutral" random events (a la Ramsey, 1931). The observation from experiment 1 that player 1s preferred betting on a red choice by player 2 to a black choice suggested that even fairly value-less colors like red and black might not be meaningless enough.

9. The SEU of row A is, more generally, $p(\{(1\text{-}30) \cap ZEJ\} \cup \{(1\text{-}30) \cap ZOJ\})u(\$5)$. Our analysis therefore assumes a distributivity property in which $p((A \cap B) \cup (A \cap C)) = p(A \cap (B \cup C))$ and an independence-type property in which $p(A \cap (B \cup C)) = p(A)$ when $p(B \cup C) = 1$. We think that violation of these properties is not likely to undermine our main finding-- since it is replicated by the other experiments, which do not require such assumptions-- but they might be interesting to check in further work.

10. The method is not incentive-compatible if subjects realize that consistently preferring the median-bet leads to future choices which include increasingly better ticket numbers. If subjects do this, outfoxing the experimenters, their measured beliefs will be highly super-additive; as Figure 5 below shows, they rarely appeared to be.

11. Yes-bias occurs when subjects tend to answer "yes" disproportionately often. Yes-biased subjects will give responses to questions about two complementary events, like "estimate the chance of rain tomorrow" and "estimate the chance of no rain tomorrow", which add to more than one. Rather than thinking of such subjects as irrational, we think of them as procedurally rational people who form beliefs in ambiguous situations by

imagining what will occur (or using some similar cognitive process). They find it easier to imagine an event occurring than an event not occurring, and the same for its complement, resulting in yes-bias.

12. Low variation of beliefs is surprising because there is substantial variation in the choices subjects actually made in the initial round of median-effort game experiments. Under SEU, variation of subjects' choices should be paralleled by comparable variation in their beliefs. In actual plays of the median-effort game, the relative frequencies of initial choices of effort levels from 1 to 7 were 0, .04, .13, .41, .18, .06, and .19 (n=108 total, from Cachon & Camerer 1994). Notice also that a subject who knew of these data would form beliefs of approximately $p(1..4)=.57$ and $p(5..7)=.43$, corresponding roughly to the average of our subjects' (normalized) elicited beliefs.

13. Define size of the belief set by the difference of its maximum and minimum elements. Then $p(A)$ has size H-L, $p(A,A)$ has size (H-L)(H+L) and $p(B,B)$ has size (H-L)(2-H-L). Then if H+L>1, $p(A,A)$ is bigger than $p(A)$ and if H+L<1 then $p(B,B)$ is bigger than $p(A)$.

14. For example, Dow and Werlang (1992) show how ambiguity-aversion creates a gap between buying and short-selling prices. Conversely, Dow, Madrigal & Werlang (1989) show how ambiguity-aversion can lead to speculative trading, reversing the stringent implications of the Milgrom-Stokey (1982) no-trade (or "Groucho Marx") theorem. (In their model, people do not trade initially because of ambiguity. When public information reduces the ambiguity, trading occurs.)

Appendix: Instructions for the median game experiment.

Instructions

This experiment is about choices people make. Your choices can affect the amount of money you will earn. You will make your choices on the computer after you have read these instructions.

You will make choices in each of several rounds, but you will not know the number of rounds until the experiment is over.

The median game

The choices at each round are related to a game played by participants in a previous experiment. The game is called the *median game*. The game was played by different people in several sessions.

In each session, there were nine players. Each player picked an integer in the range 1 through 7, without knowing the other players' choices. The integer that a player picked was called an *action*. The payoff to a player depended on his or her action and the *median action*. The median action is the middle one of all nine players' actions. In other words, there were as many choices above the median as below the median.

MEDIAN ACTION

ACTION	1	2	3	4	5	6	7
1	1.40	1.50	1.40	1.10	0.60	−0.10	−1.00
2	1.30	1.60	1.70	1.60	1.30	0.80	0.10
3	1.00	1.50	1.80	1.90	1.80	1.50	1.00
4	0.50	1.20	1.70	2.00	2.10	2.00	1.70
5	−0.20	0.70	1.40	1.90	2.20	2.30	2.20
6	−1.10	0.00	0.90	1.60	2.10	2.40	2.50
7	−2.20	−0.90	0.20	1.10	1.80	2.30	2.60

In each session, there were nine players. Each player picked an integer in the range 1 through 7, without knowing the other players' choices. The integer that a player picked was called an *action*. The payoff to a player depended on his or her action and the *median action*. The median action is the middle one of all nine players' actions. In other words, there were as many choices above the median as below the median.

After each player had picked an action, the median action was computed. Each player was paid according to the payoff table above, and each player knew the payoff table. The payoffs are given in dollars.

For example, suppose that a player picked action 5, and the median of the nine players' actions were 3. In that case, the player got the payoff of *1.40* dollars, as you can verify from the payoff table.

There were eight sessions of the median game. In each session, there were nine players, which makes a total of 72 people.

Your earnings

At each round, the amount of money you can earn depends either on choices by players of the median game, or on a random drawing, depending on your choices. Your make separate choices at each round.

At each round, there are two possible events, which are called RED-WIN and BLACK-WIN. The roll of a die determines which event occurs.

If the die comes out *Odd* (1,3,5), event RED-WIN occurs.

If the die comes out *Even* (2,4,6), event BLACK-WIN occurs.

Both events are equally likely.

Payoffs at each round will be determined by randomly drawing a ball from a container. In the RED-WIN event, red balls are winning balls. In the BLACK-WIN event, black balls are winning balls. If a winning ball is picked in the random drawing for either event, you get *5.00* dollars.

There are three containers, labelled **A**, **R**, and **B**. There are 100 balls in each. The composition of container **A** has been determined according to choices by players in one session of the median game. The session was chosen at random before this experiment.

If the median of the players' choices in the session was 1, 2, 3, or 4, there are 100 red balls in container A. In other words, there are 100 winning balls for RED-WIN and 0 winning balls for BLACK-WIN.

If the median of the players' choices in the session was 5, 6, or 7, there are 100 black balls in container A. In other words, there are 0 winning balls for RED-WIN and 100 winning balls for BLACK-WIN.

The number of winning balls in container **R** and container **B** will be specified separately for each round.

Your choices

At each round, you make two choices. You choose the container for the random drawing separately for each event, RED-WIN and BLACK-WIN. When making your choice at each round, you don't know which event occurs.

For RED-WIN, you choose either container **A** or container **R**.

For BLACK-WIN, you choose either container **A** or container **B**.

Before making your choice at each round, you are told the number of red balls in container **R**, and the number of black balls in container **B**. The composition of container A remains the same throughout, according to the median in a session of the previous experiment.

Payoffs

At the end of the experiment, the computer program will pick one of the rounds at random to determine your payoff. You don't know which round will be played out.

First, a die is rolled to determine which event – RED-WIN or BLACK-WIN – occurs.

If the die comes out Odd, RED-WIN occurs. In that case, a ball is picked from the container that you chose for RED-WIN (either **A** or **R**). If a winning (red) ball is picked, you get *5.00* dollars. Otherwise, you get nothing.

If the die comes out Even, BLACK-WIN occurs. In that case, a ball is picked from the container that you chose for BLACK-WIN (either **A** or **B**). If a winning (black) ball is picked, you get *5.00* dollars. Otherwise, you get nothing.

If a random drawing is needed to determine the payoffs, it will be carried out by computer.

Working on the computer

When told to do so, start working on the computer. Before making your choices, you must take a quiz to be sure that you understand the rules of the median game.

At the end, the program will determine your payoff. Your payoff will be displayed on the screen. You should leave it there until we have recorded it.

If you have any questions at the moment, please ask them. If you ever have questions when working on the computer, raise your hand. Do not hesitate to ask questions, because the instructions may sometimes be confusing. It is important that you understand the instructions before proceeding.

You can take as long as you like when making choices. To start the computer program, type

median

and press the **ENTER** key.

ON REGULAR COMPOSED TOURNAMENTS

Gilbert LAFFOND*
Jean LAINE**
Jean-Francois LASLIER *

INTRODUCTION

The purpose of this paper is to present and provide several results dealing with the concept of composed tournament. This concept has been introduced by Fried & Lakser (1971) and has deserved some attention only as a pure graph-theoretical notion. Using the fact that the tournament structure may be relevant for various areas in Decision Theory, including Social Choice (and especially theory of voting games), our first aim is to give some insights of such a concept from this last perspective.

A wide range of researches has been devoted to the study of alternative solution concepts for choice problems involving a tournament structure (see Laffond, Laslier & Lebreton (1992) for a progress report). Among all properties a "satisfactory" solution may share, some attention has been paid to the composition consistency property. This property has a quite natural meaning, which is to allow for a solution to be either directly computed, or to follow (whenever it

---

* Laboratoire d'Econométrie, Conservatoire des Arts et Métiers, 2, rue Conté, Paris, France
**Department of Economics, University of Keele, Keele, Staffordshire, ST5 5BG, UK
The authors wish to thank Bernard Monjardet and Michel Lebreton for very helpful comments, and all participants to the FUR VI Conference for suggestions of possible ways to imporve the presentation of an earlier draft.

is possible) a two-step procedure. This procedure precisely rests on the concept of composed tournament. In a rather unformal way, a tournament T is composed if it can be "summarized" by (or reduced to) a tournament T^* defined on a partition of T into subtournaments (called "components"). Then, given a solution Σ, the two-step procedure consists in applying in a first step Σ for T^*, i.e. selecting the "winning" subtournaments, and secondly, applying Σ within each of them. If each node of the initial tournament T is interpreted as a specific investment decision and T is composed, then each subtournament T' in the partition of T may be seen as a general project, and a node in T' as a variant of this project. A composition-consistent solution Σ is then such that it selects the best variants of the best projects. Hence our first purpose is to examine a specific property shared by tournaments, which has been introduced as a convenient way to define "satisfactory" solution concepts.

Our second purpose is to provide several new results dealing with the existence and properties of composed tournaments which belong to the specific class of regular tournaments. Existence results examine the lowest possible order of a regular composed tournament, whereas the remaining ones deal with the number and the order of its components.

The sequel is organized as follows : Part 1 is devoted to a formal presentation and some interpretations of the notion of composed tournament, as well as to a discussion of the related literature. All results are presented in Part 2. We conclude with several comments on open questions.

PART 1 : ON THE NOTION OF COMPOSED TOURNAMENT

A tournament is a pair (I,E), where I is a set and $E \subseteq I^2$ is a binary relation such that for any pair $\{x,y\} \subseteq I$, one and only one of the following situations prevails : $(x,y) \in E$, $(y,x) \in E$, $x = y$. Hence E is a complete asymmetric binary relation defined on T. We will restrict ourselves to finite tournaments. A graph-theoretical approach is to define a tournament T = (I,E) as a directed graph, where I = $\{1,...i,...n\}$ is the set of vertices or nodes (n is called the order of T) and E is the set of edges. T (resp. $T(I)$, T_n) will denote the set of all tournaments (resp. of tournaments on I, of order n).

We define for any node i the set of i's successors (resp. predecessors) by $D_T^+(i) = \{j \in I \text{ s.t. } (i,j) \in E\}$ (resp. $D_T^-(i) = \{j \in I \text{ s.t, } (j,i) \in E\}$). The integer $d_T^+(i) = |D_T^+(i)|$ (resp. $d_T^-(i) = |D_T^-(i)|$) is called i's outscore (resp. i's inscore). The outscore (resp. inscore) of T is defined by $d^+(T) = \text{Min } \{d_T^+(i), i \in I\}$ (resp. $d^-(T) = \text{Min } \{d_T^-(i), i \in I\}$. T is said to be regular whenever $d^+(T) = d_T^+(i) \ \forall \ i \in I$. Furthermore, T is said to be strong if for any two nodes i and j, there exists two sequences $S = \{i_h, 0 \leq h \leq H\}$ and $S' = \{i'_h, 0 \leq h \leq H'\}$ such that $i_0 = i = i'_{H'}$, $i'_H = j = i'_0$ and $(i_h, i_{h+1}) \in E, 0 \leq h \leq H-1$, $(i'_h, i'_{h+1}) \in E, 0 \leq h \leq H'-1$ (S and S' are called respectively path from i to j and path from j to i). It is easy to prove that a regular tournament is strong. Moreover, T is said to be irreducible if there is no partition of I into two non-empty subsets A and B such that $(i,j) \in E \ \forall \ i \in A, \ \forall \ j \in B$. It is well-known that T is irreducible iff T is strong (see e.g. Moon (1968) Theorem 2 page 5).

The tournament structure has been used in various research fields, involving Statistics (see David (1966) and Kendall (1970)), Social Choice Theory (see Moulin (1986) and the references quoted there), and especially Voting Game Theory. Let us briefly recall the formal definition of a voting game : denote by $C = \{1,...,n\}$ a finite set of candidates, and by $V = \{v_1,...,v_M\}$ a finite set of voters. A voting game is defined as an ordered pair $V = (V,C)$ where $C \subseteq (2^V - \emptyset)$ is the set of winning or all-powerful coalitions. Special attention has been paid to the specific class of quota games: a q-quota game is a voting game where $C \in \mathcal{C}$ iff $|C| > q$. The voting game associated with the majority rule is a E(0.5M+1)-quota game. If each voter has preferences on I which are represented by a strict order R_h ($1 \leq h \leq M$), a social state i will be said to dominate j (denoted $(i,j) \in R$) if there exists $C \in \mathcal{C}$ such that $(i,j) \in R_h \ \forall \ v_h \in C$. This dominance relation clearly induces a directed graph $G = (I,E)$ where I is the set of vertices and E the set of edges defined by $(i,j) \in E$ iff $(i,j) \in R$. In the case of a majority game, G will be a tournament, unless m is even and ties occur. Mc Garvey (1953) has shown that any tournament can be induced by a majority game (see also Stearns (1968). The general emptiness of the core of majority games is the main reason why numerous studies have been devoted to the search for a "satisfactory" solution concept (the reader may refer to Laffond, Laslier & Lebreton (1992) for a progress report in this area).

Due to the wide range of approaches involving a tournament structure, it is not surprising that a given concept may be studied at least twice under a different name. This is the case for the concept of composed tournament, which can be defined as follows:

Definition 1 Let $T = (I,E) \in T(I)$ and $J \subseteq I$. J is called a component for T if $J \neq \emptyset$ and $\forall (i,j) \in (I-J)^2$, $\forall h \in J$, $(i,h) \in E$ if and only if $(j,h) \in E$.

Definition 2 Let $T = (I,E) \in T(I)$. Then T is called a composed tournament if I can be partitioned into k components for T, where $1 \leq k \leq n$. Moreover, T is said to be strongly composed if I is composed and no component for T is a singleton. A partition of a composed (resp. strongly composed) tournament T into components for T is called a (resp. strong) decomposition of T.

Let $I^* = \{I_1,...,I_K\}$ be a decomposition of I for $T = (I,E)$. It is easily seen that there exists a tournament $T^* = (I^*, E^*)$, whose nodes are the elements of I^*, and edges are defined by $(I_k, I_{k'}) \in E^*$ if and only if $\exists (i_k, i_{k'}) \in I_k \times I_{k'}$ such that $(i_k, i_{k'}) \in E$. This tournament T^* will be called summary of T (through the decomposition I^*).

Then, a composed tournament $T = (I,E)$ of order n, with a decomposition $\overset{*}{I}$ into k components, can be derived from a tournament $T^* = (I^*, E^*)$ of order k, by exploding each vertex in I^* into a set of "clones", and by orienting edges between two clones of different types according to the dominance in T^*. Another way to state the idea is the following : if $T = (I,E)$ is a composed tournament of order n, then there exist $T' = (\{1,...,K\}, E') \in \mathcal{T}_K$ and K subtournaments $T_1,...,T_K$ resp. defined on non-empty and mutually disjoint sets $I_1,...,I_K$ such that $|I_i| = n_i$, $1 \le i \le n$, and $\sum_i n_i = n$, such that T' is a summary of T through $\{I_1,...,I_K\}$, and T is a (multiple) composition product of T' via $T_1,...,T_K$, where a composition product is defined in the following way :

Definition 3 Let $T' = (I', E') \in \mathcal{T}_K$ and $T = (I_1, E_1), ..., T_K = (I_K, E_K)$ be K tournaments of respective orders n_k. The multiple composition product of T' via $T_1,...,T_K$ is the tournament $T = (I,E)$ of order $n = \sum_{1 \le k \le K} n_k$ defined on $I = \bigcup_{1 \le k \le K} I_k$ by : $\forall \{k,k'\} \subseteq I'$, $\forall i \in I_k$, $\forall j \in I_{k'}$, $(i,j) \in E$ if and only if either $k=k'$ and $(x,y) \in E_k$, or $k \ne k'$ and $(k,k') \in E'$. T will be denoted by $T = \Pi(T' ; T_1, ..., T_K)$.

It is straightforward to check that a composition product defines a tournament. Moreover, it is obviously seen that a tournament is composed if and only if it can be defined as a composition product of a tournament of order > 1 via tournaments of order ≥ 1, with at least one strict inequality.

Furthermore, a composed tournament T is usually called non-simple in the Graph Theory literature, whereas components of T are called convex subsets of T (see Fried & Lakser (1971), who introduced the concept), Erdos & alii (1972a),(1972b), Moon (1972) and Imrich & Nesetril (1992)). Moon (1968) calls product of a tournament T' of order n by a tournament T" of order m the tournament T = Π(T' ; T",...,T") of order nm. We use a terminology adopted in Reid & Beineke (1978), who offer a more recent (but less complete) survey on the theory of tournaments than in Moon (1968).

It is worth stressing on the fact that the composition product of a tournament defined above is a specific formalization of a more general and abstract concept of product which may be relevant for various discrete structures (such as boolean functions, set systems and relations). Such a concept (called substitution-decomposition) is presented and studied in Mohring & Radermacher (1984). As a further proof of the diversity of terminologies adopted in the literature is that these authors call "autonomous parts" the components of a (composed) tournament.

Many results about composed tournaments are already known. Erdos & alii (1972a),(1972b) and Moon (1972) have proved that any composed tournament of order n can be embedded in a simple one by adding up only one vertex, except for two specific classes of tournaments. Several properties shared by the components of a composed tournament may be found in Astie-Vidal & Matteo (1987). These authors also provide an $O(n^3)$-algorithm which allows to determine all the component of a regular composed tournament of order n (hence allowing to determine in polynomial time whether a regular tournament is composed or not). The reader may refer to Bouchet (1987) and Cunningham (1982) for algorithms dealing with non-regular tournaments. It should be added that some results presented in Astie-Vidal & Matteo (1987) are either extended or proved with simpler arguments in the sequel.

Let us conclude this part with further comments on the concept of composed tournament, from a Social Choice perspective. As pointed out above, a very convenient approach is to consider a tournament T = (I,E) as a representation of a majority game, where (i,j) ∈ E iff a majority of voters prefers candidate i to candidate j. Let us define a Social Choice function (or solution correspondence) as a multivalued mapping Σ defined on $\mathcal{T}$ which associates with each T = (I,E) in $\mathcal{T}$ a subset Σ(T) of nodes, called the set of Σ-winners of T.

Moreover, assume that a specific solution correspondence Σ has been chosen. If T is composed, then the (majority) dominance relation E can be "summarized" in a relation E^* defined as the restriction of E to a proper subset of candidates I^*. Indeed, it is possible to compute the set of Σ-winners using a two-step procedure where (1) one computes the set of Σ-winners in the summary of T, then (2) one computes the set of Σ-winners in each of the previous "winning" components. One of the properties which are usually required for a solution Σ to be satisfactory is that it should not be sensitive to this two-step computation process, i.e. should yield the same winners if applied directly to I or if applied to the set of all components of T and then on winners in each of those components. This property is called "composition consistency". Formally, Σ is said to be composition consistent if for all $n \geq 1$ and for all $T \in \mathcal{T}_n$, $T_1, ..., T_n \in \mathcal{T}$, it satisfies $\Sigma(\Pi(T; T_1, ..., T_n)) = \cup \{\Sigma(T_h), h \in \Sigma(T)\}$ (see Laffond, Laslier & Lebreton (1992) for results on the solution correspondences sharing this property).

Such a property is related to solution correspondences, whereas the "composability" is a property dealing with tournaments, whatever the solution Σ being selected. From this point of view, our approach consists in completing all studies involving the composition consistency property by examining those tournaments for which the two-step procedure described above is possible, whatever one chooses as a solution correspondence Σ. Furthermore, the specific structure of (regular) composed tournaments has been widely used in Laffond, Laslier & Lebreton (1993) for the presentation and the study of a solution concept, called the "Bipartisan Set".

A convenient illustration of the concept of composed tournament may be borrowed from political science. Indeed, it is usual for electoral systems to follow a multi-step procedure, which involves voters' opinions first in the selection of one or several representatives of coalitions of candidates (say political parties), and then in a further selection of one or several winners among these representatives. If the tournament $T = (I,E)$ resulting from a given a profile of voters' preferences is composed, then its components may represent political parties. Hence, a partition of I into components will correspond to a political structure, i.e. a set of political parties. Moreover, this structure shares a consistency property, in the sense that pairwise comparisons (using the majority rule) between candidates are entirely determined by pairwise comparisons between their respective parties: indeed, a candidate from a party A beats a candidate from party B iff any candidate from A beats any candidate from B, according to the majority rule.

PART 2 : EXISTENCE AND PROPERTIES OF REGULAR COMPOSED TOURNAMENTS

Let us consider first the question of the existence of regular composed tournaments. It is fairly simple to prove that a regular tournament has an odd order, and that there exists no regular composed tournament whose order is strictly inferior to 9. Furthermore, a very simple way to get a RCT is the following : consider a regular tournament $T = (I,E)$ of order $n = 2k + 1$. Then explode each node $i \in I$ into a regular tournament T_i of order $2z + 1$, where $z \in N^*$. It follows that $T' = \Pi(T ; T_1, ..., T_n)$ is a RCT of order $m = (2k+1)(2z+1)$. This elementary procedure allows to obtain the following first existence result :

Theorem 1 For any non-prime odd integer $n \geq 9$, there exists a regular composed tournament of order n.

Proof : We first claim that $\forall\, n \in 2.N + 1$, $\exists\, T = (I,E)$ a regular tournament of order n. Indeed, define $T^* = (I^*, E^*)$ by $I^* = \{1,...,n\}$, and $E^* = \{(i,i+x),\ 1 \leq x \leq d,\ 1 \leq i \leq n-d\} \cup \{(n-d+1, n-d+1+x),\ x \in \{1,...,d-1,d-n\}\} \cup \{(n-d+2, n-d+2+x),\ x \in \{1,...,d-2,d-n,d-n+1\}\} \cup ... \cup \{(n,x),\ 1 \leq x \leq d\}$, where $d = 0.5n$. Hence, E^* is defined such that $(i,j) \in E^*$ if and only if $(i-j) \in \{1,...,0.5n\}$ (mod. n). Any tournament isomorphic to T^* will be said to be cyclical. It is easily seen that any cyclical tournament is regular. Now, let n be any odd non-prime integer. Then, $\exists\, m, p \in 2N + 1$ s.t. $n = mp$, where $p \leq m$.

Define $T = (I,E)$ by $T = \Pi(T^* ; T_1, ..., T_p)$, where T^* is cyclical of order p and T_i is cyclical of order m, $1 \leq i \leq p$. This completes the proof, since T is a RCT of order n

The argument above is valid only for non-prime orders. Hence, it is worth trying to answer the four following questions :
- Is there any regular composed tournament (RCT) whose order is a prime integer ?
- If so, what is the minimal order a such a tournament ?
- Is there any strongly composed regular tournament (SCRT) whose order is a prime integer ?
- If so, what is the minimal order of such a tournament ?
The next result gives addresses to the first two questions :

Theorem 2 There exists a regular composed tournament of order equal to 11.

Proof : Let $T = (I,E)$ be defined by $I = \{a_1, ..., a_4, b_1, ..., b_3, c_1, ..., c_4\}$ and
- $(a_1, a_2), (a_1, a_3), (a_2, a_3), (a_2, a_4), (a_3, a_4), (a_4, a_1) \in E$
- $(c_1, c_2), (c_1, c_3), (c_2, c_3), (c_2, c_4), (c_3, c_4), (c_4, c_1) \in E$
- $(b_1, b_2), (b_2, b_3), (b_3, b_1) \in E$
- $(a_i, b_j) \in E, i \in \{1,...,4\}, j \in \{1,2,3\}$
- $(b_j, c_k) \in E, j \in \{1,2,3\}, k \in \{1,...,4\}$
- $(c_k, a_i) \in E, k \in \{1,2\}, i \in \{1,2\}$
- $(c_1, a_3), (c_2, a_4) \in E$
- $(c_k, a_i) \in E, k \in \{3,4\}, i \in \{1,...,4\}$
- $(a_3, c_2), (a_4, c_1) \in E$

Then it is obviously seen that T is a RCT, hence the result.

It is easily checked that no RCT exists whose order is 3, 5 or 7. Hence 11 is the smallest prime order for a RCT. Moreover, Laffond

& allii (1994) have recently proved that a RCT does exist for any (odd) order greater than 13. The following proposition shows the existence of a SCRT having a prime order:

Theorem 3 There exists a strongly composed regular tournament T^* of order 61.

Proof : The construction of T^* rests on the following general procedure : let $T = (I,E) = \Pi(T'; T_1,...,T_n)$ be a RCT, where $T' = (\{T_1,...,T_n\}, E')$ and where the component $T = (I_1, E_1)$ is of order p. The T_1-extended tournament from T, denoted by $T'' = (I'', E'')$ is then defined by $T'' = \Pi(\tilde{T}; T_1, T_1', T_1'', T_2,...,T_n)$, where T_1' and T_1'' are replica of T_1, and where the summary $\tilde{T} = (\{T_1, T_1', T_1'', T_2,...,T_n\}, \tilde{E})$ is defined by:

- $(T_h, T_k) \in \tilde{E}$ iff $(T_h, T_k) \in E'$ $\forall$ $h,k \in \{1,...,n\}$
- $(T_h, T_1') \in \tilde{E}$ $\forall$ $T_h \in D_{T'}^-(T_1)$
- $(T_1', T_h) \in \tilde{E}$ $\forall$ $T_h \in D_{T'}^+(T_1)$
- $(T_h, T_1'') \in \tilde{E}$ $\forall$ $T_h \in D_{T'}^+(T_1)$
- $(T_1'', T, \text{or}_h) \in \tilde{E}$ $\forall$ $T_h \in D_{T'}^-(T_1)$
- $(T_1, T_1'), (T_1', T_1''), (T_1'', T_1) \in \tilde{E}$.

It is easily verified that T'' is regular. Now consider the tournament $T = (I,E)$ defined in the following way : let C_3 and C_5 be respectively the cyclical tournament of order 3 and 5. Moreover, let

- $T = \Pi(T'; T_1, T_2, T_3)$ where $T' = C_3$.
- $T_1 = \Pi(T_1'; T_{11}, T_{12}, T_{13})$, where $T_1' = C_3$ and each $T_{1k} = C_5$, $1 \leq k \leq 3$.
- T_3 is a replica of T_1

- $T_2 = \Pi(T_2'\,;T_{21}',...,T_{25}')$, where $T_2' = C_5$ and each $T_{2k}' = C_3$
Now denote by $\tilde{T}$ the T_{21}-extended tournament from T. Then $\tilde{T}$ is regular of order 51. Finally, denote by T^{**} the T_{11}-extended tournament from $\tilde{T}$. Thus T^{**} is a SCRT of order 61.

Iterating the construction above allows to built a SCRT for any order equal to $45 + 6x + 10y$ ($x, y \geq 0$). The reader may verify that this ensures the existence of a SCRT for any (odd) order greater than 61. This is the exact lower possible prime order of a SCRT :

Theorem 4 There is no strongly composed regular tournament whose order is a prime integer lower than 61.
Proof : It consists of an exhaustive study of all tournaments having a prime order in $\{11,...,59\}$, using the three following facts :
a) Any decomposition of a RCT involves a partition of the set of its vertices into subsets of odd cardinality (this follows directly from Astie-Vidal & Matteo (1987), theorem 1 page 8, who have pointed out that any component of a RCT is a regular subtournament of T).
b) Any decomposition of a RCT of prime order involves at least two components having different orders.
c) Let $T = (I,E)$ be a RCT of order n and let D be a decomposition of T. Denote by C^* a component in D having a maximum order c^*. Then $c^* \leq \frac{n}{3}$. A slightly more precise version of this result can be found in Astie-Vidal & Matteo (1987) (see theorem 2 page 7), at the cost of a rather long proof. A very simple argument which proves this claim is the following : let $A = D_T^-(i)$, $i \in C^*$, $B = D_T^+(i)$, $i \in C^*$. It follows from the regularity of T that $|A| = |B| = 0.5.(n - c^*)$. Moreover, $d_T^+(i) = 0.5.(n-1)$ for any $i \in I$ and $\exists j \in A$ s.t. $d_{T'}^+(j) \geq 0.5.(|A| - 1)$, where T' is the subtournament of T generated by A. Furthermore, it must be true that $d_{T'}^+(h) + c^* \leq 0.5.(n-1)$ $\forall h \in A$. Hence $0.5.(|A| - 1) + c^* \leq 0.5.(n-1)$, thus $0.5.(0.5.(n-c) - 1) + c^* \leq 0.5.(n-1)$. This implies $c^* \leq \frac{n}{3}$.

The computation of all cases is straightforward but rather long. We present here the study of two cases, leaving to the reader its replication to the remaining ones. For each case, we suppose that a SRCT does exist. Then the three facts above impose some constraints on the order of each component. Finally, it is shown that these constraints are not compatible with the regularity requirement.

CASE 1 : $n = 23$ ($\Rightarrow d^+(T) = 11$)

Then $c^* \in \{5,7\}$ from b) and c). Assume that $c^* = 7$: thus $|A| = |B| = 8$ and the only partitions of A and B into subsets of odd cardinality (using a)) are $P_A = \{A_1, A_2\}$ and $P_B = \{B_1, B_2\}$, where $|A_1| = |B_1| = 5$, $|A_2| = |B_2| = 3$. Define for $C \subseteq A$, $d'(C) = |D_T^+(j) \cap [I-(C \cup C^*)]|$, where j is some vertex in C. Then $d'(A_1) = 11 - c^* - 0.5(|A_1| - 1) = 2$, which is clearly impossible. Now assume that $c^* = 5$: thus $|A| = |B| = 9$ and the only partitions of A and B into subsets of odd cardinality are $P_A = \{A_1, A_2, A_3\}$ and $P_B = \{B_1, B_2, B_3\}$, where $|A_i| = |B_i| = 3$, $i = 1,2,3$. Then $d'(A_1) = 5$, which is incompatible with P_A and P_B.

CASE 2 : $n = 29$ ($\Rightarrow d^+(T) = 14$)

Then $c^* \in \{5,7,9\}$. Assume $c^* = 9$. Thus $|A| = |B| = 10$ and we get for A and B two possible partitions $P_A^1 = \{A_1^1, A_2^1\}$, $P_A^2 = \{A_1^2, A_2^2\}$, $P = \{B_1^1, B_2^1\}$, $P = \{B_1^2, B_2^2\}$, where $|A_1^1| = |B_1^1| = |A_2^1| = |B_2^1| = 5$, $|A_1^2| = |B_1^2| = 7$ and $|A_2^2| = |B_2^2| = 3$. If P_1^A prevails, then $d'(A_1^1) = d'(A_2^1) = 3$, hence P_B^2 prevails. This implies that $|D_T^+(i) \cap [I-B_2^2]| \le 7$, $i \in B_2^2$, a contradiction. Hence P_A^2 prevails. Then $d'(A_1^1) = 2$, which is clearly impossible. Assume now that $c^* = 7$. Thus $|A| = |B| = 11$ and we get for A and B only one partition $P_A = \{A_1, A_2, A_3\}$ and $P_B = \{B_1, B_2, B_3\}$, where $|A_i| = |B_i| = 3$, $i = 1,2$ and $|A_3| = |B_3| = 5$. Then $d'(A_3) = 5$, which implies that $|D_T^+(i) \cap [I-B_3]| \le 12$, $i \in B_3$, a contradiction. Finally, assume that $c^* = 5$. Thus $|A| = |B| = 12$, which implies that the only partitions of A and B are $P_A = \{A_1, A_2, A_3, A_4\}$ and $P_B = \{B_1, B_2, B_3, B_4\}$, where $|A_i| = |B_i| = 3$, $i \in \{1,...,4\}$. Then $d'(A_1) = 8$, which is clearly impossible

Let us turn now to several properties shared by regular composed tournaments. A first set of properties deals with the number and the properties of components involved in a decomposition. The next proposition shows that any decomposition of a RCT involves an odd number of regular subtournaments:

Theorem 5 Any decomposition of a regular composed tournament has an odd number of components. Moreover, any of its component is regular.

Proof: The first claim is an immediate corollary of results proved in Laffond, Laslier & Lebreton (1993) (see also Fisher and Ryan (1991a), (1991b)). This paper studies a solution concept for tournaments called Bipartisan Set defined in the following way: given a tournament T, it is possible to design a two-player symmetric zero-sum game, in which each player chooses an outcome (i.e. a vertex) and wins iff this outcome dominates (according to T), her opponent's choice. It can be proved that such a game has a unique mixed-strategy Nash equilibrium. The Bipartisan Set contains all equilibrium outcomes, i.e. is the support of equilibrium strategies. Furthermore, it is shown that the set of all tournaments $T = (I,E)$ having I as Bipartisan Set is the set of all tournaments which are a summary of some RCT. Finally, it is proved that the Bipartisan Set of any tournament has an odd cardinality. Hence the first assertion of the theorem. The second part of theorem 4 is already proved in Astie-Vidal & Matteo (1987) (see theorem 1 page 6). A shorter proof of their result is the following: $T = (I,E)$ be a regular tournament of order n such that $T = \Pi(T'; T_1,...,T_H)$ where the order of T' is H and $T_h = (I_h, E_h)$, $1 \leq h \leq H$. Let $n = 2m+1$, $H = 2k+1$ and $i,j \in I_h$. Then $D_T^+(i) \cap (I - I_h) = D_T^+(j) \cap (I - I_h)$. Hence $|D_T^+(i) \cap I_h| = |D_T^+(j) \cap I_h|$, which means that T_h is regular.

Other results on the number of components with a given cardinality m in a tournament of order n > m can be found in Astie-Vidal & Matteo (1987). The next result consists in a characterization of all RCT having a regular summary. A useful intermediate step toward this result is the following :

Lemma Let T be a RCT ; then there is no decomposition of T having a regular summary and at least one singleton as a component.

Proof : Let T = (I,E) be a regular tournament such that T = Π(T' ; T_1 ,...,T_H) where T' = (I',E') is regular of order 2k+1 and T_h = (I_h, E_h), 1≤h≤H. It follows from theorem 5 that each T_h is regular ; let $|I_h|$ = $2d_h$ +1, 0≤h≤H. Now suppose that $|I_1|$ = 1. For j ∈ I denote by h(j) the integer such that j ∈ $I_{h(j)}$. Since T is regular, let $d_T^+(i) = m \ \forall \ i \in I$. Then we can write :

$$d_h + \sum_{j \in D_{T'}^+(i)} [2d_{h(j)} + 1] = m, i \in I_h, h \in I = \{1,...,H\} \quad (1)$$

(1) may be rewritten in the following way, from the fact that $d_1 = 0$:

$$d_h + 2 [\sum_{j \in D_{T'}^+(i)} d_{h(j)}] = m - k, i \in I_h, h \in I = \{2,...,H\} \quad (2)$$

$$2 [\sum_{j \in D_{T'}^+(i)} d_{h(j)}] = m - k, i \in I_1 \quad (3)$$

Finally, we claim that $d_h = 0 \ \forall \ h \in I'$: indeed, (3) implies that m-k is even, hence d_h is even $\forall \ h \in I'$ using (2). Let b be the maximal integer such that $d_h \in 2^b \mathbb{N} \ \forall \ h \in \{1,...,H\}$. Then b is well-defined, except if $d_h = 0$ for any h. It follows from (3) that m-k ∈ $2^{b+1}\mathbb{N}$ and from (2) that $d_h \in 2^{b+1}\mathbb{N} \ \forall \ h$, clearly a contradiction. Thus $d_h = 0$ for all h, which means that all the components of T are reduced to singletons.

Then we get the following characterization of RCT having a regular summary :

Theorem 6 Let $T = (I,E)$ be a regular tournament of order n such that $T = \Pi(T' ; T_1 ,...,T_H)$ where $T' = (I',E') \in T_h$ and $T_h = (I_h ,E_h) \in T$, $1 \le h \le H$. Then T' is regular if and only if all the components T_h have the same order.

Proof : The sufficiency part is straightforward. In order to prove the necessity part, note first that it follows from theorem 5 that T_h is regular, $1 \le h \le H$. Denote by d_h the outscore of T_h in T. Let $d = \text{Min} \{d_h , 1 \le h \le H\}$. Then we claim that there exists a regular composed tournament $T'' = (I'',E'') = \Pi(\tilde{T} ; T''_1 ,...,T''_H)$ such that :

- $\tilde{T}$ is regular
- $\tilde{T}$ is isomorphic to T' and $|\Phi(I''_h)| = |I''_h| - 2d$, $1 \le h \le H$, where Φ denotes the isomorphism from $\tilde{T}$ to T' and I''_h is the vertex set of $\tilde{T}_h$
- Min $\{d''_h, 1 \le h \le H\} = 0$, where d''_h is the outscore of any vertex in T''_h (i.e. there exists a component of T'' which is reduced to a singleton)

Indeed, define I''_h by deleting 2d vertices in I_h, $1 \le h \le H$. Furthermore, define E'' by :
- If $i \in I''_h, j \in I''_{h'}$ where $h' \ne h$, then $(i,j) \in E'' \Leftrightarrow (h,h') \in E'$
- T''_h is any regular tournament of order $2(d_h -d)+1$, $1 \le h \le H$ (such a tournament exists, for instance the cyclical tournament).

It is easily seen that T' is a RCT, and that T is isomorphic to T'. By construction, the outscore of a vertex i has decreased of d inside its component T_h and of $d^+_T(h).d$ outside T_h . The whole tournament T'' is obviously regular, whereas one of its component is by construction a singleton, hence the claim. Now, applying the lemma above to T'' proves that all the components of T have the same order, hence the necessity part of the theorem

An immediate corollary of this result is that if a RCT has a prime number of vertices, then it will admit no decomposition with a regular summary.

FURTHER COMMENTS

The following remarks will be made as a conclusion :
1) Composability is an intrinsec property shared by a tournament, and does not refers directly to the standart problem of defining a solution concept. However, a rather close relationship obviously prevails between composability and composition consistency. In order to suggest further related research, let us consider the Copeland solution defined by $\Sigma_c(T) = \{i^* \in I \text{ s.t. } d_T^+(i^*) \geq d_T^+(i), i \in I\}$. It is well-known that Σ_c is not composition-consistent. Then, the following question naturally arises : is it possible to characterize the set T^c of all tournaments such that the Copeland solution is composition consistent when computed for these tournaments. This problem may be easily extended to any potential solution correspondence, using the following related notion of composability : a solution correspondence Σ is said to be composable for $T \in T$ if $\forall\, T' \in T_n$, $T_1, ..., T_n \in T$ such that $T = \Pi(T'\,;\, T_1, ..., T_n)$ and $\Sigma(T) = \cup\{\Sigma(T_h), h \in \Sigma(T')\}$.

Denote by $T(\Sigma)$ the set of tournaments for which Σ is composable. A tournament T in $T(\Sigma)$ is simply a tournament for which it is equivalent to compute the solution set either directly or through a two-stage procedure, which first selects the "winning components", and then selects the "winning points" within each winning component). This allows for the general problem to be stated as follows : given a solution correspondence Σ, find the set $T(\Sigma)$ of all tournaments for which Σ is composable.

It is worth noting that one may conceive such a problem in two different ways according to whether the solution Σ is or not composition consistent : indeed, the problem reduces in the first case to the characterization of composed tournaments whereas it is much more demanding in the second case.

An immediate corollary of theorem 5 consists of the following partial characterization of the set T^c of all regular tournaments for which the Copeland solution is composable (notice that it implies that there is no regular tournament in T^c having an order equal to a prime integer) : a regular tournament belongs to T^c if and only if it is composed and all its components have the same order (notice that it implies that there is no regular tournament in T^c having an order equal to a prime integer).

2) The regular case is obviously a very special one. Hence, a rather natural direction for further studies is to allow for less specific tournament structures, i.e. to examine the existence and properties of composed tournaments whose score vectors share more general properties. Nevertheless, Laffond, Laslier & Lebreton (1992) have pointed out that the class of regular composed tournament may be a useful reference for the existence and properties of specific solution concepts. It should be added that another explicit reference to regular composed tournaments can be found in Laffond & Lainé (1993), where alternative concepts of Strong Uncovered Sets are examined.

REFERENCES

A. Astie-Vidal & A. Matteo, 1987, " Non Simple Tournaments : Theoretical Properties and a Polynomial Agorithm " Proceedings of the 5th International Conference AAECC, *Lecture Notes in Computer Science*, Vol. **356**, pp. 1-15

L.W. Beineke, K.B. Reid, 1978, " Tournaments ", Chapter 7 in *Selected Topics in Graph Theory*, L.W. Beineke and R.J. Wilson (Eds), Academic Press.

A. Bouchet, 1987, " Digraph Decompositions and Eulerian Systems " *SIAM Journal of Alg. Methods*, Vol. **8**, N0 3.

W.H. Cunningham, 1982, " Decomposition of Directed Graphs " *SIAM Journal of Alg. Methods*, Vol. **3**, N0 2.

H.A. David, 1968, *The Method of Paired Comparisons*, Griffin's Statistical Monographs and Courses, Griffin, London.

P. Erdos, E. Fried, A. Hajnal & E.C. Milner, 1972, " Some Remarks on Simple Tournaments " *Algebra Universalis*, Vol. **2**, pp. 238-245.

P. Erdos, A. Hajnal & E.C. Milner, 1972, " Simple One-Point Extentions of Tournaments " *Mathematika*, Vol. **19**, pp. 57-62.

E. Fried & H. Lakser, 1971, " Simple Tournaments " *Notices of the American Mathematical Society*, Vol. **18**, p. 295.

D.C. Fisher, J. Ryan, 1991a, " Optimal Strategies for a Generalized "Scissors,Paper, and Stone " Game " *Mimeo*.

D.C. Fisher, J. Ryan, 1992b, " Tournament Games and Positive Tournaments " *Mimeo*.

W. Imrich & J. Nesetril, 1992, "Simple Tournaments and Sharply Transitive Groups", *Discrete Mathematics*, Vol. **108**, pp. 159-165.

M.G. Kendall, 1970, *Rank Correlation Methods* Griffin, London.

G. Laffond, J. Lainé, 1994, " Weak Covering Relations in Tournaments " forthcoming in *Theory & Decision* .

G. Laffond, J. Lainé, J.F. Laslier, 1994, "Existence of Regular Composed Tournaments", *mimeo*, CNAM.

G. Laffond, J.F. Laslier, M. Lebreton, 1992, " Condorcet Choice Correspondences: A Full Set-theoretical Comparison " forthcoming in *Mathematical Social Sciences*.

G. Laffond, J.F. Laslier, M. Lebreton, 1993, " The Bipartisan Set of a Tournament Game ", *Games & Economic Behavior*, Vol. **5**, pp. 182-201.

D.S. Mc Garvey, 1953, " A Theorem on the Construction of Voting Paradoxes ", *Econometrica*, Vol. **21**, pp. 608-610.

R.H. Mohring & F.J. Radermacher, 1984, " Substitution Decomposition for Discrete Structures and Connections with Combinatorial Optimization", *Annales of Discrete Mathematics*, Vol. **19**, pp. 257-356.

J.W. Moon, 1968, *Topics on Tournaments*, Holt, Rinehart and Winston.

J.W. Moon, 1972, "Embedding Tournaments in Simple Tournaments", *Discrete Mathematics*, Vol. **2**, pp. 389-395.

H. Moulin, 1986, " Choosing From a Tournament ", *Social Choice & Welfare*, Vol. **2**, pp. 271-291.

R. Stearns, 1959, " The Voting Problem ", *American Mathematical Monthly*, Vol. **66**, pp. 761-763.

MARKET GAMES WITH ASYMMETRIC INFORMATION:
THE CORE WITH FINITELY MANY STATES OF THE WORLD

Beth Allen[*]

1. Introducton

The purpose of this paper is to present a treatment of the core of an economy with asymmetric information. More generally, an important implication of this work is the introduction of information into cooperative games, both with and without transferable utility. In fact, this analysis exploits the features of games derived from exchange economies with asymmetric information to limit commitments and thus one can use the game-theoretic machinery of balanced games as a very convenient means to guarantee nonempty cores.

In this paper, the assumption that there are only (essentially) finitely many states of the world simplifies the work considerably. The finiteness hypothesis emphasizes the economic intuition for the core with asymmetric information (modelled as partitions) as it allows one to omit an otherwise long and complicated

---

[*]University of Minnesota and Federal Reserve Bank of Minneapolis. Some of the research described here was supported by NSF grants SES88-21442 and SBR-9309854. Any views expressed herein are those of the author and not necessarily those of the Federal Reserve Bank of Minneapolis or the Federal Reserve System.

argument establishing that the derived games are well defined for general sets of states of the world.[1] Instead, one is able to focus on the relation between an economy's exogenous informational structure and the balancedness of the induced games.

The contribution of this paper begins with a general formulation of the information that may be used by members of possibly asymmetrically-informed coalitions in terms of exogenously given information sharing rules. The insight then to examine the induced games directly leads to familiar intermediate characterizations. In particular, conditions for information sharing rules are provided that are equivalent to the balancedness of all derived games; a stronger condition is necessary and sufficient for all such games to be totally balanced. These results are interesting because of the close connection between balanced games and those with nonempty cores. In particular, for the transferable utility case, balancedness is equivalent to the existence of core imputations while with nontransferable utility, balancedness seems to be the best route to obtaining a nonempty core. (Similar results relate total balancedness to the possession of nonempty cores by all subgames.)

---

[1] With incentive compatibility constraints, non-convexities destroy the proof in Allen (1991a, 1991b) that the induced games are well defined. Hence, a further reason to examine the case of finitely many states is that doing so enables one to explicitly compare the core with and without incentives considerations.

The literature concerning cores of economies with asymmetric information begins with the article of Wilson (1978). More recent work by Allen (1991a, 1991b) and Yannelis (1991) is also discussed at the end of the paper. Mention should be made of the more game-theoretic contributions of Myerson (1984) and Rosenmuller (1990) who introduce incomplete information (in the sense of the Harsanyi formalism in terms of a finite type space) into cooperative games. However, these two pieces concern solution concepts other than the core.

The plan for the remainder of this paper is as follows: Section 2 presents the model and introduces the notion of information sharing rules. Then Section 3 derives the induced games. Section 4 is devoted to the issue of when these games are balanced and also whether any balanced game can be generated by a pure exchange economy with asymmetric information. Section 5 contains the main results for the core of an exchange economy with asymmetric information; its definition (with ex ante[2] blocking and arbitrary generalized information sharing rules for coalitions) and nonemptiness are examined. Comparisons of various core concepts and discussion of

---

[2] If one interprets the basic economic model as the realization of a distribution on players' types, where the description of a type specifies the agent's economic characteristics--in this context, state-dependent cardinal utility functions, state-dependent initial endowment mappings, and initial information--then I use an interim concept.

the coarse and fine cores of Wilson (1978) and the private information core of Yannelis (1991) also appear in Section 5.

2. A Basic Model

In this section, I model uncertainty and private information. Both pure exchange economies and the cooperative games (with nontransferable utility) that they generate are considered in this paper. To the extent possible, the same notation will be used for the economies and the games.

To begin, specify an abstract measurable space $(\hat{\Omega}, \mathbf{F})$ to describe the uncertainty. The set of states of the world is denoted $\hat{\Omega}$, with typical element ω. Let $\mathbf{F}$ be a σ-field of subsets of $\hat{\Omega}$, interpreted as the measurable events that economic agents eventually learn, so that events in $\mathbf{F}$ may be payoff relevant for ex post utilities.

Let I denote the set of economic agents (consumers) in the pure exchange economy. No confusion will result from taking I also to be the set of players in the games examined here. An individual player or trader is denoted by $i \in I$. The set I is assumed to be finite; write $\#I$ for its cardinality. Let 2^I denote the set of subsets of I. Nonempty subsets of the player set I are termed <u>coalitions</u> in the game. A <u>submarket</u> is a pure exchange economy consisting of only those traders $i \in I'$ for some $I' \subseteq I$, $I' \neq \emptyset$.

Each agent $i \in I$ has ex ante probability beliefs specified by a σ-additive probability measure μ_i

MARKET GAMES WITH ASYMMETRIC INFORMATION 381

defined on $(\hat{\Omega}, \mathbf{F})$. As these are subjective probabilities, they need not be identical. However, the class of null sets in $\mathbf{F}$ must be well defined. In symbols, for all $S \in \mathbf{F}$, $\mu_i(S) = 0$ implies $\mu_j(S) = 0$ for all $i, j \in I$.

Finiteness of the set of states of the world essentially results from the following assumption: For all $i \in I$, $\#\mathrm{supp}(\mu_i) < \infty$. Hence, for each $i \in I$, there is a finite subset Ω_i of $\hat{\Omega}$ such that $\Omega_i \in \mathbf{F}$, $\mu_i(\Omega_i) = 1$ and $\mu_i(\hat{\Omega}\setminus\Omega_i) = 0$. Let $\Omega = \bigcup_{i \in I} \Omega_i$. Then Ω is finite and for all $i \in I$, $\mu_i(\Omega) = 1$ and $\mu_i(\hat{\Omega}\setminus\Omega) = 0$. In the remainder of this paper, I take the finite set Ω to be the set of states of the world and I further redefine $\mathbf{F}$ if needed (by identifying atoms with states of the world) so that 2^{Ω} is the set of measurable subsets of Ω. The null set $\hat{\Omega}\setminus\Omega$ is systematically ignored. Moreover, for all $i \in I$ and all $\omega \in \Omega$, $\mu_i(\omega) > 0$.

Suppose that there is a finite number ℓ of commodities (numbered $1, 2, \ldots, \ell$) available in the economy. To summarize endowments, let $e : I \times \Omega \to \mathbb{R}^{\ell}_+$ denote an arbitrary (measurable) function and write $e_i : \Omega \to \mathbb{R}^{\ell}_+$ for consumer i's random (state-dependent) initial allocation function. Define the set E of (not necessary feasible) allocations by $E = \{(x_1(\cdot), \ldots, x_{\#I}(\cdot)) \mid$ for each $i \in I$, $x_i : \Omega \to \mathbb{R}^{\ell}$ is $\mathbf{F}$-measurable and $0 \leq x_i(\omega) \leq \sum_{j \in I} e_j(\omega)$ for almost all $\omega \in \Omega\}$. Interpret E as a convenient closed and bounded subset of measurable functions which contains all state-dependent individual allocation functions that could ever be feasible for the economy.

Consumer i's preferences are specified by a state-dependent cardinal utility function $u_i : \mathbb{R}_+^\ell \times \Omega \to \mathbb{R}$ which is continuous on $\mathbb{R}_+^\ell$. It's automatically F-measurable as a function of Ω, so that $u_i(\cdot;\cdot)$ is jointly measurable (for the Borel σ-field $B(\mathbb{R}_+^\ell)$ on i's consumption set $\mathbb{R}_+^\ell$). Concavity of $u_i(\cdot;\omega)$ on $\mathbb{R}_+^\ell$ for all $\omega \in \Omega$ will be imposed later; it is not needed in Section 3.

Each trader's initial information is represented by a (finite) partition P_i of Ω into disjoint subsets. Write $P_i(\omega)$ for the set in P_i containing $\omega \in \Omega$. Then for all $i \in I$, $\cup_{\omega \in \Omega} P_i(\omega) = \Omega$, $P_i(\omega) \neq \emptyset$ for each $\omega \in \Omega$ [since $\omega \in P_i(\omega)$], and for all ω, $\omega' \in \Omega$, either $P_i(\omega) = P_i(\omega')$ or $P_i(\omega) \cap P_i(\omega') = \emptyset$. Say that a function is P_i-measurable or measurable with respect to the partition P_i if the function is measurable with respect to the sub-σ-field $\sigma(P_i)$ of 2^Ω generated by the partition P_i. [The sub-σ-field $\sigma(P_i)$ is the smallest σ-field of subsets of Ω containing all of the $P_i(\omega)$ for $\omega \in \Omega$.] To set notation, let P^* denote the set of all (finite) partitions of Ω, so that $P_i \in P^*$ for all $i \in I$.

A trader's goal is to maximize his state-dependent conditional expected utility (which is a $C(\mathbb{R}_+^\ell, \mathbb{R})$-valued random variable--or measurable function--defined on Ω) given his available information. This information can be analyzed by incorporating it into the consumer's objective function (i.e., by calculating conditional expected utilities given the information and his beliefs). However, a better alternative for the game-theoretic analysis is, if possible, to place the information into a measurability constraint on the agent's state-dependent allocation (or state-dependent individual net trade strategy) functions because then the information enters into the definition of commodity spaces but not utilities in my market games.[3] Assume that, for all $i \in I$, the functions $e_i(\cdot)$ and $u_i(\cdot;\cdot)$ [but <u>not</u> their realizations] are known to player i; this data can also be taken as common knowledge. If $x_i : \Omega \to \mathbb{R}^\ell_+$, let $EU_i(x_i) = \sum_{\omega \in \Omega} u_i(x_i(\omega);\omega)\mu_i(\omega)$ be the (ex ante) expected utility of the state-dependent allocation $x_i(\cdot)$ to player $i \in I$.

The information available to a particular player as a member of some coalition is defined by an exogenously given information sharing rule. Formally, an <u>information sharing rule</u> $F = \{f(S) \mid S \subseteq I, S \neq \emptyset\}$ is a collection of $2^{\#I} - 1$ mappings

$$f(S) : \underbrace{P^* \times \ldots \times P^*}_{\#S \text{ times}} \to \underbrace{P^* \times \ldots \times P^*}_{\#S \text{ times}}$$

where, if $S = \{s(1), \ldots, s(\#S)\} \subseteq I = \{1, \ldots, \#I\}$,

$$f(S)(P_{s(1)}, \ldots, P_{s(\#S)}) = (Q_{s(1)}, \ldots, Q_{s(\#S)}).$$

Write $f(S)^i$ for the composition of $f(S)$ with the projection onto the P^* component corresponding to player $i \in S$, so that $f(S)^i(P_{s(1)}, \ldots, P_{s(\#S)}) = Q_i$ if $i \in S$. A <u>generalized information sharing rule</u>

---

[3] This idea is due to Van Zandt (1988).

$\hat{F} = \{\hat{f}(S) \mid S \subseteq I, S \neq \emptyset\}$ is a collection of $2^{\#I} - 1$ mappings

$$f(S) : P^* \times \ldots \times P^* \to P^* \times \ldots \times P^*$$

where $\hat{f}(S)(P_1^{\#I \text{ times}}, \ldots, P_{\#I}) = (Q_{s(1)}^{\#S \text{ times}}, \ldots, Q_{s(\#S)})$ if $S = \{s(1), \ldots, s(\#S)\}$. Write $\hat{f}(S)^i$ for the composition of $\hat{f}(S)$ with the projection onto the P^* component corresponding to player $i \in S$, so that $\hat{f}(S)^i(P_1, \ldots, P_{\#I}) = Q_i$ if $i \in S$. The difference between these concepts is a matter of whether a coalition's information can depend only on the initial information of its members. An information sharing rule requires that the information of each member of a coalition be a function only of the initial information of fellow coalition members, whereas generalized information sharing rules permit the initial information of all players in the game to affect the information available to coalition members. Of course, any information sharing rule can always be written as a generalized information sharing rule.

Three examples of information sharing rules are of obvious economic interest. <u>Coarse information sharing</u> is defined by $f(S)^i(P_{s(1)}, \ldots, P_{s(\#S)}) = \bigwedge_{j \in S} P_j$ for all $i \in S$ and all $S \subseteq I$ ($S \neq \emptyset$). The information of any coalition is given by their common information. This is appropriate for situations in which players cannot rely on each other to honestly (truthfully and completely) share information or to execute state-dependent strategy commitments that cannot be verified separately by each individual. <u>Fine information sharing</u> is defined by

$f(S)^i(P_{s(1)}, \ldots, P_{s(\#S)}) = \bigvee_{j \in S} P_j$ for all $i \in S$ and all $S \subseteq I$ ($S \neq \emptyset$). In this case, any coalition's information includes precisely the initial information of all coalition members. Here players are implicitly trusted to reveal their information to each other. Private information sharing has $f(S)^i(P_{s(1)}, \ldots, P_{s(\#S)}) = P_i$ for all $i \in S$, $S \subseteq I$ ($S \neq \emptyset$). This intermediate specification obviously lies between the extremes of fine and coarse information sharing and permits coalitions to be asymmetrically informed. In the private information story, no communication occurs and a justification could be provided by hypothesizing that the initial information partitions of other players (in particular, of other coalition members) are not common knowledge. Here coalition membership has no informational effect but involves only the trading of commodities.

3. Cooperative Games With Asymmetric Information

The goal of this section is to derive the cooperative games in characteristic function form generated by a pure exchange economy with asymmetric information. Games with transferable utility and then games with nontransferable utility are examined in turn.

A transferable utility (TU) cooperative game in characteristic function form (or, equivalently, in coalitional form) is defined by a player set I (assumed to be finite) and a function $v : 2^I \to \mathbb{R}$ satisfying $v(\emptyset) = 0$. [I do not assume that TU games are necessarily superadditive.] The characteristic function gives the "worth" of each coalition. Notice that, for fixed I, the set of all TU cooperative games is isomorphic to $\mathbb{R}^{2^{\#I}-1}$.

The next step is to explain the derivation of a cooperative game with transferable utility from a pure exchange economy with asymmetric information. One must then verify that the induced game is well defined and satisfies the requirements of the definition. Coalitions maximize the sum of attainable (ex ante) expected utilities of coalition members. One must prove that this maximum exists and is achieved by state-dependent feasible allocations that are measurable with respect to coalition members' information, as defined by the exogenously given information sharing rules. More formally, given a pure exchange economy with asymmetric information and its (generalized) information sharing rule $\hat{F}$, define $v : 2^I \to \mathbb{R}$ by $v(\emptyset) = 0$ and for each coalition S ($\emptyset \neq S \subseteq I$), set $v(S) = \max\{\bar{w} \in \mathbb{R} \mid$ for each $i \in S$, there exist $\hat{f}(S)^i(\mathbf{P}_1, \ldots, \mathbf{P}_{\#I})$-measurable $z_i : \Omega \to \mathbb{R}^\ell$ such that $z_i(\omega) + e_i(\omega) \in \mathbb{R}^\ell_+$ for (almost) every $\omega \in \Omega$, $\sum_{i \in S} z_i(\omega) = 0$ for (almost) all $\omega \in \Omega$, and $\bar{w} = \sum_{i \in S} w_i$ where $w_i = \sum_{\omega \in \Omega} u_i(z_i(\omega) + e_i(\omega); \omega)\mu_i(\omega)\}$.

Proposition 3.1. The characteristic function form game $v : 2^I \to \mathbb{R}$ with transferable utility is well defined.

Proof. By definition, $v(\emptyset) = 0$. It suffices to check that the maximum exists in the definition of $v(S)$ for any $S \neq \emptyset$. As measurability is a closed condition, the conditions above define a set of (feasible and measurable) $z_i : \Omega \to \mathbb{R}^\ell$ for $i \in S$ which is closed and bounded. Because Ω is finite, the z_i belong to some Euclidean space and therefore the set of z_i ($i \in S$) satisfying the requirements in the definition of $v(S)$ is compact. The sum of continuous utility functions is continuous. Hence, the problem reduces to the maximization of a continuous function on a compact set, so that its maximum exists and is attained.   []

<u>Remark 3.2</u>. Only continuity of the $u_i(\cdot;\omega)$ on $\mathbb{R}^\ell_+$ (for all $i \in S$ and (almost) all $\omega \in \Omega$) is used in the proof. Concavity is not needed.

Formally, a (cooperative) <u>nontransferable utility (NTU) game</u> in characteristic function form is a correspondence $V : 2^I \to \mathbb{R}^{\#I}$ satisfying $V(\emptyset) = \{0\}$ and, for all $S \subseteq I$, $V(S)$ is nonempty, closed, and comprehensive for $S \neq \emptyset$. Moreover, for $S \neq \emptyset$ the sets $V(S)$ are "cylinder sets" in that if $(\bar{u}_1,\ldots,\bar{u}_{\#I}) \in V(S)$ and $\bar{u}_i = \bar{w}_i$ for all $i \in S$, then $(\bar{w}_1,\ldots,\bar{w}_{\#I}) \in V(S)$. Comprehensiveness ($V(S) \supseteq V(S) - \mathbb{R}^{\#I}_+$) can be interpreted as "free disposability" of utility. Note that I do not require superadditivity as part of the definition of a cooperative game.[4]

To derive the NTU game associated with a pure exchange economy with asymmetric information, I must define its characteristic function $V : 2^I \to \mathbb{R}^{\#I}$ based

---

[4]Hildenbrand and Kirman (1976, Chapter 3) is a good reference for economists who are unfamiliar with these concepts.

on the data describing the economy. Accordingly, set $V(\emptyset) = \{0\}$ and for each coalition S ($\emptyset \neq S \subseteq I$), define $V(S) = \{(w_1, \ldots, w_{\#I}) \in \mathbb{R}^{\#I} \mid$ for each $i \in S$, there exists $z_i : \Omega \to \mathbb{R}^\ell$ which is $\hat{f}(S)^i(P_1, \ldots, P_{\#I})$-measurable with $z_i(\omega) + e_i(\omega) \in \mathbb{R}^\ell_+$ for (almost) all $\omega \in \Omega$ such that $\sum_{i \in S} z_i(\omega) = 0$ for (almost) every $\omega \in \Omega$ and $w_i \leq \sum_{\omega \in \Omega} u_i(z_i(\omega) + e_i(\omega); \omega) \mu_i(\omega)$ for $i \in S\}$.

<u>Proposition 3.3</u>. The correspondence $V : 2^I \to \mathbb{R}^{\#I}$ defines a cooperative game with nontransferable utility in characteristic function form.

<u>Proof</u>. By definition, $V(\emptyset) = \{0\}$. For $S \neq \emptyset$, $V(S)$ is clearly a comprehensive cylinder set due to the form of the expressions involving the w_i; they are weak inequalities and apply only to $i \in S$. Nonemptiness follows from the fact that $z_i(\omega) = 0$ necessarily satisfies the requirements defining $V(S)$ for $S \subseteq I$. To see that $V(S)$ is closed for any coalition S, notice (as in the proof of Proposition 3.1) that the z_i satisfying the conditions (for $i \in S$) for $V(S)$ form a compact set. Moreover, each player's (ex ante) expected utility is continuous. Closedness follows from the compactness of forward images of compact sets under continuous functions.

By an asymptotic cone argument, the operation of forming comprehensive hulls of compact sets does not destroy closedness. Because the operation of taking cylinder sets preserves closedness, $V(S)$ is closed for each $S \subseteq I$. []

Remark 3.4. Again, continuity but not concavity of the $u_i(\cdot;\omega)$ on $\mathbb{R}^{\ell}_{+}$ is employed in the proof. Note, however, that convexity of the V(S) sets is not claimed under the hypothesis of merely continuous utilities.

4. Market Games With Asymmetric Information

The study of market games was initiated by Shapley and Shubik (1969). The main results in this literature establish an equivalence between market games (defined to be cooperative games in characteristic function form which satisfy total balancedness) and finite pure exchange economies in which traders have concave utility functions. Strictly, speaking, a <u>market game</u> is a cooperative game having a characteristic function that can be generated by an economy with continuous concave utilities; it is <u>representable</u> by a market. I'm interested in the pure exchange case with and without transferable utility.

Balancedness of a game is equivalent to the nonemptiness of its core with transferable utility and is sufficient for a nonempty core with nontransferable utility. Balancedness imposes a type of convexity, albeit involving convex combinations of vectors in different sets [V(S) and V(S') for the NTU case] belonging to yet another set [i.e., V(I)]. Balancedness involves the concept of a balanced family of subsets, which are here taken to be coalitions.

A TU game $v : 2^I \to \mathbb{R}$ in coalitional form is <u>balanced</u> if for every collection **B** of subsets S of I and every collection γ_S of positive weights for $S \in B$, $\sum_{\substack{S \in B \\ S \ni i}} \gamma_S = 1$ for every $i \in I \Rightarrow \sum_{S \in B} \gamma_S v(S) \leq v(I)$. It is totally balanced if all subgames are balanced.

Proposition 4.1. Pick finite sets Ω and I and, for $i \in I$, let the partitions P_i and probabilities μ_i on Ω be chosen arbitrarily. Then for any fixed (generalized) information sharing rule, every totally balanced game with transferable utility is a market game with asymmetric information (with $\ell = \#I$ commodities and continuous concave state-dependent utility functions on $\mathbb{R}_+^\ell$).

Proof. If all players' endowments and utilities are constant functions of the state of the world, any pure exchange economy becomes a pure exchange economy with asymmetric information in which the μ_i, P_i, Ω and $\hat{F}$ don't matter. Combine this observation with the main theorem in Shapley and Shubik (1969). []

An NTU game $V : 2^I \to \mathbb{R}^{\#I}$ in characteristic function form is balanced if $V(I) \supseteq \sum_{T \in B} \gamma_T V(T)_T$ for every collection B of subsets of I and all non-negative weights γ_T for $T \in B$ such that $\sum_{\substack{T \in B \\ T \ni i}} \gamma_T = 1$ for all $i \in I$, where $V(T)_T = \{(w_1, \ldots, w_{\#I}) \in V(T) \mid w_j = 0$ if $j \notin T\}$. The game is totally balanced if all of its subgames are balanced.

Remark 4.2. Results loosely analogous to Proposition 4.1 are available for the case of nontransferable utility, but some technical qualifications must be added. See Billera (1974), Billera and Bixby (1974) and Mas-Colell (1975) for details.

MARKET GAMES WITH ASYMMETRIC INFORMATION

Without asymmetric information, the converse to the representation theorem (i.e., Proposition 3.1) for market games is available in TU and NTU versions: Any "classical" pure exchange economy generates a totally balanced game. The incorporation of asymmetric information, however, can lead to some games that are balanced but not totally balanced and some that are not balanced; see Allen (1991a, 1991b) for explicit examples.

However, restrictions on (generalized) information sharing rules restore balancedness. Stronger restrictions guarantee that the games are totally balanced. For these results, concavity of utilities is used.

Definition 4.3. A (generalized) information sharing rule $\hat{F}$ is <u>nested</u> if for all $i \in I$ and all coalitions S and T with $i \in S \subseteq T \subseteq I$ and $\#S \geq 2$, $\hat{f}(S)^i(P_1, \ldots, P_{\#I})$ is coarser than $\hat{f}(T)^i(P_1, \ldots, P_{\#I})$ for any initial information partitions $P_1, \ldots, P_{\#I}$. The (generalized) information sharing rule $\hat{F}$ is <u>nested at</u> $P_1, \ldots, P_{\#I}$ if for all $i \in I$ and all coalitions S and T with $i \in S \subseteq T \subseteq I$ and $\#S \geq 2$, $\hat{f}(S)^i(P_1, \ldots, P_{\#I})$ is coarser than $\hat{f}(T)^i(P_1, \ldots, P_{\#I})$.

Definition 4.4. A (generalized) information sharing rule $\hat{F}$ is <u>bounded</u> if for all $i \in I$ and all coalitions S containing i with $\#S \geq 2$, $\hat{f}(S)^i(P_1, \ldots, P_{\#I})$ is coarser than $\hat{f}(I)^i(P_1, \ldots, P_{\#I})$ for any initial information partitions $P_1, \ldots, P_{\#I}$. The (generalized) information sharing rule is <u>bounded at</u> $P_1, \ldots, P_{\#I}$ if for all coalitions $S \subseteq I$ with $\#S \geq 2$ and all $i \in S$, $\hat{f}(S)^i(P_1, \ldots, P_{\#I})$ is coarser than $\hat{f}(I)^i(P_1, \ldots, P_{\#I})$.

Since boundedness is simply nestedness for $T = I$, any nested (generalized) information sharing rule is clearly bounded, and likewise for nestedness at $P_1, \ldots, P_{\#I}$ and boundedness at $P_1, \ldots, P_{\#I}$. Also, if a (generalized) information sharing rule is nested (respectively, bounded) at $P_1, \ldots, P_{\#I}$ for all $(P_1, \ldots, P_{\#I}) \in P^* \times \ldots \times P^*_?$ then the entire (generalized) information sharing rule is nested (bounded). An interpretation of nestedness is that the addition of one or more members to any coalition cannot make an original member worse off informationally. Boundedness means that everyone has at least as much information in the coalition of the whole as in any other coalition to which the player may belong; any player's information in the grand coalition dominates that of any subcoalition.

Assumption 4.5. For all $i \in I$ and (almost) all $\omega \in \Omega$, $u_i(\cdot;\omega) : \mathbb{R}^\ell_+ \to \mathbb{R}$ is a concave function.

Remark 4.6. For the results below, nontriviality requires that the games with asymmetric information have at least three players; otherwise all information sharing rules are both bounded and nested. The $\#S \geq 2$ qualification in the definition arises from the observation that singletons can only consume their initial endowments; since $z_i(\cdot) \equiv 0$ in this case, measurability with respect to the singleton's information does not play a role.

With concave utilities and no asymmetric information, all TU or NTU games generated by exchange economies are totally balanced. If asymmetric information is present, balancedness and total balancedness are distinct conditions. Nested information sharing rules guarantee total balancedness while bounded ones insure balancedness. Moreover, each of these conditions is close to the minimal one that assures the desired property for all market games with asymmetric information and a given information sharing rule.

Proposition 4.7. Boundedness of the (generalized) information sharing rule $\hat{F}$ implies the balancedness of all (TU or NTU) market games with asymmetric information based on the (generalized) information sharing rule $\hat{F}$. Boundedness of the (generalized) information sharing rule $\hat{F}$ at $P_1, \ldots, P_{\#I}$ guarantees balancedness of all (TU or NTU) market games with asymmetric information based on the (generalized) information sharing rule $\hat{F}$ and having initial information specified by the partitions $P_1, \ldots, P_{\#I}$ of Ω.

Proof. Fix an arbitrary economy with (generalized) information sharing rule $\hat{F}$ and assume that $\hat{F}$ is bounded. I consider the TU and NTU cases in turn.

To show that the derived game $v : 2^I \to \mathbb{R}$ with transferable utility is balanced, I must show that for all balanced collections B of subsets of I with nonnegative balancing weights $\gamma_S \geq 0$ for $S \in B$ such that $\sum_{\substack{S \in B \\ S \ni i}} \gamma_S = 1$ for all $i \in I$, $\sum_{S \in B} \gamma_S v(S) \leq v(I)$. For each $S \in B$, there are state-dependent allocations

$x_i^S : \Omega \to \mathbb{R}_+^\ell$ for $i \in S$ such that $\sum_{i \in S} x_i^S(\omega) = \sum_{i \in S} e_i(\omega)$ for (almost) all $\omega \in \Omega$, if $z_i^S : \Omega \to \mathbb{R}^\ell$ is defined by $z_i^S(\omega) = x_i^S(\omega) - e_i(\omega)$, then $z_i^S(\cdot)$ is $\hat{f}(S)^i(P_1,\ldots,P_{\#I})$-measurable, and $v(S) = \sum_{i \in S} w_i^S$ where $w_i^S = \sum_{\omega \in \Omega} u_i(x_i^S(\omega);\omega)\mu_i(\omega)$. [This is just the definition of $v(S)$.] Define state-dependent allocations $x_i^* : \Omega \to \mathbb{R}_+^\ell$ for $i \in I$ by $x_i^*(\omega) = \sum_{\substack{S \in B \\ S \ni i}} \gamma_S x_i^S(\omega)$. Each $x_i^* : \Omega \to \mathbb{R}_+^\ell$ is such that if $z_i^* : \Omega \to \mathbb{R}^\ell$ is defined by $z_i^*(\omega) = x_i^*(\omega) - e_i(\omega)$, then $z_i^*(\cdot)$ is $\hat{f}(I)^i(P_1,\ldots,P_{\#I})$-measurable as the convex combination of $\hat{f}(I)^i(P_1,\ldots,P_{\#I})$-measurable functions, since each $z_i^S(\cdot)$ is $\hat{f}(S)^i(P_1,\ldots,P_{\#I})$-measurable and $\hat{f}(I)^i(P_1,\ldots,P_{\#I})$ is finer than $\hat{f}(S)^i(P_1,\ldots,P_{\#I})$ whenever $\#S \geq 2$ by boundedness; if $S = \{i\}$ is a singleton, then the constant function $z_i^{\{i\}}(\cdot) \equiv 0$ is automatically measurable. To check that the constructed allocations $x_i^* : \Omega \to \mathbb{R}_+^\ell$ are resource feasible, write $\sum_{i \in I} x_i^*(\omega) = \sum_{i \in I} \sum_{\substack{S \in B \\ S \ni i}} \gamma_S x_i^S(\omega) = \sum_{S \in B} \gamma_S \sum_{i \in I} x_i^S(\omega) = \sum_{S \in B} \gamma_S \sum_{i \in S} e_i(\omega) = \sum_{i \in I} \sum_{\substack{S \in B \\ S \ni i}} \gamma_S e_i(\omega) = \sum_{i \in I} e_i(\omega)$. By concavity of the $u_i(\cdot;\omega)$ on $\mathbb{R}_+^\ell$ for all $i \in I$ and (almost) all $\omega \in \Omega$,

$$\sum_{i \in I} \sum_{\omega \in \Omega} u_i(x_i^*(\omega);\omega)\mu_i(\omega) \geq \sum_{i \in I} \sum_{\omega \in \Omega} \sum_{\substack{S \in B \\ S \ni i}} \gamma_S u_i(x_i^S(\omega);\omega)\mu_i(\omega) = \sum_{i \in I} \sum_{\substack{S \in B \\ S \ni i}} \gamma_S w_i^S = \sum_{S \in B} \gamma_S v(S),$$

which shows that $v(I) \geq$

$\sum_{S \in B} \gamma_S(S) v(S)$, as desired.

To show balancedness of the derived game $V : 2^I \to \mathbb{R}^{\#I}$ with nontransferable utility, I must show that for all balanced collections B of subsets of I with nonnegative balancing weights $\gamma_S \geq 0$ such that $\sum_{\substack{S \in B \\ S \ni i}} \gamma_S = 1$ for all $i \in I$, $\sum_{S \in B} \gamma_S V(S)_S \subseteq V(I)$. As in the transferable utility case, examine the definition of $V(S)$ to find state-dependent allocation functions $x_i^S : \Omega \to \mathbb{R}_+^\ell$. For each $S \in B$ and each $w^S \in V(S)$, there exist $x_i^S : \Omega \to \mathbb{R}_+^\ell$ for $i \in S$ such that $\sum_{i \in S} x_i^S(\omega) = \sum_{i \in S} e_i(\omega)$ for (almost) all $\omega \in \Omega$, if $z_i^S : \Omega \to \mathbb{R}^\ell$ is defined by $z_i^S(\omega) = x_i^S(\omega) - e_i(\omega)$, then $z_i^S(\cdot)$ is $\hat{f}(S)^i(P_1, \ldots, P_{\#I})$-measurable, and $w_i^S = \sum_{\omega \in \Omega} u_i(x_i^S(\omega); \omega) \mu_i(\omega)$ where w_i^S is the component of w^S corresponding to player i if $i \in S$. Assume that $w^S \in V(S)_S$ so that one may write $w_j^S = 0$ if $j \notin S$. As before, define state-dependent allocations $x_i^* : \Omega \to \mathbb{R}_+^\ell$ for $i \in I$ by $x_i^*(\omega) = \sum_{\substack{S \in B \\ S \ni i}} \gamma_S x_i^S(\omega)$. If $z_i^* : \Omega \to \mathbb{R}^\ell$ is defined by $z_i^*(\omega) = x_i^*(\omega) - e_i(\omega)$, then for all $i \in I$, $z_i^*(\cdot)$ is $\hat{f}(I)^i(P_1, \ldots, P_{\#I})$-measurable as the convex combination of $\hat{f}(I)^i(P_1, \ldots, P_{\#I})$-measurable functions, since each $z_i^S(\cdot)$ is $\hat{f}(S)^i(P_1, \ldots, P_{\#I})$-

measurable and $\hat{f}(I)^i(P_1,\ldots,P_{\#I})$ is finer than $\hat{f}(S)^i(P_1,\ldots,P_{\#I})$ whenever $\#S \geq 2$ by boundedness; if $S = \{i\}$ is a singleton, then the constant function $z_i^{\{i\}}(\cdot) \equiv 0$ is automatically measurable. To verify resource feasibility, write $\sum_{i\in I} x_i^*(\omega) = \sum_{i\in I} \sum_{\substack{S\in B \\ S\ni i}} \gamma_S x_i^S(\omega) = \sum_{S\in B} \gamma_S \sum_{i\in S} x_i^S(\omega) = \sum_{S\in B} \gamma_S \sum_{i\in S} e_i(\omega) = \sum_{i\in I} \sum_{\substack{S\in B \\ S\ni i}} \gamma_S e_i(\omega) = \sum_{i\in S} e_i(\omega)$ exactly as before. Concavity of $u_i(\cdot;\omega)$ on $\mathbb{R}_+$ for all $i \in I$ and (almost) all $\omega \in \Omega$ implies

$$\sum_{\omega\in\Omega} u_i(x_i^*(\omega);\omega)\mu_i(\omega) = \sum_{\omega\in\Omega} u_i((\sum_{\substack{S\in B \\ S\ni i}} \gamma_S x_i^S(\omega));\omega)\mu_i(\omega) \geq \sum_{\omega\in\Omega}\sum_{\substack{S\in B \\ S\ni i}} \gamma_S u_i(x_i^S(\omega);\omega))\mu_i(\omega) = \sum_{\substack{S\in B \\ S\ni i}} \gamma_S w_i^S = w_i,$$

which demonstrates that $\sum_{S\in B} \gamma_S V(S)_S \subseteq V(I)$, as desired. []

Corollary 4.8. Nestedness of the (generalized) information sharing rule $\hat{F}$ implies that all derived (TU or NTU) market games with asymmetric information based on the (generalized) information sharing rule $\hat{F}$ are totally balanced. If the (generalized) information sharing rule is nested at $P_1,\ldots,P_{\#I}$, then all (TU or NTU) market games with asymmetric information specified by the initial information $P_1,\ldots,P_{\#I}$ that use the (generalized) information sharing rule $\hat{F}$ are totally balanced.

Proof. Apply Proposition 4.7 to the subgames defined by all submarkets--i.e., in the proof of that result, replace I by an arbitrary coalition $T \subseteq I$. []

A weaker form of nestedness and boundedness can be used to guarantee (total) balancedness of the resulting games. The insight is based on the feasibility requirement that each coalition's state-dependent net trades sum to the zero vector almost surely. This means that not all suitably measurable functions can define net trades--in particular, if only one player has information in a coalition, he cannot truly use that information but can only make constant trades. This motivates modification of my conditions. Under the additional assumption that all subjective probabilities are identical, the new forms are equivalent to the (total) balancedness of all market games with asymmetric information derived from the (essentially nested or essentially bounded) generalized information sharing rule. Essential nestedness and essential boundedness are a bit harder to check than nestedness or boundedness and the analogous proof of (total) balancedness is slightly more difficult.

<u>Definition 4.9</u>. The (generalized) information sharing rule $\hat{F}$ is <u>essentially nested at</u> $P_1,\ldots,P_{\#I}$ if for all $i \in I$ and all coalitions S and T such that $i \in S \subseteq T \subseteq I$, if $\Omega' \subset \Omega$ is such that $0 < \mu_i(\Omega') < 1$ where Ω' is a union of sets in the partition $\hat{f}(S)^i(P_1,\ldots,P_{\#I})$, and $\Omega' = \Omega_1 \cup \ldots \cup \Omega_N$ for some disjoint $\Omega_n \in \hat{f}(S)^{j(n)}(P_1,\ldots,P_{\#I})$ with $j(n) \in S\setminus\{i\}$, $n = 1,\ldots,N$, then Ω' is a union of sets in the partition $\hat{f}(T)^i(P_1,\ldots,P_{\#I})$, and each Ω_n is a union of sets in the partition $\hat{f}(T)^{j(n)}(P_1,\ldots,P_{\#I})$. If for all $(P_1,\ldots,P_{\#I}) \in P^*_1 \times \ldots \times P^*_{\#I}$ the (generalized) informa-

tion sharing rule $\hat{F}$ is essentially nested at $P_1,\ldots,P_{\#I}$, say that $\hat{F}$ is <u>essentially nested</u>.

<u>Definition 4.10</u>. The (generalized) information sharing rule $\hat{F}$ is <u>essentially bounded at</u> $P_1,\ldots,P_{\#I}$ if for all $S \subseteq I$ (with $\#S \geq z$) and all $i \in S$, if $\Omega' \subset \Omega$ is such that $0 < \mu_i(\Omega') < 1$, where Ω' is a union of sets in the partition $\hat{f}(S)^i(P_1,\ldots,P_{\#I})$, and $\Omega' = \Omega_1 \cup \ldots \cup \Omega_N$ for some disjoint $\Omega_n \in \hat{f}(S)^{j(n)}(P_1,\ldots,P_{\#I})$ with $j(n) \in S\setminus\{i\}$, $n = 1,\ldots,N$, then Ω' is a union of sets in the partition $\hat{f}(I)^i(P_1,\ldots,P_{\#I})$ and each Ω_n is a union of sets in the partition $\hat{f}(I)^{j(n)}(P_1,\ldots,P_{\#I})$. If for all $(P_1,\ldots,P_{\#I}) \in P^* \times \ldots \times P^*$ the (generalized) information sharing rule $\hat{F}$ is essentially bounded at $P_1,\ldots,P_{\#I}$, say that $\hat{F}$ is <u>essentially bounded</u>.

<u>Proposition 4.11</u>. Essential nestedness of a (generalized) information sharing rule implies its essential boundedness. Moreover, nestedness implies essential nestedness and boundedness implies essential boundedness. The same holds for these concepts at a particular $P_1,\ldots,P_{\#I}$.

<u>Proof</u>. These implications follow immediately from the definitions. []

<u>Proposition 4.12</u>. Fix the finite sets Ω and I arbitrarily and assume that $\mu_i = \mu_j$ for all $i, j \in I$. Then, as state-dependent utilities and endowments vary, all (TU or NTU) market games with asymmetric information $P_1,\ldots,P_{\#I}$ using $\hat{F}$ are totally balanced if and only if $\hat{F}$ is essentially nested at $P_1,\ldots,P_{\#I}$.

Proof. If $\hat{F}$ is not essentially nested, then there are coalitions S and T with $S \subseteq T$, a player $i \in S$ and a subset Ω' of Ω with $0 < \mu_i(\Omega') < 1$ such that Ω' can be written as a union of sets in the partition $\hat{f}(S)^i(P_1,\ldots,P_{\#I})$ and also $\Omega' = \Omega_1 \cup \ldots \cup \Omega_N$ disjointly where, for each $n = 1,\ldots,N$, there exists $j(n) \in S\setminus\{i\}$ such that $\Omega_n \in \hat{f}(S)^{j(n)}(P_1,\ldots,P_{\#I})$, but either Ω' cannot be written as a union of sets in $\hat{f}(T)^i(P_1,\ldots,P_{\#I})$ or some Ω_n cannot be written as a union of sets in $\hat{f}(T)^{j(n)}(P_1,\ldots,P_{\#I})$. Define a two-commodity economy by the following state-dependent utilities and endowments for agents in I: $e_i(\omega) \equiv (0,0)$ for all $\omega \in \Omega$, $e_j(\omega) \equiv (0,0)$ for all $j \in I\setminus S$ and all $\omega \in \Omega$, $e_j(\omega) = (1,1)$ if $\omega \in \Omega_n$ and $j = j(n) \in S\setminus\{i\}$ $e_j(\omega) = (0,0)$ otherwise, $u_j(x_j,y_j;\omega) \equiv 0$ for all $j \in I\setminus S$, $u_j(x_j,y_j;\omega) = \max((x_j + y_j)/2, 1)$ for all $\omega \in \Omega$ and all $j \in S$ with $j \neq i$, $u_i(x_i,y_i;\omega) = \max(2, x_i + y_i)$ if $\omega \in \Omega'$, and $u_i(x_i,y_i;\omega) = \max((x_i + y_i)/2, 1)$ if $\omega \notin \Omega'$. Note that these utilities are clearly concave and continuous on $\mathbb{R}^2_+$. Consider the balanced collection $B(T) = \{S, T\setminus S\}$ of subsets of T with nonnegative balancing weights $\gamma_S = 1$ and $\gamma_{T\setminus S} = 1$. Clearly $v(T\setminus S) = 0$. Also $v(S) = 2\mu(\Omega')$, [where $\mu = \mu_i$] using an allocation in which i receives one unit of each good whenever the state of the world lies in Ω'. However $v(T) = \max_{\Omega''} \{2\mu(\{\omega \in \Omega \mid \omega \in \Omega' \text{ and } \omega \in \Omega''\}) - \mu(\{\omega \in \Omega \mid \omega \in \Omega'' \text{ and } \omega \in \Omega\setminus\Omega'\}) \mid \Omega''$ can be written as a union of sets in $\hat{f}(T)^i(P_1,\ldots,P_{\#I})$ and Ω_n'' can be written as the disjoint union $\Omega_1'' \cup \ldots \cup \Omega_N''$ where, for all $n = 1,\ldots,N$, $\Omega_n'' \subseteq \Omega_n$ and Ω_n'' is a union of sets in $\hat{f}(T)^{j(n)}(P_1,\ldots,P_{\#I})\}$. The failure of essential nestedness implies that either $2\mu(\Omega') > 2\mu(\{\omega \in \Omega \mid \omega \in \Omega'$ and $\omega \in \Omega''\})$ or [if $\Omega' \subseteq \Omega''$] $\mu(\{\omega \in \Omega \mid \omega \in \Omega''$ and $\omega \in \Omega\setminus\Omega'\}) > 0$, so that $v(T) < 2\mu(\Omega')$. This shows that $\gamma_S v(S) + \gamma_{S\setminus T} v(S\setminus T) = 1(2\mu(\Omega')) + 1(0) > v(T)$, which contradicts balancedness of the subgame on T. Hence the TU market game generated by $\hat{F}$ with the above state-dependent utilities and endowments is not totally balanced.

To demonstrate necessity for NTU games, examine the NTU version of the game defined by the above economy. Observe that $V(T\setminus S)_{T\setminus S} = \{0\}$ and $w \in V(S)_S$ where $w_j = 0$ if $j \notin S$, $w_j = 1$ if $j \in S$ and $j \neq i$ and $w_i = 2\mu(\Omega')$. To prove that the NTU game is not totally balanced, it suffices to show $w \notin V(T)_T$. This follows from the TU case examined above, where I showed that there does not exist $w' \in V(T)_T$ with $\sum_{j \in T} w_j = 2\mu(\Omega')$.

For sufficiency, recall that resource feasibility means that for every coalition S, state-dependent net trades used in the definition of $v(S)$ or $V(S)$ must sum to zero in (almost) every state of the world. Hence the allocations constructed in the proofs of Proposition 4.7 and Corollary 4.8 must satisfy the measurability requirement if the information sharing rule is essentially nested. []

Remark 4.13. Observe that sufficiency does not depend on the assumption [in symbols, $\mu_i = \mu$ for all $i \in I$] that all personal probabilities are identical. For necessity, a problem can arise if agents can exchange resources so that each has more of all goods in an event that is more likely according to the agent's own probability assessment. For instance, alter the economy constructed above for the proof by eliminating satiation, suppose that there are disjoint events $\bar{\Omega}$ and $\bar{\bar{\Omega}}$ that are measurable for agents $\bar{j}$ and $\bar{\bar{j}}$ in coalition T but not in coalition S such that $\mu_{\bar{j}}(\bar{\Omega}) = 5\mu_{\bar{j}}(\bar{\bar{\Omega}})$ but $\mu_{\bar{\bar{j}}}(\bar{\bar{\Omega}}) = 5\mu_{\bar{\bar{j}}}(\bar{\Omega})$. Then a transfer of all endowment from $\bar{\bar{j}}$ to $\bar{j}$ in the event $\bar{\bar{\Omega}}$ and from $\bar{j}$ to $\bar{\bar{j}}$ in event $\bar{\Omega}$ can raise $v(T)$ enough to swamp the effect (on agent i) created in the example. For this reason, it is much simpler to assume that all personal probabilities are identical.

Corollary 4.14. For arbitrary finite Ω and I, set $\mu_i = \mu$ for all $i \in I$. Then essential boundedness of $\hat{F}$ at $P_1, \ldots, P_{\#I}$ is a necessary and sufficient condition for the balancedness of all (TU or NTU) market games with asymmetric information based on $\hat{F}$ with initial information specified by the partitions $P_1, \ldots, P_{\#I}$ of Ω.

Proof. For necessity, set $T = I$ in the proof of Proposition 4.12. Sufficiency again follows from the observation that, since resource feasibility requires that state-dependent net trades must sum to zero in (almost) every state of the world, the allocations constructed for the grand coalition in the proof of Proposition 4.7 must be measurable with respect to the $\hat{f}(I)^i(P_1,\ldots,P_{\#I})$ for $i \in I$ whenever the (generalized) information sharing rule is essentially bounded at $P_1,\ldots,P_{\#I}$. []

Remark 4.15. Again, equality of the subjective probabilities μ_i is not needed for sufficiency, while different personal probabilities complicate the situation for necessity.

Remark 4.16. Note that the game constructed in the proof of Proposition 4.12 violates superadditivity, although essential nestedness (and not just essential boundedness) of the (generalized) information sharing rule is needed to guarantee superadditivity of the induced games.

5. Cores with Asymmetric Information

Much of the economic interest in the properties of balancedness and total balancedness lies in their close connection to nonemptiness of the core. In fact, these are the only generally applicable conditions leading to the existence of core allocations in economies.

My economic justification for the core as a solution concept lies in its ability to eliminate certain allocations. Any noncore allocation can be blocked by some group of agents who could each do better by withdrawing from the original society. While one may not like all core allocations, one is nevertheless justified in ignoring noncore allocations if there are core allocations.

Informally, the core of an economy with asymmetric information consists of feasible allocations that cannot be blocked by a better feasible allocation for some coalition where "feasibility" refers to both resource constraints and information measurability constraints. Core allocations correspond to core imputations (in terms of ex ante expected utility) for the induced game with or without transferable utility.

Definition 5.1. The <u>TU core</u> of an economy with asymmetric information consists of profiles of state-dependent individual allocations $(x_1(\cdot), \ldots, x_{\#I}(\cdot))$, where, for $i \in I$, $x_i : \Omega \to \mathbb{R}_+^\ell$ is such that

(a) $\sum_{i \in I} x_i(\omega) = \sum_{i \in I} e_i(\omega)$ for (almost) all $\omega \in \Omega$,

(b) for all $i \in I$, $z_i : \Omega \to \mathbb{R}_+^\ell$ defined by $z_i(\omega) = x_i(\omega) - e_i(\omega)$ is $\hat{f}(I)^i(P_1, \ldots, P_{\#I})$-measurable, and

(c) there does not exist a coalition $S \subseteq I$ ($S \neq \emptyset$) and state-dependent allocations $x_i' : \Omega \to \mathbb{R}_+^\ell$ for $i \in S$ with $z_i'(\cdot) = x_i'(\cdot) - e_i(\cdot)$ $\hat{f}(S)^i(P_1, \ldots, P_{\#I})$-measurable such that $\sum_{i \in S} x_i'(\omega) = \sum_{i \in S} e_i(\omega)$ for (almost) all $\omega \in \Omega$ and $\sum_{i \in S} \sum_{\omega \in \Omega} u_i(x_i'(\omega); \omega) \mu_i(\omega) > \sum_{i \in S} \sum_{\omega \in \Omega} u_i(\hat{x}_i(\omega); \omega) \mu_i(\omega)$. If $(\hat{x}_1(\cdot), \ldots, \hat{x}_{\#I}(\cdot))$ is a core allocation, then $(\hat{w}_1, \ldots, \hat{w}_{\#I}) \in \mathbb{R}^{\#I}$ defined by $\hat{w}_i = \sum_{\omega \in \Omega} u_i(\hat{x}_i(\omega); \omega) \mu_i(\omega)$ is a <u>core imputation</u>. Note that, in this case, $\sum_{i \in S} \hat{w}_i \geq v(S)$ for all $S \subseteq I$.

Proposition 5.2. Fix the finite set Ω arbitrarily and set $\mu_i = \mu$ for all $i \in I$. Essential boundedness of $\hat{F}$ is a necessary and sufficient condition for the nonemptiness of the core of all economies with asymmetric information having (generalized) information sharing rule

$\hat{F}$. Moreover, for fixed initial information partitions $P_1, \ldots, P_{\#I}$, essential boundedness of the (generalized) information sharing rule $\hat{F}$ at $P_1, \ldots, P_{\#I}$ is equivalent to the nonemptiness of the core for all economies with asymmetric information based on the (generalized) information sharing rule $\hat{F}$ and having initial information specified by the partitions $P_1, \ldots, P_{\#I}$ of Ω.

Proof. By Corollary 4.14, essential boundedness of $\hat{F}$ is equivalent to the balancedness of all games derived from the (generalized) information sharing rule $\hat{F}$. A similar statement relates boundedness at $P_1, \ldots, P_{\#I}$ to the balancedness of all games with initial information $P_1, \ldots, P_{\#I}$. By the theorem of Bondareva (1962) and Shapley (1967), TU games have nonempty cores if and only if they are balanced. []

Remark 5.3. Even if the personal probabilities μ_i may differ, the sufficiency claims in Proposition 5.2 remain true.

Corollary 5.4. If the (generalized) information sharing rule $\hat{F}$ is bounded at $P_1, \ldots, P_{\#I}$, than any economy with initial information $P_1, \ldots, P_{\#I}$ having (generalized) information sharing rule $\hat{F}$ has a nonempty TU core.

Proof. By Proposition 4.11, boundedness at $P_1, \ldots, P_{\#I}$ implies essential boundedness at $P_1, \ldots, P_{\#I}$. []

Corollary 5.5. For fixed Ω and $\mu_i = \mu$ for all $i \in I$, essential nestedness of $\hat{F}$ is necessary and sufficient for the nonemptiness of the cores of all submarkets of all economies with asymmetric information having (generalized) information sharing rule $\hat{F}$. Essential nestedness at $P_1,\ldots,P_{\#I}$ of the (generalized) information sharing rule $\hat{F}$ is equivalent to nonemptiness of the cores of all submarkets of all economies with asymmetric information based on the (generalized) information sharing rule $\hat{F}$ for initial information given by the partitions $P_1,\ldots,P_{\#I}$ of Ω.

Proof. By Proposition 4.12, essential nestedness of $\hat{F}$ is equivalent to total balancedness of all games derived from the (generalized) information sharing rule $\hat{F}$ and nestedness at $P_1,\ldots,P_{\#I}$ is equivalent to the total balancedness of all games derived from economies with the initial asymmetric information $P_1,\ldots,P_{\#I}$ using the (generalized) information sharing rule $\hat{F}$. By Bondareva (1962) and Shapley (1967), a game with transferable utility and all of its subgames have nonempty cores if and only if the game is totally balanced. []

Remark 5.6. In Corollary 5.5, sufficiency does not require that the μ_i be identical.

Corollary 5.7. If the (generalized) information sharing rule $\hat{F}$ is nested at $P_1,\ldots,P_{\#I}$, then for any economy with initial information $P_1,\ldots,P_{\#I}$ and information sharing rule $\hat{F}$, the core of the economy and the cores of its submarkets are all nonempty.

Proof. By Proposition 4.11, nestedness at $P_1,\ldots,P_{\#I}$ implies essential nestedness at $P_1,\ldots,P_{\#I}$. []

Now return to the issue of the core with asymmetric information and nontransferable utility. The core of an

NTU game $V : 2^I \to \mathbb{R}^{\#I}$ is the set of all payoff vectors $(w_1, \ldots, w_{\#I}) \in \mathbb{R}^{\#I}$ such that $(w_1, \ldots, w_{\#I}) \in V(I)$ (feasibility) and there does not exist a coalition $S \subseteq I$ and $(w'_1, \ldots, w'_{\#I}) \in V(S)$ such that $w'_i > w_i$ for all $i \in S$ (coalition S cannot block).

Definition 5.8. The NTU core of an economy with asymmetric information consists of all state-dependent allocations $(x_1, \ldots, x_{\#I})$ where $x_i : \Omega \to \mathbb{R}^\ell_+$ for each $i \in I$ such that

(a) $\sum_{i \in I} x_i(\omega) = \sum_{i \in I} e_i(\omega)$ for (almost) all $\omega \in \Omega$,

(b) each $x_i(\cdot)$ is such that $x_i(\cdot) - e_i(\cdot)$ is $\hat{f}(I)^i (P_1, \ldots, P_{\#I})$-measurable, and

(c) there does not exist a coalition S ($\emptyset \neq S \subseteq I$) and allocations $x'_i : \Omega \to \mathbb{R}^\ell_+$ for $i \in S$ such that $\sum_{i \in S} x'_i(\omega) = \sum_{i \in S} e_i(\omega)$ for (almost) all $\omega \in \Omega$, each $x'_i(\cdot) - e_i(\cdot)$ is $\hat{f}(S)^i (P_1, \ldots, P_{\#I})$-measurable, and $EU_i(x'_i) > EU_i(x_i)$ for all $i \in S$.

This is the usual concept of the NTU core of a pure exchange economy except for the informational constraints that each net trade defining a core allocation must be measurable with respect to the grand coalition's information and that blocking must also be accomplished via net trades that are measurable for each member i of the blocking coalition S. Recall that my commodity space consists of (ex ante) state-dependent commodity bundles that are measurable with respect to the appropriate information. Moreover, payoffs are given by the ex ante expected utilities associated with these state-dependent allocations.

In contrast to the transferable utility case, balancedness is merely sufficient--but not necessary--for nonemptiness of the core of a game with nontransferable utility. Hence, in the NTU analogues of Proposition 5.2 and Corollary 5.5, the implication holds in only one direction.

Proposition 5.9. All games with bounded (generalized) information sharing rules have nonempty NTU cores. In fact, boundedness of the (generalized) information sharing rule $\hat{F}$ at $P_1, \ldots, P_{\#I}$ implies that any economy with the initial asymmetric information $P_1, \ldots, P_{\#I}$ using the (generalized) information sharing rule $\hat{F}$ has a nonempty NTU core.

Proof. By Proposition 4.7, boundedness of the (generalized) information sharing rule implies that the NTU game is balanced; boundedness at $P_1, \ldots, P_{\#I}$ also implies balancedness of the induced NTU game with initial information $P_1, \ldots, P_{\#I}$. By Scarf (1967), this guarantees that the (NTU) core is nonempty. []

Corollary 5.10. Nestedness of the (generalized) information sharing rule implies nonemptiness of the NTU core for the economy and all of its submarkets. Similarly, nestedness of the (generalized) information sharing rule at $P_1, \ldots, P_{\#I}$ implies nonemptiness of the NTU core for the economy and all of its submarkets having initial information $P_1, \ldots, P_{\#I}$.

Proof. Use Corollary 4.8 and Scarf (1967). []

Remark 5.11. Proposition 5.9 and Corollary 5.10 remain valid if boundedness and nestedness are replaced by essential boundedness and essential nestedness respectively.

An implication of the results in this section is the nonemptiness of the private information core for all (TU or NTU) economies with asymmetric information and their submarkets. This parallels the NTU results of Yannelis (1991) except for the fact that his treatment (using the methodology of Banach lattices) permits infinitely many commodities in each state of the world.

In addition, comparison with the original results of Wilson (1978) is instructive. My analysis leads to nonempty fine cores for all TU and NTU exchange economies with asymmetric information and their submarkets, but possibly empty coarse cores. In contrast, Wilson (1978) proved (using balancedness of an artificial related game in which the event-agent pairs become players) that his NTU coarse core is nonempty. Furthermore, he gave an explicit example of a simple pure exchange economy for which the NTU fine core is empty. The primary difference is that in Wilson's (1978) model, blocking occurs ex post whereas I use an ex ante core concept. Moreover, for his coarse core, Wilson (1978) lets the grand coalition pool information, so that $\hat{f}(I)^i(P_1, \ldots, P_{\#I}) = \bigvee_{i \in S} P_i$ (but $\hat{f}(S)^i(P_1, \ldots, P_{\#I}) = \bigwedge_{i \in I} P_i$ for $S \neq \emptyset$) in my notation, which yields a bounded (generalized) information sharing rule.

Of course, my framework with (generalized) information sharing rules includes many other core concepts. Their nonemptiness depends on whether the (generalized) information sharing rule is essentially bounded (or essentially nested if cores of submarkets are also desired). This characterization identifies the crucial conditions. Moreover, some of the various core concepts can be ordered or compared in terms of set inclusions. If for all $S \subseteq I$, $\hat{f}(S)^i(P_1,\ldots,P_{\#I})$ is coarser than $\hat{f}'(S)^i(P_1,\ldots,P_{\#I})$ for all $i \in S$ but $\hat{f}(I)(P_1,\ldots,P_{\#I}) = \hat{f}'(I)(P_1,\ldots,P_{\#I})$, then the (TU or NTU) core of an economy with the $\hat{F}$ (generalized) information sharing rule contains the core of the otherwise identical economy under the $\hat{F}'$ (generalized) information sharing rule. The reason is that the grand coalition has the same set of resource feasible and information measurable state-dependent allocations, but blocking is easier (or, at least, no less hard) under $\hat{F}'$ than $\hat{F}$ because $\hat{F}'$ gives all coalitions at least as much information.

Finally, note that the restriction to finitely many states of the world in this paper is not necessary, although finiteness of Ω does certainly simplify the technicalities. See Allen (1991a, 1991b) for details.

References

Allen, Beth, 1991a, Market games with asymmetric information and nontransferable utility: Representation results and the core, Center for Analytic Research in Economics and the Social Sciences Working Paper #91-09, University of Pennsylvania.

Allen, Beth, 1991b, Transferable utility market games with asymmetric information: Representation results and the core, Center for Analytic Research in Economics and the Social Sciences Working Paper #91-16, University of Pennsylvania.

Billera, Louis J., 1974, On games without side payments arising from a general class of markets, **Journal of Mathematical Economics 1**, 129-139.

Billera, Louis J. and Robert E. Bixby, 1974, Market representations of n-person games, **Bulletin of the American Mathematical Society 80**, 522-526.

Bondareva, Olga N., 1962, Theory of core in an n-person Game, **Vestnik Leningradskogo Universiteta, Seriia Matematika, Mekhanika i Astronomii 13**, 141-142.

Hildenbrand, W. and A.P. Kirman, 1976, **Introduction to Equilibrium Analysis**. North-Holland, Amsterdam.

Mas-Colell, Andreu, 1975, A further result on the representation of games by markets, **Journal of Economic Theory 10**, 117-122.

Myerson, R.B., 1984, Cooperative games with imcomplete [sic] information, **International Journal of Game Theory 13**, 69-96.

Rosenmuller, Joachim, 1990, Fee games: (N)TU-games with incomplete information, Institut fur Mathematische Wirtschaftsforschung Working Paper Nr. 190, Universitat Bielefeld.

Scarf, Herbert E., 1967, The core of an n person game, **Econometrica 35**, 50-69.

Shapley, L.S., 1967, On balanced sets and cores, **Naval Research Logistics Quarterly 14**, 453-460.

Shapley, Lloyd S. and Martin Shubik, 1969, On market games, **Journal of Economic Theory 1**, 9-25.

Van Zandt, Timothy, 1988, Information, measurability, and continuous behavior, Center for Analytic Research in

Economics and the Social Sciences Working Paper #88-18, University of Pennsylvania.

Wilson, Robert, 1978, Information, efficiency and the core of an economy, **Econometrica 46**, 807-816.

Yannelis, Nicholas C., 1991, The core of an economy with differential information, **Economic Theory 1**, 183-198.

INFORMATION TRANSMISSION IN SIGNALING GAMES: CONFRONTATION OF DIFFERENT FORWARD INDUCTION CRITERIA

Gisèle Umbhauer
Bureau d'Economie Théorique et Appliquée
Université Louis Pasteur Strasbourg
France

INTRODUCTION[1]

This paper deals with information transmission in a special class of signaling games often used in economic applications.

The studied games are characterized by two main properties, "dominance of higher beliefs" and "single crossing", and motivated by the market of experience goods. They are two players games; the first player, who can be of n ($\in \mathbb{N}$) types, sends a message to the second; this one observes the message, but not the type, and then chooses a response. In the market of experience goods, the first player is the producer; he sells a good which can be of n different quality levels (vertical differentiation). He sets a price for his good; the second player, the consumer, observes the price but not the quality, and then buys a certain amount of the good.

Forward induction improves the usual backward induction approach of these games, in that it allows out of equilibrium messages to be understood as strategic deviations. This property was first exposed in Kohlberg & Mertens (1986), and since developed by many authors (see for example Kohlberg's (1989) survey).

However, despite these different works, forward induction still remains a difficult concept, whose formulation is a knotty problem. Moreover, the chosen formulation may have an important impact on the obtained equilibria. The primary purpose of this paper is precisely to show that different formulations of forward induction can lead to *strikingly different levels of information*

---

1 A first version of this paper, out of my Ph.D dissertation (1989) has been presented in a CORE (Belgium) mathematical seminar, January 1992.

transmission.

The paper is written with a view to showing that the level of information revelation is strongly related to the interpretation of out of equilibrium messages. Depending on the studied forward induction criterion, this interpretation has or has not to be *consistent* with the interpretation of other messages. This fact will lead to different equilibrium results, and, what is more, it will result in different economic policies.

The paper is organized as follows. We begin by presenting the model and its Perfect Bayesian Equilibria. Next we give the results obtained with two different forward induction approachs. Thereafter we explain the obtained differences and discuss the content of the results. A further section is devoted to additional comments and to the links between our paper and related work. We close by discussing the political economy impact.

THE CLASS OF GAMES: ASSUMPTIONS AND PERFECT BAYESIAN EQUILIBRIA

* There are two players, player 1 and player 2. Player 1 can be of n types, $t_1,...,t_n$, with $n \in \mathbb{N}$ and $n > 1$ (we note T the set of types). His type occurs according to an a priori probability distribution $\rho(.)$ on T, which is common knowledge to both players and which assigns a strictly positive probability to each type.

Player 1 plays first, by sending a message m to the second player, with $m \in M$, where M is a positive interval of $\mathbb{R}$ (of the type $[a, +\infty[$ $a \geq 0$), which can depend on t (if so, we write M(t)).

Player 2 observes the message and then chooses a response r, with $r \in R$, where R is a positive interval of $\mathbb{R}$, which can depend on m (if so, we write R(m)). Player 2's beliefs on player 1's type, after observing a message m, are given by an a posteriori probability distribution $\mu(./m)$ on T; $\mu(./m)$ belongs to Δ_T, the set of probability distributions on T. We hereafter note $r(m,\mu)$, player 2's best response after observation of m for the beliefs given by $\mu(./m)$; if $\mu(./m)$'s support is a singleton $\{t\}$, we simply write r(m,t). We will suppose that player 2's best response exists and is unique for each type of message and beliefs.

The game ends with player 2's action. u(t,m,r), respectively v(t,m,r), is player 1's payoff, respectively player 2's payoff, if player 1 is of type t and plays m, and player 2 plays r.

* To these usual assumptions, we add four assumptions:

Assumption 1

i) $\forall\, t \in T,\ \exists\, \underline{m}_t \in M(t)\ /$
$\forall\, \mu \in \Delta_T,\ u(t,\underline{m}_t,r(\underline{m}_t,\mu))=0$ and $u(t,m,r(m,\mu))<0$ for $m<\underline{m}_t$;

ii) $\forall\, \mu \in \Delta_T\ \exists\, \tilde{m}_\mu \in \bigcap_{i=1\ \text{to}\ n}\,]\underline{m}_{t_i},\ \infty[\ /$
$\forall\, t \in T,\ u(t,\tilde{m}_\mu,r(\tilde{m}_\mu,\mu))=0$ and $u(t,m,r(m,\mu))<0$ for $m>\tilde{m}_\mu$;

iii) $u(t,m,r(m,\mu))$ is continuous and strictly concave in m for fixed t and μ.

Assumption 2: dominance of higher beliefs

$\forall t \in T,\ \forall m/\ m > \underline{m}_t,\ \forall \mu\ \text{and}\ \mu' \in \Delta_T\ /\ \sum_{t \in T} t\mu'(t/m) > \sum_{t \in T} t\mu(t/m)$:
$u(t,m,r(m,\mu)) < u(t,m,r(m,\mu'))$.
If $\sum_{t \in T} t\mu'(t/m) = \sum_{t \in T} t\mu(t/m)$ then
$u(t,m,r(m,\mu)) = u(t,m,r(m,\mu'))$ for each m of $M(t)$.

Assumption 3:

$\forall\, \mu \in \Delta_T,\ \forall\, m/\ m < \tilde{m}_\mu,\ \forall\, t,t' \in T,\ \text{with}\ t'>t$:
$u(t,m,r(m,\mu)) > u(t',m,r(m,\mu))$.

Assumption 4: single crossing

$\forall\, m,m'\ \text{with}\ m'>m,\ \forall\, r \in R(m),\ \forall\, r' \in R(m'),\ \forall\, t,t' \in T,\ \text{with}\ t'>t$:
$u(t,m',r') \geq u(t,m,r)\ \Rightarrow\ u(t',m',r') > u(t',m,r)$.

Assumption 1 ensures a well shaped function $u(t,m,r(m,\mu))$, u being strictly positive for m between $\underline{m}_t$ and $\tilde{m}_\mu$. $\underline{m}_t$ is to be interpreted as the lowest message player 1 of type t can send to get a positive payoff, regardless of player 2's response; $\tilde{m}_\mu$ is the highest message for which player 2 (with beliefs given by μ) chooses a response which leads to a positive payoff for player 1, regardless of type. Assumption 2, called dominance of higher beliefs, means that player 1's payoff is an increasing function of player 2's mean expected type. So every type of player 1 is better off being taken for a higher type. Assumption 3 means that, for a fixed message m and fixed beliefs μ, $u(t,m,r(m,\mu))$ is a decreasing function of t. Together with assumption 1, it ensures that $\underline{m}_t$ is an increasing function of t; it follows that the condition $\tilde{m}_\mu \in \bigcap_{i=1 \text{ to } n}]m_{-t_i}, \infty[$ (in assumption 1) simply becomes $\tilde{m}_\mu > m_{-t_n}$. Assumption 4, called single crossing property, ensures that if a type t can achieve a higher payoff with a higher message, then a higher type can all the more achieve a better payoff with it.

In the model of experience goods, t represents the quality level of the good, t_i being lower than t_j if and only if $i<j$. Therefore t_1 represents the lowest quality and t_n the highest one. t is also called the type of the producer producing a good of quality t. If c(t) represents the average cost of production of one unit of good of quality t, m the price set by the producer and r the amount bought by the consumer, then $u(t,m,r)=(m-c(t)).r$ is the usual producer's profit function. By setting $c(t_i) < c(t_j)$ if and only if $i<j$, which means that a higher quality good is more costly to produce than a low quality one, we get assumption 3. $\tilde{m}_\mu$ is the highest price for which the consumer accepts to buy a positive amount of the good, when his beliefs are given by μ. m_{-t} is nothing else than c(t), that is to say the lowest price the type t producer can set to make a profit. Assumption $\tilde{m}_\mu > m_{-t_n}$, regardless of μ, merely ensures that each type of producer can get a strictly positive profit, regardless of player 2's beliefs. For assumption 2 to hold, it is sufficient to suppose that the optimal amount bought by the consumer is an increasing function of the expected quality. Assumption 4 follows from the shape of the profit function (especially from the fact that c(t) grows with t). This single crossing property here simply means that, if a type t is able to get a higher profit with a price m' higher than a price m, then a higher quality type is able too.

* These assumptions lead to Figure 1, which gives the general form of function u(.,.,.) for two different systems of beliefs and two consecutive types.

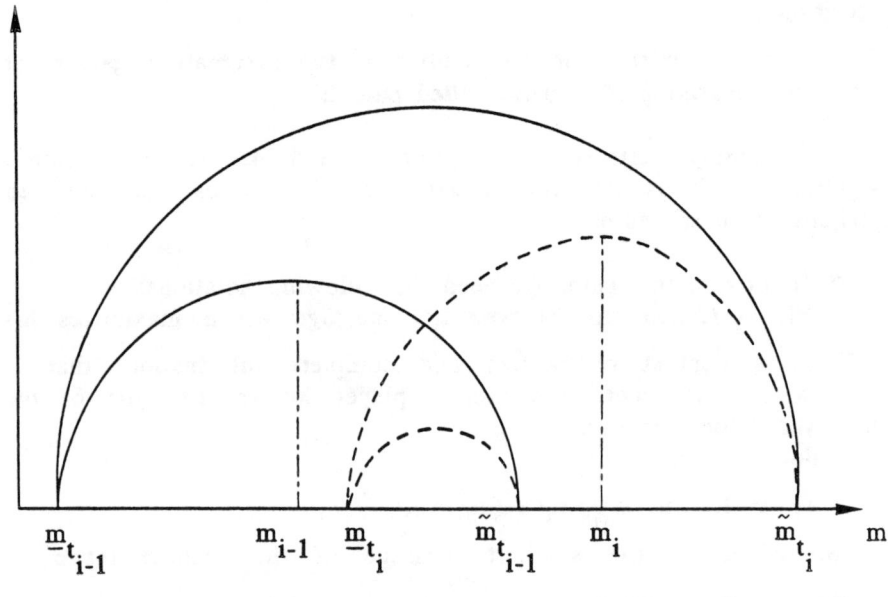

Figure 1

Legend:

- The full curves represent type t_{i-1}'s payoff when player 2 assigns m to t_{i-1}(curve 1), to type t_i(curve 2); curve 1 is below curve 2.
- The dashed curves represent type t_i's payoff when player 2 as signs m to t_{i-1}(curve 1), to type t_i (curve 2); curve 1 is below curve 2.

Let us now turn to the Perfect Bayesian Equilibria (PBE hereafter) of this class of games.

We only focus on *equilibrium paths*. By equilibrium path we mean the sequence of actions which are played with a strictly positive probability, when the equilibrium is played. This choice is motivated by the fact that many equilibria do only differ in their out of equilibrium actions, and not in their equilibrium path.

The above assumptions lead to the following result:

Proposition 1

There always exists, for the studied n types signaling games, at least one separating PBE path, called path E'.

Proof: It mainly rests on assumption 2 and 4. As it is rather straightforward it is not reproduced here, but it can be obtained on request from the author.

* To precise this path, we need the following notations:
- $\forall i$, $i=1,\ldots,n$, m_i is type t_i's message which maximizes his payoff in a context of perfect and complete information, that is to say a context where the second player knows the type of the first player before playing.
- For $i=1$, $m'_i = m_i$;
- $\forall i$, $i=2,\ldots,n$, $m'_i = \max(m_i, \bar{m}_i)$,

where $\bar{m}_i$ is the smallest message of the highest range of messages m which satisfy:

$u(t_{i-1}, m'_{i-1}, r(m'_{i-1}, t_{i-1})) \geq u(t_{i-1}, m, r(m, t_i))$.

Figures 2a and 2b depict the two possible configurations of m'_i, m_i and $\bar{m}_i$ for a fixed m'_{i-1}.

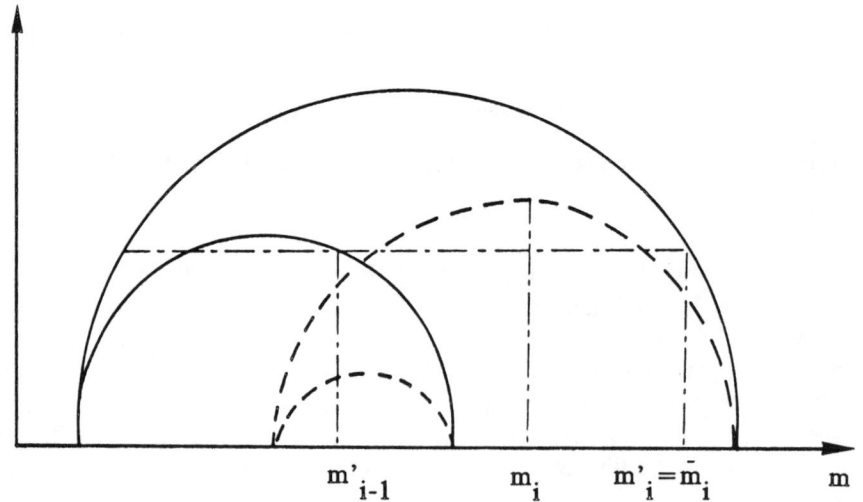

Figure 2a

INFORMATION TRANSMISSION IN SIGNALLING GAMES

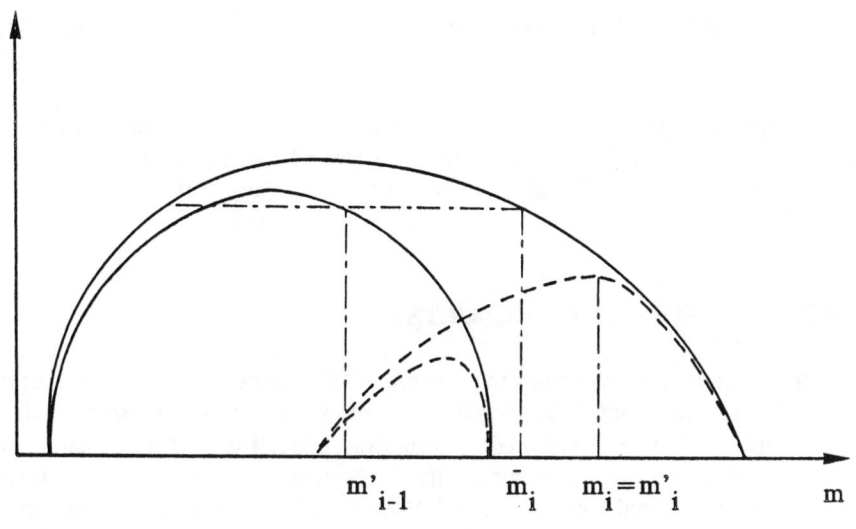

Figure 2b

Common legend:

- The full curves represent t_{i-1}'s payoff when player 2 assigns m to t_{i-1} (curve 1), to t_i (curve 2); curve 1 is below curve 2.
- The dashed curves represent t_i's payoff when player 2 assigns m to t_{i-1} (curve 1), to t_i (curve 2); curve 1 is below curve 2.

It follows the definition of E'.

Definition 1

E' is the separating PBE path which is characterized by:
$\forall i$, $i=1,\ldots,n$, player 1 of type t_i plays m'_i and player 2 plays $r(m'_i,t_i)$ after each message m'_i.

A system of beliefs which sustains E' is given by:

$\forall m/\ m < m'_1$ $\mu(t_1/m)=1$ and $\mu(t_j/m)=0$, for every $j \neq 1$;

$\forall i$, $i=1,\ldots,n-1$, $\forall m/\ m'_i \leq m < m'_{i+1}$, $\mu(t_i/m)=1$ and $\mu(t_j/m)=0$, for every $j \neq i$;

$\forall m/\ m'_n \leq m$, $\mu(t_n/m)=1$, and $\mu(t_j/m)=0$, for every $j \neq n$.

This equilibrium path has the following property: it is the

separating path which maximizes the separating payoff of each type of player 1.

* Of course, in the general case, there exists an infinity of PBE paths. Such a result is rather awkward in political economy as it does namely not allow to predict the future equilibrium situations.

FORWARD INDUCTION RESULTS

It is now well known that some PBE paths are less enforceable than others, in that they are sustained by unreasonable out of equilibrium beliefs. Backward induction equilibria allow such beliefs because they systematically interpret out of equilibrium actions as irrational moves (see Selten (1975) for the concept of momentary insanity). It follows that strategic deviations are impossible, and that deviations from a PBE path can therefore *convey no information*.

Forward induction, on the contrary, allows strategic deviations and a consequent information transmission through deviating actions. Indeed, it (roughly) requires the following behavior: if a player observes a deviation from the equilibrium path, he looks for a rational explanation of this deviation (he therefore interprets a deviation as an irrational move, only if no rational explanation can be found). Then he behaves optimally, taking this explanation into account.

Forward induction therefore allows for a *new source of information transmission: information transmission through deviations*. As a result, many PBE paths will be eliminated.

* However, the obtained results heavily depend on the *logic* behind the used forward induction criterion. More precisely the forward induction criteria can be split into two families. The first one studies the informational content of a deviation without calling in question the informational content of the equilibrium actions. To put it more precisely, it assumes that the *equilibrium actions always convey the information they are supposed to convey in the equilibrium path*. On the contrary, the second one claims that one cannot study the meaning of a deviating action without calling in question the meaning of *all* the other actions, *namely the equilibrium ones*. They require the beliefs to be *globally consistent*, which implies that an equilibrium path can only be removed by another equilibrium path. In other terms, these criteria claim that a signal sent by a deviation may affect the signal sent by other actions, possibly equilibrium ones. It follows that the equilibrium messages may convey a different information than the one they are supposed to convey in the equilibrium path.

Up to now most of the forward induction criteria belong to the first family (it includes, among others, the criteria of Cho & Kreps (1987a,b), Banks & Sobel (1987), Grossman & Perry (1986), Kohlberg (1989) and the forerunner concept of Kohlberg & Mertens (1986)). We will, in this paper, only focus on Kohlberg's Forward Induction with Admissibility (FIA hereafter) criterion. This choice is not crucial for the results: other criteria of this class would have behaved similarly (see Cho & Sobel(1990) for more details in a similar class of games).

As far as we know, only very few criteria belong to the second family: among them are our Consistent Forward Induction Equilibrium Path concept (CFIEP hereafter) (see Umbhauer (1989)-(1991)) and Mailath, Okuno-Fujiwara & Postlewaite's (Journal of Economic Theory forthcoming) Undefeated Equilibrium concept. We focus in this section on the results obtained with the CFIEP concept; nevertheless, in a further section, we will compare these results to the independently developed results of Mailath et al.

We will not discuss in this paper the motivations that lead to the first or the second family of criteria (for such a discussion see Van Damme (1990) and Umbhauer (1991)). We just compare the obtained results.

* We firstly give the results obtained with Kohlberg's FIA (also called Self-Enforcing) criterion.

Definition 2 (out of KOHLBERG (1989))

> A PBE path (see KOHLBERG (1989) for a more precise definition and explanation) is Self Enforcing if it is robust to the successive elimination of inferior or (weakly) dominated strategies (where an inferior strategy is a strategy that is never a best response at any admissible (i.e. without (weakly) dominated strategies) equilibrium with the outcome (i.e. the distribution on the endpoints of the game tree) of that equilibrium path).

Proposition 2

> The only Self Enforcing PBE path of the studied class of games is the separating path E'.

Proof: see Appendix 1.

* We now expose the results obtained with the CFIEP criterion for the case n=2 (more general results are given in a further section).

We firstly recall the definition of this criterion. To this end we introduce the following notations: $u_t(E^*)$ is type t's payoff in the equilibrium path E^*, $\bar{u}(t/m)$ is his payoff if he plays m (which is not necessarily his equilibrium message) in the equilibrium path $\bar{E}$, and $\bar{\pi}(m/t)$ is t's probability of playing m in this path.

Definition 3

> A PBE path E^* is a CFIEP if and only if:
> For any message m, out of E^*'s support of equilibrium messages, there does not exist a PBE path $\bar{E}$, which satisfies:
> α) m ∈ $\bar{E}$'s support of equilibrium messages;
> β) For $N = \{t \in T / \bar{\pi}(m/t) > 0 \text{ and } \bar{u}(t/m) > u_t(E^*)\}$ and
>
> $S = \{r \in \arg\max_{r \in R(m)} \sum_{t \in N} v(t,m,r).\rho(t).\bar{\pi}(m/t)/(\sum_{t \in N} \rho(t)\bar{\pi}(m/t))\}$
>
> (i), (ii) and (iii) are satisfied:
> (i) N is not empty;
> (ii) ∀ t ∈ T\N, $\bar{u}(t/m) \leq u_t(E^*)$;
> (iii) ∃ r ∈ S / ∀ t ∈ N, $u(t,m,r) \geq u_t(E^*)$.

Roughly, this criterion requires two conditions:

The first one (condition α), requires that the beliefs assigned to an out of equilibrium message belong to a PBE; this condition is the global consistency requirement.

The second one (condition β) expresses the forward induction principle. Hence beliefs assigned to an out of equilibrium message m must allow for the possibility that player 1, by playing m, is trying to get a higher payoff than the planned equilibrium one. Player 2 especially knows that it is only in the interest of a type of N, that is to say a type of player 1 who can be better off by deviating, to provoke the deviation. Therefore condition β requires, among other things, that the types of N will deviate even if player 2 behaves in accordance with the above knowledge (that is to say plays a response r of S).

For a detailed comment of this criterion, see Umbhauer (1991) and the following sections.

To state the next proposition, we need one more notation: m_ρ, which is the message which maximizes type t_2's payoff when player 2's a posteriori beliefs are the a priori ones.

Proposition 3

In the case $n=2$, the CFIEP leads to the following selection:

If $u(t_2, m_\rho, r(m_\rho, \rho)) < u(t_2, m'_2, r(m'_2, t_2))$, then the only CFIEP is the separating PBE path E' (with $n=2$).

If $u(t_2, m_\rho, r(m_\rho, \rho)) > u(t_2, m'_2, r(m'_2, t_2))$, then the only CFIEP is the pooling PBE path E_ρ, characterized by: player 1 plays m_ρ regardless of type, and player 2 plays $r(m_\rho, \rho)$ after m_ρ.

If $u(t_2, m_\rho, r(m_\rho, \rho)) = u(t_2, m'_2, r(m'_2, t_2))$, then there are two CFIEP, E' and E_ρ.

Proof: see Appendix 2.

INFORMATION REVELATION AND THE LOGIC BEHIND THE RESULTS

 * The Self Enforcing criterion does only select one PBE path, and what is more, it always selects, regardless of the values of the parameters of the game, the same *perfect information revelation* path. It follows that the second player, by observing the message played by the first one, *perfectly* knows his type. On the contrary, the CFIEP criterion, even in the case $n=2$, selects one equilibrium path, whose level of information transmission *varies with respect to the values of the parameters*. So, for one range of values, it selects the same separating equilibrium path than the Self Enforcing criterion, whereas, for the other range, it selects a pooling equilibrium path, that is to say a *no information revelation* equilibrium path. Appendix 2 let reasonably conjecture that the above result generalizes in the case $n \in \mathbb{N}$, leading to a larger number of levels of information transmission, the level varying with respect to the values of the different parameters.

The reason why these results are different is best explained by going into the logic behind the two criteria.

 * To this end we especially explain why the Self Enforcing criterion, as opposed to the CFIEP one, systematically eliminates every non separating PBE path.

Consider one of these paths, E*, where a set of types (different from a singleton) play a same message m*; Let t_k be the highest type who plays this message. Given the assumptions on u(.,.,.), every message m higher than m* is an inferior strategy for every type lower than t_k. But, eliminating m from the strategies' sets of the types lower than t_k, leads the second player to assign m to a type (or a set of types) higher or equal to t_k. It follows that $\Sigma t \mu^*(t/m^*)$ (where $\mu^*(./.)$ is E*'s system of beliefs) is *strictly* lower than $\Sigma t \mu'(t/m)$, where $\mu'(./m)$ is the system of beliefs obtained by eliminating m from the types t_j strategies' sets (j<k). Consequently, by continuity of u in m and dominance of higher beliefs, there exists a positive and sufficiently small ε such as:

$u(t_k, m^* + \varepsilon, r(m^* + \varepsilon, \mu')) > u(t_k, m^*, r(m^*, \mu^*))$.

Hence t_k will deviate and, as a result, E* is eliminated.

This reasoning especially points out that the system of beliefs assigned to m* in E* is *never called in question* by the new system of beliefs assigned to m (>m*). In other terms the signal sent by m does not modify the signal sent by m*; m* always sends the message it is supposed to send in the tested equilibrium path.

* In contrast, according to the CFIEP criterion, a new system of beliefs, to eliminate a tested path, has to be globally consistent, that is, it has to be sustained by the actions and beliefs it implies. The latter *may call* the equilibrium system of beliefs *in question*.

So the CFIEP concept begins by testing the global consistency of every new system of beliefs, namely μ', which may eliminate E*.

For a start, assume that μ' is globally consistent. We showed above that μ' incites t_k to deviate to a message $m^* + \varepsilon$. *Yet this fact compels player 2*, if he observes m*, to assign this message to a set of types *strictly lower* than t_k. That is, the system of beliefs assigned to m>m* leads player 2 to *change* the equilibrium system of beliefs assigned to the equilibrium message m*. It *may now however happen*, due to this change, that a subset A of types lower than t_k are better off with $m^* + \varepsilon$ (to which is assigned the belief $\mu'(./m^* + \varepsilon)$), than with m* (to which is assigned the new system of beliefs implied by $\mu'(./m^* + \varepsilon)$). If A actually exists, then the types of A are also incited to deviate to $m^* + \varepsilon$, which *belies* μ''s global consistency, as μ' only assigns $m^* + \varepsilon$ to types higher or equal to t_k. In this case, μ' can not be used to eliminate E*.

It follows that the CFIEP criterion does not necessarily eliminate every non separating equilibrium path.

ECONOMY AND INTUITION

* The main feature of the Self Enforcing selection is the perfect information revelation of the selected path. In contrast, the main feature of the CFIEP selection, at least in the case n=2, is that the selected path is *the one which maximizes the highest type's payoff*; it is *as though the highest type could select the level of information transmission*.

The above results can be intuitively explained as follows: The studied games exhibits two kind of asymmetries:

- Firstly high types and low types do not favour the same levels of information revelation, in that *a high type*, for a fixed message m, *is better off being recognized*, whereas *a low type is better off being taken for a higher one*. As a result, high types generally prefer a high degree of revelation whereas low types prefer a low degree of revelation.

- This first type of asymmetry gives rise to a second one: *the asymmetric incentives to deviate*. Indeed, when the second player observes an out of equilibrium message, he tries to know who sent it. To put it more precisely, a meaningful deviation is a deviation that allows player 2 to recognize the deviator, so as to accordingly react to the message. But, as a high type generally more prefers to be recognized than a low one, it follows that *high types are more often led to undertake strategic deviations*. As a result, high types play a more important role (than low ones) in the choice of the finally played equilibrium path.

Hence it is intuitive that the forward induction principle selects equilibrium paths that are favoured by the highest types; this is in accordance with the CFIEP result (for the case n=2). As, for a large range of values of the parameters, the high types' most prefered paths are those with a high degree of information revelation, the above reasoning also justifies, at least in part, the high degree of revelation which characterizes the Self Enforcing selection.

The intuitive explanation is however not in support of the *uniformity* of the Self Enforcing selection. Indeed the selected path is the same, regardless of the values of the parameters and especially of the value of n; so perfect revelation prevails in any case, for n=2, as well as for n near ∞. This result is difficult to justify: indeed, although high types often favour perfect revelation, they do not prefer it *always*, in that *perfect revelation may be too costly*. Indeed, for certain ranges of values of the parameters, m'_i (t_i's message in E') is much higher than m_i (t_i's message in a context of complete and perfect information), causing t_i's payoff in E' to be very low; if so, it may happen that high types prefer an intermediate level of information transmission, leading some of them, for example, to play the same message than the nearest lower type.

* To better highlight the importance of this last remark, we go into the *economic content* of the obtained results, by going back to the model of experience goods for n=2.

The Self-Enforcing PBE path, for this model, is such as, *regardless* of the average production costs, and *regardless* of the a priori beliefs of the consumer, each type of producer chooses a differenciating price policy, that is to say a price policy such as the consumer always observes the quality of the good before purchase (this result is usually referred to as the Riley (1979) outcome).

This price policy is readily justifiable for pessimistic a priori beliefs and a high quality average production cost much higher than the low quality one. It is however less justifiable in the opposite case. A differenciating price policy is indeed *costly*, for *both* the consumer and *the high quality producer*, if it leads this producer to set a price which is much higher than the one which maximizes his payoff in a context of perfect and complete information (m'_2 much higher than m_2). If so, one can expect that a high quality producer prefers a pooling or semi separating price policy; such a policy can indeed ensure him a higher payoff, *even if he is not recognized*, as it allows him to set a lower price, (nearer to the complete information one), which may be followed by a high amount of quantity, especially if the a priori probability assigned to the high type is high.

On the contrary, the CFIEP selection is in agreement with these expectations: it indeed depends on the a priori beliefs of the consumer, and on the high quality producer's perceived cost of a differenciating price policy, this cost being an increasing function of the difference m'_2-m_2 (see Umbhauer (1989)). It namely satisfies the following properties:

- The more the a priori probability assigned to the high quality producer grows, the more the CFIEP concept selects a pooling price policy equilibrium path. To put it more precisely, if $p(t_2)$ is high, the CFIEP is the path where both types of producer play the price m_p. This is due to the fact that this policy leads, for the high quality producer, to a profit which is nearer and nearer to the profit of a context of complete and perfect information, as $p(t_2)$ grows. Indeed, $m_p \to m_2$ (respectively $r(m_p, p) \to r(m_2, t_2)$), as $p(t_2) \to 1$. Moreover, as m'_2 and m_2 do not depend on $p(.)$, $m'_2 - m_2$ does not shrink to 0 as $p(t_2) \to 1$. It follows that, for high values of $p(t_2)$, the high quality producer prefers the pooling price policy.

- The more $c(t_2)$ grows, the more the CFIEP criterion selects the differenciating price policy. It is due to the fact that $m'_2 - m_2$ is a decreasing function of $c(t_2)$ (m'_2 does not depend on $c(t_2)$, and m_2 is an increasing function of this term). Hence the high quality producer's perceived cost of the differenciating price policy is a decreasing function of $c(t_2)$, causing this policy to be selected for high values of $c(t_2)$.

GENERALISATION AND COMMENTS ON RELATED WORK

* It is not easy to find the CFIEP(s) for the general case $n \in \mathbb{N}$, in that condition β is difficult to check.

* For a start, let us go into condition β)ii. This condition, which limits the elimination possibilities, has been introduced to avoid endless discussions as to how another out of equilibrium message (than the one under consideration) has to be interpreted.
To explain this point, consider a tested PBE path E*, and a PBE path E, whose support of equilibrium messages includes two out of E* equilibrium messages, m and m'. For simplicity, suppose also that N, the set of types playing m in E *and getting a higher payoff* than in E*, is equal to K, the set of types that play m in E. It follows that player 2's threat after m is E's equilibrium response, which leads the types of N to deviate (condition β)iii

holds).

Suppose now, in addition, that there exists a type t_i, such as the following conditions are satisfied:
- t_i plays m' in E;
- he gets a higher payoff with m' in E than with m in E;
- *he gets a higher payoff with m in E than his E* equilibrium payoff;*
- there does not exist a PBE path E', such as N for m' satisfies: t_i belongs to N and t_i is better off with m' even if player 2 focuses his beliefs on N.

It arises from this additional assumption that t_i *may be incited to deviate to m even if m ensures him a lower payoff than m'; this deviation would however compel player 2 to reconsider his threat after m.* By requiring condition β)ii, according to which each type of T\N gets a lower payoff with m than the E* payoff (hence the additional assumption never holds), we avoid this problem.

This rather strong condition has however a drawback: it is difficult to check in the general case.

* Let us, in this paragraph only, suppress condition β)ii *(suppression we do not agree with)*, with a view to obtaining more general results. This suppression reveals to be useless, in that the *possible difference between N and K* makes difficult to check condition β)iii.

The only result we obtain by so doing is given in proposition 4.

Proposition 4

Set: $K(t_n) = \left\{ \text{(PBE paths)} E \;/\; E \in \arg\max_{E^* \in PBEpaths} u_{t_n}(E^*) \right\}$;

For i from n-1 to 1 set:

$K(t_i) = \left\{ E \;/\; E \in \arg\max_{E^* \in K(t_{i+1})} u_{t_i}(E^*) \right\}$

If this iterative process only selects the separating path E', then every other PBE path is eliminated by the modified CFIEP version.

Proof: The idea behind the proof is to establish that, in each *modified* CFIEP (CFIEP without condition β)ii), each type t gets the same payoff than in E'. The fact that the above process only selects E' completes the proof (a detailed proof can be obtained on request from the author).

The above iterative process follows directly from the intuitive reasoning (see a previous section). Indeed, it firstly selects the equilibrium paths which maximize the highest type's payoff. In this set of paths it then selects the paths which maximize the highest type minus 1's payoff. In this new set it selects the paths which maximize the highest type minus 2's payoff and so on, down to t_1. For the case n=2, the above process leads to the same selection than the CFIEP criterion.

Proposition 4 is however not a far reaching one. Hence, even without condition β)ii, it is not easy to find the selected equilibrium paths in the general case n∈ℕ, for n>2.

* The reason is that N, the set of types who play the out of equilibrium message m in the new PBE path E *and* get a higher payoff with m than the tested equilibrium one, may be a *proper subset* of K, the set of types who play m with positive probability in E.

This remark leads us to compare our work with the independently developed work of Mailath et al. (Journal of Economic Theory forthcoming). These authors share the central idea that an equilibrium path can only be dismissed by another equilibrium path, but their Undefeated Equilibrium concept (UE hereafter) differs from the CFIEP in other respects.

We firstly compare the obtained results and then proceed to explain the reasons of the observed differences. Since the UE shares the same central idea than the CFIEP, the trend of the results is the same: the UE concept also leads to a larger number of levels of information transmission than the Self Enforcing criterion. Nevertheless, important differences can be observed:

- The UE concept, *only developed for pure strategies equilibria*, allows, in a similar class of games, a *more general result*, in that every equilibrium defined by the process in proposition 4 is an UE (these equilibria are however not always the only UE).

- The UE selection is not so powerful as the CFIEP one. Namely, for the case n=2, the *CFIEP leads to unicity* (except for a non generic class of games); in contrast, the UE concept leads to an *infinity of UE paths* when the CFIEP concept selects the pooling path E_ρ.

These differences mainly arise from the fact that Mailath et al require, for a new equilibrium E to dismiss the tested one E*, that all types which play m in E (with m belonging to E's support of equilibrium messages but not to E*'s one) get a higher or the same payoff than the E* one. Hence each deviating type has to get a higher (or the same) payoff by deviating. In other words, Ñ has to be equal to K, where Ñ is the set of types who play m *and* get a higher or the same payoff by playing it (N⊆Ñ, in that N is the set of types who play m and get a *higher* payoff than the equilibrium one).

In contrast, we do not require this equality, in that we think that the deviation of one type (say t_2) *can compel* another type (say t_1) to deviate, *even if this type is worse off by deviating*. The reason is that, owing to t_2's deviation, player 2 *may play a new response after the equilibrium message, such as t_1 is worser off by playing the equilibrium message than by deviating*. That is why, contrary to Mailath et al., we allow N and also Ñ to be proper subsets of K.

This difference especially well explains why, in the case n=2, when E_ρ is the only CFIEP, Mailath et al. can not eliminate an infinity of other pooling PBE paths (we recall that, in this case, E_ρ is t_2's preferred equilibrium path). The explanation runs as follows:

Consider a pooling PBE path, E", where t_1 gets a higher payoff than in E_ρ and t_2 (necessarily) a lower one.

E_ρ can not be eliminated by E" with the UE concept: indeed, $K=\{t_1,t_2\}$ but t_2 gets a strictly lower payoff with m" in E" (i.e. K≠Ñ). Similarly, E" can not be eliminated by E_ρ: $K=\{t_1,t_2\}$ but t_1 gets a strictly lower payoff with m_ρ in E_ρ (i.e. K≠Ñ).

In contrast, the CFIEP only selects E_ρ. Let us explain why E" is eliminated. To this end look at the system of beliefs (E_ρ's one) which assigns the out of equilibrium message m_ρ to both types of player 1 with the a priori probabilities. This system leads player 2 to play $r(m_\rho,\rho)$ after m_ρ, thereby inciting t_2 to actually play m_ρ; by so doing it compels player 2 to assign m" to t_1 (and no more to both types as in E″) and hence to play $r(m″,t_1)$ after m″. It follows that, although t_1 gets a lower payoff with m_ρ followed by $r(m_\rho,\rho)$ than in E″, he would be worse off by keeping on playing m″ than by deviating to m_ρ. Therefore he also deviates to m_ρ, thereby justifying the system of beliefs. To put it more precisely, E″ is eliminated by E_ρ although N ($=\tilde{N}$) is *strictly included* in K.

The reverse is not true: E_ρ can not be eliminated by E″ (with the CFIEP criterion). Indeed, assigning m″ to both types with the a priori probabilities would only incite t_1 to deviate ($N=\tilde{N} \subset K$); hence player 2 would be led to assign m_ρ to t_2, which would incite this type to *keep on* playing m_ρ; as a result player 2 would finally be compelled to assign m″ to t_1 which dissuades this type from deviating (technically speaking, condition β)iii does not hold). Therefore, nobody deviates from E_ρ.

CONCLUSION

In contrast to the backward induction principle, the forward induction principle allows out of equilibrium messages to convey new information. Hence it gives rise to new sources of information transmission, which can help to choose a path of actions. However, we established in this paper that the selected paths, and the consequent level of information revelation, heavily depend on the logic behind the different forward induction criteria.

Whereas the Self Enforcing criterion (and most of the other criteria which do not require global consistency) lead to a perfect information revelation for the studied class of games, regardless of the values of the parameters of the games, the CFIEP concept (and the UE one) lead to a larger range of levels of information transmission.

Yet this difference is important in economy. It may have repercussions on political economy.

Criteria like the Self-Enforcing concept, by leading to a perfect information revelation result, may lead to liberal recommendations; indeed, as the play of the game automatically leads to a (usually viewed as highly desirable) perfect information revelation situation, no authority is needed to ensure this revelation.

We however pointed out in this paper that the logic behind this kind of criteria, and hence the results obtained with these criteria, is not the only possible one. This remark, that led to forward induction criteria like the CFIEP concept, also led to a larger range of possible levels of information transmission. This last result does not convey the above-mentioned liberal implications.

REFERENCES

BANKS J. & SOBEL J.(1992): Equilibrium selection in signaling games, *Econometrica*, **55**, pp.647-661.
CHO I.K.(1987a): A refinement of sequential equilibria, *Econometrica*, **55**, pp.1367-1389.
CHO I.K. & KREPS D.M.(1987b): Signaling games and stable equilibria, *Quarterly Journal of Economics*, **102**, pp.179-221.
CHO I.K. & SOBEL J.(1990): Strategic stability and uniqueness in signaling games, *Journal of Economic Theory*, **50**, pp.381-413.
GROSSMAN S.J. & PERRY M.(1986): Perfect sequential equilibrium, *Journal of Economic Theory*, **39**, pp.97-119.
KOHLBERG E.(1989): Refinement of Nash equilibrium: the main ideas, Mimeo Harvard.
KOHLBERG E. & MERTENS J.F.(1986): On the strategic stability of equilibria, *Econometrica*, **54**, pp.1003-1037.
MAILATH G.J., OKUNO-FUJIWARA M. & POSTLEWAITE A.:On belief based refinements in signaling games, *Journal of Economic Theory*, Forthcoming.
RILEY J.(1979): Informational equilibrium, *Econometrica,* **47**, pp.331-359.
SELTEN R.(1975): Reexamination of the perfectness concept for equilibrium points in extensive games, *International Journal of Game Theory*, **4**, pp.25-55.
UMBHAUER G.(1989): Information incomplète et qualité des produits, Thèse de Sciences Economiques, Université Louis Pasteur, Strasbourg I, France.
UMBHAUER G.(1991): Forward induction, consistency and rationality of ε perturbations, revised B.E.T.A. Working Paper, **9104**, Université Louis Pasteur, Strasbourg I, France.
VAN DAMME E.(1990): Refinements of Nash Equilibrium, 6th World Congress of the Econometric Society, Barcelona, Spain.

APPENDIX 1

* We prove that E' is the only Self Enforcing PBE path.

* It is clear from single crossing that, if t_i and t_{i+2} play a same message m* in a PBE path E*, t_{i+1} plays this message too.

* We now prove that a pooling or semi separating PBE path can not be Self-Enforcing.

Consider such a PBE path E*. There are necessarily two types t_i and t_k, who play a same message m*. Let t_i be the smallest type playing m* and t_k the highest one.

It follows from above that each t_j, with $i \leq j \leq k$, plays m* in E*.

- It results from single crossing that each message m, with $m > m^*$, is an inferior strategy for each t_j, with $i \leq j < k$.

- Let us prove that m is an inferior strategy for each t_j, with $1 \leq j < i$.

t_j does not play m*. Suppose that t_j plays, perhaps among other messages, the message m^*_j.

If $u(t_j, m^*_j, r(m^*_j, \mu^*)) \leq u(t_j, m, r)$ (1)

(where μ^* is E*'s system of beliefs and r is a response after m, sustaining E*), then

$u(t_j, m^*, r(m^*, \mu^*)) \leq u(t_j, m^*_j, r(m^*_j, \mu^*)) \leq u(t_j, m, r)$ (2)

Single crossing applied to (2) implies:

$u(t_k, m^*, r(m^*, \mu^*)) < u(t_k, m, r)$, which is impossible because r has to sustain E*.

It follows that (1) is a bad assumption and that m is an inferior strategy for t_j.

- Owing to the above results, the Self Enforcing criterion excludes m from t_j's strategies' set, with $1 \leq j < k$. As a result, player 2's system of beliefs has to assign m to a set of types t_j, with $j \geq k$. Let μ_m be such a system of beliefs. Since $\mu^*(./m^*)$'s support is a set of types t, with $t_i \leq t \leq t_k$, we get, by dominance of higher beliefs: $u(t_k, m^*, r(m^*, \mu^*)) < u(t_k, m^*, r(m^*, \mu_m))$.

The continuity of u in m for fixed type and beliefs ensures

the existence of m, with $m = m^* + \varepsilon$ (ε positive and low), such as:
$u(t_k, m^*, r(m^*, \mu^*)) < u(t_k, m, r(m, \mu_m))$
Hence t_k deviates to m and E* is not Self Enforcing. ∎

* We finally prove that E' is the only possible Self Enforcing separating PBE path.

Let E* be another separating PBE path. E* is characterized by:
t_i plays m^*_i, (i=1,...,n), and player 2 plays $r(m^*_i, t_i)$ after observing m^*_i, (i=1,...,n).

- It is obvious that, necessarily, $m^*_1 = m'_1 = m_1$.

- We prove that E*, characterized by: t_j, with $1 \le j \le i$, plays m'_j, t_k, with $i < k \le n$, plays m^*_k, and player 2 plays $r(m'_j, t_j)$ after m'_j and $r(m^*_k, t_k)$ after m^*_k, necessarily satisfies: $m^*_{i+1} = m'_{i+1}$.

Let us suppose $m^*_{i+1} \ne m'_{i+1}$.

○ If so, m'_{i+1} is an inferior strategy for t_j, with $1 \le j < i+1$. Indeed, to sustain E*, player 2's response r after m'_{i+1} has to satisfy: $u(t_{i+1}, m^*_{i+1}, r(m^*_{i+1}, t_{i+1})) \ge u(t_{i+1}, m'_{i+1}, r)$ (3)

We also have:

$u(t_j, m'_j, r(m'_j, t_j)) \ge u(t_j, m^*_{i+1}, r(m^*_{i+1}, t_{i+1}))$ (4)

<u>Case 1</u>: $m'_{i+1} > m^*_{i+1}$

Single crossing and (3) imply:
$u(t_j, m^*_{i+1}, r(m^*_{i+1}, t_{i+1})) > u(t_j, m'_{i+1}, r)$ (5)
(4) and (5) ensure that m'_{i+1} is an inferior strategy for t_j.

<u>Case 2</u>: $m'_{i+1} < m^*_{i+1}$

It follows from the construction of the m'_i that:
$u(t_{i+1}, m^*_{i+1}, r(m^*_{i+1}, t_{i+1})) < u(t_{i+1}, m'_{i+1}, r(m'_{i+1}, t_{i+1}))$

r in (3) is a response of an admissible equilibrium; it has therefore to be justified by a system of beliefs. Hence, in order to fit condition (3), r has to satisfy $r = r(m'_{i+1}, \mu)$, with μ such as $\sum_{t \in T} t\mu(t/m'_{i+1}) < t_{i+1}$ (by dominance of higher beliefs). It follows that:

$u(t_j, m'_j, r(m'_j, t_j)) \geq u(t_j, m'_{i+1}, r(m'_{i+1}, t_{i+1})) > u(t_j, m'_{i+1}, r)$
(by dominance of higher beliefs).

Consequently, m'_{i+1} is an inferior strategy for t_j. ∎

o It follows that m'_{i+1} can not be assigned to t_j with $j < i+1$. As a result, player 2's system of beliefs after m'_{i+1} is μ, with $\sum_{t \in T} t\mu(t/m'_{i+1}) \geq t_{i+1}$. This result and dominance of higher beliefs lead to: $u(t_{i+1}, m'_{i+1}, r(m'_{i+1}, \mu)) \geq u(t_{i+1}, m'_{i+1}, r(m'_{i+1}, t_{i+1}))$
$> u(t_{i+1}, m^*_{i+1}, r(m^*_{i+1}, t_{i+1}))$.

Hence t_{i+1} deviates to m'_{i+1} and E* is not Self Enforcing.

o It follows that, if E* is Self Enforcing, then $m^*_{i+1} = m'_{i+1}$. ∎

It is clear from the above results, by induction on i, that E' is the only possible Self Enforcing separating equilibrium path.

* Consequently, E' is the only possible Self Enforcing equilibrium path. Since a Self Enforcing equilibrium path always exists, E' is the only Self Enforcing equilibrium path.

APPENDIX 2

* We prove proposition 3.

* There are at most three types of semi separating PBE paths:
- The first type is characterized by: t_1 (respectively t_2) plays m_1 and m* (respectively m*), and player 2 plays $r(m_1, t_1)$ after m_1 and $r(m^*, \mu)$ after m*, $\mu(./m^*)$ being obtained by bayesian updating.
- The second type is characterized by: t_1 (respectively t_2) plays m* (respectively m* and m**), and player 2 plays $r(m^{**}, t_2)$ after m** and $r(m^*, \mu)$ after m*, $\mu(./m^*)$ being obtained by bayesian updating.
-The third type is characterized by: t_1 (respectively t_2) plays m_1 and m* (respectively m* and m**), and player 2 plays

$r(m_1,t_1)$ after m_1, $r(m^{**},t_2)$ after m^{**}, and $r(m^*,\mu)$ after m^*, $\mu(./m^*)$ being obtained by bayesian updating.

This result is derived from single crossing which ensures that t_1 and t_2 can not play more than 1 same message m^* in a PBE path. None of the semi separating PBE paths is a CFIEP. The proof mainly rests on single crossing and dominance of higher beliefs. It is not reproduced here but can be obtained on request from the author.

* We now prove that E' is the only possible separating CFIEP path. To this end, we consider a separating PBE path E* where t_2 plays m^*_2 different from m'_2 (we already know that t_1 necessarily plays m_1).

E' satisfies the following conditions:

- m'_2, which is out of E*'s support of equilibrium messages, is played in E'.

- $N=\{t_2\}$, that is, only t_2 plays m'_2 in E' and gets, by so doing, a higher payoff than the E* payoff (property of m'_2).

- $S=\{r(m'_2,t_2)\}$: player 2's threat, given N, is $r(m'_2,t_2)$.

- t_2 gets a higher payoff (than the E* one) with m'_2 followed by $r(m'_2,t_2)$. In contrast, t_1, only type of T\N, gets with m'_2 in E' a lower or the same payoff than the E* one.

It follows that E* is eliminated by E', and that each separating PBE path different from E' is not a CFIEP. ∎

We now consider three cases:

▷ **Case 1:** $u_1(t_2,m_\rho,r(m_\rho,\rho)) < u_1(t_2,m'_2,r(m'_2,t_2))$

In this case it is a trivial matter to show that each pooling PBE path is eliminated by the separating path E'. It follows that no pooling PBE path is a CFIEP.

In contrast E' is a CFIEP.

In order to prove it, consider any other PBE path E where an out E''s support of equilibrium message m is played: necessarily, either $N = \emptyset$ or $N = \{t_1\}$, as t_1 is the only type who can possibly get a higher payoff in another PBE path. In this last case player 2 threatens to play $r(m, t_1)$ after m, which dissuades t_1 from deviating (condition β)iii does not hold). Hence, in both cases, E can not be used to eliminate E').

It is clear from all the previous results that E' is the only CFIEP. ∎

▷ **Case 2:** $u_1(t_2, m_\rho, r(m_\rho, \rho)) > u_1(t_2, m'_2, r(m'_2, t_2))$

- For one, E_ρ, the pooling path where both types of player 1 play m_ρ (followed by $r(m_\rho, \rho)$), is a PBE path (it immediately results from single crossing, dominance of higher beliefs, and the fact that, in this case, m'_2 is necessarily equal to $\tilde{m}_2$).

- For another, E' and every pooling PBE path E*, different from E_ρ, are not CFIEP. The proof runs as follows:

  ○ Firstly E' is eliminated by E_ρ. Indeed, m_ρ is out of E''s support of equilibrium messages, m_ρ is played in E_ρ, $N = \{t_1, t_2\}$, T\N is empty, and player 2's threat, given N, is $r(m_\rho, \rho)$, which ensures a higher payoff to both types. It follows that E' is not a CFIEP.

  ○ Secondly consider any pooling PBE path E*, where both types of player 1 play a message m*, different from m_ρ.

  E_ρ satisfies: m_ρ is out of E*'s support of equilibrium messages, m_ρ is played in E_ρ, and, necessarily, $N = \{t_1, t_2\}$ or $N = \{t_2\}$ (as m_ρ maximizes t_2's payoff for the system of beliefs $\rho(.)$).

  If $N = \{t_1, t_2\}$, both types get a higher payoff (than the E* one) by playing m_ρ, and player 2's threat, given N, is $r(m_\rho, \rho)$, which ensures a higher payoff to both types. As T\N is empty, all the required conditions to eliminate E* are satisfied.

  If $N = \{t_2\}$ both types deviate to m_ρ but only t_2 gets a higher payoff by playing this message. Therefore player 2's threat, given N, is $r(m_\rho, t_2)$, which ensures a higher payoff to t_2 (by dominance of higher beliefs). Moreover, t_1, only type of T\N, gets a lower payoff (than the E* one) by playing m_ρ in E_ρ. It follows that E_ρ satisfies all the required conditions to eliminate E^*.

Hence no pooling PBE path, different from E_ρ, is a CFIEP.

- We finally prove that E_ρ is a CFIEP. To this end, consider a PBE path E, where player 1 plays a message m, different from m_ρ. Necessarily, either $N = \emptyset$ or $N = \{t_1\}$ (as t_1 is the only type who can possibly get a higher payoff in another PBE path). In this last case, player 2 threatens to play $r(m, t_1)$ after m, which dissuades t_1 from deviating (in other terms condition β)iii of the criterion does not hold). It follows that, in both cases, E can not be used to eliminate E_ρ. ∎

- It follows that E_ρ is the only CFIEP. ∎

▷ **Case 3:** $u_1(t_2, m_\rho, r(m_\rho, \rho)) = u_1(t_2, m'_2, r(m'_2, t_2))$

There are two CFIEP: E' and E_ρ. The proof is similar to the above ones.

THEORY AND DECISION LIBRARY

SERIES B: MATHEMATICAL AND STATISTICAL METHODS
Editor: H. J. Skala, *University of Paderborn, Germany*

1. D. Rasch and M.L. Tiku (eds.): *Robustness of Statistical Methods and Nonparametric Statistics.* 1984   ISBN 90-277-2076-2

2. J.K. Sengupta: *Stochastic Optimization and Economic Models.* 1986
ISBN 90-277-2301-X

3. J. Aczél: *A Short Course on Functional Equations.* Based upon Recent Applications to the Social Behavioral Sciences. 1987
ISBN Hb 90-277-2376-1; Pb 90-277-2377-X

4. J. Kacprzyk and S.A. Orlovski (eds.): *Optimization Models Using Fuzzy Sets and Possibility Theory.* 1987   ISBN 90-277-2492-X

5. A.K. Gupta (ed.): *Advances in Multivariate Statistical Analysis.* Pillai Memorial Volume. 1987   ISBN 90-277-2531-4

6. R. Kruse and K.D. Meyer: *Statistics with Vague Data.* 1987
ISBN 90-277-2562-4

7. J.K. Sengupta: *Applied Mathematics for Economics.* 1987
ISBN 90-277-2588-8

8. H. Bozdogan and A.K. Gupta (eds.): *Multivariate Statistical Modeling and Data Analysis.* 1987   ISBN 90-277-2592-6

9. B.R. Munier (ed.): *Risk, Decision and Rationality.* 1988
ISBN 90-277-2624-8

10. F. Seo and M. Sakawa: *Multiple Criteria Decision Analysis in Regional Planning.* Concepts, Methods and Applications. 1988   ISBN 90-277-2641-8

11. I. Vajda: *Theory of Statistical Inference and Information.* 1989
ISBN 90-277-2781-3

12. J.K. Sengupta: *Efficiency Analysis by Production Frontiers.* The Nonparametric Approach. 1989   ISBN 0-7923-0028-9

13. A. Chikán (ed.): *Progress in Decision, Utility and Risk Theory.* 1991
ISBN 0-7923-1211-2

14. S.E. Rodabaugh, E.P. Klement and U. Höhle (eds.): *Applications of Category Theory to Fuzzy Subsets.* 1992   ISBN 0-7923-1511-1

15. A. Rapoport: *Decision Theory and Decision Behaviour.* Normative and Descriptive Approaches. 1989   ISBN 0-7923-0297-4

16. A. Chikán (ed.): *Inventory Models.* 1990   ISBN 0-7923-0494-2

17. T. Bromek and E. Pleszczyńska (eds.): *Statistical Inference.* Theory and Practice. 1991   ISBN 0-7923-0718-6

THEORY AND DECISION LIBRARY: SERIES B

18. J. Kacprzyk and M. Fedrizzi (eds.): *Multiperson Decision Making Models Using Fuzzy Sets and Possibility Theory.* 1990 ISBN 0-7923-0884-0
19. G.L. Gómez M.: *Dynamic Probabilistic Models and Social Structure.* Essays on Socioeconomic Continuity. 1992 ISBN 0-7923-1713-0
20. H. Bandemer and W. Näther: *Fuzzy Data Analysis.* 1992
ISBN 0-7923-1772-6
21. A.G. Sukharev: *Minimax Models in the Theory of Numerical Methods.* 1992
ISBN 0-7923-1821-8
22. J. Geweke (ed.): *Decision Making under Risk and Uncertainty.* New Models and Empirical Findings. 1992 ISBN 0-7923-1904-4
23. T. Kariya: *Quantitative Methods for Portfolio Analysis.* MTV Model Approach. 1993 ISBN 0-7923-2254-1
24. M.J. Panik: *Fundamentals of Convex Analysis.* Duality, Separation, Representation, and Resolution. 1993 ISBN 0-7923-2279-7
25. J.K. Sengupta: *Econometrics of Information and Efficiency.* 1993
ISBN 0-7923-2353-X
26. B.R. Munier (ed.): *Markets, Risk and Money.* Essays in Honor of Maurice Allais. 1994 ISBN 0-7923-2578-8
27. D. Denneberg: *Non-Additive Measure and Integral.* 1994
ISBN 0-7923-2840-X
28. V.L. Girko, *Statistical Analysis of Observations of Increasing Dimension* (forthcoming) ISBN 0-7923-2886-8
29. B.R. Munier and M.J. Machina (eds.): *Models and Experiments in Risk and Rationality.* 1994 ISBN 0-7923-3031-5

KLUWER ACADEMIC PUBLISHERS – DORDRECHT / BOSTON / LONDON